Contents

PART 4   **Reading Textbooks   385**

PART 5   Critical Reading   525

PREFACE

As you enthusiastically greet your class each semester, you know that your students may not bring many formal reading strategies with them to the college reading classroom, but they do bring a wealth of life experience. And if students haven't had certain experiences themselves, they have probably lived them vicariously in the media. Because many students have enjoyed using multimedia such as television, movies, and the Internet more than they have reading print materials, *Activate: College Reading* draws on these media experiences to help students learn reading strategies and stay engaged in reading.

A Book Designed for the YouTube Generation

Lesson 1, for instance, shows students how they use a before, during, and after process when watching a television program (or movie) and then demonstrates how to apply the same process to reading. Media is used as a means to help students gain knowledge before reading a selection. For each reading at the beginning and end of Parts 1–5, and for all six readings in Part 6, students can view a video on a closely related topic. They can then approach the selection with this "prior" knowledge, thus increasing the likelihood that they will comprehend the reading. The videos are online on the Reading CourseMate website, accessed via login.cengage.com.

activate

COLLEGE READING

IVAN G. DOLE
North Lake College

LESLIE TAGGART

WADSWORTH
CENGAGE Learning

Australia • Brazil • Japan • Korea • Mexico • Singapore • Spain • United Kingdom • United States

Activate: College Reading
Ivan G. Dole, Leslie Taggart

Senior Publisher: Lyn Uhl

Director: Annie Todd

Development Editor: Marita Sermolins

Assistant Editor: Melanie Opacki

Editorial Assistant: Matt Conte

Media Editor: Amy Gibbons

Marketing Manager: Kirsten Stoller

Marketing Coordinator: Ryan Ahern

Marketing Communications Manager: Stacey
    Purviance

Content Project Manager: Corinna Dibble

Senior Art Director: Jill Ort

Senior Print Buyer: Betsy Donaghey

Rights Acquisition Specialist, Image: Mandy
    Groszko

Rights Acquisition Specialist, Text: Katie Huha

Production Service: Lachina Publishing Services

Text Designer: Lachina Publishing Services

Cover Designer: Nancy Goulet

Cover Images: Thinkstock, a division of Getty
    images (www.thinkstockphotos.com) and
    Shutterstock

Compositor: Lachina Publishing Services

For product information and technology assistance, contact us at
Cengage Learning Customer & Sales Support, 1-800-354-9706

For permission to use material from this text or product,
submit all requests online at **cengage.com/permissions.**
Further permissions questions can be emailed to
permissionrequest@cengage.com.

Library of Congress Control Number: 2010930764

Student Edition:
ISBN-13: 978-1-4130-3315-1
ISBN-10: 1-4130-3315-6

Wadsworth
20 Channel Center Street
Boston, MA 02210
USA

Cengage Learning is a leading provider of customized learning solutions
with office locations around the globe, including Singapore, the United
Kingdom, Australia, Mexico, Brazil, and Japan. Locate your local office at:
international.cengage.com/region

Cengage Learning products are represented in Canada by
Nelson Education, Ltd.

For your course and learning solutions, visit
www.cengage.com.

Purchase any of our products at your local college store
or at our preferred online store **www.cengagebrain.com.**

Printed in the United States of America
2 3 4 5 6 7 14 13 12 11

Your students can also find on Reading CourseMate two kinds of audio files that help make reading a more engaging experience. First, each "Read and Talk" reading (found at the beginning of each part in Parts 1–5 and the beginning of each theme in Part 6) is read aloud so students can listen to as well as read them. Second, each red vocabulary word has a corresponding audio file so students can hear how the word is pronounced. Not only do these audio files aid students who have auditory learning preferences, but they also help students gain confidence using the new vocabulary in conversation.

Videos Related to Readings

Vocab Words on Audio

Read and Talk on Demand

Reading Topics Students Love and Will Learn to Love

Activate includes many readings on topics that students like to talk about: Hollywood stars; recent movies (based on books, of course!); inspiring sports figures like Bethany Hamilton, Kyle Busch, and Joe Kapp; the power of music; *CSI* and *CSI: Miami;* the Oscars; Facebook and MySpace; cell phones; the environment; and body image. By acknowledging and respecting students' current interests, we allow them to divorce content from process. After they learn the process of active reading, we change the content to show them the many interesting ideas and experiences that more academic sources engage. *Activate* includes many excerpts from college textbooks and other more academically inclined sources, on topics as varied as mummies, poverty, digestion, artistic creativity, surviving airplane crashes, nonverbal communication, the use of robots to catch poachers, setting and achieving goals, and hundreds of other topics relevant to academic and everyday life. There are even brief excerpts from novels to entice students to read for enjoyment.

Access the Reading CourseMate via www.cengagebrain.com/shop/ISBN/1413033156 to hear vocabulary words from this selection and view a video about this topic.

Mistakes, I've Made a Few

Kyle Busch

1   At the beginning of the season, I told myself that as a **rookie** driver, I was going to make some mistakes. I sure haven't fallen short on that prediction.

2   I'm just lucky to have a **veteran** team behind me that catches me when I stumble and helps me get back on my feet. That has happened a couple of times lately, and I don't know where I'd be if I didn't have my crew to keep me straight.

3   Some of you might have read about what happened to us at Dover, where I hit another car when I was leaving my pit stall and damaged the fender on my car. I came back into the pits, and the team fixed me up. We had a _____ that ended up _____ to my team

Reading Journal

rookie Use your logic based on the rest of the sentence. Is a *rookie* driver new or experienced?

● Listen to the words Busch says to himself.

veteran The word *rookie* in the previous paragraph is an antonym to *veteran*. What does *veteran* mean?

● Make a mental movie of the ideas here and in the next two paragraphs.

or her body and see it in a distorted and unrealistic way. Michael may have seen his nose as being ugly or fat. His BDD caused him to view his nose in an extremely unrealistic and unhealthy way.

Frank Edwards/Archive Photos/Getty Images

Michael Mariani-Pool/Getty Images

Michael Germana/Everett Collection

everything including her vocal ability to her grandmother, w[ho] encouraged her to pursue her dreams.

    Before *American Idol*, in 2003, Jennifer was signed to a 7-mon[th] contract to perform on a Disney cruise playing the role of Calliop[e]. When that ended, she decided not to renew her contract and inste[ad] flew to Atlanta to try out for *American Idol*. She left a sure thing [in] order to take a chance at a bigger dream. The prize for the winn[er] of *Idol* is a record contract.

    Jennifer reached 7th out of 70,000 *Idol* hopefuls. In typic[al] Simon Cowell fashion, he sent her away with the **stern** word[s] "You're out of your depth. I don't think you're capable of doi[ng] any better." Ouch. However, others, such as Barry Manilow a[nd] Elton John, recognized her amazing abilities. When season 3 of *Id[ol]* ended, she went on tour with the top 10 finalists, and was gratef[ul] for having the opportunity.

Summary: _____

_____

Thinking Required!

A byword of the Dole/Taggart reading series is critical thinking. In *Activate: College Reading*, students are asked to start thinking on page 1 and they never stop thinking. Several critical thinking features are built into the book:

- **The "Why?" question** is asked after many multiple-choice question and other kinds of questions in the book. Students are asked to explain their thinking in writing after they have selected an answer by going back into the reading selection and finding information to support their answer. This allows students to practice analysis and learn to provide evidence for their ideas, a skill they will use in every college course. Students' answers can also provide instructors with valuable feedback about what students are noticing or ignoring as they read.

> ___ 2. Which of the following statements is the best main idea of the list at the end of the passage?
>   a. To be successful, set big goals that you can achieve in one to two years.
>   b. Write down your goals.
>   c. Goal setting is important.
>   d. Pat Summitt has a strategy for setting goals that will help you succeed.
>
> **WHY?** What information in the selection leads you to give that answer? _____
>
> _____
> _____
> _____

- **"Spotlight on Inference"** features provide students with step-by-step instructions that demystify the process of inference, on which all reading depends. For instance, using word parts to build word meanings is a rather complicated process that is spelled out in the "Spotlight on Inference" that appears in Lesson 4.

> ### Spotlight on Inference: Working with Word Parts
>
> When you use word parts to figure out the meaning of a word, you often have to use **inference**. Inference is the process of putting together the bits of information you read to see what they add up to. You do this by using your logic and your prior knowledge. Here is an example using the word **contiguous**.
>
>
>
> | prefix | + | root | + | suffix |
> |--------|---|------|---|--------|
> | con- | | tig | | -uous |
> | together | | touching | | full of |
>
> When you put the meanings of the word parts together, you get "full of touching together" or "touching together fully." Now, you could draw any number of conclusions

- **Lessons 15 and 16 specifically cover critical thinking topics.** Lesson 15 introduces each of the six critical thinking levels of Bloom's (Revised) Taxonomy separately and shows students how they have been using the levels throughout the course and the book. Lesson 16 teaches students to distinguish fact and opinion and has further coverage of inference.

- **Critical thinking underlies vocabulary questions** that appear after part-end readings and four of the readings in Part 6. Instead of providing students with a list of vocabulary words and definitions before a reading, *Activate* points to context clues and word part clues during reading so students can figure out the meanings of words. (See the margin of page 208 for an example.) This critical thinking process is true to how experienced readers figure out word meanings on the fly. Another example is "Relationships Between Words." After students figure out word meanings, they are asked to respond to items that link two or more new words in a relationship; in order to respond they must go through a process of remembering, understanding, applying, analyzing, and evaluating—the first five levels of Bloom's Taxonomy.

Figure 5.1 Bloom's taxonomy with questions.

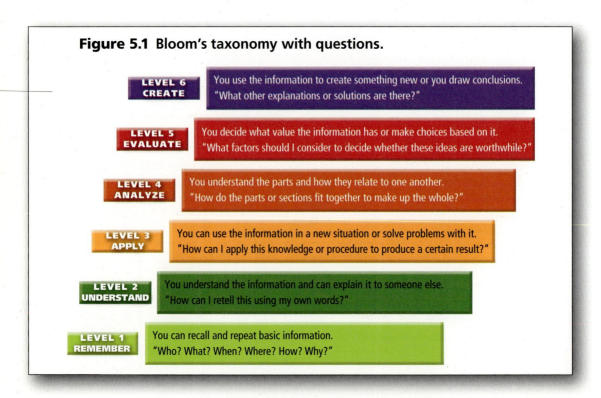

LEVEL 6 CREATE
You use the information to create something new or you draw conclusions.
"What other explanations or solutions are there?"

LEVEL 5 EVALUATE
You decide what value the information has or make choices based on it.
"What factors should I consider to decide whether these ideas are worthwhile?"

LEVEL 4 ANALYZE
You understand the parts and how they relate to one another.
"How do the parts or sections fit together to make up the whole?"

LEVEL 3 APPLY
You can use the information in a new situation or solve problems with it.
"How can I apply this knowledge or procedure to produce a certain result?"

LEVEL 2 UNDERSTAND
You understand the information and can explain it to someone else.
"How can I retell this using my own words?"

LEVEL 1 REMEMBER
You can recall and repeat basic information.
"Who? What? When? Where? How? Why?"

Vocabulary Development in Every Part of the Book

Four distinct lessons on vocabulary form the vocabulary development process outlined in Part 2 of *Activate: College Reading*: using word parts, defining words in context, using the dictionary, and examining the author's tone. The coverage in each lesson is brief, yet detailed enough so that students can then apply the lessons when reading the "Test" selections at the end of each part. Every end-of-part "Test" reading starting in Part 2 includes a multipart vocabulary development component, as do four readings in Part 6.

- Where needed, a "Common Knowledge" box defines background concepts the author assumes everyone knows.

- Vocabulary words are printed in red in each reading. Marginal notes point out the presence of context clues and/or word part clues for each vocabulary word. In rare instances, students are asked to consult a dictionary for a definition.

Access the Reading CourseMate via **www.cengagebrain.com/shop/ISBN/1413033156** to hear a reading of this selection and view a video about this topic.

A Tense Moment in Iraq

Daniel Goleman

Reading Journal

Dean Conger/CORBIS

1   During the early days of the second American invasion of Iraq, a group of soldiers set out for a local mosque to contact the town's chief **cleric**. Their goal was to ask his help in organizing the distribution of relief supplies. But a mob gathered, fearing the soldiers were coming to arrest their spiritual leader or destroy the mosque, a holy **shrine**.

2   Hundreds of **devout** Muslims surrounded the soldiers, waving their hands in the air and shouting, as they pressed in toward the

cleric Look for a synonym for *cleric* two sentences later.

shrine Use the words *mosque* and *holy* to help you figure out what a *shrine* is.

devout Look at the emotion expressed by the mob in the previous sentence to determine the meaning of *devout* in this context.

- "Vocabulary in New Contexts" helps students transfer word vocabulary knowledge from the context in which they learned them to new contexts. This section includes five different types of activities:
  1. "**EASY Note Cards**" asks students to make note cards for vocabulary words according to the system set up in Lesson 5.
  2. "**Relationships Between Words**" are sentences that include two or more vocabulary words; students have to decide if the situation in each sentence makes sense or not, and explain their answers.
  3. "**Language in Your Life**" consists of brief statements in which students relate a vocabulary word to something in their own experience.
  4. "**Language in Use**" includes fill-in-the-blank sentences all related to one topic, and students are asked to insert the appropriate vocabulary words.
  5. "**Spotlight on Word Parts**" shows how a vocabulary word from the reading is composed of word parts, and then other words that use the featured word part are defined. Students are asked to distinguish the words in sentence contexts.

Relationships Between Words

Circle yes or no to answer the question. Then explain your answer.

1. If a person were described as "**fiendish**," could his or her behavior be considered **hideous**?

   Yes   No

   Explain. _____

2. Would hearing that she had been **vindicated** after being falsely accused **alleviate** a person's pain and anxiety?

   Yes   No

   Why or why not? _____

Spotlight on Word Parts: *Pro-*

As you have learned, *profound* means "deep and insightful." The word *profound* is composed of two parts:

   pro- means "from, forward, forth, or before" + **found** means "bottom or deep"

When you put the two parts together, you get "from the deep."

   The word part **pro-** is used in many other words.

   proceed = move forward
   progress = walk forward
   profit = gain from
   produce = bring forth
   profuse = give forth in abundance

Circle the correct word in each of these sentences.

   1. California vineyards have a reputation for (proceeding / producing / progressing) excellent wines.

An Entire Part Devoted to Text Structure

Students often have trouble distinguishing the main idea of a paragraph from its topic and from its supporting details. So Part 3 is devoted to the MAPP reading plan. MAPP reinforces the concept that ideas are connected and that a reader's primary job is to understand the relationship of these ideas. This reading strategy is simple and direct, and it helps students understand the hierarchy of ideas at the same time as it requires the active participation of the reader.

MAPP: A Plan for Reading

Mark = **Mark** the answers to your questions.

About = Topic: What is the reading **about**?

Point = Main Idea: What is the **point**?

Proof = Supporting Detail: What is the **proof**?

A Progression of Skills Within a Holistic Framework

Activate: College Reading focuses students' attention on one skill at a time to give them the best opportunity to fully integrate each skill before moving on. Each section in Parts 1–5 includes targeted activities ("Interactions") and ends with a review of the main points of the section. Each lesson ends with four activities—two "Activate Your Skills" and two "Master Your Skills"—that not only give students additional practice but also can be used to test individual skills. Each part ends with a "Summary Activity" that is a comprehension check of the ideas in the part, an application in which the skills of the part are used to read a longer selection, and then, for instructors who want to give their students practice reading comprehension tests throughout the term, a test that includes all the major reading skills.

ACTIVATE YOUR SKILLS 1
Asking Questions and Marking Answers

A. What six words can you use to form questions from the titles and headings as you are reading?

1. _____

Form a question from each title or heading from the college textbook *Voyages in World History* by Hansen and Curtis.

Time of Upheaval, 1966–1974 _____

Postal Relay System _____

ltiple Centers of Europe, 500–1000 _____

_____

5. _____ nids _____

6. T_____ cally Modern Humans Leave Africa _____

_____

The framework for all this skill development is the active reading process introduced in Lessons 1–3 and then revisited in the major readings. Students practice a full reading process in every end-of-part reading and four of the readings in Part 6. Before they read, they survey the reading, guess its purpose, predict the content, and activate their prior knowledge. While they read, students are reminded to picture or hear what the author is saying, put ideas into their own words, predict what the author is going to say next, search for connections to their own lives, and be open to learning new ideas. After they read, they do different tasks depending on the lessons in that part.

Test 3: Reading Comprehension

ONLINE NEWSPAPER ARTICLE

Your instructor may ask you to take practice tests throughout the semester to help you decide which topics you need to study the most. All the tests in this book include questions about all the major reading comprehension skills after the reading selection.

● Pre-Reading the Selection

The following selection, "The Power of Music," was printed in the October 29, 2007, issue of Boston.com, the online version of the *Boston Globe* newspaper.

Surveying the Reading

What parts of the reading should you survey? _____

_____

Go ahead and survey the reading that begins on page 373.

Guessing the Purpose

Based on the title of the article and the place of publication, do you think the author's purpose is to persuade, inform, or entertain? _____

Supplements

Instructor's Manual with Test Bank

This three-hole punched and perforated Instructor's Manual includes lesson summaries and various activities designed especially for every section of every lesson of the book, offering instructors a wealth of resources from which to choose, tutoring suggestions, lab activities and discussion, and multiple test banks for each lesson.

CourseMate Reading CourseMate

Cengage Learning's Reading CourseMate brings course concepts to life with interactive learning, study, and exam preparation tools that support the printed textbook. Watch student comprehension soar as your class works with the printed textbook and the textbook-specific Web site. Reading CourseMate goes beyond the book to deliver what you need!

Reading CourseMate includes:

- An interactive eBook
- Interactive teaching and learning tools including
  - Quizzes
  - Flashcards
  - Videos
  - Timed Reading
  - And more
- Engagement Tracker, a first-of-its-kind tool that monitors student engagement in the course.

Tailored for *Activate: College Reading,* Reading CourseMate also provides audio versions of "Read and Talk" readings with embedded videos on topics pertinent to the readings included in *Activate.* The videos give students the prior knowledge they might be lacking and increases their cultural literacy. Look for this icon in the text, which denotes resources available within CourseMate, and access them via login.cengage.com.

aplia Aplia for *Activate: College Reading*

Aplia for *Activate: College Reading,* an online reading and learning solution, uses compelling material, interactive assignments, and detailed explanations to give students the structure and

motivation to become better readers. With Aplia for *Activate*, students practice indentifying main points and supporting details, honing critical thinking skills, reviewing vocabulary, and improving comprehension.

Each lesson assignment begins with an engagement page that features an interactive multimedia application to spark students' interest. The engagement page also includes a quote, introduction to the lesson, and comprehension questions that correspond to the multimedia feature.

The core concepts page covers the main objectives of the textbook, such as strategies to increase a student's reading comprehension, surveying and identifying the purpose, main idea and supporting details of a reading, and identifying word parts such as suffixes and prefixes. The material uses multiple-choice, check box, scenario, identification, and comprehension questions.

Compelling readings provide questions of varying difficulty with detailed explanations that let students try a problem again if they get it wrong the first time. Students can also interact with the text by using built-in tools that allow them to annotate, underline, and highlight. The in-text vocabulary review uses ten new and challenging words taken from the readings and reviews. The reading page also includes review of the synonyms and antonyms of each vocabulary word.

To learn more about Aplia for *Activate: College Reading*, visit **www.aplia.com/ developmentalenglish**.

Acknowledgments

We would like to thank the many people at Cengage Learning who have collaborated with us in the development, production, and marketing of *Activate: College Reading*. Annie Todd, Director of Developmental English and College Success, has once again bravely and safely led us through the unknown. Her confidence inspires us, her trust motivates us, and her wit makes us laugh. Marita Sermolins, our development editor, has worked hard to help us stay organized, informed, and on track. Her many hours of organizing, scheduling, coordinating, summarizing, reorganizing, and rescheduling have been invaluable. Kirsten Stoller, Senior Marketing Manager, has a seemingly endless reserve of energy, creativity, and enthusiasm for talking about our book that is truly inspirational. Corinna Dibble, Content Project Manager, guided the book through production with careful attention to both schedule and accuracy. Amy Gibbons, Media Editor, managed the production of the book's Web site and lent it some of her own original style. Melanie Opacki, Assistant Editor, has helped us through the first two books of our series, answering our questions with cheer and good will.

The in-house team is only part of the collaborative process that occurs in the making of every college textbook. We have read, held to our hearts, and gnashed our teeth over the many helpful comments from instructors from around the country who participated in the development of *Activate: College Reading* by reading numerous drafts, asking pointed questions of our work, and suggesting adjustments to lessons that have helped make this book one that we hope many instructors and students will find value in. Thank you to the following discerning instructors for their assistance:

Lenice Abbott, Waubonsee Community College

Angelia Adams, Richmond Community College

Idell Adams, Baton Rouge Community College

Sandra Albers, Leeward Community College

Karin Alderfer, Miami Dade College

Tamera Ardrey, North Lake College

Tina Ballard, Elgin Community College

Lisa Barnes, Delaware County Community College

Christine Barrilleaux, Tallahassee Community College

Alfred Basta, Kaplan University

Gail Bauer, Richland Community College

Thomas Beery, Rhodes State College

Carla Bell, Henry Ford Community College

Linda Berreau, St. Cloud Technical and Community College

Linda Black, St. Johns River Community College

Eleanor Bloom, Chemeketa Community College

Michael Boyd, Illinois Central College

Regina E. Boyd, Itawamba Community College

Sylvia Boyd, Phillips Community College of the University of Arkansas

Acquanetta Bracy, Alabama State University

Napoleon Brooks, Union County College

Maureen A. Cahill, Tidewater Community College

Kathleen Carlson, Brevard Community College

Marlys Cordoba, College of the Siskiyous

Karen Cowden, Valencia Community College

Barbara Doyle, Arkansas State University

Pam Drell, Oakton Community College

Rhoda Fagerland, St. Cloud State University

Rochelle Favale, College of DuPage

Meribeth Fields, Central Florida Community College

Deborah Fuller, Bunker Hill Community College

Amy Garcia, Fullerton College

Georgia Gaspar, Rio Hondo College

Patricia Grega, University of Alaska Anchorage

Geraldine Gutwein, Harrisburg Area Community College

Mary Harper, Broward College

Lois Hassan, Henry Ford Community College

Valerie R. Hicks, Community College of Baltimore County Catonsville

Patricia L. Hill-Miller, Central Piedmont Community College

Letitia Hudlow, Jackson State Community College

Suzanne Hughes, Florida State College at Jacksonville

Martin Hyatt, ASA Institute

Julie Jackson-Coe, Genesee Community College

Marguerite Jones, Central Florida Community College

Julie Kelly, St. Johns River Community College

Patty Kunkel, Santa Fe College

Diane N. Lerma, Palo Alto College

Amelia Lopez, Harold Washington College

Jane Maguire, Valencia Community College

Lisa Martin, Piedmont Technical College

Teresa Massey, Chemeketa Community College

Donna Mayes, Blue Ridge Community College

L. Adam Mekler, Morgan State University

Marlene Merritt, Seminole Community College

Dianne Miller, Phoenix College

Roxanne Morgan, American River College

Yvette Myrick, Community College of Baltimore County

Mary C. Newman, College of DuPage

Julie Odell, Community College of Philadelphia

Hattie L. Pinckney, Florence-Darlington Technical College

Carolyn Poole, San Jacinto College

Elizabeth Renn, Guilford Technical Community College

Dawn Sedik, Valencia Community College, West Campus

Jeffrey Siddall, College of DuPage

Mitzi Sloniger, Riverside Community College, Norco

Valerie Solar, East Los Angeles College

Lorraine Stansel, McLennan Community College

Marjorie Sussman, Miami Dade College

Sharon Swallwood, St. Petersburg College

Priscilla Underwood, Quinsigamond Community College

Nicole Williams, Community College of Baltimore County

Lynda Wolverton, Polk State College

Helen E. Woodman, Ferris State University

Leslie would like to thank Ivan for his always refreshing reservoir of creativity and his devotion to truth. It's been my pleasure to listen to Ivan's stories from the reading classroom and to hear his respect and deep concern for his students. To Chuck, Sara, Harmony, and Phoenix, thank you for your good-natured, ever-present support, without which I couldn't make it through a single day of writing.

Ivan would like to thank Leslie for her relentless pursuit of perfection. Her skilled eye, keen insight, and ability to connect the dots have improved the creativity of our frequent discussions and the quality of our many pages. No one knows more than I how fortunate I am to be partnered with such a high-caliber professional who is also a friend. Ivan also wants to thank his family. Without you to be proud of me, this book would not mean as much. To my wife, Deneé, you are an incredible woman, and I thank God that you are in my life today and always; thanks for leaving the closet light on for me! Bella and Lilli, I love you so much . . . Daddy's done; let's play!

Plan for Success

In order to plan for success, you need to know a few things. First, you need to know who your instructor is and how to contact him or her. Second, you need to make a connection with some of your classmates, so you can get homework if you are absent or discuss assignments or talk through any questions you may have. Next, you need to be aware of the syllabus guidelines, especially as they relate to grading policies. You also need to think about and clarify any short- and long-term goals that you are working toward. Finally, having specific steps in your plan for success is essential. We wish you the best as you begin.

Find Out About Your Instructor

What is your instructor's name? _____

What is your instructor's e-mail address? _____

What is your instructor's office phone number? _____

What are your instructor's office hours? _____

Get to Know Your Classmates

Write down the name and contact information of at least two students in your class whom you can call or e-mail for any work you miss or have questions about. This list can be adapted as you make friends with your classmates.

1. _____

2. _____

3. _____

Read and Understand Your Class Schedule or Syllabus

What are three important goals for this course? _____

_____

_____

_____

What is the course policy on attendance? _____

How is your grade determined? _____

What is your instructor's drop policy? _____

Circle yes or no to indicate whether a certain kind of information is on your class schedule or syllabus.

1. The name of a required textbook   Yes   No

2. Student learning outcomes or objectives   Yes   No

3. The date of the midterm exam   Yes   No

4. A grading scale   Yes   No

5. The date of the final exam   Yes   No

6. Holidays   Yes   No

7. A lab requirement   Yes   No

8. A weekly reading assignment   Yes   No

9. A weekly vocabulary assignment   Yes   No

10. Information about Student Services   Yes   No

Write down other important dates or requirements your class schedule or syllabus includes:

1. _____

2. _____

3. _____

4. _____

5. _____

Ask questions on anything you are unsure of.

What Are Your Short-Term and Long-Term Goals?

Goals generally fall into one of five different categories:

1. Mental—learning, reading, studying

2. Physical—health, diet, exercise, sleep

3. Relational—family, friends

4. Financial—save, budget, make more money

5. Spiritual—grow in faith, explore your beliefs

We will define short-term goals as any goal that you can accomplish within the next year. Please write down one short-term goal you have for each category. We will help you with the first one!

1. Mental: To pass this class with an A. _____

   _____

2. Physical: _____

   _____

3. Relational: _____

   _____

4. Financial: _____

   _____

5. Spiritual: _____

   _____

We will define long-term goals as any goal that you can accomplish within the next two to five years. Please write down one long-term goal you have for each category. We will help you with the first one!

6. Mental: To graduate with a certificate or degree in _____

   _____

7. Physical: _____

   _____

8. Relational: _____

   _____

9. Financial: _____

   _____

10. Spiritual: _____

    _____

Investigating What Makes Students Successful

Life as a student is busy. You may be trying to balance school, a part- or full-time job, your family, perhaps even young children. The demands on you are great. However, you have enrolled in college for a purpose. You have a goal in mind. You want to earn a degree, get a better job, or maybe make more money to provide a comfortable life for you and your family. Whatever your reason, you have chosen to improve yourself through education, and that is a wonderful goal.

Understand that the main purpose of school is learning. No matter how many roles you are juggling, school will demand your attention. You will have to choose priorities in order to be successful in school—just enrolling will not be enough.

Being in school is like running a marathon. Unlike a sprinter, who races all out for a short distance, marathon runners must pace themselves so they can go the whole distance. As a student, you are signing up for a whole semester, and you must pace yourself from beginning to end in order to be successful.

Your goal in this and every course you take is to earn an A, right? OF COURSE! Here are some strategies to help you achieve your short-term goal of getting an A and your long-term goal of graduating.

1. **Believe in yourself.** Belief in oneself is not a magic formula for automatic success. However, do not underestimate the power of belief. It affects your emotions, thoughts, assumptions, and behavior. **Write one specific way that you can believe in yourself.**

   _____

2. **Know what motivates you.** Remember why you are here. What is your goal? What are you working for? Keep your short- and long-term goals in mind. Reward yourself for jobs well done. It can be a small reward—watching your favorite TV show after completing homework. Or it can be a bigger reward—going out with your friends, or anything else that will motivate you to make a short-term sacrifice to achieve your academic goal. **Write one thing that you can use to motivate yourself to do well in this class.**

   _____

3. **Be organized.** Make sure you have a folder for important documents from each of your classes. Know assignment due dates. Turn assignments in on time and in the format your instructor has requested. Buy a planner or use your smartphone. Enter study times in your planner or calendar so that you make time to do your work. Have an organized place where you do your homework. Make a commitment to create a weekly schedule for schoolwork, and stick to it. **Write down when you will be doing the homework for this class each week.**

   _____

4. **Prioritize**. Make to-do lists and order them.

   1—for the most important items that need to be done today

   2—for items that are important but not as urgent as the number 1's

   3—for things that are least urgent but still need to be done soon

   Write down a specific plan for how you will prioritize your schoolwork.

   _____

5. **Be active**. Participate actively in class. Ask questions and be prepared to discuss ideas with classmates. If you do not understand something, ask your instructor. Chances are someone else has the same question. Also, be present as you are studying. Do not passively read, but actively engage your mind so you do not waste your time or energy by just going through the motions. **Write one specific way you will be active in class.**

   _____

6. **Don't procrastinate**. Do homework the day it is assigned rather than the night before it is due. You will be a much more effective student if you study a little each day rather than try to cram it all in at the last minute. Also, when you procrastinate, you tend to have emergencies. By planning, prioritizing, and organizing, you can avoid a lot of stress because you have a game plan and are following it. **Write down an idea of how you can avoid procrastination.**

   _____

7. **Network**. Who can you use to your advantage to help you in your academic success? Are your parents a good resource? Are your friends encouraging you or distracting you from school? Are you utilizing your instructors? Have you identified the good students in your classes with whom you can form study groups? Do you know what resources your school offers, such as labs, advising, counseling, career services, and so forth? **Write down one person and one resource you can use to become a more accountable student.**

   _____

8. **Keep your health in mind**. Do not underestimate the power of a good night's sleep, a healthy diet, and exercise. All of these will help you manage stress, stay focused on your studies, and keep a positive attitude. **Write down one way you can maintain or improve your health.**

   _____

9. **Take the initiative**. Read ahead. Ask questions. Make connections. If you are absent, come to the next class with any missed work done. Review your material a few minutes each day in order to be better prepared for class discussions, quizzes, and tests. Make the effort to talk to your instructor and develop a rapport with him or her. **Write down one strategy that will help you take the initiative.**

   _____

10. **Always do your best**. If you always do your best, then you are a success, even if you do not get the highest grade. Be honest. Do not cheat, which actually leads to failure. Treat others the way you wish to be treated and chances are they will return the gesture. **Write down something that gets in the way of you doing your best. Then write down one idea for how to overcome this temptation.**

   _____

Discuss the ten items from the preceding list with a partner. Talk about how each of you can be a successful student this semester. See how your ideas are similar to a classmate's or if one of you has thought of a different idea that may be motivating to others.

activate

COLLEGE READING

"Mama always said life was like a box of chocolates. You never know what you're gonna get."

Tom Hanks said this as Forrest Gump in the movie of the same name.

CostinT/iStockphoto.com (laptop)
bluestocking/iStockphoto.com (pens/pencils)

Active Reading

Have you ever gotten a fancy box of chocolates that included a shape or location "key" for the piece of chocolate you picked? You could get an idea of what was in the chocolate before you took a bite, so you could choose one you actually wanted to taste!

This "key" reflects the same idea that motivates us to watch movie previews, view a TV guide, read the table of contents, or survey the headings and titles of an article. We want to have an idea of what we are going to watch or read.

. . . .

Share Your Prior Knowledge

Tell a classmate about a movie you really want to see because of the preview.

Survey the Lessons

Take a moment to turn to the table of contents and survey the headings in Lessons 1 to 3 in Part 1 so you know what to expect. Name one thing you already know about:

_____

Name one thing you need to read more about to understand better:

_____

Everett Collection

Find chapter-specific interactive learning tools for *Activate,* including quizzes, videos, and more, through CengageBrain.com.

Videos Related to Readings

Vocab Words on Audio

Read and Talk on Demand

Read and Talk

In college, reading is just the beginning of how you will share new ideas with others in your class. So the first reading in each part of this book is meant to give you the chance to talk about reading. Read the article, and then use the four discussion questions to talk about your ideas with your classmates and your instructor. Make this an opportunity to create new friendships and knowledge through the art of listening to the ideas of others, the enjoyment of discussing your thoughts, and the fun of reading something new.

Access the Reading CourseMate via www.cengagebrain.com/shop/ISBN/1413033156 to hear a reading of this selection and view a video about this topic.

CSI's Adam Rodríguez Looks Beyond "Miami"

Francis Rodríguez

1   Adam Rodríguez's Detective Eric Delko may be vanishing from *CSI: Miami* in the upcoming eighth season (in 2009), but the Cuban/Puerto Rican actor is **reappearing** everywhere else, it seems. "*CSI* was an amazing opportunity to develop my career," the Yonkers-born Rodríguez said over the phone from Los Angeles. "I'm ready to explore any kind of [good] projects down the road on TV or the big screen."

reappearing Appearing again.

Frazer Harrison/Getty Images

dramedy A movie that has equal parts of drama and comedy.

2   So far, it's going according to his plan. The 34-year-old can currently be seen opposite singer Mary J. Blige and Taraji P. Henson in Tyler Perry's **dramedy** *I Can Do Bad All by Myself,* which opened Friday, September 11th, 2009, and was the highest-grossing film of

the weekend. He's also joining ABC's *Ugly Betty* for the upcoming season, **premiering** October 9th. He will play an old flame of Betty's sister, Hilda, TVGuide.com reported. And he's in three films yet to be released: the Latino thriller *A Kiss of Chaos, Let the Game Begin* (with Stephen Baldwin) and *Caught in the Crossfire,* a police corruption drama with rapper 50 Cent.

premiering Showing a movie or other performance to the public for the first time.

3   "It's not a secret that Latinos work harder," said the actor, who splits time between Los Angeles and New York. "I've been working hard and waiting. Patience and hard work are paying off."

4   When he's not acting, Rodríguez likes to write poems and play guitar. He says music holds a special place in his life, something that attracted him to sharing a film with R&B queen Blige. "I've been a fan of Blige's work for years," he said. "The music really plays a key role in the story, and that made even easier the connection for me. We had a genuine bond."

5   Today, his main passion clearly is acting, but that was not always the case. In his youth, he hoped to play professional baseball, until he suffered a spinal injury. "The injury made clear that the dream of becoming a baseball player was **intercepted**," he said. "When I turned 19, I said to myself: 'I'm going to take acting classes and dedicate myself to this passion.'"

intercepted Interrupted the progress of.

6   Though he says he has been enjoying the Hollywood life, he misses the city. "I feel at home when I'm there," he said. "If I'm in New York, you'll find me hanging out with my friends and spending time with my family," he explained. "One thing is for sure: The Latin food and the music"—he likes Marc Anthony and Gilberto Santa Rosa—"will be included."

—"Miami's Heat" by Francis Rodriguez, *The New York Daily News*, September 16th 2009

Talking About Reading

Respond in writing to the questions below and then discuss your answers with your classmates.

1. Have you ever seen Adam Rodríguez on *CSI: Miami* or anywhere else? What did you think of his acting? What do you think makes a good actor or actress? _Yes I have seen him in Tyler Perry moves, he was pretty good. A good actor or actress is someone who have their ardence full attention_

2. This article states that Rodríguez had wanted to be a pro baseball player, but then he hurt his back. Do you know anyone, like Adam Rodríguez, who started off on one track but then had to set a different goal? What happened? *Yes my sister started out as a police officer then change goal and become a nurse.*

3. Rodríguez says that patience and hard work have paid off for him. *CSI: Miami* was an amazing opportunity to develop his career, but he is ready to move on now. In what areas of life have you noticed that patience and/or hard work have paid off?

   when going to college. when you just started something you feel like giving up but you just have to be patience and with hard work it will paid off.

4. Rodríguez says he likes to act, write poems, play guitar, spend time with friends and family in New York, and enjoy Latin food and music. Turn to your neighbor and give him or her five "fast facts" about yourself. Write notes to yourself first if you want to. _____

   _____

Reading Is an Active Process

At the beginning of each episode, the crime scene investigators on *CSI: Miami* are faced with a mystery they need to solve. To find the answers they seek, they have to ask tough questions, examine evidence, and use their heads. They actively search for clues and then think about what the clues mean.

You use the same skills when you view TV shows or movies.

- **Before a TV program comes on**, you may think ahead to what will happen on the program. If it's *CSI: Miami*, you may wonder what tonight's mystery is going to be. Will the investigators have to figure out who the murderer is, whose DNA sample was found at the scene of the crime, or who died in a car crash?

- **During the TV program**, you may be thinking about which person is most likely to be the killer. You might be commenting to friends about who seems suspicious, what the investigators and medical examiners are doing, what they are saying to each other, and which ones you like best.

- **After the TV program,** you may be talking about whether the story made sense, whether you believed the story the whole way through, and whether this episode was better or worse than the previous one.

Active reading is similar to this way of watching TV. It is a process that can include steps to take before reading, steps to take while reading, and steps to take after reading. During all the steps, an active reader works like a *CSI* investigator to uncover the real meaning of a reading selection.

Before You Read or View, Take Four Actions.

Before you read or view, you can quickly take four actions that dramatically improve comprehension (that is, understanding):

1. Survey the reading selection or program to get an overview of what will be coming.

2. Guess the purpose of the reading selection or program.

3. Predict what's going to happen.

4. Think about your prior knowledge of the subject matter.

We will discuss each action one at a time. It will take some time to describe each action. However, you should take just a few moments to apply all four actions before you start reading a selection.

1. Survey to Get an Overview of What's Coming.

Surveying a reading is like watching a preview. When you go to a movie, often you have already seen the preview for it several times. The preview shows you some of the highlights of the movie. You often know who the main characters are (and which actors play them), you've viewed some of the scenery and settings, and you have a sense of the film's genre—whether the movie is going to be a fast-paced action adventure, a romantic comedy, or a horror flick.

Similarly, if you take a few moments to survey or preview a reading selection, you will tremendously improve your chances of comprehending the reading selection. When you preview, you do not read the whole selection, you only examine selected parts. Following are the parts to look at.

write this in book

Read These Parts Quickly When You Survey.

- **The title:** What do these words reveal about the subject? Some titles also have a subtitle. For example, here is a title from a health book: "Working Out on Campus: Student Bodies in Motion." The main title is "Working Out on Campus," and the subtitle is "Student Bodies in Motion." You should read both parts of the title to gather information when you survey.

- **The headings:** Read each heading and, for a moment, think about how it relates to the title. You can tell the headings from the regular text in different ways:

  1. Headings may sit on their own lines.

  2. Headings may be in **bold** or *italic* type.

  3. Headings may be printed in all capital letters.

  4. Headings may be printed in a different color than the regular text or in a larger size.

- **The first sentence of each paragraph:** Read each first sentence quickly to get a sense of what that paragraph will cover.

- **Words that are in boldface or *italic* type:** These words are likely to be some of the most important ideas the author wants you to remember. In textbooks, words that are in **bold type** are often followed by a definition of that word.

- **Images and their captions:** If photos, graphs, or charts are part of the reading, look at them and read their captions. The caption is the title or sentence that explains the visual. We will talk more about visuals and captions in Lesson 14.

Example of Surveying

In the following reading selection, the parts that are highlighted in yellow are the parts you read when surveying. Take a moment to think about each highlighted piece of text as you read it.

Engage in Your Learning Process

1   Most people have mastered "the look"—with which you stare blankly at someone while trying to act interested. In reality, your mind is wandering more than listening or learning. It could be that the person speaking is not very interesting or that you are just tired or unmotivated that day.

2   No matter the situation, it is your responsibility to understand what the person is saying. In a learning situation, the key is to engage with the speaker. To engage means to get either mentally or physically involved and to participate actively. Active participation (1) increases concentration, (2) improves listening, (3) seems to make the time go quicker, and (4) positively affects overall learning.

3   How can you actively take part in a learning situation? Five key ways to engage in the learning process are discussed in the following sections.

4   **BE THERE AND DO IT.** One obvious way to increase your potential for learning is to be physically and mentally present. Whether you are learning in a classroom or lab or searching the Internet, learning sessions are a very important part of the learning process. Since learning is an individual activity, there is no substitute for being there. In every learning situation, you have the choice of acting like a sponge or a rock. Learners who act like sponges soak up the information through active participation, demonstrate a positive learning attitude, and possess an eagerness to learn. On the other hand, learners who act like rocks generally have a negative learning attitude and are, in effect, just occupying space. It should be no surprise that sponges learn more than rocks.

5   **SIT CLOSE TO THE ACTION.** This is an easy way to ensure your participation in the learning process. Sitting up front limits distractions from others and gives you a clear view of the instructor and the instructor a clear view of you. Learners in front usually sit up taller than those in the back and thus appear more eager and ready to learn. Though you may feel a little uncomfortable at first, try sitting in front in your next class. You just might find yourself concentrating better and learning more.

6   **FEARLESSLY ASK AND ANSWER QUESTIONS.** To ask an intelligent question and to respond intelligently, you have to be listening and concentrating. Too many learners feel that asking questions makes them look stupid. Actually, learners who don't ask questions don't learn nearly as much or as easily as those who do.

7   Remember that you aren't expected to know it all; that's why you are studying—to learn. Your job as a student is to ask questions so you can learn more. Though you may feel a little uncomfortable asking questions in front of others, many times, they are happy the question was asked, as they themselves had the same question in mind but were afraid to ask. In the workplace, active questioning is essential for clarifying work tasks and communicating efficiently with others.

8   Questions can be asked during instruction, after class, during office hours, or in a scheduled appointment. As long as the question is answered, it doesn't matter where or when it is asked. Remember to keep an ongoing list of the questions you have so you don't forget them.

9   Not all questions need to be asked aloud. When you are curious about a topic, write down your questions. Decide which ones someone else can answer and which ones you can research yourself. Asking questions and working to find the answers will help you learn even more.

10   Questions are easy to ask when you use the **5W's and H: who, what, when, where, why, and how.** For example, if you are taking a computer course and the day's topic is "Font Styles and When to Use Them," you might think about the following questions:

1. Who uses the fonts?

2. What are the font styles?

3. When should the font be changed?

4. Where do I get fonts?

5. Why should fonts be used?

6. How many fonts are available?

Think of yourself as a young child, a curious student of the entire world. By learning to ask questions, you will understand the world better while learning more in less time.

11   **TAKE NOTES. Taking effective notes is like taking a picture for later reference of anything you see, hear, or read.** Learners who take notes are more focused, have information to study from, and—most importantly—daydream less. Even if you are not required to take notes, creating your own notes will help you learn more. Knowing how to take good notes will transform the act of reading—which for many is a passive activity—into an active process. Note taking while reading forces you to concentrate because you are actively seeking out important information. *More concentration means less mind wandering. Less mind wandering means more learning in less time.*

12   **GET HELP. Even the most active learners need some help sometime.** Assistance can come from your instructor, boss, or fellow learners. The time to ask for help is not the day of or the day before an exam or a project deadline. Starting to prepare at least a week ahead will ensure that the help you need is available when you want it. Classroom instructors generally do not have a lot of sympathy for students who wait until the last minute to ask for help. Bosses have even less tolerance for employees who wait to ask for help.

—Beale, *Success Skills: Strategies for Study and Lifelong Learning,* 3rd edition

INTERACTION 1–1	Reviewing What You Learned from Your Survey

Using only the information from the parts of the reading highlighted in yellow, answer the following questions on your own or with a partner.

1. What process is being described in this reading? _____

_____

2. What are five ways to actively take part in this process?

- _____
- _____
- _____
- _____
- _____

3. Aside from the headings, what words or letters are in **bold type** in this reading selection? _____ What does this mean? _____

4. What sentences are in *italics*? _____

_____

_____

5. Someone once said that the only stupid question is the question you don't ask. Would the author of this selection agree with that statement? Why or why not?

_____

_____

_____

_____

Remember: Previewing selected parts of a reading before you start reading it straight through is a tremendous boost to reading comprehension.

INTERACTION 1–2   Surveying a Movie Review

1. Which of the elements that you should read while surveying are in the movie review that follows? Check them.

____ Title

____ Headings

____ First sentences of paragraphs

____ Words in bold or italic type

____ Visuals and captions

2. Highlight or underline the parts of this movie review that you should read while surveying.

New Moon Delivers . . . Six Packs

Suzie Soule

1   The Twilight Saga continues with the *New Moon* movie that arrived in theaters Friday, November 20, 2009. This year's most anticipated film really delivers to the fans of the Twilight Saga. I loved *New Moon* because of its trueness to the book. It will be a harder task for the next installment, *Eclipse*. Even if you are not a Twi-hard (a fan of the Twilight Saga), you can appreciate the movie.

2   *New Moon* correlated with the book by telling the story of why Edward left Bella—because he feared for her life with Vampires. Unless you have read the books, you might be lost as to what is going on with the movie. The camera angles and effects were a little too complicated and took away from the story.

3   The best parts of the movie were the gratuitous shirtless Quileutes. Audible expressions were heard from the female viewers in the theater when Jacob Black (Taylor Lautner) takes off his shirt for the first time in the movie. Costuming for the movie must have been easy because there were a lot of cut off jean shorts. Jacob Black is caring for Bella Swan (Kristen Stewart) and she tells him, "You're kind of beautiful, you know?" Yes, we know. His body was amazing. Especially when you compare [it] to how Jacob looked in *Twilight*.

Photos 12/Alamy

4   *New Moon* also delivers great special effects. The Quileutes' morphing into werewolves was very smooth. The fight scenes with the Volturi

were good as well. Christopher Heyerdahl, as the Volturi Marcus, was very chilling. Dakota Fanning did a great job as Jane. I look forward to seeing more of her in *Breaking Dawn*.

5   Overall the movie was what I expected from the second installment of the Twilight Saga. *New Moon* delivers what women want . . . beautiful men with great bodies. (For the critics, there have been gratuitous topless women in movies for decades. It's about time that women get a chance to see some skin.) *New Moon* also delivers a love story that is so strong it affects the people physically. It is the classic story of star-crossed lovers with [the] twist of a love triangle between a girl-next-door, a vampire and a werewolf.

—"New Moon Delivers ... Six Packs" by Suzie Soule.
Associated Content—Yahoo. November 21, 2009

Using only the material you highlighted or underlined, answer the following questions.

3. What movie is being reviewed? _____

   _____

4. What series is it a part of? _____

   _____

5. What is the writer's favorite part of the movie? _____

   _____

6. What are two places in your highlighted material that give you the answer to question 5?

   • _____

   • _____

7. What are two other reasons the writer liked the movie?

   • _____

   • _____

2. Guess the Purpose of the Program or Reading Selection.

Some TV programs and movies are meant to entertain you with an interesting story about the characters' lives. They might get you to laugh or to feel sad or to be angry. If the main purpose of the program or movie is to engage your emotions, then we say its purpose is to **entertain** you.

Other times, you may watch a program in order to learn something new. For instance, a show on The History Channel and a news program both have the general purpose of teaching you something. Their purpose is to **inform** you.

A third general purpose of some TV shows and some reading material is to **persuade** you to believe something different from what you currently believe or to act in a way that you don't currently act. The most obvious form of persuasive programming on TV is a commercial. The purpose of commercials is to get you to buy something.

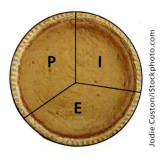

Jodie Coston/iStockphoto.com

One way to remember the three general purposes of a program or a reading is to think of purpose as a PIE: *P* is for the persuasive purpose, *I* is for the informative purpose, and *E* is for the entertainment purpose.

Sometimes writers or producers may want to serve only one thin slice of PIE—one purpose—in a particular program or reading. However, many times they give you a more generous helping (a larger slice) of PIE. For example, a magazine article may have two purposes: to entertain and to inform.

Consider two kinds of information when you are guessing the purpose of a reading before you read it:

- The source—for example, a textbook, *Cosmopolitan* magazine, a cookbook.

- The ideas you read while you are surveying. Does the author seem to be trying to persuade you to change how you think or act? Is he or she explaining a process or teaching you something? Or entertaining you? Think about the author's words and what they suggest.

INTERACTION 1–3	Deciding on the Purposes of Programs

Discuss the general purpose(s) of each of the following kinds of TV programming with your classmates and circle the purposes. Then, if a show has more than one purpose, decide which one seems most important and put a "1" next to it.

1. Cooking shows   4. Cartoons

2. Reality TV shows   5. Nature shows

3. Political speeches

INTERACTION 1–4	Deciding on the Purposes of Reading Material

Discuss the general purpose(s) of each of the following kinds of reading materials with your classmates and circle the purposes. Then, if the reading material has more than one purpose, decide which one seems most important, and put a "1" next it.

1. TV Guide

2. College textbook

3. Novel (fiction)

4. Advertisement in the mail

5. Sports section of a newspaper

Remember: When you are preparing to read, spend a moment thinking about the likely purpose of the reading selection. Later, after you read, decide whether you were right.

3. Predict What's Going to Happen.

The beginning of a movie often sets up the "problem" that the movie will later solve. A crime is committed, and the movie will be about catching the crook. Or a boy loves a girl who loves a different boy, and the movie will be about how the three of them sort things out. As soon as the scene is set with the problem, we as viewers try to figure out what's going to happen next. Who committed the crime? Who does the girl really love?

The same thing happens as you are reading. While you are surveying or previewing a reading selection, you can start to think about what is going to happen. If you have surveyed a heading, you will start to think about what the author will say in that section. If you have surveyed the first sentence of a paragraph, you will wonder what the author is going to say in the rest of that paragraph. This curiosity is natural, and sometimes it may happen without you even realizing it. Other times, you may have to make predictions more deliberately.

INTERACTION 1–5	Predicting the Content of a Reading Selection

The following heading and sentences come from a college communications textbook. They are the material that you would read during a quick survey before reading. After each highlighted part, make a prediction about what the authors will discuss.

Self-Image

1. Based on this heading alone, what might the authors talk about in this part of the textbook chapter? _____

_____

_____

We form impressions about ourselves based on our own perceptions.

2. What might the authors talk about here? _____

_____

_____

> We place a great deal of emphasis on the first experience we have with a particular kind of event.

3. What might the authors talk about here? _____

_____

_____

> When we have positive experiences, we are likely to believe we possess the personal characteristics that we associate with that experience, and these characteristics become part of our picture of who we are.
>
> —Adapted from Verderber, Verderber, & Sellnow, *COMM*

4. What might the authors talk about here? _____

_____

_____

5. Think about the first time you tried something new and were successful at it. What did you believe about yourself as a result? _____

_____

_____

Remember: When you are surveying the title, headings, first sentences, bold and italic words, and visuals of a reading, think for a moment about what the author is probably going to be talking about. This prepares your mind to understand the material.

4. Think about Your Prior Knowledge of the Subject Matter.

Earlier in this lesson you surveyed a reading called "Engage in Your Learning Process." But this is not the first time you've gotten information about learning. You have heard advice from teachers, parents, or others about how to learn. Because you knew this information *before* you read, it's called your *prior* knowledge. Take a moment to think about some of the advice you've heard about how to learn.

In addition to what people have told you about how to learn, you have probably developed some ideas yourself through the years about how to learn. This prior knowledge is based on your own experience. Think about what you have learned through experience about how you learn.

In addition to the things you've heard from others and learned from experience, you have been observing others at school for a long time. What have you figured out about how to learn from observing others who are good at it?

All of this knowledge that you bring to your viewing or reading is called your **prior knowledge**. (*Prior* means "before.") You want to activate, or set in motion, your prior knowledge as much as you can before you start reading. Doing this takes advantage of a natural pattern of learning for people. The pattern is to fit what you are learning about into what you already know.

INTERACTION 1–6	Activating Your Prior Knowledge

Titles of articles, chapters, and books are listed here. For each title, predict what the reading selection might be about—its topic. Then list three things you already know about that topic. It's okay if your knowledge is vague or incomplete. Just write whatever you know.

1. Book title: *The Book of Basketball*

   Prediction about the topic: _____

   Three pieces of prior knowledge:

   - _____
   - _____
   - _____

2. Article title: "Calorie-Burning Fat? Studies Say You Have It"

   Prediction about the topic: _____

   Three pieces of prior knowledge:

   - _____
   - _____
   - _____

3. Title of a section in a textbook: "The Health Care System"

Prediction about the topic: _____

Three pieces of prior knowledge:

- _____
- _____
- _____

4. Book title: *Joker One: A Marine Platoon's Story of Courage, Leadership, and Brotherhood*

Prediction about the topic: _____

Three pieces of prior knowledge:

- _____
- _____
- _____

5. Book title: *Snakebit: Confessions of a Herpetologist*

Prediction about the topic: _____

Three pieces of prior knowledge:

- _____
- _____
- _____

Review: Actions to Take Before Reading

Four actions that you can complete before reading will dramatically improve your reading comprehension:

- Survey the reading selection to get an overview of what will be coming.
- Guess the purpose of the reading selection.
- Predict what's going to happen.
- Think about your prior knowledge of the subject matter.

ACTIVATE YOUR SKILLS 1
Taking Four Actions Before You Read

1. In the textbook selection that follows, look for the elements you should read while surveying. Check the ones that are in this particular reading.

_____ Title

_____ Headings

_____ First sentences of paragraphs

_____ Words in bold or italic type

_____ Images and captions

2. Highlight or underline the parts of this textbook selection that you should read while surveying.

Movies at Work

1   Today the center of the movie industry is movie production. Most of the movies that are distributed by the major studios and exhibited at your local theater result from independent companies that produce movies under agreements with individual studios. Although these production companies work independently, and each company is organized differently, jobs in movie production fall mainly into the following categories:

1. Screenwriters
2. Producers
3. Directors
4. Actors
5. Production
6. Marketing and administration

2   The beginning for each movie is a story idea, and these ideas come from *screenwriters*. Screenwriters work independently, marketing their story ideas through agents, who promote their clients' scripts to the studios and to independent producers.

3   Typically, *producers* are the people who help gather the funding to create a movie project. Financing can come from banks or from individuals who want to invest in a specific movie. Sometimes producers or actors help finance the movies they make. Once the funding for the story is in place, a *director* organizes all the tasks necessary to turn the script into a movie. The director works with the producer to manage the movie's budget.

4   Obviously, *actors* are important to any movie project. Sometimes the producer and director approach particular stars for a project even before they seek funding, to attract interest from the investors and also to help assure the investors that the movie will have some box office appeal.

5   *Production* includes all the people who actually create the movie—camera operators, set designers, film editors, script supervisors and costumers, for example. Once the movie is finished, the *marketing* people seek publicity for the project. They also design a plan to advertise and promote the movie to the public. As in any media industry, people who work in *administration* help keep all the records necessary to pay salaries and track the employees' expenses, as well as keep track of the paperwork involved in organizing any business.

—Biagi, *Media Impact: An Introduction to Mass Media*, 8th edition

Using only the material you highlighted or underlined, answer the following questions.

3. What is this selection about? _____

4. What are people who write movie stories called? _____

5. Who figures out where the money will come from to fund a movie? _____

6. What are five other jobs in the movies that this reading selection mentions?

   • _____

   • _____

   • _____

   • _____

   • _____

7. What is the main purpose of this selection?

8. Predict what paragraph 2 will discuss. _____

   _____

9. List two things you already know about how movies are made, even if that knowledge seems vague or incomplete.

   • _____

   • _____

ACTIVATE YOUR SKILLS 2
Taking Four Actions Before You Read

1. In the textbook selection that follows, look for the elements you should read while surveying. Check the ones that are in this particular reading.

   _____ Title

   _____ Headings

   _____ First sentences of paragraphs

   _____ Words in bold or italic type

   _____ Images and captions

2. Highlight or underline the parts of this textbook selection that you should read while surveying.

Families Often Control Latin American and Caribbean Media

1   In Latin America, media are part of the same power structure that controls politics, business, and industry. Family dynasties often characterize Latin American media ownership.

2   Romulo O'Farrill, Jr., chairman of the board of Televisa in Mexico, owns more than 150 TV stations and eight newspapers. Mario Vásquez Raña owns more than 50 Mexican newspapers. His name became familiar in the United States in 1986 when he bought a controlling interest in United Press International, but he sold his interest a year later.

Print Media

3   In Santiago, Chile, the Edwards family has owned *El Mercurio* since 1880; now the El Mercurio newspapers total at least 14. *O Estado de São Paolo* in Brazil, owned by the Mesquita family, has represented editorial independence in the region for more than 50 years and is often mentioned as one of the country's best newspapers. Argentina's *La Prensa* refuses government subsidies and has survived great conflicts with people like former dictator Juan Perón, who shut down the newspaper from 1951 to 1955.

4   Home delivery for newspapers and magazines is uncommon in Latin America. The centers of print media merchandizing are street corner kiosks, where vendors offer a variety of publications. *Manchete,* published in Brazil, is one of the most widely circulated national magazines, similar in size and content to *Life* magazine.

Audio and Video Media

5   Broadcasting operates in a mix of government and private control. Government often owns a few key stations and regulates stations that are privately owned, but the pattern is varied. Cuba's broadcast media are controlled totally by the government, for example. In Costa Rica and Ecuador, almost all the broadcast media are privately owned. In Brazil, private owners hold most of the radio stations and television networks, including TV Globo Network, which claims to be the world's fourth largest network (after the United States' original three TV networks).

—Biagi, *Media Impact: An Introduction to Mass Media*, 8th edition

Using only the material you highlighted or underlined, answer the following questions. Circle T for true and F for false.

3. Many newspapers and TV stations in Latin America are owned by powerful families.   T   F
4. To answer question 3, you could check the title.   T   F
5. *El Mercurio* is a newspaper in Mexico.   T   F
6. To answer question 5, you could check the first sentence of paragraph 3.   T   F
7. This selection discusses print, audio, and video media.   T   F
8. This selection discusses media in North America, South America, and Latin America.   T   F
9. The words in *italics* are the names of TV stations.   T   F
10. Select one of the sentences you said was false. Write the number of the question:

    9 The words in italics are the name of tv station

    Correct the statement here: _____

    _____

    _____

MASTER YOUR SKILLS 1
Taking Four Actions Before You Read

First, apply the four actions to use before reading. After you complete the four actions, answer the questions that follow the reading.

2012: Another Cheesy Disaster Movie

Linda Cook

1   Here's a movie that's dopey, cheesy and sometimes downright silly.

2   But it's a disaster movie—it's supposed to be ridiculous! Because this is all about spectacle, and *2012* has plenty of that. If you enjoyed Roland Emmerich's *The Day After Tomorrow*, then you'll also want to take in his *2012*.

3   The late filmmaker Irwin Allen, crowned "The Master of Disaster," would be proud. You know the drill, if you've watched disaster movies before. You start with a nice bunch of people in various places, and then you follow them as the rest of humanity—or at least most of it—is lost to fires, volcanoes and tsunami.

4   We first meet the insistent Dr. Adrian Helmsley (Chiwetel Ejiofor), one of the advisors to the President (Danny Glover). He has discovered that the world is headed toward annihilation within three years, and it's now 2009. Helmsley's assignment is to try to figure out a way to save the lives of thousands of people when the earth finally starts to self-destruct.

5   His boss is Carl Anheuser (Oliver Platt), a no-nonsense, unemotional type who barks orders and tries to do the best he can for the most people despite the individual connections and circumstances at hand. The President's daughter (Thandie Newton) strikes up a friendship with Helmsley, and worries about the safety of her father.

6   Elsewhere, Jackson Curtis (John Cusack) is taking his two kids to a national park when he hears about a huge earthquake that is laying siege to his home in Los Angeles. In Yosemite, he meets the wild-eyed but seemingly sensible Charlie Frost (Woody Harrelson) who tells Jackson that the world is indeed about to end—turns out the Mayans were right about 2012.

7   So Jackson ends up teaming up with his kids, his ex-wife Kate (Amanda Peet), and her plastic surgeon boyfriend Gordon (Tom McCarthy) who just happens to know how to fly a plane. They're trying to make it to a spot where, Charlie has informed them, there's a plan in place to save at least a piece of humanity.

8   The special effects are really good, and believe me, that's the main reason to go see this movie. It's certainly not a show focused on character development or serious drama. The dialogue is sometimes laughable and the situations are outrageous.

9   But if you want to see some great special-effects, this is a fun way to spend an afternoon or evening.

Rated: PG-13 for scenes of death and destruction and foul language.
Running time: 2 1/2 hours.
Stars: John Cusack, Chiwetel Ejiofor, Amanda Peet, Oliver Platt, Thandie Newton, Danny Glover and Woody Harrelson.
Director: Roland Emmerich.
Screenwriter: Roland Emmerich and Harald Kloser.

—Linda Cook, "Love disaster and destruction? '2012' won't disappoint."
From the *Quad City Times*, Davenport, IA. Nov. 17, 2009.

Use only the material you highlighted or underlined to answer the questions about the movie review.

1. What movie is this review about? _____

2. What kind of movie is it? _____

3–4. What other movies of this kind have you seen?

    • _____

    • _____

5. What do movies of this kind have in common? _____

    _____

6. After you surveyed the review, did you predict that the writer would suggest readers go see the movie?   Yes   No   Maybe

7. Why did you give that answer? _____

    _____

8–13. Who are six characters in the movie, and which actors play them?

    • _____

    • _____

    • _____

    • _____

    • _____

    • _____

14–15. Have you seen any of these actors in other movies? If so, name the actor and the movie.

    • _____

    • _____

16–17. What are the author's purposes in this movie review?

Circle any that apply. (P I E)

18–20. What are three words the author uses to describe this movie?

    • _____

    • _____

    • _____

MASTER YOUR SKILLS 2
Taking Four Actions Before You Read

The reading that follows is from a college psychology textbook called *Psychology: Themes and Variations*. First, apply the four actions to use before reading. After you complete the four actions, answer the questions that follow the reading.

Observational Learning

1   Most people learning to drive know exactly where to put the key and how to get started. How are these responses acquired? Through *observation*. Most new drivers have years of experience observing others drive, and they put those observations to work.

Ted Horowitz/Corbis Edge/CORBIS

Observing a Good Deal Strengthens Assertiveness

2   Suppose you observe a friend behaving assertively with a car salesperson. You see your friend's assertive behavior reinforced by the exceptionally good buy she gets on the car. Your own tendency to behave assertively with salespeople might well be strengthened as a result. Notice that the reinforcement is experienced by your friend, not you. The good buy should strengthen your friend's tendency to bargain assertively, but your tendency to do so may also be strengthened indirectly. This process, called **observational learning**, has been investigated extensively by Albert Bandura (1977, 1986).

Physical Punishment Increases Aggressive Behavior

3   Bandura's theory of observational learning can help explain why physical punishment tends to increase aggressive behavior in children, even when it is intended to do just the opposite.

Parents who depend on physical punishment often punish a child for hitting other children—by hitting the child. The parents may sincerely intend to reduce the child's aggressive behavior, but they are unwittingly serving as *models* of such behavior. Although they may tell the child, "hitting people won't accomplish anything," they are in the midst of hitting the child in order to accomplish something. Because parents usually accomplish their immediate goal of stopping the child's hitting, the child witnesses the reinforcement of aggressive behavior. In this situation, actions speak louder than words—because of obsvervational learning.

Basic Processes of Observational Learning

4   Bandura has identified four key processes that are crucial in observational learning. The first two—attention and retention—highlight the importance of cognition in this type of learning.

- *Attention*. To learn through observation, you must pay attention to another person's behavior and its consequences.

- *Retention*. You may not have occasion to use an observed response for weeks, months, or even years. Hence, you must store a mental representation of what you have witnessed in your memory.

- *Reproduction*. Enacting a modeled response depends on your ability to reproduce the response by converting your stored mental images into overt behavior. This may not be easy for some responses. For example, most people cannot execute a breathtaking windmill dunk after watching Kobe Bryant do it in a basketball game.

- *Motivation*. Finally, you are unlikely to reproduce an observed response unless you are motivated to do so. Your motivation depends on whether you encounter a situation in which you believe that the response is likely to pay off for you.

—Adapted from Weiten, *Psychology: Themes and Variations*, 7th edition

1. What is the most important purpose of this reading selection? _____
   _____

2. What clue did you use to decide on the most important purpose? _____
   _____

3. What kind of learning does this reading selection discuss? _____
   _____

4. Where in the reading selection did you find the answer to question 3? _____
   _____

5. How many headings does this reading have? _____

_____

6. Write down the first heading and make a prediction about what the section will cover.

- Heading: _____

- Prediction: _____

_____

7. Write down the second heading and make a prediction about what the section will cover.

- Heading: _____

- Prediction: _____

_____

8. Write down the third heading and make a prediction about what the section will cover.

- Heading: _____

- Prediction: _____

_____

9. Think about a time when you learned from observing how someone else acted. Write a few sentences about that time. _____

_____

_____

_____

10. Some observational learning leads to results that aren't good for the person who is learning. Using information you got from this reading and from your prior knowledge, list two kinds of situations in which this might happen.

- _____

- _____

As you read, focus your attention on the meaning of the words, sentences, and paragraphs you are reading. You can help yourself stay focused and attentive in the following ways:

Picture or hear what the author is saying. Create a photo, a movie, or a soundtrack in your mind.

> *Suppose you read:* A US Airways jet was forced to crash land in the Hudson River after it hit a flock of geese.

> *You would create a movie in your mind:* A jet hit a flock of geese. The jet started falling. The plane landed in a river. (Each person would imagine somewhat different details. People who knew more about the crash would picture it more accurately than others.)

AP Photo/Edouard H. R. Gluck

Put ideas into your own words. See if you can restate what the author is saying.

> *Suppose you read:* To raise people's awareness about global warming, the World Wildlife Fund has organized Earth Hour, one hour in which major buildings around the world will turn off their lights. Participating buildings in the United States include the Empire State Building, the Golden Gate Bridge, and the St. Louis Gateway Arch.

You might restate these ideas by saying to yourself: Some big buildings all around the world, including three in the United States, are going to turn off their lights for an hour to draw people's attention to the problem of global warming. The World Wildlife Fund has planned this event, which is called Earth Hour. (Some details are missing. If they were important to know, you would go back and reread to find them.)

- **Predict what the author is going to say next.** What is this about, and where is it going?

    Suppose you read: Chuck Faesy thought his fence-building days were over.

    You might predict: He thought they were over? So I guess they weren't. I predict the next sentence will tell how Chuck Faesy had to build another fence.

- **Search for connections to your own life and to other ideas and situations.** How is this information or event like something you already know?

    Suppose you read: Franklin Delano Roosevelt's first Inaugural Address is now known for only one sentence: "The only thing we have to fear is fear itself."

    —From Zakaria, "There's More to Fear Than Fear,"
    Newsweek, February 2, 2009

    You could make various connections: You might think of Barack Obama's inauguration and what he said. You might think of other famous speeches and the sentence that is most remembered from them. Or you might think about the quotation and try to connect it to times in your life when you were afraid. Is the quotation true? Is the only thing we have to fear—fear?

- **Be open to learning something new that doesn't fit easily into information you already have.** How is this situation or idea different from something you're familiar with?

    Suppose you read: Harvard psychologist Howard Gardner does not agree with traditional definitions of "intelligence." He argues that there are eight different kinds of intelligence and says that intelligence is not inborn.

    You might consider: Perhaps when you were in elementary school, certain children were considered the "bright" ones. Gardner's idea is different. It suggests that everyone has a certain kind of intelligence. Depending on your experiences, you might need to rethink certain situations that happened earlier in your life.

| INTERACTION 1–7 | Staying Active and Focused While You Read |

Use the strategy shown in parentheses before each of the following sentences to understand the author's meaning. If the strategy helps you understand that sentence, put a √ on the line after it. If it doesn't help you, put an X on the line.

1. (Hear) The world around us is full of sounds. _√_

   (Search for connections) All of them are meaningful in some way. _√_

   (Hear) Stop for a moment and listen to the sounds around you. _√_

   (Learn something new) What do you hear? _√_

   (Predict) Why didn't you hear those sounds a moment ago? _was not listening_

   (Learn something new) We usually filter out "background noise" for good reason, but in doing so we deaden our sense of hearing. _____

   —Adapted from Titon, et al., *Worlds of Music*, Shorter 3rd Ed. (2009)

2. (Predict) For many Americans, gun ownership provides a comforting feeling of safety. _____

   (Learn something new) In the six-month period following the terrorist attacks of September 11, 2001, for example, handgun sales increased by 455,000 over the same period the year before. _____

   (Put ideas in your own words) The vast majority of Americans who own guns are law-abiding citizens who keep their firearms at home for self-protection. _____

   (Picture) Law enforcement efforts are mostly concerned with keeping guns out of the hands of those—such as children, the mentally ill, and criminals—who might use guns to harm themselves or others. _____

   —Gaines & Miller, *Criminal Justice in Action: The Core*, 5th edition

3. (Predict) A *tamalera* is a mandatory piece of tamale-making equipment that functions as a giant steamer, and I wasn't certain I could buy one in Utah. _____

   (Search for connections) You are toast without one, especially if you are making mass quantities of tamales to give away to family and friends, which is the only reason my mom makes tamales. _____

(Picture) A tamalera resembles an aluminum trash can, including the handles and lid, but it is half the size. _____

(Picture) It is shiny, almost like silver, with a shelf inside. _____

(Search for connections) You fill it with a gallon or two of water, set it to slow boil, and steam your tamales there for a couple of hours. _____

—Huerta, *Educational Foundations*

INTERACTION 1–8   Deciding on a Reading Strategy to Use While Reading

The readings that follow are from a variety of sources. As you begin reading, decide which "during reading" strategy you want to try. Write down the strategy. Try a different strategy for each paragraph.

Strategies to Use While Reading

- Picture or hear.
- Put ideas into your own words.
- Predict.

- Search for connections.
- Learn something new.

---

1. Strategy you are trying: ___Picture or hear___

> Last summer, Creigh Deeds, who was then the Democratic candidate for governor of Virginia, killed a 270-pound black bear with his car near the little Appalachian town of Millboro, where the two of us grew up in the 1970s. The bear had lumbered out of the woods and Deeds couldn't brake fast enough. The bear died instantly. The candidate's car didn't fare much better. The news went out over the police scanner, and within a few hours most everyone in rural Bath County knew all about it. It wasn't long before Deeds started receiving urgent phone calls from locals. They weren't worried about him. They wanted to know what he was going to do with the bear. "People kept coming up to me for days," Deeds recalled recently when I traveled around the state with him. "'Can I have your bear, Creigh, can I have your bear?'" They wanted to use it to train their bluetick hounds for hunting, or to make a rug, or to eat.
>
> —Tuttle, "Mr. Deeds Goes to Town," *Newsweek*, October 26, 2009

How well did that strategy work for this paragraph?   Very well   Okay   Not well

2. Strategy you are trying: _Predict_____

Bean and Sausage Soup

Sausage lends hearty flavor to this Italian-flavored soup. For best results, add the sausage near the end of the cooking time, as indicated, just long enough to heat it through. For color, you can brown the sausage first in a skillet, if you like, and drain off the excess fat, but it isn't really necessary.

—Haughton, *The Best Slow Cooker Cookbook Ever*

How well did that strategy work for this paragraph?   Very well   Okay   Not well

3. Strategy you are trying: _Search for connections_____

Mummies Revealed

X-rays are perhaps the most important tool used today to examine Egyptian mummies. Before X-rays were possible, no one could see what lay hidden beneath the tightly wrapped mummies without unwrapping them. So, for many years, scientists unwound mummies to study them, but they destroyed them in the process. X-rays gave archaeologists a way to "see" inside the mummies without damaging them.

—McClafferty, *The Head Bone's Connected to the Neck Bone*

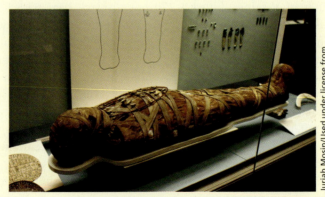

Juriah Mosin/Used under license from
Shutterstock.com

How well did that strategy work for this paragraph?   Very well   Okay   Not well

4. Strategy you are trying: _____

Poverty

We need to remind ourselves why so many children are orphans today: because their parents were not able to get treatment for AIDS, most likely because they could not afford it, or because they lived in a country which was too poor to provide basic health care. We must know that one of the greatest assaults on human dignity is poverty, where you wake up not knowing where you're going to get your next meal. When you cannot have decent accommodation for yourself and your children. When you cannot feed them, and send them to school. That is the greatest assault on human dignity.

—Nelson Mandela, former president of South Africa

How well did that strategy work for this paragraph?   Very well   Okay   Not well

5. Strategy you are trying: _____

The Police Force

For many years, the typical American police officer was white and male. As recently as 1968, African Americans represented only 5 percent of all sworn officers in the United States, and the percentage of "women in blue" was even lower. Only within the past thirty years has this situation been addressed, and only within the past twenty years have many police departments actively tried to recruit women, African Americans, Hispanics, Asian Americans, and other members of minority groups. These efforts have produced steady, though not spectacular, results. Minority representation as a whole in American police departments increased from 14.6 percent in 1987 to 23.6 percent in 2003. During that time, the percentage of female police officers rose from 7.6 to 11.3 percent, the percentage of African American officers grew from 9.3 to 11.7 percent, and the percentage of Hispanic or Latino officers expanded from 4.5 to 13 percent.

—Gaines & Miller, *Criminal Justice in Action: The Core*, 5th edition

How well did that strategy work for this paragraph?   Very well   Okay   Not well *write in your notes*

Review: Ways to Stay Active and Focused While Reading

As you read, stay active and focused using the following techniques:

- Picture or hear what the author is saying.

- Put ideas into your own words.

- Predict what the author is going to say next.

- Search for connections to your own life and to other ideas and situations.

- Be open to learning something new that doesn't fit easily into information you already have.

INTERACTION 1–9   **Combining Strategies: Before and While You Read**

The selection that follows is taken from a college health textbook called *An Invitation to Health.* To read the selection, use the "before reading" and "during reading" strategies you learned. Answer the questions that follow each paragraph.

Self-Efficacy and Locus of Control

1   Do you see yourself as master of your fate, asserting control over your destiny? Or do so many things happen in your life that you just hang on and hope for the best? The answers to these questions reveal two important characteristics that affect your health: your sense of *self-efficacy* (the belief in your ability to change and to reach a goal) and your *locus of control* (the sense of being in control of your life).

1. What two major concepts (ideas) does this reading selection discuss?

- _That you should take control of your life_

- _____

2. Before you read this selection, did you know what either of these ideas means?   Yes   No

3. Define each idea.

- _Self-Efficancy is to control what goes on in your life_

- _Locus Control- is to take control of your life_

4. Connect these ideas to something you already know about: yourself. Circle the answers that best describe your level of self-efficacy and your locus of control.

Self-efficacy: Low   Medium   High
Locus of control: Low   Medium   High

> 2   Your confidence in your ability to cope with challenge can determine whether you can and will succeed in making a change. In his research on self-efficacy, psychologist Albert Bandura of Stanford University found that the individuals most likely to reach a goal are those who believe they can. The stronger their faith in themselves, the more energy and persistence they put into making a change. The opposite is also true, especially for health behaviors. Among people who begin an exercise program, those with lower self-efficacy are more likely to drop out.

5. Is it easier to keep a successful exercise program going if your self-efficacy is high or low? Why? *If your self-efficacy is high it would be easier to keep a successful exercise program but if your self-efficacy is low you will give up easy*

6. Think of someone you know who has high self-efficacy and a strong locus of control. Give an example of how this person acted when he or she wanted to change something in his or her life. *Robert the use to sell on the street and a friend ask him to give up that like? was heard for him at first because it ds the only life he knew, but he did*

7. What does faith in a person's self lead to that helps him or her succeed? *Faith goes a long way you have to have faith in your self first for things to happen.*

> 3   If you believe that your actions will make a difference in your health, your locus of control is internal. If you believe that outside forces or factors play a greater role, your locus of control is external. Hundreds of studies have compared people who have these different perceptions of control. "Internals," who believe that their actions largely determine what happens to them, act more independently, enjoy better health, and are more optimistic about their future. "Externals," who perceive that

> chance or outside forces determine their fate, find it harder to cope with stress and feel increasingly helpless over time. When it comes to weight, for instance, they see themselves as destined to be fat.
>
> —Hales, *An Invitation to Health*, 12th edition

8. Who is more optimistic, a person with an internal locus of control or a person with an external locus of control? Why? <u>A person with internal</u> <u>locus because the have stronger will power</u>

9. Use the strategy of being open to learning something new. How is the information in this reading selection different from ideas you were familiar with before you read it? _____

_____

_____

10. Rate how easy or difficult this selection (paragraphs 1–3) was to understand with 1 being difficult and 5 being easy.

very hard to understand   very easy to understand

1   2   3   (4)   (5)

Remember: The rest of the lessons in this book will suggest strategies you can use to improve your comprehension. It is you, however, who will need to decide to use them.

ACTIVATE YOUR SKILLS 1
Staying Active and Focused While You Read

A. Use the strategy of picturing and hearing to read the following paragraph. Actively try to understand what you are reading.

Joe lay on his covers, dressed in blue jeans and a T-shirt, a small man with scarred and wiry arms and prominent collarbones. He had an unkempt beard and unruly hair, and when he smiled nervously at the doctors trooping in, I saw he still had most of his teeth but probably wouldn't for long. Farmer introduced himself and the members of his team. Then he sat down at the head of Joe's bed, on a corner of the mattress, folding himself half around Joe in an agile way that made me think of a grasshopper. He leaned over Joe, gazing down at him, pale blue eyes behind little round lenses. For a moment, I thought Farmer might climb into bed with him. He placed his hand on Joe's shoulder instead and stroked it.

—Kidder, *Mountains Beyond Mountains*

Answer the following questions.

1. Where is Joe, probably? _____

2. Why do you say so? _____

3. Does Joe take good care of himself?   Yes   No

4. Why do you say so? _____

   _____

5. Who do you think Farmer is? _____

6. Why do you say so? _____

   _____

7. Is Joe at ease among the doctors?   Yes   No

8. Why do you say so? _____

   _____

9. Does Farmer act the way a doctor usually acts in this situation?   Yes   No

10. Why do you say so? _____

   _____

B. Read the following paragraph, paying close attention to it. Talk with a partner about what each numbered section means. Then each of you write down the ideas using your own words.

(1) As we get older, a few of the many potential abilities are put into service; most disappear. We see this in a child's ability to dance, to draw, to dazzle in many ways, ways that are often gone by adolescence. This process happens through biological, cultural, linguistic selections early in life. (2) The world in which we find ourselves actually wires up the brain differently because of experience. The world selects what's needed. (3) For example, people develop to digest the food of their region. A fellow graduate student of mine, born in Japan, had to leave the room if Velveeta were even opened, so sick did he become at the smell of rotten milk. (I always wanted to give him blue cheese to see what would happen.) The mind gets customized for each locale.

—Ornstein, *The Evolution of Consciousness*

1. _____
   _____
   _____
   _____

2. _____
   _____
   _____
   _____

3. _____
   _____
   _____
   _____

ACTIVATE YOUR SKILLS 2
Staying Active and Focused While You Read

A. Read each sentence, and then write down a question or prediction about what the author might discuss next.

1. Lynn Lingenfelter's life changed forever on November 11, 1983. *When his family move to another country*

2. Along with a friend, he headed into the woods that day near his family's home to hunt small game, something the two had done dozens of times before. _So it_ _bring back meores_

3. They were climbing a steep mountain slope when Lynn's friend lost his footing. Even before Lynn heard the pop of his companion's .22-caliber rifle, he felt a thump in his back, "As though I'd been slugged with a baseball bat." _he got shot_ _in the back_

4. Almost beside himself with panic and fear, Lynn's friend ran to get help. When he returned, it was with Lynn's younger brother, Mike. _____

5. "They found me lying on the ground, stone cold and blue. I wasn't breathing. By coincidence or fate, Mike had learned CPR in health-education class just a few days earlier. He got me breathing again and held me tight to keep me warm until the paramedics got there and took me to the hospital." _to dress my wound_

—Phillips & D'Orso, *Body for Life*

B. Read the following paragraphs from a business management textbook. Each time you come to a blank line, make a note about either (1) a connection from what you just read to something you know about, or (2) something you just learned for the first time.

If you found a wallet containing $100, would you return it with the money? (6) _____ _____. Informal studies typically show that 57 to 80 percent of people would and that women and people in small towns are more likely to return the wallet with the money. (7) _____

As an employer, you can increase your chances of hiring the honest person who returns the wallet with the money if you give job applicants integrity tests. *Overt integrity tests* estimate job applicants' honesty by directly asking them what they think or feel about theft or about punishment of unethical behavior. (8) _have taken one._ For example, an employer might ask an applicant, "Would you ever consider buying something from somebody if you knew the person had stolen the item?" or "Don't most people steal from their companies?" (9) _no_ _no_ Surprisingly, because they believe that the world is basically dishonest and that dishonest behavior is normal, unethical people will usually answer "yes" to such questions. (10) _____

—Williams, *Management*, 4th edition

MASTER YOUR SKILLS 1
Staying Active and Focused While You Read

Use the strategies you've learned to stay active and focused while you read the following selection. Then answer the questions.

Is It Safe to Talk on the Phone While Driving?

1   According to the National Highway Traffic Safety Administration, driver distraction from various causes plays a role in 20 to 30 percent of all motor vehicle crashes. People who use mobile phones while driving are four times more likely to have a serious crash.

2   Most college students with cell phones use them when driving. A third of these have been involved in a serious car accident. In some states, it is now illegal to talk on a cell phone while driving.

3   Although many believe that hands-free car phones are less hazardous, researchers have shown this is not the case. Talking on a wireless phone while driving a car is just as dangerous with a hands-free or a handheld phone. The reason is that talking while driving distracts the brain as well as the eyes—much more so than talking to another person in the vehicle. Conversation on any type of phone disrupts a driver's attention to the visual environment, leading to what researchers call "inattention blindness," the inability to recognize objects encountered in the driver's visual field. This form of cognitive impairment may distract drivers for up to two minutes after the phone conversation has ended.

—Hales, *An Invitation to Health*, 12th edition

1. How do you answer the question posed in the title? Is it safe to talk on the phone while driving?   Yes   No

2. What are two reasons the author gives in her answer to this question?

   • _____

   • _____

3. Is it safer to drive if you are using a hands-free phone?   Yes   No

4. Why did you give that answer? _____

   _____

5. What is "inattention blindness"? _____

_____

6. As soon as you hang up, does driving get your full attention again?   Yes   No

7. Explain your answer to question 6. _____

_____

8. How much more likely is it that you will have a serious crash if you talk on a cell

phone while driving? _____

_____

9. Who says that driver distraction plays a role in 20 to 30 percent of all car crashes?

_____

10. How often do you talk on your cell phone while driving?

Every time I drive   A lot   Not often   Never

11. What is one new thing you learned from reading this textbook selection? _____

_____

_____

MASTER YOUR SKILLS 2
Staying Active and Focused While You Read

Before Reading. Survey the following reading selection. After you read the first sentence of each paragraph, decide what reading strategy might work well for that paragraph and write it on the line provided.

Strategies to Use While Reading

▪ Picture or hear what the author is saying.

▪ Put ideas into your own words.

▪ Predict what the author is going to say next.

▪ Search for connections to your own life and to other ideas and situations.

▪ Be open to learning something new that doesn't fit easily into information you already have.

While Reading. Use the reading strategy you selected while reading the paragraph. As you read each paragraph, answer the questions that follow it.

Paragraph 1

Pictures of Homeless People in the Media

News article: They live—and die—on a traffic island in the middle of a busy downtown street, surviving by panhandling drivers or turning tricks. Everyone in their colony is hooked on drugs or alcohol. They are the harsh face of the homeless in San Francisco.

Paragraph 1. Strategy you selected before reading: _____

Answer these questions while you read:

1. Who is this paragraph about? _____

2. Where do they live? _____

Paragraph 2

News article, continued: The traffic island where these homeless people live is a 40-by-75 foot triangular chunk of concrete just west of San Francisco's downtown. . . . The little concrete divider wouldn't get a second glance, or have a name—if not for the colony that lives there in a jumble of shopping carts loaded with everything they own. It's called Homeless Island by the shopkeepers who work near it and the street sweepers who clean it; to the homeless, it is just the Island. The inhabitants live hand-to-mouth, sleep on the cement and abuse booze and drugs, mostly heroin. There are at least 3,000 others like them in San Francisco, social workers say. They are known as the "hard core," the people most visible on the streets, the most difficult to help.

—Kevin Fagan, "Shame of the City/Homeless Island."
From *The San Francisco Gate*, November 30, 2003

Paragraph 2. Strategy you selected before reading: _____

Answer these questions while you read:

3. Who calls the traffic island "Homeless Island"? _____

4. Who are known as the "hard core"? _____

Paragraph 3

The news article above is an example of how the media (such as TV, magazines, and newspapers) frame stories about homeless people. The full article includes statements about how the homeless of San Francisco use drugs, lack ambition, and present a disreputable appearance on the streets. This type of framing of stories about the homeless is not unique. According to the media scholar Eungjun Min, media images typically portray the homeless as "drunk, stoned, crazy, sick, and drug abusers." Such pictures of homeless people limit our understanding of the larger issues surrounding the problem of homelessness in the United States.

Paragraph 3. Strategy you selected before reading: _____

Answer these questions while you read:

5. What is the news article an example of? _____

_____

6. How do the media usually show homeless people? _____

_____

Paragraph 4

> Most media framing of <u>newspaper</u> articles and <u>television</u> reports about the problem of home-lessness can be classified into one of two major categories: <u>thematic</u> framing and <u>episodic</u> framing.

Paragraph 4. Strategy you selected before reading: _____

Answer these questions while you read:

7. What two kinds of media are discussed? *newspaper and television*

_____

8. What two types of media framing are mentioned? *thematic and*
   episodic

Paragraph 5

> Thematic framing refers to news stories that focus mostly on statistics about the homeless population. Examples include stories about changes in the U.S. poverty rate and articles about states and cities that have had the largest increases in poverty. Most articles of this type are abstract and impersonal, primarily presenting data and some expert's interpretation of what those data mean. Media representations of this type convey a message to readers that "the poor and homeless are faceless."

Paragraph 5. Strategy you selected before reading: _____

Answer these questions while you read:

9. What kind of news stories does "thematic framing" refer to? _____

_____

10. What is one example of such a news story? _____

_____

Paragraph 6

By contrast, episodic framing presents public issues such as poverty and homelessness as concrete events, showing them to be specific instances that occur more or less in isolation. For example, a news article may focus on the problems of one homeless family, describing how the parents and kids live in a car and eat meals from a soup kitchen. Often, what is not included is the big picture of homelessness: How many people throughout the city or nation are living in their cars or in shelters? What larger factors (such as reductions in public and private assistance to the poor, or high rates of unemployment in some regions) contribute to the problem of homelessness in this country?

Paragraph 6. Strategy you selected before reading: _____

Answer these questions while you read:

11. How does "episodic framing" present public issues such as poverty and

    homelessness? _____

    _____

12. What is often not included in "episodic framing"? _____

    _____

Paragraph 7

How stories about the homeless are framed in the media influences how we view the less fortunate in our society. If we come to see the problem of homelessness as nothing more than isolated data or as situations that affect only a few people, then we are unable to make a balanced judgment of the larger social problems involved. How are the poor and homeless represented in news reports and the television entertainment shows you watch? Are the larger social issues surrounding homelessness discussed within the context of these shows? Should they be?

—Kendall, *Sociology in Our Times*, 7th edition

Paragraph 7. Strategy you selected before reading: _Predict_

Answer these questions while you read:

13. What does the ways the homeless are "framed" in the media influence? _How we_ _veiw the less fortunate in our society_

_____

14. What happens if we view homelessness as data or isolated incidents? _If we come_ _to see the problem of homelessness as nothing more_ _than isolated data or as situation that affect only_ _a few people_

What do you do after you watch a TV program, a movie, or a YouTube video? Your action probably depends partly on why you were watching it to begin with.

- **If you were watching to be entertained,** you may think back on a favorite part of the story, or you may think about the movie or program as a whole to decide what you feel about it.

- **If you were watching to be informed,** you may ask yourself what you learned, and why it matters to you.

- **If you were watching to be persuaded,** you might ask yourself if you were convinced, and why.

When you are reading in college, your most likely purpose is to become more informed—to learn something new. You will probably have to be able to show on a test that you have learned the material, too. There are three related tasks that you can do to review the information that you have read:

- **Think about the ideas in the reading selection.** Each time you finish a section of a textbook chapter, a magazine or newspaper article, or a chapter in a nonfiction book, stop and think. Here are three helpful hints:

  1. **5W's and H.** Ask yourself who, what, when, where, why, and how. In other words, review and remember the basic information you read.

  2. **Connect.** Make connections between the ideas in the reading and your own prior knowledge. This will help you understand the reading selection.

  3. **Search for patterns.** You might find repeated words or ideas that help you understand the topic or patterns the author has used to organize the ideas. This will help you analyze the reading selection.

- **Talk about the ideas in the reading selection.** Talking helps people understand ideas in a way that just thinking to yourself does not. First, you and your classmates may have noticed different things about the ideas, so it's good to combine your knowledge. Second, talking is a method of *rehearsing* your knowledge. Just as a dancer or actor needs to rehearse before a performance, college students need to rehearse their knowledge before a class discussion or test. One effective way to rehearse is to have one person ask the other person questions. You can switch back and forth between asking and answering.

- **Write about the ideas in the reading selection.** Writing is another form of rehearsal. It can be even more useful than talking if you are preparing for a test because most tests are written. However, writing is more than a test prep method. When you write, you find out how much you know about a topic. You can also look at what you wrote and think about whether it all makes sense. You can write important terms and their definitions. You can write a summary of a section (we'll teach you how in Lesson 14). You can also write down your questions about what an author has said.

Reviewing and rehearsing your knowledge are important when you need to remember what you read.

Review: Three Ways to Rehearse Information After You Read

- Think about the ideas in the reading selection.
- Talk about the ideas in the reading selection.
- Write about the ideas in the reading selection.

INTERACTION 1–10	Think, Talk, and Write After You Read

Read the selection from a Web site and answer the questions that follow.

How to Survive a Plane Crash

Charles W. Bryant

1   It's every air traveler's nightmare. Sudden turbulence throws you backward. The beverage cart flies by and crashes into the rear of the cabin. You're losing altitude quickly, and your seatbelt is jammed between the seats. Oxygen masks drop from above, but you didn't pay attention to preflight instructions. People scream, pray, and clutch each other as the plane descends downward at an improbable angle. You think you're going to die.

2   The good news is that an airplane crash doesn't necessarily mean certain death. In fact, of the 568 U.S. plane crashes between 1980 and 2000, more than 90 percent of crash victims survived.

3   In the event of an air disaster, there are things you can do that can increase your odds of living. Keeping a calm, cool head amidst panic and disorder isn't easy, but key to your chances. So are the clothes you wear, the luggage you bring, and where you stow it. Some research even indicates that the seat you choose might help.

4   The most common question asked of crash experts is "Is there a safest seat?" Official sources say that it makes no difference because no two plane crashes are alike. *Popular Mechanics* magazine did some exhaustive research that seems to point to the rear of the plane as the safest spot. They studied data of every U.S. commercial jet crash in the last 36 years and found that passengers in the rear of the plane are 40 percent more likely to survive than those in the first few rows. The Federal Aviation Administration's position is that there is no safest seat. The FAA also concluded in a 2005 report that there's no evidence that any one carrier is any safer than the next.

5   In the event of a crash, there are things you can do to give you a better shot at making it out alive. Following are five tips that everyone should know before they get on their next flight:

- After you board, find the two closest exits and count the rows between them and your seat. In the event of darkness or smoke, feel the seats and count until you reach the exit row.

- Ready for the impact. The official FAA crash position is to extend your arms, cross your hands and place them on the seat in front of you, and then place your head against the back of your hands. Tuck your feet under your seat as far as you can. If you have no seat in front of you, bend your upper body over with your head down and wrap your arms behind your knees. Always stow your carry-on bag under the seat in front of you to block the area.

- Wear long pants, sleeves and closed-toed shoes. This will help protect you from glass, metal and the elements.

- If you're with your family, talk to your children about what to do in the event of an emergency. Divide the responsibility of helping your children between you and your spouse. It's easier for one parent to help a single child than for both to try to keep everyone together.

- Pay attention to the preflight instructions, as all planes are different. When the oxygen mask drops, put it on yourself first before attempting to help someone else. If you fall unconscious, you have no chance of helping your travel mate.

—From http://adventure.howstuffworks.com/ how-to-survive-a-plane-crash.htm/printable.

Think About the 5 W's and H

1. What is the purpose of this article?

　　　　To persuade　　　To inform　　　To entertain

2. Who is this article about? _____

3. What is it about? _____

4. When did 568 U.S. plane crashes occur? _____

5. Where does *Popular Mechanics* say is the safest place to sit in a plane? _____

　_____

6. Why should you count the seat rows between you and the two closest exits?

　_____

7. Why should you place your carry-on luggage under the seat in front of you?

　_____

8. Why should you put on your own oxygen mask before helping others with theirs?

　_____

9. How can you protect yourself from glass and metal in a crash? _____

　_____

Search for Patterns and Write

10. How many of the tips given in paragraph 5 for having a better chance of survival are things you would have to do before a disaster started to happen? _____

   What are they?

   - _____

   - _____

   - _____

   - _____

Connect and Talk

11. Have you ever been in a plane that was shaking, dropping quickly, or otherwise acting in a way you didn't expect?   Yes   No

12. What was your reaction—what did you do? Discuss your reactions with your classmates.

   _____

   _____

ACTIVATE YOUR SKILLS 1
Think, Talk, and Write After You Read

Read each paragraph and then answer the questions that follow.

Paragraph 1

Going for Your Goals

Think of goals as road maps that give you both a destination and a planned itinerary for getting there. "To set goals means to set a course for your life," says psychologist James Fadiman, author of *Unlimit Your Life: Setting and Getting Goals*. "Without goals, you remain what you were. With goals, you become what you wish." As studies of performance in students, athletes, and employees have shown, the one single characteristic that separates high- and low-achievers is having a clear, specific goal.

1. What does the author say is the one difference between high and low achievers?

   _____

2. How can goals act like road maps? _____

   _____

Paragraph 2

> ■ **Set your sights on a destination or target.** You wouldn't board a bus without knowing where you want to go, but it's easy to drift through life with only a vague sense of where you're heading. Unfortunately, goals that don't lead somewhere—like wanting to be healthy—tend to go nowhere. A specific, focused, realistic goal—like developing your upper body strength or reaching a certain weight—can fast-forward you into the future.

3. Check the two examples the author gives of specific, focused, realistic goals:

   _____ Wanting to be healthy

   _____ Wanting to develop your upper body strength

   _____ Wanting to reach a certain weight

4. Who do you know who seems to drift through life with only a vague sense of where he or she is heading? _____

   Who do you know who sets specific, focused, realistic goals? _____

   _____

Paragraph 3

> ■ Take a step and stretch. With your target goal in sight, set "step-and-stretch" goals. Think of them like stair steps that lift you out of your comfort zone and keep you moving forward. Every goal should be a reach from where you are that will bring you to the next level. Break down each step goal into projects, and every project into tasks. Ask yourself the following questions, and write down the answers.
>
> ■ What skills do I need to achieve this?
>
> ■ What information and knowledge must I acquire?

- What help, assistance, or resources do I need?
- What can block my progress? (For each potential barrier, list solutions.)
- Whom can I turn to for support?
- Who or what is likely to get in my way?
- How am I most likely to sabotage myself?

As you develop your game plan, make sure that each goal is within your control. "Other people should not have to change in order for you to meet your goal."

5. What kind of goal do you think the author has in mind here—a big goal or a small goal?   Big   Small

6. Why do you say that? _____

_____

Paragraph 4

- **Express your goal as an affirmation.** Once you've pictured your goal in detail, express it as an affirmation, a single positive sentence. As decades of psychological research have shown, affirmations serve as powerful tools for behavioral change. One key to their success is the present tense. "In your mind's inner grammar, the present tense predicts the future while the words 'I will' delay it," says Fadiman. "The impact is subtle but critical when you're setting goals."

7. What is an affirmation? _____

8. What is a key to developing a successful affirmation? _____

_____

Paragraph 5

- **Visualize the hurdles.** During training, many athletes visualize crossing the finish line or scoring the winning point. Gold medal Olympian Edwin Moses used a different technique: He visualized every hurdle in a 400-meter race, calculating the distance between each, and seeing himself clearing each one. Goal-getters do the same. If you think ahead to what might go wrong, you can come up with ways of going over, under, around, or through whatever obstacles you encounter. If you don't anticipate and problem-solve, obstacles turn into excuses.

9. Why should you visualize the hurdles? _____

10. Who does the author use as an example of visualizing the hurdles? _____

Paragraph 6

■ **Go all the way.** Despite good intentions and considerable progress, many people give up their goals just before the rainbow's end—and congratulate themselves for getting that far. "Would you ever board a plane for Chicago and say, 'Well, you got three-quarters of the way there!' as if that were good?" asks psychologist Christian, who urges goal-seekers to persist, persevere, and "not settle for almost-there." If you stall on the final stretch, do a quick reality check. Maybe you need to add some smaller-step goals, seek more support, or simply allow yourself more time.

—Hales, *An Invitation to Health,* 12th edition

11. What should you do if you have almost reached your goal but feel like giving up?

_____

12. What are some possible solutions? _____

_____

After Reading the Entire Selection

13. **Connect and Talk.** When you want to achieve something in your life, how do you go about getting or doing it? With your classmates, discuss some of the steps you take to reach your goals. _____

_____

_____

14. **Connect and Write.** Think of an area of your life in which you want to change something. On separate paper, write your goal. Then follow the steps given in the reading selection to make your goal work better as a destination and as a map. Be sure to answer the questions in paragraph 3 as completely as you can.

15. **Search for Patterns and Write.** Go back through paragraphs 2 to 6. Write the first bold sentence of each paragraph here.

Para. 2: _____

Para. 3: _____

Para. 4: _____

Para. 5: _____

Para. 6: _____

How is each sentence stated? _____

_____

ACTIVATE YOUR SKILLS 2
Think, Talk, and Write After You Read

Use "before reading" and "during reading" strategies on the following textbook selection. After you read, answer the questions that follow.

Nonverbal Communication

1   Humans communicate without words in a number of important ways, including hand gestures, facial expressions, eye contact, touching, space usage, scents, gait, and stance. A brief examination of hand gestures, posture, and touching will help convey the importance of this form of human communication.

Hand Gestures

2   Consider how many hand gestures we use every day. We cup our hand behind the ear as a nonverbal way of communicating that we cannot hear. We thumb our noses at those we don't like. We can thumb a ride on the side of the highway. We can wave hello or good-bye. We tell people to be quiet by holding our forefinger vertically against our lips. We give the peace

sign by holding up our forefinger and middle finger, but send a very different message when we flash half of the peace sign. Or, by making a circle with our thumb and forefinger we can communicate that everything is "A-OK."

Sharon Dominick/iStockphoto.com

3   However, problems arise with these gestures when we cross national boundaries. Although the "A-OK" sign carries a positive, upbeat message in North America, it refers to money in Japan, zero (worthless) in France, male homosexuality in Malta, and an obscene gesture in parts of South America. Thus, a single hand gesture carries with it many different meanings throughout the world. There are also many examples of the opposite phenomenon—namely, the use of different gestures to send the same message. For example, the nonverbal ways of communicating admiration for an attractive woman vary widely throughout the world. The Frenchman kisses his fingertips, the Italian twists an imaginary moustache, and the Brazilian curls one hand in front of another as if he is looking through an imaginary telescope.

Posture (Body Stance)

4   The way that people hold their bodies often communicates many kinds of information. When communicating, people tend to orient their bodies toward others by assuming a certain stance or posture. A person can stand over another person, can kneel, or can "turn a cold shoulder," and in each case something different would be communicated by the body posture. The meaning attached to different body postures varies from one culture to another and is learned in the same way that other aspects of a culture are internalized. To illustrate this point, we can look at differences in body posture that people assume when relaxing. People in the United States, for example, are sitters, whereas people in some parts of rural Mexico are squatters. This basic cultural difference has actually been used by the U.S. Border Patrol to identify illegal immigrants.

Touching

5   Touching is perhaps the most personal and intimate form of nonverbal communication. Humans communicate through touch in a variety of ways or for a variety of purposes, including patting a person on the head or back, slapping, kissing, punching, stroking, embracing, tickling, shaking hands, and laying-on of hands. Every culture has a well-defined set of meanings connected with touching. That is, each culture defines who can touch whom, on what parts of the body, and under what circumstances.

—Ferraro, *Cultural Anthropology*, 6th edition

Think

1. What is this reading about?

   Communication   Verbal communication   Nonverbal communication

2. Who is this reading about?

   Humans   North Americans   South Americans   Europeans

3. When do North Americans use the hand wave? _____

4. Where might a North American get into trouble giving the "A-OK" hand sign? Why?

   • _____

   • _____

5. Why should a traveler be careful about the hand gestures he or she uses? _____

   _____

6. How do Italian men indicate that they find a woman attractive? _____

   _____

Talk

7. Talk with your classmates about the uses of the following hand gestures in North America and in any other places you and your classmates come from. What do they mean? When are they used? Are they polite or rude?

   • Pointing a finger. _____

- Holding out the palm of your hand toward a listener. _____

  _____

- Tapping your index finger against your lips. _____

  _____

- Moving your index finger around in a circle by your ear. _____

  _____

- Raising your hand in the air. _____

  _____

8. Recall each of the kinds of touch the author describes. In a group, discuss with whom, when, where, and under what conditions each kind of touch is acceptable in each country that you and your classmates are from.

Write

9. When does kneeling happen in your country or your culture? What does it mean?

   _____

   _____

10. Another type of nonverbal communication that the author mentions in paragraph 1 is eye contact. Name three situations in which eye contact plays a role in communication in your culture.

    - _____

    - _____

    - _____

MASTER YOUR SKILLS 1
Think, Talk, and Write After You Read

Using the strategies you have learned, read the textbook excerpt shown here. Then answer the questions that follow.

A Boy Soldier Tells His Story

1   Twenty-six-year-old Ishmael Beah can not only tell the story of being in a rap band when he was eight years old but also the story of his capture and forced life as a teenaged "boy soldier" in his native Sierra Leone, Africa. In his public presentations and his discussions about his book, *A Long Way Gone*, Beah describes his life as a thirteen-year-old after his village was destroyed and he was forced to stay awake for days, popping pills, smoking marijuana, sniffing "brown-brown" (cocaine mixed with gunpowder), and killing indiscriminately. He describes a time when "taking a gun and shooting somebody had become as easy as drinking a glass of water," torture was a way of life, and leaving captivity was not a choice: "Leaving was as good as being dead." He says, "In Western culture, people have romanticized war and violence. But none of it is glorious. When you're there, it's madness. It's your life, or someone else's."

2   When he was sixteen, UNICEF workers rescued Beah and other boy soldiers and took them to Freetown, Sierra Leone's capital. After a slow, torturous recovery in a rehabilitation center, he moved in with an uncle, started attending school, and even managed to enjoy life, going to pubs and soccer matches with his cousins. In 1996, he received an invitation to speak in New York City at the United Nations' First International Children's Parliament on war-affected children. There he met Laura Simms, an American author invited to the event to help the children tell their stories. Not long after he returned home, the war found its way to Freetown, and an illness took his uncle's life. Desperate, Beah contacted Simms and asked her to adopt him. She agreed, and Beah emigrated to New York.

3   When he decided to write a book to tell his story, he found the process difficult: "Many times I would start writing about what I did, and then have to step away and write about something easier, like my mother's cooking. What gave me the strength to continue, to face myself and relive my experiences, was reminding myself there are children living it right now." Despite the pain, he says, "I knew the importance of it, to expose what continues to happen to a lot of children. That gave me the strength to sit down and do it." He feels there are no excuses for not working to stop other children from being abducted and forced to fight in wars. Now in law school, Beah is often asked to speak about his experiences and his work advocating for children. His narratives often feature a common theme: He feels lucky to have escaped the war and lived to tell others. "For me healing is not forgetting. It's just learning to live with it, transform it."

—Griffin, *Invitation to Public Speaking*, 3rd edition

1. What is the title? _____

2. Who is the boy soldier? _____

3. How old was he when he was forced to become a soldier? _____

4. What country is Beah from? _____

5. How old was he when he was rescued? _____

6. Who did Beah meet in 1996? _____

7. What happened when Beah left New York and returned to Freetown? _____

_____

8. Why was it difficult for Beah to write his life story? _____

_____

9. What helped him to continue writing? _____

_____

10. What does Beah do now? _____

MASTER YOUR SKILLS 2
Think, Talk, and Write After You Read

Using the strategies you have learned, read the online magazine article shown here. Then answer the questions that follow.

Crystal Renn's Disappearing Act:
Why the "V" Magazine Spread Sends
Mixed Messages About Bigger Bodies

Sarah Kliff

1   When I stumbled onto the "One Size Fits All" photo essay in the January 2010 issue of *V* magazine, featuring plus-size model Crystal Renn, I was initially pleased. The spreads featured Renn and a skinnier counterpart in nearly identical clothing and poses. Renn looked awesome and, frankly, outdid her skinnier counterpart in a number of the photos.

Sylvain Gaboury/FilmMagic/Getty Images

2   Then, I did a little research, and it suddenly dawned on me: Renn is by no means plus size. While she is admittedly larger than the average model, Renn's body does not represent the rest of us. In fact, she has dimensions that most American women would envy: a 31-inch waist, which turns out to be six inches smaller than that of the average American woman, according to statistics from the Centers for Disease Control and Prevention. Not to mention that at 5 feet 9, she's about a half foot taller than the average American woman as well. When it comes to body diversity, Renn's spread is a big step for fashion, and a teeny, tiny nudge for the rest of humankind. (Plus-size models are smaller than plus-size people; though many plus-size models work at a size 12 or 14, the plus-size category begins at size 6.)

3   So *V* features a woman who is taller than most of us, and smaller in the waist than most of us, looking a lot skinnier than she was a few months ago, and says that represents "all" sizes looking good. In a sense, that seems even more frightening to me than all the skinny models we see day after day. When we open up an issue of *Cosmo* or *Vogue*, at least we know the women we see are way beyond the norm, by no means obtainable. But running a fashion spread that says "one size fits all," with two models who are both a size or two (or 10) smaller, is even more dismaying.

4   Renn's appearance is part of *V*'s special all-shapes-and-sizes issue, which frustrates me on a (no pun intended) larger level. Running a "special issue" to feature larger women makes an upfront declaration that this is not the norm, these are not regular models and, come next month, they will return to their regularly scheduled program. I love that *Glamour* ran a

picture of size 12 Lizzi Miller right in the middle of a regular issue—and am encouraged that they've been incorporating plus-size models in other spreads. But doesn't running a feature like "These Bodies Are Beautiful at Any Size," as *Glamour* did in their November issue, just say these models are included for their size, not necessarily their beauty? Putting plus-size models in their own special issue only proves what we already knew: fat has yet to become fashionable.

—Sarah Kilff, "Crystal Renn's Disappearing Act: Why the 'V' Magazine Spread Sends Mixed Messages about Bigger Bodies." From Newsweek 12/23/09 issue.

1. What is the title of the photo essay that this article is about? _One size fit all_

2. Who is the model the author mostly talks about? _Crystal renn_ .

3. According to the author, why would American women envy Renn? _____

_____

4. About how tall is the average American woman? _5:3_

_____

5. When the author looks at models in *Vogue*, what does she think about? _____
that those who woman are way above the room

6. Is the author glad that *V* ran a whole issue featuring "all shapes and sizes" of women?   Yes   No

7. Why or why not? _because she does feel comfortable in the same cloth as crystal_

8. What other magazine ran a similar issue? _Glamour_

9. What was the title of the feature in that magazine? _These Bodies are Beautiful at any size_

10. According to the author, has fat become fashionable?   Yes   (No)

Summary Activity: Active Reading

Part 1 has discussed how to read as an active process, showing you tasks you can do before, during, and after reading to increase your reading comprehension. Fill in the Reading Guide by completing each idea on the left with information from Part 1 on the right. You can return to this guide throughout the course as a reminder of how to use the reading process to your advantage.

Reading Guide to Using an Active Process

Complete this idea	with information from Part 1.
Before reading, you can take four actions to dramatically improve your comprehension:	1. _____ 2. _____ 3. _____ 4. _____
Comprehension means _____.	5. _____
The parts of a reading selection to pay attention to while surveying are	6. _____ 7. _____ 8. _____ 9. _____ 10. _____
The author always has a purpose. The three general purposes the author may have are	11. _____ 12. _____ 13. _____
Prior knowledge is knowledge that you had _____ you read.	14. _____
As you read, stay active and focused. You can use five strategies to help you:	15. _____ 16. _____ 17. _____ 18. _____ 19. _____

Complete this idea	with information from Part 1.
After reading, review and rehearse the information you read in three ways:	20. _____ 21. _____ 22. _____
The questions you can ask yourself after you read that will help you check your understanding are	23. _____ 24. _____ 25. _____ 26. _____ 27. _____ 28. _____
In addition to the questions you ask after reading, two other kinds of thinking you can do to aid your comprehension are to	29. _____ 30. _____

Think about what your reading habits were before you read Part 1. How did they differ from the reading suggestions here? Write your thoughts.

_____

_____

_____

_____

Application: Active Reading   **WEB SITE**

● Pre-Reading the Selection

Michael Jackson, the King of Pop, died on June 25, 2009, right before he was going to start a fifty-concert tour beginning in London. As a tribute to his incredible success as a singer, *American Idol* showed a rerun of a program they had originally produced on March 10, 2009. This article was written in response to that first showing.

Surveying the Reading

What parts of the reading selection should you survey? _____

_____

Go ahead and survey the reading on page 68.

Guessing the Purpose

Based on the information above about *American Idol* and the title of the article, "No Michael Jacksons Here," what do you suppose the author's purpose is: to persuade, inform, or entertain? _____

Predicting the Content

Based on your survey, what are three things you expect the reading selection to discuss?

- ● _____

- ● _____

- ● _____

Activating Your Knowledge

Search your memory for knowledge that you have on any of the following topics: Michael Jackson and his music, *American Idol*, Adam Lambert, Allison Iraheta, and Danny Gokey. Write down at least two of these pieces of prior knowledge.

- ● _____

- ● _____

- ● _____

● Reading with Pen in Hand

Now read the selection. Pay attention to and mark any ideas that seem important, and respond to the questions and vocabulary items in the margin.

Access the Reading CourseMate via **www.cengagebrain.com/shop/ISBN/1413033156** to hear vocabulary words from this selection and view a video about this topic.

Reading Journal

● Listen to a Michael Jackson song in your head if you know any of them.

digress The author was talking about *American Idol* and then started talking about Michael Jackson. After "But I digress . . ." the author says "Back to . . ." What does *digress* probably mean?

● Picture or hear what the author is describing.

● Make a mental movie of the judges giving these comments.

originality The sentence before this one has a word that means something similar to *originality*. What's the word?

● Do you agree that Gokey should be judged only on singing?

No Michael Jacksons Here

1   It was Michael Jackson night on *American Idol* Tuesday evening and, after watching the performances, one is glad the King of Pop has decided to tour again. Why? Because nobody does Michael Jackson quite as well as Michael Jackson. Truthfully, I would rather Michael Jackson put out a new album—and he may—but we will have to wait and see. But I **digress** . . . Back to the Michael Jackson musical onslaught that occurred on *American Idol* as the Final 13 took the stage.

Felix Hoerhager/Dpa/Landov

2   Lil Rounds started things off. She's no Michael Jackson. Her voice was far too powerful for the song she chose, but the judges gave her enthusiastic reviews. She didn't deserve them, but her performance of "The Way You Make Me Feel" wasn't bad—it just wasn't as good as the judges wanted everyone to think it was.

3   Then Scott MacIntyre sang "Keep the Faith," a song that was nearly unrecognizable as a Michael Jackson song—and that's exactly the way it should have been done. The judges had mixed reviews. Simon Cowell told him it was a bad song choice because no one had ever heard the song before. Scott MacIntyre said he was attempting to be different and Simon told him that was all right but not on *American Idol*. Now, haven't I heard him constantly saying things about **originality**, personal slants and twists, being oneself, etc.? (Yes, we all have.)

4   Then Danny Gokey surprised this writer and the judges with his version of "PYT (Pretty Young Thing)." Simon told him the singing was fine but the dancing was hideous. For a nerdy-looking guy,

he seemed to do all right (this coming from a guy who can't line-dance). But this is a singing competition.

5   Michael Sarver sang "You Are Not Alone." Good vocals. Strong. And good enough to make it to the next round.

6   Jasmine Murray then did "I'll Be There," which is a difficult song to perform now after Mariah Carey did it. Simon said she seemed liked "a little girl trying to be a grown-up." Personally, I think it was the dress. Too cutesy.

○ Listen to Mariah Carey singing "I'll Be There" in your head.

7   Kris Allen came out with his acoustic guitar and did a really nice job with "Do You Remember the Time?" Simon Cowell told him the guitar made him look clumsy. Cowell also said Allen made a mistake revealing that he had a wife so early in the competition. And Simon could be right, but Kris Allen didn't make a mistake if he chose for looks. The woman is beautiful.

○ Imagine watching the conversation between Allen and Cowell.

8   Allison Iraheta performed "Give In to Me," which was original enough to make it her own, especially with her unique vocal stylings. The judges complimented her **stage presence**. They mentioned that it was difficult to remember that she was only 16 when she performs. It's the voice . . .

○ For the next paragraphs, picture what the author is describing.

stage presence If someone has "presence," he or she commands attention. What does *stage presence* mean?

9   Then Anoop Desai walked out, all high-collared, and channeled his inner Michael. But Paula Abdul was first to tell him that "Beat It" was the one Michael Jackson song that seemed to be off-limits to everyone, simply because nobody seemed to be able to do it like him or better than he did it. Simon called it "**karaoke**." Randy Jackson and Kara DioGuardi agreed that it was a poor choice for him. But this sit-at-home critic liked it. It was smooth, well sung, and didn't sound like MJ. He gave an energetic performance. It wasn't anywhere near his best, but it wasn't as bad as the judges said it was.

karaoke Use a print or online dictionary to find the meaning of this word if you don't know it.

10   Little Jorge Nuñez performed "Never Can Say Good-bye" and the judges **panned** it, saying it just seemed too old-fashioned. But it wasn't all that bad. Not bad enough to get kicked off the show . . .

panned The next sentence offers a clue to the meaning of *panned*. What does it mean?

11   And speaking of getting kicked off the show . . . That brings us to contestant number ten out of the Final 13. Megan Joy Corkrey's version of "Rockin' Robin" (didn't know Michael Jackson sung that, did ya?) was probably the worst all-around performance the writer has seen on *American Idol* since Sanjaya was on the show. Not only was her voice flat through much of the performance, her little cutesy-butt-twisty thing she was doing was simply annoying

○ Make a mental movie using the details the author supplies.

and distracting. Megan Corkrey's problem, besides not being able to sing better than a burlesque understudy, is that she doesn't seem to be able to decide whether she wants to sing or smile. The judges loved her, which only makes you wonder if they're all on drugs, weren't paying attention, or the **acoustics** at the Kodak Theatre are actually that bad.

12   Adam Lambert did what Adam Lambert has been doing since he auditioned for *American Idol*. He blew his competition away. The judges praised his performance. His version of "Black or White" was so over-the-top, Simon Cowell said that it worked, that it was in a "different league" than the rest of the night's performances. Paula Abdul said, "Never in the history of *American Idol* have we ever seen someone so comfortable on that stage." And she just might be right.

13   Matt Giraud performed some soft Michael Jackson: "Human Nature." Perhaps one of the more quiet Michael Jackson songs, it proved to be the perfect **counterpoint** for Adam Lambert's rousing performance. Matt Giraud is comfortable and has great control.

14   The last of the Final 13 stepped out sexy and in control. Alexis Grace belted out "Dirty Diana" like the song was written about her. She seemed to lose a little of her **vocal** control near the end, but it was still a powerful performance. Simon told her she probably didn't do as well as she thought she did. And he's probably right. But she did well enough to make it into the Final 12.

15   So the Michael Jackson-themed show ended with an overall round of **mediocre** performances and no groin injuries. There were three notable exceptions: the performances of Adam Lambert, Allison Iraheta, and Danny Gokey. There were several passable ones, the best of which were Matt Giraud, Lil Rounds, Scott MacIntyre and Kris Allen. The poorest by far was the godawful vocals and little-girl-performing-for-granny performance by Megan Corkrey. She should be the one going home, but if there is one thing a regular viewer of *American Idol* has learned in eight seasons, there is really no telling who the voting public will abandon. If you need proof, just go back to Season 6 and ask yourself how someone as awful as Sanjaya Malakar did not get abandoned until he had made it into the Final 7.

—Saul Relative, "Adam Lambert and Danny Gokey Dominate American Idol Final 13." *Associated Content—Yahoo*. March 11, 2009.

Marginal notes:

acoustics Use your logic based on the context to determine the meaning of *acoustics*.

● Listen in your head to the conversation.

● Imagine watching Giraud in this paragraph and Grace in the next one.

counterpoint Look at the adjectives for Giraud's singing: *soft, quiet*. Lambert's is called *rousing*. What does *counterpoint* mean?

vocal Grace is a singer, so what do you expect her to have control of? What does *vocal* mean?

mediocre The next sentence says there were exceptions to the mediocre performances, and the three best performers are listed. What does *mediocre* probably mean?

● Based on what the writer said previously, are these rankings understandable?

● After Reading: Think, Talk, Write

Think: 5W's and H

List the basic information you learned by reading this selection.

1. Who is the selection about? _____

2. What is the selection about? _____

3. When did the events in the selection occur? _____

4. Where did these events occur? _____

5. Why did the author say in paragraph 1 that he is "glad the King of Pop has decided to tour again"? _____

6. How did the author show that none of the performers were as good as Michael Jackson? _____

Think: Connect

Make connections between the ideas in the reading and your own prior knowledge.

   Think of another program you have watched in which people compete against one another. Put the title at the top of the last column in the following table. Then fill out both columns with information that answers the questions about each show.

	American Idol	Other show:
7. How many people compete in a season?		
8. What do contestants do?		
9. How would you rate the need for actual talent in order to win? Why?		
10. How popular is the show?		

Think: Search for Patterns

Look for the patterns that the author has used to organize the information.

11. Paragraphs 2–14 each focus on what? _____

12. What kinds of facts does the author give about every performer?

_____ Name

_____ Age

_____ Song the singer sang

_____ What the judges had to say about the performance

What words does the author use to express his opinion about each song discussed in the following paragraphs?

13. Paragraph 3: _____

14. Paragraph 5: _____

15. Paragraph 6: _____

16. Paragraph 8: _____

Talk About the Ideas in the Reading

With a partner, talk over the next question. Then write your answers in the space provided. In this author's opinion, who was the best performer? Who was the worst? What does the author say about each one?

17. Best: _____

18. Worst: _____

_____

Write About the Ideas in the Reading

19. Who got eliminated from (kicked off) the show that the author is discussing? Why? Write a sentence. _____

20. Does it seem that singing is the only part of the performance that the judges consider in their scoring?   Yes   No

What information from the reading selection makes you give this answer?

_____

_____

_____

Spotlight on Inference: Beliefs Behind Opinions

Behind every opinion there is a belief about the way things *should* be. For example, the author says about Lil Rounds: "Her voice was far too powerful for the song she chose." For the author to say that, he must believe that singers should choose songs that match the power of their voices. For each opinion, state the belief that lies behind it.

1. Author's opinion (paragraph 6): "Jasmine Murray then did 'I'll Be There,' which is a difficult song to perform now after Mariah Carey did it."

   Belief behind the opinion: _____

   _____

2. Simon Cowell's opinion (paragraph 7): "Cowell also said Allen made a mistake revealing that he had a wife so early in the competition."

   Belief behind the opinion: _____

   _____

3. Simon Cowell's opinion (paragraph 3): "Simon Cowell told him it was a bad song choice because no one had ever heard the song before."

   Belief behind the opinion: _____

   _____

Test 1: Reading Comprehension NONFICTION BOOK

Your instructor may ask you to take practice tests throughout the semester to help you decide which topics you need to study the most. All the tests in this book include questions about all the major reading comprehension skills after the reading selection. Many of these skills you have not studied yet. Here in Part 1, a brief description and an example of each reading comprehension skill are provided before you are asked to answer a question.

● Pre-Reading the Selection

The excerpt that begins on page 75 is taken from a nonfiction book called *How to Watch TV News*. The book was written by a college professor and a television newsperson. The excerpt is titled "The Commercial."

Surveying the Reading

What parts of the reading selection should you survey? _____

_____

Go ahead and survey the reading.

Guessing the Purpose

Based on the title of the excerpt and the title of the book it comes from, do you think the authors' purpose is mostly to persuade, inform, or entertain? _____

_____

Predicting the Content

Based on your survey, what are three things you expect the reading selection to discuss?

- _____
- _____
- _____

Activating Your Knowledge

Think about the commercials you see on television. What do they teach you about how to be a good person or what is important in life? Write down two or three lessons you've learned from watching commercials.

- _____
- _____
- _____

● Reading with Pen in Hand

Now read the selection. As you read, pay attention to and mark any ideas that seem important, and respond to the questions and vocabulary items in the margin.

Access the Reading CourseMate via www.cengagebrain.com/shop/ISBN/1413033156 to hear vocabulary words from this selection and view a video about this topic.

The Commercial

Neil Postman and Steve Powers

1   Commercials are about the serious **manipulation** of our social and psychic lives. There are, in fact, some critics who say that commercials are a new although degraded means of religious expression in that most of them take the form of parables (teaching stories), teaching people what the good life consists of. It is a claim not to be easily dismissed.

2   Let us take as an example an imaginary commercial for a mouthwash but one that replicates a common pattern. We'll call the product Fresh Taste. The commercial will run for thirty seconds, and, like any decent parable, will have a beginning, a middle, and an end. The beginning will show a man and woman saying good-bye at her door after an evening out. The woman tilts her head expecting to be kissed. The man steps back, in a state of polite **revulsion**, and says, "Well, Barbara, it was nice meeting you. I'll call sometime soon." Barbara is disappointed. And so ends Act I, which is accomplished in ten seconds. Act II shows Barbara talking to her roommate. "This always happens to me, Joan," she laments. "What's wrong with me?" Joan is ready. "Your problem," she says, "is with your mouthwash. Yours is too mediciny and doesn't protect you long enough. You should try Fresh Taste." Joan holds up a new bottle, which Barbara examines with an optimistic gleam in her eye. That's Act II. Also ten seconds. Act III, the final ten, shows Barbara and the once-reluctant young man getting off a plane in Hawaii. Both are in the early stages of ecstasy, and we are to understand that they are on their honeymoon. Fresh Taste has done it again.

3   Let's consider exactly what it has done. To begin with, the structure of the commercial is as compact and well-organized as the

Reading Journal

manipulation This word consists of an action, *manipulate*, and an ending that makes it into a thing. If someone manipulates you, what does he or she do?

● Predict what this reading selection will discuss.

● Make a mental movie of the commercial the author describes.

revulsion Think about what the woman and the man do. Is *revulsion* more similar to "attraction" or "disgust"?

● Restate in your own words what the author says here.

parable of the Prodigal Son, maybe even better organized and certainly more compressed. The first ten seconds show the problem: Barbara has trouble with her social life but is unaware of the cause. The second ten seconds show the solution: Barbara has bad breath, which could be **remedied** by her buying a different product. The last ten seconds show the moral of the story: if you know the right product to buy, you will find happiness.

remedied This word represents an action. It is based on the word for a thing—*remedy.* Another word for remedy is "medicine." What does *remedied* mean here?

Michael Fernahl/iStockphoto.com

alteration Often, an author repeats the same idea using different words in sentences that are near each other. Read the next two sentences. What other word probably means the same as *alteration?*

● Picture and hear the change in the commercial. What effect does the change have on you?

4   Imagine, now, a slight **alteration** in the commercial. The first ten seconds remain the same. The change comes in Act II. Barbara wonders what's wrong with her but gets a somewhat different answer from Joan. "What's wrong with you?" Joan asks. "I'll tell you what's wrong with you. You are boring. You are dull, dull, dull. You haven't read a book in four years. You don't know the difference between Mozart and Bruce Springsteen. You couldn't even name the continent that Nigeria is on. It's a wonder that any man would want to spend more than ten minutes with you!" A chastened Barbara replies, "You are right. But what can I do?" "What can you do?" Joan answers. "I'll tell you what you can do. Start by taking a course or two at a local university. Join a book club. Get some tickets to the opera. Read *The New York Times* once in a while." "But that will take forever, months, maybe years," says

Barbara. "That's right," replies Joan, "so you'd better start now." The commercial ends with Joan handing Barbara a copy of Freud's *Civilization and Its Discontents*. Barbara looks forlorn but begins to finger the pages.

5   This, too, is a parable but its lesson is so different from that of the first commercial that there is no chance you will ever see anything like it on television. Its point is that there are no simple or fast solutions to life's important problems; specifically, there is no chemical that can make you desirable: attractiveness must come from within. This idea, which is a commonplace in the Judeo-Christian tradition, is the exact opposite of what almost all commercials teach.

> ● Search for connections to what you know. Why won't you ever see such a commercial on TV?

6   The average American TV viewer will see about thirty thousand commercials next year. Some of them are quite straightforward and some are funny, some are spoofs of other commercials and some are mysterious and exotic. But many of them will have the structure of our hypothetical commercial, and will urge the following ideas: Whatever problem you face (lack of self-esteem, lack of good taste, lack of attractiveness, lack of social acceptance), it can be solved, solved fast, and solved through a drug, a detergent, a machine, or a salable technique. You are, in fact, helpless unless you know about the product that can remake you and set you on the road to paradise. You must, in short, become a born-again consumer, redeem yourself, and find peace.

> ● Search for connections. What commercials have you seen that have the same message as the one discussed in this reading selection?
>
> **hypothetical** Here, the authors use a new word for the fake commercial they've been talking about. What did they call this kind of commercial in the first sentence of paragraph 2?

—"The Commercial," from *How to Watch TV News*, Revised Edition, by Neil Postman and Steve Powers

● Check Your Skills While Continuing to Learn

The questions that follow will check your understanding (comprehension) of the reading selection. They address all the skills you will learn throughout the book. Here in Part 1, each skill is first described briefly. Then a sample question, answer, and reason for the answer are given. You can use these questions to see which skills you need to practice carefully.

A Suggested Learning Process

- Read and think about the skill.
- Study all three parts of the example: the question, the answer, and the explanation.

- Look back at the reading selection so you can understand the example.
- Answer the second question as a check for yourself of how well you can already apply this skill.

• Comprehension Questions

Write the letter of the answer on the line. Then explain your thinking.

Main Idea

Think of the main idea as the "point" of the paragraph or passage. To find the main idea, notice which sentence explains the author's most important point about the subject. The other sentences in the paragraph should offer explanations, examples, and details about the main idea. The details are more specific than the main idea.

Example

___a___ 1. What is the best statement of the main idea of paragraph 2?

    a. The commercial will run for thirty seconds, and, like any decent parable, will have a beginning, a middle, and an end.

    b. The beginning will show a man and woman saying good-bye at her door after an evening out.

    c. Act II shows Barbara talking to her roommate.

    d. Act III, the final ten, shows Barbara and the once-reluctant young man getting off a plane in Hawaii.

WHY? What information in the selection leads you to give that answer? Answer A is the main point of this paragraph, which describes the beginning, middle, and end of the commercial. The other answers each talk about the beginning (sentence B), middle (C), and end (D).

Practice

_____ 2. What is the best statement of the main idea of paragraph 3?

    a. The structure of the commercial is as compact and well-organized as the parable of the Prodigal Son, maybe even better organized and certainly more compressed.

    b. The first ten seconds show the problem: Barbara has trouble with her social life but is unaware of the cause.

c. The second ten seconds show the solution: Barbara has bad breath, which could be remedied by her buying a different product.

d. The last ten seconds show the moral of the story: if you know the right product to buy, you will find happiness.

WHY? What information in the selection leads you to give that answer? _____

_____

_____

_____

Supporting Details

Think of the supporting details as the "proof" for the main idea. To locate the supporting details, find the main idea and then look for the information the author uses to explain it in more detail. Sometimes, if a main idea covers more than one paragraph, you will find the supporting details in several paragraphs.

Example

_b_   3. Which of the following details most directly supports this main idea from paragraph 4? *Barbara wonders what's wrong with her but gets a somewhat different answer from Joan.*

a. Imagine, now, a slight alteration in the commercial. The first ten seconds remain the same.

b. You are boring. You haven't read a book in four years. You don't know the difference between Mozart and Bruce Springsteen.

c. The commercial ends with Joan handing Barbara a copy of Freud's *Civilization and Its Discontents.*

d. Barbara looks forlorn but begins to finger the pages.

WHY? What information in the selection leads you to give that answer? The main idea is that Barbara wonders what is wrong with her, and Joan tells her something different than changing her mouthwash. Answer B is a list of three things Joan thinks are "wrong" with Barbara. The details in A set the scene but don't support the main idea. C and D are both minor details that don't directly support the main idea.

_____

Practice

_____   4. The main idea of paragraph 6 is this: *But many of them will have the structure of our hypothetical commercial, and will urge the following ideas.* Which sentence does *not* directly support this statement?

a. Whatever problem you face, it can be solved, solved fast, and solved through a drug, a detergent, a machine, or a salable technique.

b. You are, in fact, helpless unless you know about the product that can remake you and set you on the road to paradise.

c. You must, in short, become a born-again consumer, redeem yourself, and find peace.

d. The average American TV viewer will see about thirty thousand commercials next year.

WHY?   What information in the selection leads you to give that answer? _____

_____

_____

_____

Author's Purpose

The author's general purpose may be to persuade (change the reader's mind or behavior), inform (share information with the reader), or entertain (make the reader feel a certain way, often through stories), or it may be a combination of these purposes. At specific points in a text, an author may use a variety of methods to achieve the general purpose. You should always assume that the author has a particular reason for what he or she wrote.

Example

_c_   5. What is the authors' purpose in paragraph 2?

a. To inform readers that using the right mouthwash is important.

b. To entertain readers by helping them laugh at someone else's problem.

c. To inform readers by describing the usual structure of commercials.

d. To persuade readers to buy Fresh Taste.

WHY?   What information in the selection leads you to give that answer? The authors are describing an imaginary commercial so that readers will understand its structure in three acts and what each act accomplishes.

_____

Practice

_____   6. What is the authors' purpose overall?

      a. To entertain readers with their own stupidity.

      b. To persuade readers that their lives are being manipulated by commercials.

      c. To persuade readers that commercials are trying to sell them something.

      d. To inform readers that buying the right product equals happiness.

WHY? What information in the selection leads you to give that answer? _____

_____

_____

_____

Relationships

The ideas in a reading selection are related to one another in different ways. For instance, one sentence might discuss the causes of an event mentioned in a different sentence. Some relationships have to do with time, space, comparisons and contrasts, causes and effects, and so on. You may see the relationships between the ideas in different parts of one sentence, in different sentences, or even in different paragraphs. Many times, these relationships are indicated with signal words or transitions such as _but, and, however, for example_, and so on.

Example

_b_   7. What pattern is used to organize the supporting details in Paragraph 3?

      a. Space order

      b. Time order

      c. Comparison

      d. Definition

WHY? What information in the selection leads you to give that answer? Words that signal time order here are _to begin with, the first ten seconds, the second ten seconds_, and _the last ten seconds._

_____

_____

Practice

_____ 8. In the following part of a sentence from paragraph 6, what is the relationship between the first four words and the words in parentheses? *Whatever problem you face (lack of self-esteem, lack of good taste, lack of attractiveness, lack of social acceptance), it can be solved, . . .*

a. The first words are an example of the words in parentheses.

b. The words in parentheses offer a contrast with the first words.

c. The words in parentheses are the causes of the first words.

d. The words in parentheses are examples of the first words.

WHY? What information in the selection leads you to give that answer? _____

_____

_____

_____

Fact, Opinion, and Inference

A fact is a true statement that can be verified by using another source of information: *It is 85 degrees outside.* An opinion is a person's personal reaction: *It's too hot to play baseball.* An inference is an idea the reader gets from the other ideas that the author has stated: *That person must be from up north.* To be valid, an inference must be a logical extension of what the author has written.

Example

_c_ 9. Which statement is an opinion?

a. Commercials are an attempt to get people to make purchases.

b. Some commercials last thirty seconds.

c. Barbara should join a book club.

d. Freud wrote a book called *Civilization and Its Discontents.*

WHY? What leads you to give that answer? The word *should* is an indication that answer C is an opinion. Some people might disagree with this opinion. Answer A is a fact that many people know. B is suggested in this reading selection and can be verified in other sources, such as textbooks. D is mentioned at the end of paragraph 4.

Practice

_____ 10. Which of the following statements is a fact?

   a. You are dull, dull, dull.

   b. The average American TV viewer will see about thirty thousand commercials next year.

   c. Advertisers on television want people to think deeply and read great books.

   d. Commercials try to show people they can solve their problems by buying certain products.

WHY? What information in the selection leads you to give that answer? _____

_____

_____

_____

_____

● Vocabulary in New Contexts

Review the vocabulary words in the margins of the reading selection and then complete the following activities.

Relationships Between Words

Circle yes or no to answer the question. Then explain your answer.

1. If a person found out that his best friend had **manipulated** him, might he feel **revulsion**?

   Yes   No

   Why or why not? _____

2. Would **revulsion** be an appropriate response if the best friend somehow **remedied** the situation?

   Yes   No

   Why or why not? _____

   _____

3. Would an **alteration** in the friendship be likely if the best friend did <u>not</u> try to **remedy** the situation?

Yes   No

Why or why not? _____

_____

Language in Your Life

Write short answers to each question. Look at vocabulary words closely before you answer.

1. Name one **alteration** you would like to make in your life. _____

_____

2. Name one **hypothetical** situation you would like to be in. _____

_____

3. Name one time when you **remedied** a difficult situation. _____

_____

4. Name a time a person you know felt **revulsion**. _____

_____

5. Name a time when you thought you were being **manipulated**. _____

_____

Language in Use

Select the best word to complete the meaning of each sentence.

alterations	hypothetical	manipulate	remedies	revulsion

1. All _____ are intended to help patients get better.

2. Medicines cause _____ in the body's systems or the body's chemistry.

3. Children often feel a sense of _____ when they see Pepto-Bismol (a popular medicine for upsets in the digestive system) on a spoon headed toward their mouths.

4. A child may try to _____ the situation by claiming quickly that his or her stomach feels better—really.

5. To a child who doesn't have much sense of cause and effect, the benefits of the thick pink syrup must seem purely _____.

PART 2

"Intelligence plus character—that is the goal of true education."

These words are from Dr. Martin Luther King Jr., used at the end of the movie *Stomp the Yard*.

He will challenge
their traditions.

Their traditions will
change his life.

Screen Gems/The Kobal Collection/
Picture Desk

Find chapter-specific interactive learning tools for *Activate*, including quizzes, videos, and more, through CengageBrain.com.

Videos Related to Readings

Vocab Words on Audio

Read and Talk on Demand

Vocabulary Development

Whether you are motivated to attend college because you hope to get a better job, your parents are "forcing" you to go, you love to learn, or you want to change the world, a true education changes the way you view and understand the world around you. And at the core of every true education is a good vocabulary.

Having a good vocabulary allows you to express your ideas and feelings in a way that others will understand. It allows you to participate in the life of our culture through understanding what others have to say about government, education, the arts, and the sciences. And it allows you to read the ideas of people from long ago or far away whose thoughts still have something valuable to offer, whether at work, at home, or at school.

This part of the book focuses on developing your vocabulary by using word parts, context clues, and the dictionary, and by understanding the author's tone. All are important skills to develop in your quest to change the world . . . or at least to change **your** world! Good luck!

. . . .

Share Your Prior Knowledge

Share your educational goal with a classmate. Then discuss what character is, and how you think an education helps build character (or, more specifically, will help build yours). Come up with one or two ideas.

Survey the Lessons

Take a moment to turn to the table of contents and survey the headings in Lessons 4 to 7 in Part 2 so you know what to expect. For each lesson, name one thing you think you already know about that topic:

Lesson 4: _____

Lesson 5: _____

Lesson 6: _____

Lesson 7: _____

Name one thing you want to read more about to understand better:

_____

Read and Talk   ESSAY

In college, reading is just the beginning of how you will share new ideas with others in your class. So the first reading in each part of this book is meant to give you the chance to talk about reading. Read the article, and then use the four discussion questions to talk about your ideas with your classmates and your instructor. Make this an opportunity to create new friendships and knowledge through the art of listening to the ideas of others, the enjoyment of discussing your thoughts, and the fun of reading something new.

Access the Reading CourseMate via **www.cengagebrain.com/shop/ISBN/1413033156** to hear a reading of this selection and view a video about this topic.

Child Hero: Bethany Hamilton

Tyler H.

1   On October 31st, 2003, young surfer Bethany Hamilton suffered a big loss. But it wasn't a loss in one of her many surfing heats, she lost her arm! It was Halloween morning in Hawaii, and it was sunny and a perfect day for surfing. Bethany decided that she would go surfing near Tunnels Beach with her best friend Alana Blanchard and Alana's father and brother. There were also six other surfers practicing nearby. She was catching great waves and all of a sudden, her life changed in an instant. She got bit by a 14-foot tiger shark! The shark bit her just 4 inches below

AP Photo/Ronen Zilberman

her left shoulder and took the rest of her arm off! She definitely wasn't expecting that to happen to her on Halloween!

2   Bethany was planning on being a professional surfer before her accident in the waves. She was ranked 8th in the world for amateur surfers beforehand. "She is probably the best young surfer I have ever seen," said Bobo Bollin, who works at the Hanalei Surf Company. "She was going to be the women's world champion and I think she still will be." Her whole family has always been surfers and has always been involved with her surfing. Bethany only turned 14 on February 8th, 2004, so it was a young age to have something that bad happen to her, but she still has her whole life ahead of her.

3   Bethany Hamilton definitely qualifies to be a survivor hero according to T. S. Barron's book, "A Hero's Trail." She was bit by a tiger shark while surfing, and was able to compose herself and swim to safety. She also overcame the loss of her left arm and rose to the challenge of going surfing out in the ocean again. This all happened within a month! Her life was at risk when the tiger shark bit her arm completely off and her instincts helped her get to safety and she was successful. Her bravery and courage are evident and those are true hero qualities.

4   Bethany Hamilton showed that she was a true hero by saving her life. She is now a role model to many people for what she has done. She turned a negative into a positive, which many people can't do! She did this by taking the tragedy that occurred and remained positive and continued to go forward with her dream. This inspired millions of people all across the world to try to find something good in something that only seems bad. She is obviously a survivor hero and is keeping her surfing career "alive" as well. She went back to surfing and only has one arm, and that is amazing!

—From "Child Hero: Bethany Hamilton," by Tyler H. (The My Hero Project).

Talking About Reading

Respond in writing to the questions below and then discuss your answers with your classmates.

1. Bethany Hamilton has become a role model for young athletes. Do you have role models in different areas of your life? Who are they? _____

_____

_____

2. The author calls Bethany a "survivor hero." What do you think would be the difference between a plain "survivor" and a "survivor hero"? _____

_____

_____

3. Have you heard of any other examples of people who might be thought of as survivor heroes? What did they do? _____

_____

_____

4. Many heroes are "unsung heroes," meaning that they have never become famous. If you had to name one unsung hero you have known, who would you name? What about that person's life makes her or him a hero in your eyes? _____

_____

_____

Improve Your Vocabulary to Make Reading Easier

Did you notice that in "Child Hero," the author says that Bethany was able to *compose* herself after being bitten by the shark? If you only know one of the definitions of the word *compose*—that is, to write an essay, for example, or to create a piece of music—this use might not make sense to you. But if you understand that *compose* means "put together," then its use here becomes understandable. Being bitten by a shark would make many people fall apart, so to speak, and Bethany's ability to put herself back together quickly may have saved her life.

Three ways to develop your vocabulary so that you can understand the many meanings of words are covered in Part 2:

- Using word parts
- Defining words in context
- Using the dictionary

Once you have learned a word, the next step is to use it in your daily life. You could *read* twenty new words a day and never learn one of them. The only way to truly learn a new word is to actively make it a part of your writing and speech—that is, to use it in new contexts.

- **Use new words in writing.** As you write in your college courses, use the vocabulary you are learning. You can also use new words in a vocabulary notebook, a journal, letters, e-mails, blogs, and IMs—anywhere you write.

- **Use new words in speaking.** You can transfer new words into your speaking vocabulary by learning how they are pronounced. For help, use the audio files that accompany the readings in each part of this book online at **www.cengagebrain.com/shop/ISBN/1413033156.** Listen to the words, practice them on your own, and then introduce them into your conversation.

Before You Read, Use Word Parts to Expand Your Vocabulary.

The single most powerful way to quickly expand your vocabulary is to learn word parts. Learning one word part can increase your understanding of hundreds of unfamiliar words. In this lesson you will learn some of the most productive word parts in the English language. If you learn all the word parts covered in this lesson, you will know the meanings of thousands of words you have never seen before.

Test Your Prior Knowledge.

Before we go on, however, take a little test to see how much you already know about word parts. We think you already know quite a bit.

1. How do you know what **girlfriend** means? _____

_____

2. What does the -s at the end of **movies** mean? _____

3. What does the **un-** at the beginning of **unsafe** mean? _____

_____

4. If the word **beautiful** is broken into two parts, **beauty + -ful,** which part carries the root meaning of the word? _____

As you probably noted when you answered question 1, some words are composed of two different words that each can stand alone and mean something. These are called **compound words.**

Question 2 is a different case. Here, a word that can stand on its own—*movie*—is combined with a letter that cannot stand alone as a word. But the -s still adds meaning to the word. It means "more than one." Some word parts have to be attached to others. When the word part is attached at the end of the word, it's called a **suffix.** Some words have more than one suffix.

The **un-** in *unsafe* (question 3) is similar to the -s in *movies*: it can't stand alone as a word. The difference, of course, is that **un-** comes at the beginning of the word, not at the end. These word parts are **prefixes.** In fact, the **pre-** in **prefix** is itself a prefix that means "before." Just as with suffixes, some words have more than one.

Finally, in question 4, *beauty* carries the root meaning of the word. This root comes from a Latin word—as do many English words. Many English words also come from Greek. In this chapter, you'll learn both Latin and Greek roots. Some roots stand alone as words, like *beauty*. But some roots need to be attached to other word parts to suggest a meaning to readers.

Definitions of Word Parts

- **Root:** The root carries the main meaning of a word. A word usually has at least one root. It can have more than one. The root can be found at the beginning, middle, or end of a word.

- **Prefix:** Placed before a root, the prefix changes the meaning of the word. Not all words have prefixes. Some words have one prefix; others have more than one.

- **Suffix:** Placed after a root, the suffix often changes the part of speech (such as noun or verb) and thus changes the way the word acts in the sentence. Not all words have suffixes. Some words have one suffix; others have more than one.

Figure 2.1 Words Composed of Word Parts

As you can see from Figure 2.1, a word has at least one root, but it may or may not have prefixes or suffixes. And it may have more than one of each. Read across each line to put the word parts together to form a whole word.

prefix	+	prefix	+	root	+	root	+	suffix	+	suffix
				mind						
				mercy				ful		
				beauty				ful		ly
		un		real				ist		ic
		re		mind				er		
re		con		struct				ed		
				demo		graph		y		

When you combine roots with other word parts, sometimes their spelling changes. For example, if you combine *mercy* and *ful*, the resulting word is spelled *merciful*. It has an *i* instead of a *y*. Word parts often have alternative spellings depending on what other word parts they are attached to.

Look for Meaning in Word Parts.

A reference list of roots, prefixes, and suffixes that you can use while you read is provided on pages 105–107. In this section we'll look at a small number of roots and some of the other word parts they can be combined with. You'll see how to analyze the word parts and then how to infer the meaning from the word parts and the reading context.

Roots: Sight, Hearing, and Touch

Let's start with some roots that have to do with using your senses of sight, hearing, and touch.

Study the three roots. (When roots are given with a slash between them, that means they are spelled in different ways.) As you read each root, picture using the sense listed under the heading "Basic meaning."

Root	Basic meaning	Example words
vid/vis	see	video, visible, visionary
aud	hear	audio, audible, audience
tact/tang/tig	touch	contact, tangible, contiguous

Combining Word Parts

Notice that each root can be combined with the suffix -**ible**. This suffix can also be spelled -**able**, and that's what it means: "able to be."

- **Visible** means "able to be seen."

- **Audible** means "able to be heard."

- **Tangible** means "able to be touched."

You can tell from these examples that sometimes you have to put the meaning of the suffix in front of the meaning of the root for the combined meaning of the whole word to make sense.

Spotlight on Inference: Working with Word Parts

When you use word parts to figure out the meaning of a word, you often have to use **inference.** Inference is the process of putting together the bits of information you read to see what they add up to. You do this by using your logic and your prior knowledge. Here is an example using the word **contiguous.**

prefix	+	root	+	suffix
con-		tig		-uous
together		touching		full of

When you put the meanings of the word parts together, you get "full of touching together" or "touching together fully." Now, you could draw any number of conclusions about what this means. So the next step in figuring out the word's meaning is to look at the context. Suppose you read this sentence:

> Canada and the United States are **contiguous** countries.

Given this context, you could infer that **contiguous** means "sharing a boundary" or "neighboring." The two countries share a border—they touch together fully. Notice the border on the map.

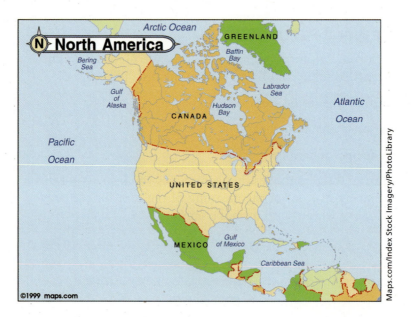

Roots: Leading, Carrying, and Pulling

Study these three roots. Make a mental movie of each action to help you remember it.

Root	Basic meaning	Example words
duc/duce/duct	lead, bring, take	induction, produce, conduct
port	carry	comport, export, import
tract/trah	pull, drag, draw	contract, extract, protract, retraction

Combining Word Parts

Notice that each root can be combined with the prefix **com-,** which is also spelled **con-.** This prefix means "together," as you saw in the word *contiguous.*

- **Conduct** means "lead together."
- **Comport** means "carry together."
- **Contract** means "draw together."

Notice that in the meaning of these words, the root is put before the prefix. When you are analyzing word parts, play with the order of the word parts until you arrive at a phrase that makes sense.

More Prefixes

Other prefixes are used in the example words in the table above:

- **in-/im-/il-/ir-** meaning "not"
- **in-** meaning "in"
- **ex-** meaning "out"
- **pro-** meaning "forward" and "forth"

You can see from the first two items in the list that sometimes a prefix can have more than one meaning. If you see a word that begins with **in-,** for example, you need to test each possible meaning. Read the sentence and the surrounding sentences carefully to decide which meaning is more logical.

INTERACTION 2–1   Identifying the Meanings of Word Parts

Use the word parts you have learned in this lesson thus far for this interaction. Divide each word into its parts, using plus signs between them. Then write a phrase that brings these bits of information together in a way that makes sense.

1. **portable**   Word parts: _____

                     Phrase: _____

2. **contact**   Word parts: _____

                     Phrase: _____

3. **unexportable** Word parts: _____

                     Phrase: _____

4. **inaudible**   Word parts: _____

                     Phrase: _____

5. **produce**   Word parts: _____

                     Phrase: _____

6. **protract**   Word parts: _____

                     Phrase: _____

7. **extract**   Word parts: _____

                     Phrase: _____

8. **intractable**   Word parts: _____

                     Phrase: _____

9. **induce**   Word parts: _____

                     Phrase: _____

10. **intact**   Word parts: _____

                        Phrase: _____

| **INTERACTION 2–2** | **Using Context to Check Your Understanding of a Word's Meaning** |

In Interaction 2–1, you divided each bold word into word parts and decided on its meaning. Now read each sentence to gain a context for the word. Write the meaning of the word on the line after the sentence.

1. The 50-gallon containers of water were **portable** only by using the special wheeled cart the villagers had built. _____

_____

2. Please **contact** me immediately if you experience a problem. _____

_____

3. Ever since children were poisoned by "milk" from China, that country has found several of its products to be **unexportable.** _____

_____

4. After the speakers blew out, the band was **inaudible.** _____

_____

5. Can you **produce** your identification, please? _____

_____

6. The lawyer was preparing herself for a **protracted** battle to convince the judge of her client's viewpoint. _____

_____

7. Her parents tried to **extract** a promise that she would never steal again. _____

   _____

8. But she was **intractable,** refusing to speak and glaring at each parent in turn. ___

   _____

9. If a woman has been pregnant for 42 weeks and still hasn't given birth, the drug Pitocin may be used to **induce** labor. _____

   _____

10. Be sure you buy a DVD that's in an **intact** package. _____

    _____

Review: Meaning in Word Parts

Not all words are composed of word parts. However, for words that are, the meaning of the word can be understood by combining the meaning of each part.

- Roots carry the main meaning of the word. Prefixes attach to the beginning. Suffixes attach to the end. A word may have any number of roots, prefixes, and suffixes, or none at all.

- Use inference. Inference is the process of putting bits of information together to see what they add up to. Your logic and your prior knowledge are active when you infer meaning from word parts.

- To make meaning from word parts, you often have to switch the order of the part meanings to arrive at a definition that makes sense.

- Context matters. Words often have more than one definition, and the sentence that the word is in will help you decide which meaning the author intends.

Look at Prefixes for Changes to Meaning.

Roots carry the basic meaning of the word, but prefixes change that meaning. Look at the following table of prefixes. Memorize these five prefixes, and you will gain a partial understanding of more than 60 percent of all English words that have prefixes. Notice that half of them can mean "not."

As you read the example words, divide them into word parts to figure out what they mean. For even better practice, write them on a separate piece of paper and divide them into word parts with plus signs between each part.

Prefix	Basic meaning	Example words
un-	not	unkind, unproductive, unstoppable
re-	again; back	reduce, reproduce, retract
in-/il-/im-/ir-	not	inactive, illegal, impossible, irresistible
dis-	not; apart	disrespect, distrust, distract
en-/em-	cause to	enlarge, enrage, embolden

On pages 105–107 is an alphabetical list of word parts you can refer to as you read.

INTERACTION 2–3   **Stating Word Meanings**

State the meaning of the following words based on their word parts.

1. retrain _____

2. irreligious _____

3. unforgettable _____

4. impolite _____

5. retract _____

6. endanger _____

7. disconnect _____

8. illogical _____

9. reproduce _____

10. empower _____

Review: Prefixes

The root of a word carries the basic meaning, and prefixes change that meaning.

Look at Suffixes to See How Words Act in Sentences.

Suffixes often change the part of speech of words and, thus, how the words act in the sentence.

Suffixes That Can Indicate Actions—Verbs:

- **-s:** plays, ends, happens (**-s** on a verb indicates actions that happen again and again)

  *But note that -s on a noun means "more than one."

- **-ing:** laughing, remembering, choosing (**-ing** indicates action happening now)

- **-ed:** touched, lighted, described (**-ed** indicates action that happened in the past)

When you see a verb in a sentence, you can ask, "Who or what is doing this? When is this happening?" Figuring out who is doing what in a sentence will improve your reading comprehension.

Suffixes That Indicate Conditions or Processes—Nouns:

- **-ance/-ence:** guidance, dependence, tolerance
- **-hood:** neighborhood, manhood, statehood
- **-ion/-sion/-tion:** suspension, vacation, completion, partition

When you see a noun in a sentence, you can ask, "What is this thing doing? What relationship is there between this noun and other nouns?" To understand sentences fully, you need to understand the relationships between words.

Suffixes That Indicate Characteristics of Something—Adjectives:

- **-ly** (characteristic of): fatherly, miserly, homely
- **-less** (without): motherless, waterless, loveless
- **-ing, -ed:** Also used as verb endings, these endings can indicate adjectives that are describing people, places, things, and ideas: caring brother, expected visitor.

When you find an adjective, you can ask, "Who or what is this word describing?"

Suffixes That Can Indicate How, When, or Where An Action Is Done—Adverbs:

- **-ly** (characteristic of): nicely, instinctively, suddenly
- **-fully** (full of): faithfully, joyfully, fearfully
- **-wise** (in a certain direction or position; with respect to): clockwise; likewise

When you see an adverb in a sentence, ask, "What verb or other words is this describing?"

See pages 105–107 for a list of suffixes that you can consult while you are reading.

INTERACTION 2–4	Selecting the Best Suffix

For each word in *italics*, select a suffix from the list below that helps the word act the way it needs to in the sentence. Notice that in three words, the final letter has been removed because the spelling changes when the suffix is added.

-ance	-ence	-hood	-ing	-less	-ly	-s	-ion	-tion

1. Although they had started their marriage deeply in love, their partnership became *joy*_____ after they lost a child.

2. Her utter *depend*_____ on her mother made her itch for her freedom.

3. He *commute*_____ to his office, 45 minutes each way.

4. The farmer carefully controlled his herd's *reproduc*_____ to make sure that only the cows who gave a lot of milk had calves.

5. She was outwardly patient but *inward*_____ frustrated.

6. The *extract*_____ of every bit of silver from the mine meant that all the miners lost their jobs.

7. She was *laz*_____ around the house on her day off.

8. He was holding his hurt wrist *protective*_____.

9. She asked for the rabbi's spiritual *guid*_____.

10. He spent most of his *child*_____ with his grandmother.

Review: Suffixes

Suffixes often change the part of speech of a word, and thus change how a word acts in a sentence. Suffixes can indicate:

- Actions—these are verbs.
- Conditions or processes—these are nouns.
- Characteristics of things—these are adjectives.
- How, when, or where an action is done—these are adverbs.

Word Parts Glossary

The following 146 commonly used word parts are organized alphabetically so they will be easy to find while you read. Read down the column that describes the word part you are searching for. Remember that sometimes a word starts with a root rather than a prefix.

Prefixes	Roots	Suffixes
ab-/abs-: away	annu: year	-able: able to
ad-: to, toward	anthrop: human	-age: condition or state of
ante-: before	aster/astro: star	-al: characteristic of
anti-: against	aud: hear	-ance: state, condition, action
auto-: self	bio: life	-ate: act upon
bi-: two	cap: take, seize	-ative: adjective form of a noun
circum-: around	cede/ceed/cess: go, yield, surrender	-cracy: government
com-/con-: together; bring together	chron: time	-ed: happened in the past (on a verb), or characteristic of (on an adjective)
counter-: opposite	cog/gnosi: know	-en: made of
de-: reverse, remove, reduce	corp: body	-ence: condition or state of
demi-: half	dem: people	-ent: causing or being in a certain condition
dis-: not; apart	dict: say	-eous: possessing the qualities of
en-/em-: cause to	dorm: sleep	-er: comparative (faster = more fast)
ex-/e-/ec-/ef-: out; up	duc/duce/duct: lead, bring, take	-er: person who
fore-: before	fact: make	-es: noun plural (boxes)
hemi-: half	flu: flow	-est: superlative (happiest = most happy)
hyper-: above, more	geo: earth	-ful: full of

(Continued)

Prefixes	Roots	Suffixes
hypo-: under, less	graph: write	-hood: condition or process of (neighborhood)
in-/im-: in, into	gress: walk	-ial: characteristic of
in-/im-/ir-/il-: not	gyny: woman	-ible: able to
inter-: between, among	ject: throw	-ic: characteristic of
intra-: within	junct: join	-ical: characteristic of
macro-: large, long	log/logue: word, thought, speech	-ing: present participle of verb (enjoying)
mal-: bad, wrong	man/manu: by hand	-ion: condition, process of
micro-: small	merc: money received for work; price	-ious: possessing the qualities of
mid-: middle	mit/mitt/miss: send	-ish: characteristic of
mis-: wrongly	morph: form	-ise: verb ()
mis-/miso-: hatred	mors/mori/mort: dead	-ism: state, quality, or condition
mono-: one	nom: name, term	-ist: one who; characterized by
non-: not	path/pat: feeling, suffering	-ity: state of
over-: too much	ped/pedo: children	-ive: adjective form of a noun (massive)
pan-: all	pel: drive	-ize: make
poly-: many	pend: hang	-less: without
post-: after	philo/phil: love	-ly: characteristic of
pre-: before	phobia: irrational fear	-ment: state of
pro-: forward	phon: sound	-ness: state of, condition of
pseudo-: false	plic: fold	-nym: name
re-: again, back	port: carry	-ology: field of study
semi-: half	sat/satis: enough	-or: person who
sub-: under	scrib/script: write	-ous: possessing the qualities of
super-: above	sta: stand	-s: verb (swims); noun plural (trees)
sur-: more, above, over	struct: build	-sion: condition, process of
syn-/sym-: together, with; united	tact/tang/tig: touch	-some: characteristic of

Prefixes	Roots	Suffixes
trans-/tres-: across	theo: God	-tion: condition, process of
tri-: three	tract/trah: pull, drag, draw	-ty: state of
un-: not	trib: pay, bestow	-wise: in a specified direction, manner, or position
under-: too little	ven/veni/vent: come	-worthy: worthy of
ultra-: beyond, exceeding	vert: turn	-yze: verb (analyze)
uni-: one	vis/vid: see	
	viv: life	

- What if a word part is not in the Word Parts Glossary? Look in a college dictionary (see page 151). The word parts are often given toward the beginning or end of an entry. Because word parts show which languages a word comes from, you will often see an abbreviation of the word *Latin* or *Greek* with the word parts. See *Lat.* in the dictionary entry on page 151 for an example.

- What if you don't understand the combination of word parts? First, look at the sentences around the word to see if they can help. We will talk more about context in Lesson 5. Second, look in a dictionary. We will talk about using a dictionary in Lesson 6.

INTERACTION 2–5   **Deciding on the Meaning of Words in Sentences**

For each word in **bold,** use the Word Parts Glossary as a reference and write the meaning of each word part. Then decide what the whole word means and write the definition.

1. The lightbulb was **suspended** from the ceiling by a single fraying wire.

   Meaning of word parts: _____

   _____

   Meaning of word: _____

   _____

2. I don't mean to interrupt, but please let me **interject** a comment here.

   Meaning of word parts: _____

   _____

Meaning of word: _____

_____

3. The man living alone in that cave isn't a peaceful, meditating monk; he's a **misanthrope.**

   Meaning of the word parts: _____

   _____

   Meaning of the word: _____

   _____

4. The first **transcontinental** railroad in the United States was completed in 1869.

   Meaning of the word parts: _____

   _____

   Meaning of the word: _____

   _____

5. Every ten years, the U. S. government counts all the people living in the country. The census provides a **demographic** snapshot of the people of the United States.

   Meaning of word parts: _____

   _____

   Meaning of word: _____

   _____

6. An **edict** went out from the government that no one would be allowed in or out of the country.

   Meaning of the word parts: _____

   _____

   Meaning of the word: _____

   _____

7. The study of language includes *morphology,* which is the study of the structure of words (including word parts), and *phonology.*

   Meaning of the word parts: _____

   _____

   Meaning of the word: _____

   _____

8. Worshippers in three of the world's largest religious groups—Islam, Christianity, and Judaism—are **monotheists.**

Meaning of the word parts: _____

_____

Meaning of the word: _____

_____

9. At their **commitment** ceremony, the couple gave each other rings.

Meaning of the word parts: _____

_____

Meaning of the word: _____

_____

10. Help me understand the **chronology** of the crime. At 4:42, you arrived home. At 4:45, you heard a shot. What happened after that?

Meaning of the word parts: _____

_____

Meaning of the word:_____

_____

INTERACTION 2–6 **Naming College Studies**

Many subjects you can study in college end with the suffix **-ology.** How many *-ology* words that are college subjects can you make from the roots in the Word Parts Glossary? What do they mean? Write the words and their meanings on the lines below.

1. _____

2. _____

3. _____

4. _____

5. _____

6. _____

Here are some other fields of study. What do you think people in these fields study?

7. sociology _____

8. psychology _____

9. climatology _____

10. archaeology _____

INTERACTION 2–7   **Using Word Parts to Read Popular Novels**

Use the Word Parts Glossary, your logic, and your prior knowledge to make sense of the **bold** words. The excerpts are taken from popular novels.

> It had been the longest, coldest winter of my life. Day after day under a pale, **worthless** sun. And the hunger—hunger that burned and gnawed, an **insatiable** master.
>
> —Maggie Stiefvater, *Shiver*

1. **Worthless** means _____

_____

2. **Insatiable** means _____

_____

> Even though **trespassing** in the woods is **illegal** and poaching carries the **severest** of penalties, more people would risk it if they had weapons.
>
> —Suzanne Collins, *The Hunger Games*

3. **Trespassing** means _____

_____

4. **Illegal** means _____

_____

5. **Severest** means _____

_____

> The initiate's journey, like all such journeys, had begun at the first degree. On that night, in a ritual similar to this one, the **Worshipful** Master had blindfolded him with a velvet hoodwink and pressed a ceremonial dagger to his bare chest, demanding "Do you seriously declare on your honor, **uninfluenced** by **mercenary** or other unworthy motive, that you freely and **voluntarily** offer yourself as a candidate for the mysteries and privileges of this **brotherhood**?"
>
> —Dan Brown, *The Lost Symbol*

6. **Worshipful** means _____

_____

7. **Uninfluenced** means _____

_____

8. **Mercenary** means _____

_____

9. **Voluntarily** means _____

_____

10. **Brotherhood** means _____

_____

> **Review: Word Parts to Expand Your Vocabulary**
>
> Use the Word Parts Glossary to look up the meanings of word parts that make up an unfamiliar word. You can use word parts in the following ways.
>
> - To understand the basic meaning of the word, find out what the root means.
> - To understand major changes to the root's meaning, find out what the prefix means.
> - To understand how a word will act in a sentence, find out what the suffix means.
>
> Keep in mind that the spelling of a word part often varies depending on what other word parts it is combined with.

ACTIVATE YOUR SKILLS 1
Using Word Parts to Expand Your Vocabulary

Circle one word in each sentence that seems to be composed of word parts. Then use the Word Parts Glossary and your prior knowledge to decide what it means.

1. Our family just did our biannual house cleaning. _____
   two times a year

2. My son has an overactive mind. _____
   too active moving

3. The money we raised this year far surpassed our goal. _____
   go over

4. The author used a pseudonym. _____
   False name

5. Empower yourself by speaking truth. _____
   to have strent

6. Next, turn your body counterclockwise. _____
   Opposite of clockwise

7. Are human beings mortal? _____
   Can die

8. A little <u>forethought</u> could have saved you a lot of trouble. _____

_____ *think before you act* _____

9. My boss likes to <u>dictate</u> my actions. _____

_____ *controle* _____

10. The mosquito was <u>bothersome</u>. _____

_____ *annoying* _____

ACTIVATE YOUR SKILLS 2
Using Word Parts to Expand Your Vocabulary

For each **bold** word, write the word parts, their meanings, and a phrase that puts together the meanings in a way that makes sense. If you need to use a dictionary, do so.

> Despite 20 years of **reassuring** research, many people still avoid **caffeinated** coffee because they worry about its health effects. In **moderation**—a few cups a day—coffee is a safe beverage that may offer some health benefits, including lowering the risk for type 2 diabetes. Coffee may also reduce the **likelihood** of gallstones, Parkinson's disease, and colon cancer.
>
> —Hales, *An Invitation to Health*, 12th edition

1. <u>reassuring</u>   3 word parts: *back again* *re* *assure* *reinforce make sure*

_____ *ing continuous* _____

Word part meanings: _____

Phrase that makes sense: *Mrs E reassuri us that*
we will all pass her class

2. **caffeinated**   3 word parts: *Caffeine   ate   ed*

_____ *ed upon   happen in the pas* _____

Word part meanings: _____

Phrase that makes sense: *My Coffie was*
Caffeinted

3. **moderation**   2 word parts: _Moderate - tion_
    not extreme   process of
    Word part meanings: _process of not extreme_

    Phrase that makes sense: _____

4. **likelihood**   2 word parts: _likely   hood_
    probable   process of
    Word part meanings: _probability_

    Phrase that makes sense: _____

You're driving down a lonely desert road outside of Palm Springs. Your car **inexplicably** stalls. Suddenly, a flying saucer lands next to you. A four-foot-tall green alien exits the craft and, in perfect English, says, "Human being! I wish to visit five interesting things in California and Arizona. No more, no less! What must I see? They must please me, or I will **disintegrate** you!"

—Mancini, *Selling Destinations: Geography for the Travel Professional*, 4th edition

---

5. **inexplicably**   5 word parts: _in ex plic able ly_
    not   out fold able to char g
    Word part meanings: _____
    not able to be explained
    Phrase that makes sense: _____

6. **disintegrate**   2 word parts: _dis integrate_
    not   to gether
    Word part meanings: _____

Phrase that makes sense: _____

_____

> Hospitals use several methods to attract new nurses. They offer signing bonuses, hire temporary nurses, and **vigorously** recruit nurses in distant places rather than raise base salary. All of these methods allow hospitals to pay nurses less than the value of their **contribution.** As a result, hospitals are permanently **understaffed,** and nurses are **chronically** overworked and underpaid.
>
> —Adapted from Getz, *Investing in College*

7. vigorously   3 word parts: _Vigo rous lu_
Strength quality char of

Word part meanings: _____
have the quality of forcef

Phrase that makes sense: _____

_____

8. contribution   3 word parts: _Con tribu tion_
together pou process

Word part meanings: _____
Everybody is giving

Phrase that makes sense: _____

_____

9. understaffed   3 word parts: _Under Staff ed_
too little people pass

Word part meanings: _____
not enoug people

Phrase that makes sense: _____

_____

10. **chronically**   3 word parts: _Chron ical ly_
time   _Char of Char_

Word part meanings: _Char of time_

Phrase that makes sense: _____

_____

MASTER YOUR SKILLS 1
Using Word Parts to Expand Your Vocabulary

A. Using the Word Parts Glossary and your prior knowledge, finish each definition for words 1–4. Then circle the correct word in sentences 5–8.

1. **junction** = result of or process of _join together_
2. **partition** = result of or process of _be bold_
3. **suspension** = result of or process of _being suspended_
4. **elevation** = result of or process of _being evated_
5. The (junction / elevation / suspension) bridge was built in 1984.
6. In 1947, India was (suspended / joined / partitioned) into India and Pakistan.
7. Travelers from two states exited their trains at the railroad (partition / junction / elevation).
8. The (elevation / junction / suspension) was 2,532 feet above sea level.

B. Finish each definition for words 9–13. Then circle the correct word in sentences 14–18.

9. **progress** = step _to step forword_
10. **transgress** = step _to step across_
11. **regress** = step _to step back_
12. **egress** = step _to step out_
13. **ingress** = step _to step up_
14. The leaders made great (digress / progress / ingress) toward peace.
15. When the teenager became afraid, he (ingressed / regressed / transgressed) and started acting like he was a two-year-old.

16. A person who has sex with someone outside his or her marriage (egresses / ingresses / <u>transgresses</u>) religious laws.

17. (<u>Ingress</u> / Progress / Transgress) to the building was controlled by security guards.

18. The only (progress / digress / <u>egress</u>) from the park was to the south.

C. State the definition of the **bold** word in the sentence.

19. Their friend **interceded** when they had an argument. _____

_____

20. An **ultramodern** way to go online is with an iPad. _____

_____

MASTER YOUR SKILLS 2
Using Word Parts to Expand Your Vocabulary

A. Match the word on the left with the definition on the right. Use each definition only once. Use the Word Parts Glossary and a dictionary if you need to.

G	1. recall	a. draw a line around
D	2. propel	b. make a person leave a country
J	3. democracy	c. done by hand
A	4. circumscribe	d. drive forward
F	5. transmit	e. turn to a new religion
I	6. vivify	f. send from one person to another
B	7. deport	g. remember
C	8. manual	h. take away
E	9. convert	i. bring to life
H	10. abscond	j. government by the people

B. Determine the meaning of each **bold** word and write it down. All the selections are from the book *Hunger: An Unnatural History,* by Sharman Apt Russell.

11. Our body is a circle of messages: communication, feedback, updates. Hunger and **satiety** are the most basic of these. _State of having enough to eat_

_____

12. We know that it is relatively easy to **repress** the signal for enough. _____

_____ to hold back _____

13. A gene **malfunctions,** and a three-year-old girl weighs a hundred pounds: her body does not tell her when to stop eating. _not working_

14. The signal for hunger is much, much harder to turn off. We are **omnivores** with an oversized brain that requires a lot of energy. _consume everything (Plants and Animals)_

15. We are not **specialized** in how we get our food. _are not pickly_

16. Our love of fat and sugar has been **associated** with the same chemical responses that underlie our addictions to alcohol and drugs; this cycle of addiction may have developed to encourage eating behavior. _Connected to_

17. Human beings evolved for a bad day of hunting, a bad week of hunting, a bad crop, a bad year of crops. We were hungry even in that first Garden of Eden, what some **anthropologists** call the "Paleoterrific," a world full of large animals and relatively few people. _People who study human behavior_

18. Our diet didn't get better as our population grew and the big-game species died out. In the Mesolithic, we foraged more **intensively** for plants and hunted smaller game with new tools like nets and snares. _extremely Carefully_

19. In the **Neolithic,** we invented agriculture, which sparked the rise of cities. There is no evidence that any of these changes reduced the odds of starvation or malnutrition. _Early Cultures_

20. It's no wonder we are programmed to pound the table and demand dinner. The exceptions to this are usually extreme: infection, disease, **terminal** illness. _Fatal (limited time)_

While You Read, Define Words in Context.

As you work through this lesson, you will learn strategies to help you determine the meanings of words you do not know based on the **context** in which they are used. If you have completed Lesson 4, you have probably noticed that the word *context* is composed of a prefix and a root: **con- + text.** Since *con-* means "together," and *text* means "weave," you can figure out that *context* means "the words woven together with the new word." Words weave together to make meaning, and the meaning of a word changes—a lot or a little—depending on its context. The context is the word's setting or environment.

Find Context Clues While Reading.

Context clues are hints about the meaning of a word that are located in the surrounding words or sentences. When you are trying to figure out what a word means, look in the sentences surrounding the word. Clues to your word's meaning can be found anywhere within a paragraph, but they are often found in one or more of the following three places:

1. The actual sentence in which the unknown word appears.

2. The sentence before the one in which the word appears.

3. The sentence after the one in which the word appears.

Here is an example of a context clue for the word *conceive*.

Some people should not drink. For example, women who are pregnant or trying to conceive should not drink any alcohol.

If you didn't know what the word *conceive* means, you could figure it out from the sentence it appears in. The words "are pregnant" is a context clue that helps you understand "trying to conceive." Conceive means "get pregnant." Notice that this definition is not very technical.

However, it does the job: it gives you enough understanding so you can keep reading. That is the goal to aim for.

Recognize Four Kinds of Context Clues.

We will focus on four common kinds of context clues: examples, antonyms, synonyms, and your own logic interacting with the words on the page. Context clues are **EASY**:

Example = illustration of
Antonym = opposite
Synonym = word that means the same thing
Your Logic = prior knowledge/inferencing

You won't necessarily use the context clues in this order, but the word EASY will help you remember some different strategies to try when you don't know the meaning of a word.

Examples

Look for **examples** that might give you clues to a word's meaning. Examples may describe or explain an unknown word. At times, the author may use signal words like these to let you know an example is coming.

Words that signal examples:

for example, for instance, such as, to illustrate

Laura's "conversations" are more like monologues. For example, the last time I talked with her, she spent half an hour describing her new apartment. I couldn't get in a single word.

As you can see, the word *monologue* has something to do with talking a lot and not letting the other person say anything. You can tell because of the examples given: *she spent half an hour describing her new apartment* and *I couldn't get in a single word.* Based on these examples, you can tell that a monologue is a long speech made by one person.

INTERACTION 2–8	Using Example Context Clues with Signal Words

Each sentence includes a **boldfaced** vocabulary word.

    A. Circle the example signal words.
    B. Underline the example that provides a clue to the word's meaning.
    C. Guess the meaning of the vocabulary word and write it on the line.

1. Some college students major in the **social sciences,** such as communications (the study of how people talk and otherwise communicate with each other) and sociology (the study of how people act when they're together).

Social sciences are <u>How people act when they are together</u>

2. A sociologist studies how people act in **social** contexts. For example, some sociologists study how people act in family groups, and others study how people are affected by their religious membership or local community.

Social means <u>Comunicate with group</u>

3. Sociologist Mattijs Kalmijn has studied the social **factors** that influence whom people fall in love with and marry. To illustrate, one factor that matters is how large the person's community is. The larger it is, the more likely it is that a person will marry someone from inside the group.

Factors are <u>Tale</u>

4. Other sociologists study what makes a marriage stable, and they find that **economic** factors influence whether a marriage will continue or end in divorce. For instance, the lower the income of a family, the more likely it is that the marriage will be unstable. Also, satisfaction generally increases for both partners when both are working and making money.

Economic means <u>money</u>

5. Other factors also play a **role** in marital satisfaction. For example, the amount of sex a couple has, how the partners divide up the housework and childcare, and whether they have children and how old the children are all matter.

A role is a ~~is the port that you play~~

—Adapted from Brym & Lie, *Sociology*, 3rd edition

INTERACTION 2–9   **Using Vocabulary in a New Context**

Here are the vocabulary words you worked with in Interaction 2–8:

| economic | factors | role | social | social sciences |

Choose from these words to fill in the blanks in the sentences that describe the photo.

Nice One Productions/CORBIS

    These football fans are at a tailgating party, which is a _____ situation. A college professor who is a sociologist might want to study how they act. The fans play a _____ in the game by cheering for their team. Of course, other _____ are even more important in deciding who wins, such as how well the team plays.

Signal Words May Not Be Present

Signal words may not always be used. However, if you think about the meaning of a sentence, you may find out that the author has still given examples without making it so obvious. Sometimes you can figure out if there are examples by adding example signal words to different places to see if they make sense. If they do, that's an example context clue. Notice how you can insert "for example" into the following sentence to help you determine the meaning of *monologues*.

> Laura's "conversations" are more like monologues. [**for example**] The last time I talked with her, she spent half an hour describing her new apartment. I couldn't get a word in edgewise.

This won't always work, but it works often enough that you can use it to search for example context clues. However, use your common sense. Sometimes the way a sentence is put together doesn't allow you to insert *for example* or *such as,* but it can still include examples.

INTERACTION 2–10	Using Example Context Clues Without Signal Words

Each item includes a **boldfaced** vocabulary word.

> A. Add example signal words where they fit best—if possible. *Hint:* Signal words can't be used in two of the sentences.
> B. Underline the example that provides a clue to the word's meaning.
> C. Guess the meaning of the vocabulary word and write it on the line.

1. Joey is a **cautious** person. When his friends jumped on burros to ride to the bottom of the Grand Canyon, Joey asked the park ranger a dozen questions about the path down the mountain before he decided to join them.

   Cautious means _____

2. The woman's clothing made her **conspicuous**. She wore a pink feathered collar, purple fringed shawl, and bright green, thigh-high boots covered with rhinestones.

   Conspicuous means _____

3. The **imprint** from the intruder's sneaker remained in the soft earth of the garden; the police officers could clearly see the pattern of treads.

   Imprint means _____

4. The mother's **nurturing** attitude was obvious in the home-cooked meal she made every night, the way she allowed her children's friends to stay in her home for weeks on end, and the understanding attitude she expressed when her oldest daughter got into trouble.

Nurturing means _____

5. The medicine was so **potent** that a single dose cured the disease.

Potent means _____

INTERACTION 2–11　　**Using Vocabulary in a New Context**

Here are the vocabulary words you worked with in Interaction 2–10:

| cautious | conspicuous | imprint | nurturing | potent |

Choose from these words to fill in the blanks in the sentences that describe the photo.

Nina Leen/Time Life Pictures/Getty Images

　　The man in this photo is Karl Lorenz, an Austrian ethologist (a scientist who studies how animals act). Lorenz discovered that if geese or other birds hatch out of their eggs and see a person rather than a mother goose, they will _____ on the person. That is, they will form a deep impression that he is their mother. It is unknown how much it matters if the person is _____ to the birds or not. (And as you probably know, scientists tend to be _____ about saying that one thing causes another.) The imprint is _____: the birds will follow the person everywhere. Lorenz was probably a bit _____ since everywhere he went, he was followed by a gaggle of geese!

Antonyms

Antonyms are words that have opposite meanings, such as *high* and *low*. Sometimes you can figure out the meaning of a word by finding its antonym in a context that shows the author means to contrast (show the difference between) the two words.

> **Words that signal contrast:**
> *on the other hand, in contrast, however, but, yet,*
> *instead, even though, although, unlike*

> Bullies often seem confident, yet they are actually insecure.

The word *yet* signals a contrast between the two parts of the sentence that are divided by the comma. To figure out the meaning of *insecure*, you can use that signal word as a clue. You might also notice that the sentence shows contrast in its wording: <u>seem</u> confident . . . , are <u>actually</u> insecure.

The word with an opposing meaning is *confident*. So *insecure* means (roughly) "not confident." This is a **working definition** for the word *insecure*. Notice that we found the opposite word, and then put *not* in front of it. You can also use the word *doesn't* instead of *not* to help you form a working definition.

Suppose you knew the word *insecure* but not the word *confident*. A working definition for *confident* would be "not insecure." The *in-* in *insecure* means "not," and so does the word *not* itself. When you put two *not*'s together in English, they cancel each other out. So, "not insecure" means "secure."

| **INTERACTION 2–12** | **Using Antonym Context Clues** |

Each sentence includes a **boldfaced** vocabulary word.

    A. Underline the antonym that provides a clue to the word's meaning.
    B. If there are signal words that indicate contrast, circle them.
    C. Guess the meaning of the vocabulary word and write it on the line.

1. It is difficult to drop bad habits like smoking and overeating. Although outside rewards such as praise from friends and family can be helpful, it's the **internal** decision to change that is most important and lasting.

   A. What is your "working definition" for **internal**? _____

   B. What does **internal** mean? _____

2. Your **resolve** to eat less may be hard to keep if your mother is always offering you homemade fudge and brownies, yet indecision makes it even harder.

   A. What is your "working definition" for **resolve**? _____

   B. What does **resolve** mean? _____

3. Each **obstacle** can cause frustration, but each step forward increases the possibility of success.

   A. What is your "working definition" for **obstacle**? _____

   B. What does **obstacle** mean? _____

4. **Anticipating** how you will deal with each temptation will help you succeed. In contrast, if you aren't expecting to have to deal with temptations, you are more likely to fail.

   A. What is your "working definition" for **anticipating**? _____

   B. What does **anticipating** mean? _____

5. You can **sustain** your new, healthy behaviors by giving yourself frequent rewards. On the other hand, you may be tempted to stop your new habit if you spread out the rewards over too long a time period.

   A. What is your "working definition" for **sustain**? _____

   B. What does **sustain** mean? _____

   —Adapted from Hales, *Invitation to Health,* 12th edition

| **INTERACTION 2–13** | **Using Vocabulary in a New Context** |

Here are the vocabulary words you worked with in Interaction 2–12:

| anticipating | internal | obstacle | resolve | sustain |

Choose from these words to fill in the blanks in the sentences that describe the photo.

Randy Faris/Flirt/CORBIS

A track and field event that is sometimes overlooked is running the hurdles. Hurdling is difficult. It requires a runner to jump over an _____ (called a hurdle) while _____ speed. The runner has to _____ when to start the jump in order to avoid running into the hurdle. In addition to the physical demands of running the hurdles, the runners must keep their _____ strong in order to succeed.

Synonyms

Synonyms are words that have a similar meaning or the same meaning, such as *huge* and *enormous*. Sometimes you can figure out the meaning of a word by finding its synonym in a context that shows the author means to compare (show the similarities between) the two words. Other times the author actually defines the word, so be on the lookout for phrases that mean the same thing as the word.

Words that signal similarity:
like, as, also, as well, or, in other words, similar to, that is, in the same way

Hamid's words and actions revealed him to be a candid person; **in other words,** he was open and truthful.

The words *in other words* signal that the author is going to repeat the same idea using different words. The word *candid* means the same thing as "open and truthful." These words are synonyms.

| INTERACTION 2–14 | Using Synonym Context Clues |

Each sentence includes a **boldfaced** vocabulary word.

    A. Underline the synonym (or definition) that provides a clue to the word's meaning.
    B. If there is a signal word to signal the synonym, circle it.
    C. Guess the meaning of the vocabulary word and write it on the line.

1. **Blogs** are like online journals. Some people discuss personal topics on their blogs, and others discuss the news of the day.

    Blogs are _____

2. **Vlogs** are also a way for people to share their ideas online, except that vlogs are video journals instead of written ones.

    Vlogs are _____

3. Similar to blogs and vlogs, **podcasts** can be recorded by individuals and posted online for others to hear.

    Podcasts are _____

4. These **media** are fairly new, but in the same way that they allow individuals and nonprofit groups to state their opinions, older communication channels such as public-access television and the public broadcasting service (PBS) have also given people a way to air their views.

    Media are _____

5. Just as these new media may be distributed globally on the Internet, they may also be disseminated more locally. Some college professors, for instance, now post podcasts of their lectures to an online class Web site so that students can listen to them again later.

Disseminated means _____

<table>
<tr><td>**INTERACTION 2–15**</td><td>**Using Vocabulary in a New Context**</td></tr>
</table>

Here are the vocabulary words you worked with in Interaction 2–14:

blogs	disseminated	media	podcasts	vlogs

Choose from these words to fill in the blanks in the sentences that describe the photo.

Courtesy of Carrie Chaney

This _____ is called [carrotspeak]. It is written by Carrie Chaney Richmond and is _____ via the Internet. You can also find _____ (video) and _____ (audio) online.

Your Logic

We said earlier that context clues for the meaning of a word are found in the surrounding words or sentences—that is, in the context of the reading selection. However, the reader's context plays a role, too, especially the context of how you think—your logic.

Your ability to understand logical connections as you interact with the words on the page will help you make meaning as you read.

Starting with what you already understand, actively try to figure out what you don't yet know. This process of making **inferences** is one you should always be using as you read. Here is an example.

A **characteristic** of fairy tales told in the United States is that they begin with the words "Once upon a time."

If you grew up in the United States, you know from your prior experience with fairy tales that many of them begin with the words "Once upon a time." So those words are a typical feature of fairy tales. **Characteristic** means "typical feature." If you grew up elsewhere, then you can figure out the meaning by substituting a similar idea from folk tales or stories told in your own culture.

INTERACTION 2–16	Using Your Logic and Prior Knowledge

Each sentence includes a **boldfaced** vocabulary word.

    A. Underline the part of the sentence that provides a clue to the word's meaning.

    B. Use your logic and any prior knowledge you may have to guess the meaning of the word and write it on the line.

1. Animals are **adapting** to global warming, which they must do if their species are to survive.

  A. What does **adapting** mean? _____

  B. How did your logic and prior knowledge help? _____

_____

_____

2. Sheep that live on islands off the west coast of Scotland have **diminished** in size because smaller animals are no longer being killed off in a long, harsh winter.

  A. What does **diminished** mean? _____

  B. How did your logic and prior knowledge help? _____

_____

_____

3. The purple pitcher mosquito, found in the mid-Atlantic states up through Canada, has begun hibernating later as the winter arrives later. Christina Holzapfel, a biologist, says, "As the environment changes, individuals that can't change are **lopped off.**"

A. What does **lopped off** mean? _____

B. How did your logic and prior knowledge help? _____

_____

_____

4. The **reproductive** cycle of the field mustard weed in California has allowed it to respond faster to the changing climate. Species that can reproduce rapidly—like insects and weeds—will adapt more easily to the pace of climate change than large mammals and old trees.

A. What does **reproductive** mean? _____

B. How did your logic and prior knowledge help? _____

_____

_____

5. The world's climate has always changed, and species have always evolved to survive it. But the sheer speed of human-made climate change today is **unprecedented**.

A. What does **unprecedented** mean? _____

_____

B. How did your logic and prior knowledge help? _____

_____

_____

—Adapted from Walsh, "Why Are Scotland's Sheep Shrinking?" *Time*, July 20, 2009

INTERACTION 2–17	Using Vocabulary in a New Context

Here are the vocabulary words you worked with in Interaction 2–16:

adapting	diminishes	lopped off	reproductive	unprecedented

Choose from these words to fill in the blanks in the sentences that describe the photo.

Patrice Coppee/Workbook Stock/Getty Images

These farmers on the island of Martinique are using their machetes to _____ stalks of sugar cane. Each stand of cane can be harvested several times, but the crop _____ each time, and then a new stand must be planted to maintain a good-sized crop. Since some sugar cane no longer produces seeds, farmers today plant stem cuttings as the _____ method.

Review: Context Clues to Understand New Words

Use context clues to help you figure out what words mean while you are reading, including these four EASY-to-remember ones:

- E = Examples
- A = Antonyms (words with opposite meanings)
- S = Synonyms (words with similar meanings)
- Y = Your logic

Remember that context clues are often found in the same sentence as the mystery word, in the sentence before it, or in the sentence after it.

Look for Signal Words.

You have practiced working with signal words when you know which kind to expect. But of course, when you are reading you can't be sure what you will find. Here is an Interaction in which the kinds of context clues, and signal words, are varied.

INTERACTION 2–18	Looking for Signal Words

Each sentence includes a **boldfaced** vocabulary word.

>   A. Circle signal words. (Three sentences do not include any signal words.)
>   B. Underline words that provide a clue to the word's meaning.
>   C. Write the meaning of the word on the line.

1. In the book *Survive!*, Lee Stroud tells readers they can prepare themselves for emergency situations if they **contemplate** problems that could come up when they go hiking, climbing, or boating. If, on the other hand, they do not think about possible accidents, they are really asking for trouble.

   A. What does **contemplate** mean? _____

   B. What kind of context clue was used? _____

2. In a survival situation, starting and **maintaining** a fire can be tricky. For instance, keeping a fire going all night takes about five times as much wood as most people expect.

   A. What does **maintain** mean? _____

   B. What two kinds of context clues were used? _____

3. A person can **tolerate** going without water for only about three days. Then dehydration causes severe headaches and a drop in the energy level needed to get out of a bad situation.

   A. What does **tolerate** mean? _____

   B. What kind of context clue was used? _____

4. How easy it is to find food varies, depending, in part, on a person's knowledge of what is **edible** and what is poisonous.

   A. What does **edible** mean? _____

   B. What kind of context clue was used? _____

5. People who don't have **phobias** about spiders and snakes will probably find it easier to pull together quick shelters from fallen leaves, grasses, and tree boughs. Those who do have such phobias can use long sticks to avoid touching hidden creatures.

   A. What does **phobias** mean? _____

   B. What kind of context clue was used? _____

INTERACTION 2–19   **Using Vocabulary in a New Context**

Here are the vocabulary words you worked with in Interaction 2–18:

contemplate	edible	maintain	phobias	tolerate

Choose from these words to fill in the blanks in the sentences that describe the photo.

Gavin Hellier/Robert Harding/Getty Images

When you visit a foreign country, it can be hard to decide which foods you will love and which foods you will only _____. In Japan, many kinds and styles of fish are considered _____. The fugu, or blowfish, for example, can be deadly if it is not prepared by an expert. If someone has a fear of eating fugu, could we call it a _____? Certainly, the fear may be intense, but is it unreasonable?

Review: Signal Words to Understand Context Clues

Watch out for signal words that may lead you to a context clue for words whose meanings you don't know. Signal words can point to:

- Examples: *for example, for instance, such as, to illustrate*
- Contrast (difference): *on the other hand, in contrast, however, but, yet, instead, even though, although, unlike*
- Comparison (similarity): *like, as, also, as well, or, in other words, similar to, that is, in the same way*

Create EASY Note Cards to Study Words.

You need a way to keep your study of vocabulary organized, and it's a smart idea to keep reminding yourself of the meanings of new words so you can commit them to memory. Creating and then studying EASY note cards is a simple way to learn and remember enough about a new word so that you can start to use it comfortably.

Here is an example of an EASY note card.

The word

(the part of speech--
noun, verb, adjective, adverb)

FRONT

Example-- Write a sentence using the word that
shows you know its meaning.

Antonym (if there are any)

Synonym (if there are any)

Your Logic-- Use your logic to make up a definition
in your own words.

BACK

Here is a sample note card for the word "compose," which was discussed earlier in Part 2 in relation to Bethany Hamilton.

Compose
(verb)

FRONT

Example: Marita composed a picture in the sand using a
stick, and then her brother ran through it and
ruined it.

Antonyms: fall apart, disturb

Synonyms: put together, make up, arrange, write, create

Your logic: Compose—arrange something to create something
new

BACK

As you learn about each word, you may find that other words are related to it. You can add this information to the front of the card as you learn it. You may also choose to draw a picture on the front of the card that reminds you of the meaning, or you can write how to pronounce the word. If you write the pronunciation, you can base it on the pronunciation key on page 156 or you can use your own method, as shown on this card.

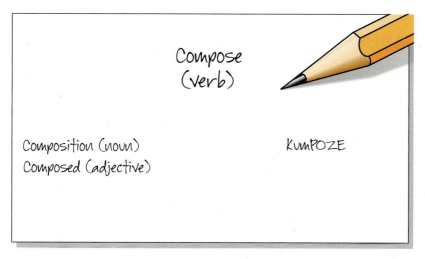

Compose
(verb)

Composition (noun)
Composed (adjective)

KumPOZE

FRONT

INTERACTION 2–20	Composing EASY Note Cards

With your classmates, form five groups. Listed below are twenty-five vocabulary words that have been discussed in this chapter. Each group should take one set of words found here.

1. **In your group,** read each word out loud and talk about what it means. If your group remembers what it means, each person should write a brief definition next to the word.

Group 1: Words from Interaction 2–8 on page 121

social sciences (noun) _____

social (adjective) _____

factor (noun) _____

economic (adjective) _____

role (noun) _____

Group 2: Words from Interaction 2–10 on page 123

cautious (adjective) _____

conspicuous (adjective) _____

imprint (noun) _____

nurturing (adjective) _____

potent (adjective) _____

Group 3: Words from Interaction 2–12 on page 125

internal (adjective) _____

resolve (noun) _____

obstacle (noun) _____

anticipate (verb) _____

sustain (verb) _____

Group 4: Words from Interaction 2–14 on page 128

blog (noun) _____

vlog (noun) _____

podcast (noun) _____

media (noun) _____

disseminate (verb) _____

Group 5: Words from Interaction 2–16 on page 130

adapt (verb) _____

diminish (verb) _____

lop off (verb) _____

reproductive (adjective) _____

unprecedented (adjective) _____

2. **In your group,** each person should start an EASY note card for the words the group didn't remember. Write the word and its part of speech (given above) on the front of the card. Go back to the Interaction each word is from, reread the item, and see how much information you can fill in on the back of the card.

3. **On your own or in your group,** use a computer that is online to go to http:// thesaurus.reference.com and type in each word to find synonyms and antonyms to write on the back of the card. If you can't get online, use a print thesaurus such as *Roget's Thesaurus* along with a good college dictionary (see page 151). Write down synonyms and antonyms only if you know what they mean. (Notice that you need to pay attention to the part of speech in order to find the right synonyms and antonyms.)

4. **On your own,** compose a definition using your own words. Don't copy the definition—it's easier to remember if you put the definition into your own words.

5. **On your own,** select two other groups of words from the list above that you want to learn. Compose an EASY note card for each word, following the directions above.

6. **On your own,** study your EASY note cards each day. When you are sure you know a word, set that card aside and continue with the others. Every two weeks, put all the words back together and test yourself to make sure you remember them all. For each word, think about whether you have heard or read any related words that you can add to the front of the card.

ACTIVATE YOUR SKILLS 1
Defining Words in Context While You Read

Using the EASY method, read the following sentences from an education textbook called *Those Who Can, Teach,* by Ryan Cooper. Decide what each bold word probably means and write your definition on the line provided. Not all kinds of clues will appear in all sentences.

A great variety of **motivations** lead people to select teaching as their **occupation**, and often the same person has more than one reason for choosing teaching.

1. **Motivation** means _a reson to do something_
2. **Occupation** means _work_

Individuals' responses to the question, "Why teach?" can run the **gamut** from "Will teaching satisfy me?" to "How can I help others?"

3. An **individual** is _person_
4. **Gamut** means _cover a range_

The **extrinsic** rewards of teaching—the salary, the status, and the power—are not great. But the **intrinsic** rewards—the joy of helping others, the knowledge that teachers contribute to society, and the enjoyment of working with young people—can make teaching a pleasure.

5. **Extrinsic** means _physical reward_
6. **Intrinsic** means _more joy_

As much as possible, students of teaching should observe in schools and participate in various activities that give them real **encounters** with children and adolescents. They may find that young people are much different from the images they have **manufactured**.

7. **Encounters** are _experence_
8. **Manufactured** means _made_

Teachers can help their students **transform** their lives. For example, Erin Gruwell, the teacher who was **portrayed** in the 2007 movie *Freedom Writers,* helped a group of teens who didn't have much hope for their futures become critical thinkers, aspiring college students, and citizens for change.

9. **Transform** means _Change_

10. **Portrayed** means _Shown represented_

ACTIVATE YOUR SKILLS 2 *do*
Defining Words in Context While You Read

Using the EASY method, read the following passages. Decide what each boldfaced word probably means. After each definition that you write, circle which kind or kinds of context clues helped you figure out the word's meaning:

E = Example
A = Antonym
S = Synonym
Y = Your logic

Excerpt from the Novel *Twilight*

One of the best things about Charlie is he doesn't **hover.** He left me alone to unpack and get settled, a feat that would have been altogether impossible for my mother. It was nice to be alone, not to have to smile and look pleased; a relief to stare **dejectedly** out the window at the sheeting rain and let just a few tears escape. I wasn't in the mood to go on a real crying jag. I would save that for bedtime, when I would have to think about the coming morning.

—Stephenie Meyer, *Twilight*

1. **Hover** means _____ E A S Y

2. **Dejectedly** means _____ E A S Y

The Need for Sleep

You stay up late cramming for a final. You drive through the night to visit a friend at another campus. You get up for an early class during the week but stay in bed until noon on weekends. And you wonder: "Why am I so tired?" The answer: You're not getting enough sleep.

Superstock

Whenever we fail to get adequate sleep, we **accumulate** what researchers call a sleep **debit**. With each night of too little rest, our body's need for sleep grows until it becomes **irresistible**. The only solution to the sleep debt is the obvious one: paying it back. College students who extended their nightly sleep time were more alert, more productive, and less likely to have accidents. And because sleepy people tend to be irritable and **edgy**, those who get more rest also tend to be happier, healthier, and easier to get along with.

—Hales, *An Invitation to Health*, 12th edition

3. **Accumulate** means _____   E A S Y

4. **Debit** means _____   E A S Y

5. **Irresistible** means _____   E A S Y

6. **Edgy** means _____   E A S Y

Safeguarding Your Online Reputation

Nothing is temporary online. The **virtual** world is full of opportunities to interact and share with people around the world. It's also a place where nothing is **temporary** and there are no "take-backs." A lot of what you do and say online can be retrieved online even if you delete it— and it's **a breeze** for others to copy, save, and forward your information.

—USA.gov; The Nemours Foundation

7. **Virtual** means _____ E A S Y

8. **Temporary** means _____ E A S Y

9. **A breeze** means _____ E A S Y

Storms

Storms often **disrupt** travel plans. Sometimes you can know when they're more likely to **occur** and thus recommend the best time to visit certain destinations.

Hurricanes are among the most violent of storms. Usually born near the equator, hurricanes **migrate** in rather unpredictable patterns. They can cover hundreds of square miles with high winds (74 mph or more) and heavy rains for a day or two in one place before moving on. When they're born near the Caribbean or Mexico, they're called *hurricanes;* when they **originate** in the western Pacific, they're called *typhoons;* the southward-heading ones around Australia and in the Indian Ocean are called *cyclones,* the official generic name for all such storms.

Hurricanes rarely maintain strength if they move far inland over a continent; instead, they **degenerate** into large rainstorms.

—Mancini, *Selling Destinations: Geography for the Travel Professional,* 4th edition

10. **Disrupt** means _____ E A S Y

11. **Occur** means _____ E A S Y

12. **Migrate** means _____ E A S Y

13. **Originate** means _____ E A S Y

14. **Degenerate** means _____ E A S Y

MASTER YOUR SKILLS 1
Defining Words in Context While You Read

Read the following excerpts from a college textbook by Anthony J. Bertino called *Forensic Science,* and then answer the vocabulary questions.

> **Direct evidence** includes firsthand observations such as eyewitness accounts or police dashboard video cameras. For example, a witness states that she saw a defendant pointing a gun at a victim during a robbery. In court, direct evidence involves testimony by a witness about what that witness personally saw, heard, or did. Confessions are also considered direct evidence.

1. What three kinds of context clues help you understand the meaning of *direct evidence?*

   _____ Examples

   _____ Antonyms

   _____ Synonyms

   _____ Your logic

2. Explain each kind of context clue you checked above. You can give an example of the context clue or describe how you used it.

   • _____

   _____

   _____

   • _____

   _____

   _____

   • _____

   _____

   _____

3. Which of the following can be considered direct evidence?

_____ Testimony by a witness to an event

_____ A suspect's gun at a crime scene

_____ Confessions

_____ A videotape of a crime

4. Which statements about direct evidence are true?

_____ Direct evidence is not admissible in court.

_____ Direct evidence comes from people who saw a crime occur.

_____ Direct evidence is probably more important than indirect evidence.

_____ Direct evidence can be spoken.

Circumstantial evidence is indirect evidence that can be used to imply the fact but that does not directly prove it. No one, other than the suspect and victim, actually sees when circumstantial evidence is left at the crime scene. But circumstantial evidence found at a crime scene may provide a link between a crime scene and a suspect. For example, finding a suspect's gun at the site of a shooting is circumstantial evidence of the suspect's presence there.

5. What synonym is given for *circumstantial evidence*? _____

_____

6. What is the antonym for *indirect evidence*? _____

_____

7. What example of circumstantial evidence is given? _____

_____

8. Give your own example of circumstantial evidence. _____

_____

_____

Circumstantial evidence can be either physical or biological in nature. Physical evidence includes impressions such as fingerprints, footprints, shoe prints, tire impressions, and tool marks. Physical evidence also includes fibers, weapons, bullets, and shell casings. Biological evidence includes body fluids, hair, plant parts, and natural fibers.

9. What is the main context clue used here? _____

_____

10. Look carefully at all the examples of physical and biological evidence. What is the difference between the two kinds of evidence? _____

_____

MASTER YOUR SKILLS 2
Defining Words in Context While You Read

Read the following excerpts from popular novels. For each bold word, figure out as much as you can about its meaning and write down your guess. Then write down any words from the sentence you used to figure it out.

I **clasp** the **flask** between my hands even though the warmth from the tea has long since **leached** into the frozen air. My muscles are **clenched** tight against the cold. If a pack of wild dogs were to appear at this moment, the odds of **scaling** a tree before they attacked are not in my favor.

—Suzanne Collins, *Catching Fire*

1. clasp _____grab_____

_____

2. flask _____Container_____

_____

3. leached _____evoprote_____

_____

4. clenched _____ close tite _____

_____

5. scaling _____ climb _____

_____

Separating the Meadow from the woods, in fact **enclosing** all of District 12, is a high chain-link fence topped with barbed-wire loops. In theory, it's supposed to be **electrified** twenty-four hours a day as a **deterrent** to the **predators** that live in the woods—packs of wild dogs, lone cougars, bears—that used to threaten our streets. But since we're lucky to get two or three hours of electricity in the evenings, it's usually safe to touch. Even so, I always take a moment to listen carefully for the hum that means the fence is live. Right now, it's silent as a stone. **Concealed** by a clump of bushes, I flatten out on my belly and slide under a two-foot stretch that's been loose for years. There are several other weak spots in the fence, but this one is so close to home I almost always enter the woods here.

—Suzanne Collins, *The Hunger Games*

6. enclosing _____ circle _____

_____

7. electrified _____ put electri _____

_____

8. deterrent _____ shild to turn away _____

_____

9. predators _____ wild animal _____

_____

10. concealed _____ cover up _____

_____

There are two-toed sloths and three-toed sloths, the case being determined by the **forepaws** of the animals, since all sloths have three claws on their hind paws. I had the great luck one summer of studying the three-toed sloth *in situ* in the equatorial jungles of Brazil. . . . Its only real habit is **indolence**. It sleeps or rests on average twenty hours a day. Our team tested the sleep habits of five wild three-toed sloths by placing on their heads, in the early evening after they had fallen asleep, bright red plastic dishes filled with water. We found them still in place late the next morning, the water of the dishes **swarming** with insects. . . .

The three-toed sloth is not well informed about the outside world. On a scale of 2 to 10, where 2 represents unusual dullness and 10 extreme **acuity**, Beebe (1926) gave the sloth's senses of taste, touch, sight and hearing a rating of 2, and its sense of smell a rating of 3.

—Yann Martel, *Life of Pi*

11. **forepaws** _front paws_

12. *in situ* (**a Latin phrase**) _in_

13. **indolence** _lazy_

14. **swarming** _full of_

15. **acuity** _sharpness_

She raised her head to another icy blast, and noticed it was twilight. It would be dark soon, and her feet were numb. **Frigid** slush was soaking through her leather foot coverings despite the **insulating** sedge grass she had stuffed in them. She was relieved to see a dwarfed and stunted pine.

Trees were rare on the steppes; they grew only where there was **moisture** enough to sustain them. A double row of pines, birches, or willows, sculptured by wind into stunted asymmetrical shapes, usually marked a watercourse. They were a welcome sight in dry seasons in a land where groundwater was **scarce.** When storms howled down the open plains from the great northern glacier, they offered protection, **scant** though it was.

—Jean M. Auel, *The Valley of the Horses*

16. **frigid** _cold_

17. **insulating** _to keep inside_

18. **moisture** _wet_

19. **scarce** _small amount_

20. **scant** _little bite_

When you are reading, first try to use word parts and context clues to understand the meaning of a word. If those clues don't work, and you think the word is important to know so you can understand the reading selection, look up the word in the dictionary.

Understand Different Types of Dictionaries.

Print, online, and cell phone app dictionaries are available today. You should know how to use all three types. Even when you look a word up in a dictionary, you will need to stay aware of the context of the word in the reading selection. Words often have more than one definition, and knowing which one to use depends on the context.

- **Print Dictionaries.** Print dictionaries come in different sizes:
  - **Pocket dictionaries** include brief definitions of words used frequently. For example, *Webster's New Pocket Dictionary* contains 35,000 definitions. One limitation of pocket dictionaries is that they give only one or two definitions for most words, when many words have multiple definitions. A strength of pocket dictionaries is that they are small and easy to carry, so you can carry them in your backpack.

Sample entry from *Webster's New Pocket Dictionary* (2007)

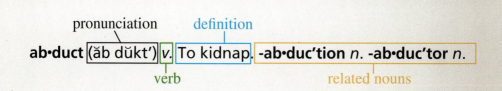

pronunciation definition
ab•duct (ăb dŭkt′) *v.* To kidnap. -**ab•duc′tion** *n.* -**ab•duc′tor** *n.*
verb related nouns

- **Collegiate dictionaries** include more and different kinds of information. *Webster's New College Dictionary,* for instance, gives fuller definitions than the pocket dictionary. It also gives examples of words in use. Other features that collegiate dictionaries typically have are comparisons of synonyms and their precise meanings, word histories, and illustrations of some words.

Sample entry from *Webster's New College Dictionary* (3rd edition, 2008)

verb forms

word history and word parts

ab·duct (ăb dŭkt) *vt* **-duct·ed,-duct·ing, -ducts.** [Lat. *abducere, abduct: ab-,*

general definition

away + ducere, to lead.] 1. To carry off by force. 2. *Physiol.* To draw away

from the median line of a bone or muscle or from an adjacent part or limb.

-abduc'tion *n.* **-abduct'or** *n.*

definition related to field of physiology

TommL/istockphoto.com

- **Comprehensive dictionaries** are bigger and more valuable still. In addition to the features that collegiate dictionaries include, comprehensive dictionaries define more words; give more examples of words used in context; sometimes provide photographs of people, places, and other subjects; and include sections on word roots from different languages. *The American Heritage Dictionary of the English Language* is an example of a comprehensive dictionary.

Sample feature from *American Heritage Dictionary of the English Language* (4th edition, 2000)

Synonyms accompany, conduct, escort, chaperon These verbs mean to be with or to go with another or others. *Accompany* suggests going with another on an equal basis: *She went to Europe accompanied by her colleague. Conduct* implies guidance of others: *The usher conducted us to our seats. Escort* stresses protective guidance: *The party chairperson escorted the candidate through the crowd. Chaperon* specifies adult supervision of young persons: *My mom helped chaperon the prom.*

TommL/istockphoto.com

You can see from this example that the more specific information you need, the bigger the dictionary you should consult. For quicker or more casual use, go to a smaller dictionary.

- **Online Dictionaries.** Online dictionaries may be based on textual definitions (definitions given in words) or visual definitions. In either case, audio files may be provided that allow you to hear how a word is pronounced.

  - **Online text-based dictionaries** are available at the following Web addresses:

    - Merriam-Webster Online   www.merriam-webster.com
    - Your Dictionary   www.yourdictionary.com
    - Dictionary   http://dictionary.reference.com

The online format is useful because you can hear the word spoken in an audio file. It's also convenient to simply type in the word you are looking for instead of leafing through the pages of a book. However, you will often see advertisements when you look up or listen to words, which can be distracting.

Sample definition from *Merriam-Webster Online*

Note that some dictionary sites include other kinds of reference works. Make sure you select the dictionary.

- **Online visual dictionaries** are available in several types. They are limited by the number of words that can be represented in pictures. An example is *Visual Dictionary Online* from Merriam-Webster at http://visual.merriam-webster.com. The dictionary includes about 20,000 words and 6,000 related images. Visual dictionaries may be especially helpful if you need to understand how complex parts fit together, such as in the example that follows. They can also be useful for people who are native speakers of languages other than English.

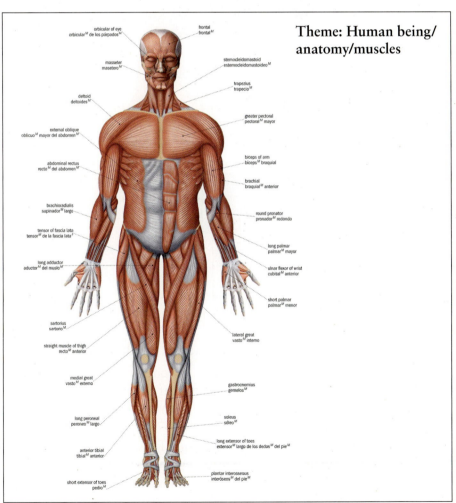

Theme: **Human being/ anatomy/muscles**

Sample entry from *Visual Dictionary Online*

• **Dictionary Apps for Smart Phones.** Many students now access dictionaries on their smart phones using cell phone apps (applications). If you have a smart phone, such as an iPhone, BlackBerry, Motorola RAZR, or another, you can probably find a dictionary app for it. Some apps are free, some are just a couple of dollars, and others cost much less than a print version of the same dictionary. Some apps require an Internet connection, but others do not. Here are a few choices that were available in 2010.

ICP-DE/Alamy

Some dictionary apps:

• Dictionary (for iPhones; free). About 120,000 words.

• Dictionary.com (for BlackBerry, iPhone, and Android; free). About 300,000 words. This dictionary is based on the *Random House Unabridged Dictionary* and includes content from Dictionary.com and Thesaurus.com.

• WordBook English Dictionary and Thesaurus (for iPhones; $1.99). About 150,000 words. Definitions are not as carefully written as in major dictionaries, such as the *American Heritage Dictionary*.

- American Heritage Dictionary, 4th edition (for iPhones and iPod Touches; $29.99). About 300,000 terms—or the entire 2,000-plus page print dictionary.

Just as a pocket-sized print dictionary may not include all the words you need in your college studies, you may not want to rely on free dictionary apps when precise definitions matter. For defining words on the fly, however, they are probably fine.

Review: Types of Dictionaries

Dictionaries come in a wide range of sizes and formats. Use one that is appropriate for your purpose and need.

- For convenient, quick use, use a cell phone app, online text dictionary, or pocket print dictionary.

- When precision is needed—for example, when you are writing a college essay—use a collegiate or comprehensive dictionary.

- If you need to see a diagram to understand how complex parts fit together, use an online visual dictionary.

- To hear a word being pronounced, use an online dictionary. Some cell phone apps also include this feature.

Know What Kinds of Information You Can Find in a Dictionary Entry.

You have seen several examples above of the kinds of information dictionaries provide in a word's definition. Here is a more complete list.

- **Basic form.** The entry word is the basic form of the word, minus any endings that indicate plurals of nouns or tenses of verbs. So if you need to find *harangues,* you look up *harangue.* If you need to find *crippling,* you look up *cripple.*

- **Syllables.** The entry word is divided by little dots or diamonds that show where syllables are: die·sel. If you are writing by hand and want to divide a word at the end of a line, only do so where a syllable break occurs.

- **Pronunciation.** The pronunciation of the word is given in parentheses: (dēzəl, -səl) or between back slashes: \ \. To understand the symbols that are used, look for the pronunciation key. This key is usually found at the bottom or side of the dictionary page. It may also be found in the first pages of the dictionary.

Sample List of Abbreviations

Symbol	Example of word with that pronunciation
ă	pat
ā	pay
âr	care
ä	father
ĕ	pet
ē	be
ĭ	pit
ī	pie
îr	pier
ŏ	pot
ō	toe
ô	paw
oi	boy
ou	out
o͝o	took
o͞o	boot
ŭ	cut
ûr	urge
th	thin
th	this
hw	which
zh	vision
ə	about, item
◆	regionalism

Stress marks: ′ (primary); ′ (secondary), as in **dictionary** (dĭk′shə-nĕr′ē)

—Pronunciation key from *The American Heritage Dictionary*, 4th edition

- **Part of speech.** The part of speech is given, usually abbreviated, often in italic type. Here are the main ones:

  n. = noun (person, place, thing, idea)

  v. = verb (action or state of being)

  v.i. or *intr.* = intransitive verb (verb that doesn't need an object, like *die*)

  v.t. or *tr.* = transitive verb (verb that does need an object, like *make*)

  adj. = adjective (describes a noun)

  adv. = adverb (describes a verb, adjective, or another adverb)

  Here is an example of an entry for a noun from *The American Heritage Dictionary* (4th edition):

smart bomb *n.* A bomb that can be guided by radio waves or a laser beam to its target.

- **Definitions and sometimes examples.** Some words have just one or two definitions, but others may have hundreds. The definition you are looking for is the one that fits the context of the sentence you have read.

  Some definitions are in general use. Others are used only in particular fields of study or professions. See the second definition of *handshake* from *The American Heritage Dictionary* (4th edition) for an example.

hand·shake (hănd′shāk′) *n.* 1. The grasping of hands by two people, as in greeting or leave-taking. 2. *Computer Science* An exchange of signals between two devices when communications begin in order to ensure synchronization.

When examples are given, they are often put in italic type or within brackets so you can tell them apart from the definitions.

out·growth (out′grōth′) *n.* 1. The act or process of growing out. 2. A product of growing out; a projecting part or offshoot: *an outgrowth of new shoots on a branch.* 3. A result or consequence: *Inflation is an outgrowth of war.*

—From *The American Heritage Dictionary*, 4th edition

- **Idioms and other common phrases.** Some dictionaries first give all the definitions of the word alone, and then they give all the definitions of that word combined with others in common phrases. *The American Heritage Dictionary* (4th edition), for instance, gives definitions under the word **run** for phrases such as *run against, run along, run away,* and *run down* (and many, many more).

- **Etymology of the word.** The *etymology* is a word's history. To illustrate, here is an etymology for the word *abandon* from *Webster's New College Dictionary* (3rd edition):

  ME *abandounen* < OFr. *Abandoner* < *a bandon*: a, at (< Lat. *ad*) + *bandon* control.

  This word history goes backward in time. It begins with Middle English (ME, spoken from about 1150 to 1500) and then traces the word back to Old French (OFr.) and then back to Latin (Lat.). Etymologies can provide a fascinating glimpse into how a word gradually took on its present meaning and how languages have influenced one another.

INTERACTION 2–21	Using a Dictionary Entry While You Read

Read the following sentence.

> The bank has **stipulated** that the loan amount can't exceed $10,000.

Now read this dictionary entry for the word *stipulate* from *The American Heritage Dictionary* (4th edition).

> **stip·u·late** (stĭp′yə-lāt′) *v.* –lat·ed; -lat·ing, -lates. –*tr.* **1a.** To lay down as a condition of an agreement; require by contract. **b.** To specify or arrange in an agreement: *stipulate a date of payment and a price.* **2.** To guarantee or promise (something) in an agreement. –*intr.* **1.** To make an express demand or provision in an agreement. **2.** To form an agreement. [Latin *stipulāri, stipulāt-,* to bargain.] –*stip′u·la′tor* n.

Answer the following questions.

_____ 1. What part of speech is *stipulate*?
   a. noun
   b. verb
   c. adjective
   d. adverb

_____ 2. Which sentence best describes *stipulate*?
   a. It is a transitive verb.
   b. It is an intransitive verb.
   c. It has both transitive and intransitive uses.
   d. It is neither transitive nor intransitive.

_____ 3. Of the intransitive definitions, which one best fits how *stipulate* is used in the sentence above?
   a. 1
   b. 1a
   c. 1b
   d. 2

4. What's the meaning of the Latin root that the word *stipulate* comes from?

_____

5. Which syllable of *stipulate* is emphasized when it is spoken? _____

_____

| INTERACTION 2–22 | Using a Dictionary While You Read |

Read the following paragraph. Look up the four **bold** words in a dictionary—in print, online, or on your phone. Write a brief definition for each word.

> When there is a **devastating** accident, people's explaining away the signs of the **impending** disaster always seems **implausible** to others. Afterward, there is a **tendency** to read about what has taken place and to criticize: "How could those people be so stupid? Fire them. Pass a law against it. Redo the training."
>
> —Norman, *The Design of Everyday Things*

1. devastating _____

2. impending _____

3. implausible _____

4. tendency _____

Read the following excerpt from Chapter 2 of *Brian's Return,* a novel by Gary Paulsen.

It came to a head in of all places the front entryway of Mackey's Pizza Den. Brian had become **aloof,** sometimes unaware of the social life around him, and without knowing it had upset a boy named Carl Lammers. Carl was a football player, a large boy—his nickname was Hulk—and also a bully who **envied** Brian's celebrity. Brian didn't know him. Apparently Carl thought Brian had said something bad about him and he was coming out of Mackey's Pizza Den just as Brian was walking in with a boy and girl from school. The boy was small and thin—he was named Haley—and the girl was named Susan and she thought Brian was great and wanted to know him better and had invited him for a pizza so she could talk to him. Haley had been standing nearby and thought the invitation included him, to Susan's disappointment.

Carl had asked Susan on a date once and she had refused him. Seeing her with Brian made his anger that much worse.

He saw Brian through the glass of the door, saw him walking with Susan, and Carl threw his whole weight into his shoulder and slammed the door open, trying to knock Brian off balance.

It all went wrong. Brian was too far to the side and the door missed him. It caught Haley full on, smashing his nose—blood poured out immediately— and slammed him back into Susan. The two of them went flying backward and Susan fell to the ground beneath Haley and twisted her kneecap.

"Oh . . . ," she moaned.

For a moment everything seemed to hang in place. The door was open, Carl standing there and Brian off to the side, his face **perplexed**—he had been thinking about the woods when it happened—and Susan and Haley on the ground, blood all over Haley's face and Susan moaning, holding her knee.

"What—?" Brian turned back to Carl just as Carl took a swing at his head. Had it connected fully, Brian thought, it would have torn his head off. Dodging before it caught him, he missed the total force of the blow, but even then it struck his shoulder and knocked him **slightly** back and down on one knee.

Then things came very quickly. Haley was blinded by the blood in his eyes but Susan saw it all and still didn't believe it.

"Something happened," she said later. "Something happened to Brian— Carl just disappeared . . ."

In that instant Brian totally **reverted.** He was no longer a boy walking into a pizza parlor. He was Brian back in the woods, Brian with the moose,

> Brian being attacked—Brian living because he was quick and focused and intent on staying alive—and Carl was the threat, the thing that had to be stopped, attacked.
>
> Destroyed.

Give the definition for each **bold** word. Then note if you had to use a dictionary to find it.

1. **aloof** _____

   Yes   No

2. **envied** _____

   Yes   No

3. **perplexed** _____

   Yes   No

4. **slightly** _____

   Yes   No

5. **reverted** _____

   Yes   No

Review: Kinds of Information in a Dictionary Entry

Dictionary definitions are found under the basic form of a word. Entries typically include the following kinds of information:

- How to break the word into syllables.
- How to pronounce the word.
- What part of speech the word is.
- Definitions, some of which are general definitions and others that are specific to a particular field of study.
- Sometimes, examples of a word in use.

Dictionary entries in larger dictionaries may include other kinds of information, such as the word history (called the *etymology* of the word).

ACTIVATE YOUR SKILLS 1
Selecting the Right Definition for the Context

Read the sentences, which are all from *Cahokia: Mirror of the Cosmos* by Sally A. Kitt Chappell. Then select the dictionary definition that best fits the **bold** word as used in the sentence.

> From the top of Monks Mound the horizon of the wide world beyond forms a perfect circle. At dawn the rising sun embraces this **cosmos** with an arc of gold, a reminder of the past once cradled in this land on the broad shores of the Mississippi.

1. **cosmos**   __✓__ the universe as an orderly whole

               _____ herbs in the composite family

> At the beginning of the second **millenium,** a civilization more sophisticated and powerful than any other in the Western Hemisphere north of Mexico emerged and **flourished** in the Midwest.

2. **millenium**   __✓__ a span of one thousand years

                   _____ a hoped-for period of peace

3. **flourished**   _____ made bold, sweeping movements

                   __✓__ grew well; thrived

> The center of **communal** life for these Native American "Mississippians" was in the place we now call the Cahokia Mounds, in southwestern Illinois.

4. **communal**   _____ related to living in a commune

                   __✓__ related to a community

> At the turn of the **millenium,** about A.D. 1050, the population of Cahokia and its **environs** was larger than that of London.

5. environs   _____ environment

                __✓__ area surrounding a city

Their technology was that of the Stone Age. Yet without the wheel, beasts of burden, or metal-working, their **stratified** society **fostered** widespread commerce, refined artistic expression, and monumental architecture.

---

6. **stratified**   _____ deposited or arranged in layers

                     __✓__ separated into social status levels

7. **fostered**   _____ received the care of a parent

                     __✓__ promoted the growth and development of

---

The center of this six-square-mile area, the **climax** of this Native American world, was a great four-**tiered** pyramid covering fourteen acres and rising one hundred feet into the sky—the tallest structure in the United States until 1867.

---

8. **climax**   _____ the turning point in a play

                    __✓__ the point of greatest intensity or development

9. **tiered**   __✓__ having a series of rows, one above the other

                    _____ ranked

A wide variety of **indigenous** plants thrived there in the days before agriculture.

---

10. **indigenous**   __✓__ originating naturally in an area

                        _____ intrinsic; innate

ACTIVATE YOUR SKILLS 2
Finding Definitions in a Dictionary

Use a dictionary to find a definition for the word in **bold** that makes sense in the sentence. Then write down another definition of that word that does not fit the context.

1. The **sinuous** river slid through the stony mountains.

   Definition in sentence: _____

   Another definition: _____

2. It is my **practice** to begin the day by reading the Bible.

   Definition in sentence: _____

   Another definition: _____

3. The Nielsons are of Danish **descent.**

   Definition in sentence: _____

   Another definition: _____

4. She gave him a **perfunctory** smile before vanishing into her office.

   Definition in sentence: _____

   Another definition: _____

5. The story of how they survived the winters is long and **involved.**

   Definition in sentence: _____

   Another definition: _____

6. The town **endured** the lack of water caused by the long drought.

   Definition in sentence: _____

   Another definition: _____

7. This is a **knotty** problem that I need to think about.

   Definition in sentence: _____

   Another definition: _____

8. They were **mindless** of the avalanche danger as they snowboarded.

   Definition in sentence: _____

   Another definition: _____

9. He **scrambled** to keep his balance on the icy pond.

   Definition in sentence: _____

   Another definition: _____

10. It is **incumbent** upon you to attend the president's ball.

    Definition in sentence: _____

    Another definition: _____

MASTER YOUR SKILLS 1
Using a Dictionary After You Read

Read the following selections from the book *Women's Diaries of the Westward Journey* by Lillian Schlissel. As you are reading, use word parts or context clues to guess the meanings of the words in color. Write your guesses in the margin.

1. province: _____

2. nullified: _____
3. assertion: _____
4. tilled: _____

5. decreed: _____

The "New Country" to Americans in 1840 was the land of the Oregon and California Territories. California, that far-off Mexican **province**, was said to be an earthly paradise where the sun always shone and fruit grew wild. Trappers of the Hudson's Bay Company in Oregon reported an unending supply of furs, rich river banks for fishing, and valley land for farming. The claim of the Indians to the lands they had lived on for over a thousand years was universally **nullified** by the **assertion** that they had neither **tilled** the land nor built upon it. Americans saw only "free land," and they were drawn toward it as if by a magnet. They believed in the destiny that **decreed** the nation's sweep across the entire continent.

Check your guess about what each word means by looking it up in a print, online, or smartphone dictionary. Write the definition that best fits the context.

6. **province** _____

7. **nullified** _____

8. **assertion** _____

9. **tilled** _____

10. **decreed** _____

11. particularly: _____

12. represented: _____
13. entrenched: _____

14. dominated: _____
15. plied: _____

The Pacific Northwest Territory, **particularly** the Willamette Valley, a triangle formed by the Columbia River and the 46th parallel, was an area too rich to be ignored. England's interests were **represented** by the Hudson's Bay Company, and a thousand Englishmen were firmly **entrenched** on small farms that dotted the Puget Sound valley. Americans **dominated** shipping. So many Yankee ships **plied** the coast waters that the Indians came to call any sailor a "Boston."

Check your guess about what each word means by looking it up in a print, online, or smartphone dictionary. Write the definition that best fits the context.

16. particularly   _____

17. represented   _____

18. entrenched   _____

19. dominated   _____

20. plied   _____

MASTER YOUR SKILLS 2
Integrating Vocabulary Development

Read the following passages. For each word in red, use context clues, word parts, the dictionary, or all of these to figure out the meaning. Write each definition, and check off which method or methods you used to understand the word's meaning.

Excerpt from Chapter 1 of the Novel *Jellicoe Road*

I'm dreaming of the boy in the tree and at the exact moment I'm about to hear the answer that I've been waiting for, the flashlights yank me out of what could have been one of those perfect moments of clarity people talk about for the rest of their lives. If I was prone to dramatics, I could imagine my sighs would have been heard from the boundaries of the school to the town down below.

The question begs to be asked, "Why the flashlights?" Turning on the light next to my bed would have been less conspicuous and dramatic. But if there is something I have learned in the past five years, it's that melodrama plays a special part in the lives of those at the Jellicoe School. So while the mouths of the year twelves move and their hands threaten, I think back to my dream of the boy, because in it I find solace. I like that word. I'm going to make it my word of the year. There is just something about that boy that makes me feel like I belong. *Belong. Long to be.* Weird word, but semantics aside, it is up there with *solace.*

—Melina Marchetta, *Jellicoe Road*

1. clarity

   Definition: _____

   Methods used: _____ context clues _____ word parts _____ dictionary

2. prone

   Definition: _____

   Methods used: _____ context clues _____ word parts _____ dictionary

3. conspicuous

   Definition: _____

   Methods used: _____ context clues _____ word parts _____ dictionary

4. solace

   Definition: _____

   Methods used: _____ context clues _____ word parts _____ dictionary

5. semantics

   Definition: _____

   Methods used: _____ context clues _____ word parts _____ dictionary

The Wrong Place at the Wrong Time

The BBC is **undoubtedly** one of the best **broadcasters** in the world, with a proud history and popular website. But even the "Beeb" isn't **immune** to screwing up once in a while. Consider the case of its "Internet expert" Guy Goma, who participated in a studio discussion in 2006 regarding music downloads and Apple Computer's victory at the London High Court against Apple Corps, the record label for the Beatles. None of the **producers** noticed anything funny about Goma until he responded to one of the questions by saying, "I don't know. I'm not at all sure what I'm doing here." Turns out that Goma thought he was going to be interviewed for an IT job at the BBC, not interviewed on air.

A producer, however, thought that Goma was actually the **bona fide** Internet expert Guy Kewney after the receptionist mistakenly pointed Goma in his direction. And to make matters worse, Goma didn't get the job he was after either.

—Kelly & Levy, from "Top Ten Internet Blunders," *Time*, October 15, 2009

6. undoubtedly

Definition: _____

Methods used: _____ context clues _____ word parts _____ dictionary

7. broadcasters

Definition: _____

Methods used: _____ context clues _____ word parts _____ dictionary

8. immune

Definition: _____

Methods used: _____ context clues _____ word parts _____ dictionary

9. producers

Definition: _____

Methods used: _____ context clues _____ word parts _____ dictionary

10. bona fide

Definition: _____

Methods used: _____ context clues _____ word parts _____ dictionary

Is the Family in Decline?

Today, when people speak about the **decline** of the family, they are **referring** to the *nuclear family*. The nuclear family is composed of a **cohabiting** man and woman who maintain a socially approved sexual relationship and have at least one child. Others are referring more narrowly to what might be called the *traditional nuclear family*. The traditional nuclear family is a nuclear family in which the wife works in the home without pay while the husband works outside the home for money. This makes him the "primary **provider** and ultimate **authority**" (Popenoe, 1988: 1).

—Brym & Lie, *Sociology,* 3rd edition

11. decline

Definition: _____

Methods used: _____ context clues _____ word parts _____ dictionary

12. referring

   Definition: _____

   Methods used: _____ context clues   _____ word parts   _____ dictionary

13. cohabiting

   Definition: _____

   Methods used: _____ context clues   _____ word parts   _____ dictionary

14. provider

   Definition: _____

   Methods used: _____ context clues   _____ word parts   _____ dictionary

15. authority

   Definition: _____

   Methods used: _____ context clues   _____ word parts   _____ dictionary

---

Message From an Octopus

Octopuses are **sticklers** for fresh food, and one day Jean remembers that she was feeding a group of California mud flat octopuses (*binaculoides*) a meal of squid and shrimp. The food was a little past its peak of freshness. She would give each animal its first portion of food, and then go back to the beginning of the line of tanks to give them a second serving. When she got back to the first tank, a female octopus was waiting at the front of the tank. At this point, Jean says the octopus made eye contact with her while taking the piece of shrimp in one of her tentacles. **Maintaining** eye contact all the while, she then crawled over to the drain at the bottom of the tank and **unceremoniously** shoved the offending meal into the opening, where it was carried away. What makes the story so funny and **arresting** is the eye contact and the **dexterity** that enabled the animal to hold the spoiled shrimp while she slithered across the bottom of the tank. There is something about eye signals and manual dexterity that suggests intelligent behavior.

—Eugene Linden, *The Octopus and the Orangutan*

---

16. sticklers

   Definition: _____

   Methods used: _____ context clues   _____ word parts   _____ dictionary

17. maintaining

    Definition: _____

    Methods used: _____ context clues   _____ word parts   _____ dictionary

18. unceremoniously

    Definition: _____

    Methods used: _____ context clues   _____ word parts   _____ dictionary

19. arresting

    Definition: _____

    Methods used: _____ context clues   _____ word parts   _____ dictionary

20. dexterity

    Definition: _____

    Methods used: _____ context clues   _____ word parts   _____ dictionary

How can you tell if people are happy, sad, mad, or experiencing some other emotion? The short answer is that you can use **inference.** Based on what people say and how they say it, you can infer how they are feeling. (Or sometimes, they'll just tell you!) Here's the long answer.

- You can listen closely to a speaker's tone of voice and, using your prior knowledge of hearing many people use different tones of voice under different circumstances, understand what that tone implies (suggests without saying).

- You can listen to the actual words a person says, and, based on your memories of experiences you have had (again, your prior knowledge), you can understand what shade of meaning he or she is using. If someone says "I'm glad to meet you," the phrase means something different than if he or she says, "I'm so delighted to meet you!" The first sentence usually means the person is just being polite. The second suggests that the person has been waiting to meet you for some time or has a special reason for wanting to meet you.

- You can imagine what the person is trying to accomplish with her or his words. The person's emotions probably have something to do with her or his purpose for speaking.

Written language also has a tone—and it, too, can be happy, sad, mad, or a thousand other emotions. The difference is, of course, that you are reading words, not listening to and seeing a person. But the basic idea is the same. The author chooses specific words to get you to understand and even to feel the feelings he or she is trying to evoke in you. One way authors do this is by imagining what associations you will have to certain words. What memories, emotions, or experiences will a word call up for readers?

Spotlight on Inference: Drawing on Memories and Associations to Make Meaning

Read the following sentences from Aldous Huxley's novel *Brave New World,* and think about what the author wants you to think and feel about what he is describing.

> The overalls of the workers were white, their hands gloved with a pale corpse-coloured rubber. The light was frozen, dead, a ghost.

The author could have chosen any color in the world for the workers' overalls. Why did he choose the color white? What other things do you know of that are white?

One is snow. Related to snow is winter. In the next sentence, the author calls the light "frozen," so that confirms the association with winter. What does "corpse-coloured" tell you? The author also calls the light "dead, a ghost."

These kinds of associations are important to consider when you think about tone. The overall effect that Huxley suggests in these two sentences is that of a lifeless, unmoving, cold situation. Even though we don't know what the workers do or where they are, we do know that Huxley wants us to understand that there is nothing there that seems alive or colorful.

Huxley uses words that create certain feelings in his readers. This kind of tone is called **subjective.** Let's see how you can decide if an author's tone is subjective or not.

Understand the Difference Between Denotation and Connotation.

Denotation is the literal meaning of a word. It is straightforward. When you see denotation, think "d"—denotation is the **dictionary definition.** When you look up a word in the dictionary, the definition is the denotation of that word.

vig·or·ous (vĭg'ər-əs) *adj.* 1. Strong, energetic, and active in mind or body; robust. 2. Marked by or done with force and energy.

—*American Heritage Dictionary*, 4th edition

Connotation, on the other hand, adds other associations to a word. When you see connotation, think "conn": connotation is the **connection** or association of a word to certain emotions or attitudes. Some words have positive connotations, and others have negative connotations. Connotations are related to the context in which a word appears.

TomML/istockphoto.com

Spotlight on Inference: Understanding Connotations

Here are three words and their denotations, or dictionary definitions.

trudge   walk in a heavy-footed way
walk   move by taking steps with the feet at a slower pace than a run
stride   walk with long steps in a vigorous way

Now read each sentence below. Based on the different verbs that are used, what does each sentence connote? What feelings is the student having about taking her final exam?

A. The student **walked** in to take her final exam.

B. The student **trudged** in to take her final exam.

C. The student **strode** in to take her final exam.

No particular emotion is suggested by the verb *walked* in sentence A. The word doesn't have any connotations in this situation. In sentence B, the verb *trudged* suggests that the student may be depressed at the thought of taking her test, which might further suggest that she doesn't feel she will do well on it. In sentence C, the student's energetic act of *striding* may suggest she feels confident and is ready to take the test.

You use **inference** to determine what a word connotes. You base your reading of connotations on your prior experiences. Your memories of taking tests, your experiences of walking in different ways, and how these things are connected to certain emotional states, all come into play. The other important part of understanding connotation is knowing what words mean. Use the strategies you've learned throughout Part 2 when you don't know the meanings of words.

INTERACTION 2–24	Noting the Connotations of Words

Each of the following items starts with the definitions (denotations) of two words. Then the words are used in sentences. For each sentence, decide what feelings or attitudes (connotations) are suggested by the word in **bold**. Some words won't suggest any.

1. house   dwelling place
   home   dwelling place

   Crying, she said, "I have to go back to my **house** now." _____

   _____

   Crying, she said, "I have to go back **home** now." _____

   _____

2. beautiful   having a delightful appearance

cute   delightfully pretty

Their apartment was **beautiful.** _____ C _____

_____

Their apartment was **cute.** _____ D _____

_____

3. cut   separate into parts with a sharp instrument

hack   chop with irregular blows

The hair stylist **cut** off her client's long hair. _____

_____

The hair stylist **hacked** off her client's long hair. _____

_____

4. slither   move like a snake

thrust   push quickly and forcefully

The man's hand **slithered** into the cash register. _____

_____

The man **thrust** his hand into the cash register. _____

_____

5. contented   happy with things as they are; satisfied

ecstatic   intensely happy or joyful

She was **contented** that she had won the scholarship. _____

_____

She was **ecstatic** that she had won the scholarship. _____

_____

6. confidence   self-assurance; certainty

bravado   false show of courage or bravery

He talked to his parents with **confidence** about his decision to quit his job. _____

_____

He talked to his parents with **bravado** about his decision to quit his job. _____

_____

7. bolt   get startled and run away
   scamper   run lightly and quickly

The child **bolted** through the crowded streets, her eyes noticing everyone and everything. _____

_____

The child **scampered** through the crowded streets, her eyes noticing everyone and everything. _____

_____

8. took   carried away
   abducted   carried away by force

He **took** the child from the swing. _____

_____

He **abducted** the child from the swing. _____

_____

9. lounge   pass time in a lazy way
   hustle   move energetically or rapidly

While his wife got all the bags packed, the dishes done, and the house locked up, Jim **lounged** around making phone calls. _____

_____

While his wife got all the bags packed, the dishes done, and the house locked up, Jim **hustled** around making phone calls. _____

_____

10. event   social gathering
   gala   lavish or extravagant social event

The **party** was held in the city park. _____

_____

The **gala** was held in the city park. _____

_____

Connotations Suggest a Subjective Tone.

When an author uses words that have connotations, you can assume that the tone is subjective. **Subjective** means that the author is putting himself or herself into the writing as one of the subjects. It's like someone in a conversation giving her opinion. Her opinion becomes part of what you then respond to. Of course, sometimes the author gives opinions directly instead of by using words with connotations—for example, by using phrases such as *I believe, I think, people should,* and *in my opinion.* In either case, the tone is subjective.

Example of subjective tone

Parents should shower attention on their children.

author's opinion   connotation

Lack of Connotations Suggests an Objective Tone.

You may have noticed in Interaction 2–24 that a few bold words did not suggest any connotations. You might call these words the "plain" version of all the choices the author could have made. A lack of connotations suggests that the tone is objective. **Objective** means the author is ignoring his or her own opinions and is focusing on the object of the writing—the facts or ideas he or she is reporting.

Example of objective tone

Many parents pay attention to their children.

"plain" words

INTERACTION 2–25	Understanding Tone Based on Connotation

A. In the following excerpts, underline words that have connotations or that suggest the author's opinion.

B. Decide whether the tone is subjective or objective.

1.   Something awful has happened—so awful that I can hardly bear to write it. Oh, how could they, how could they?

—Smith, *I Capture the Castle*

subjective   objective

2.　　An estimated twenty million people inhabited the interior [of Southern and Central Africa] when Livingston first arrived. The tribes lived in villages, great and small. Their mud and grass huts with a single low doorway would be clustered within a protective fence of thorn bushes or sharpened sticks.

　　　　　　　　　　　　　　　　　　—Dugard, *Into Africa*

　　　　　subjective　　　　objective

3.　　According to a recent study in *The Journal of Applied Psychology*, there is another kind of exam that may be more predictive of how successful students will be in medicine: personality testing.

　　　　　　—Chen, "Do You Have the 'Right Stuff' to Be a Doctor?"
　　　　　　　　　　　　New York Times, January 14, 2010

　　　　　subjective　　　　objective

4.　　Some snow in a Buffalo neighborhood turned a deep shade of pink after a cloud of powder was released during demolition of a business that used to make food coloring. As surprised parents and pet owners wondered whether to ban outdoor play, state health and environmental officials collected samples.

　　　　　　—Associated Press, *Ft. Worth Star-Telegram*, January 17, 2010

　　　　　subjective　　　　objective

5.　　She was on her throne, the chair at the head of the mahogany dining table. It's a wonder of the world she has fit her parents' furniture into that room, including a cupboard for dishes. The old carved chairs are so enormous she looks like a child, feet swinging below her ruffled skirts and not quite reaching the floor.

　　　　　　　　　　　　　　—Kingsolver, *The Lacuna*

　　　　　subjective　　　　objective

Review: Denotation and Connotation

Two kinds of word meanings are denotative and connotative.

- Denotative meaning is the dictionary definition of a word. Connotative meaning is the emotional tone of a word.

- Connotations vary depending on the context in which a word is used.

- When an author uses words with connotations, the tone of a reading selection is subjective. The author has put himself or herself into the writing as a subject.

- When an author does not use words with connotations, the tone of a reading selection is objective. The author focuses on what happened, not on his or her opinion about what happened.

Consider a Word's Degree of Intensity.

Several kinds of words can have connotations. To take examples from Interaction 2–24, one noun that has connotations is the word *home,* and one verb with connotations is the word *scamper.* There is another kind of word, however—the adjective—that has the job of stating outright what the characteristics of a person, place, thing, or idea are. Some examples from Interaction 2–24 are *cute* and *beautiful,* *contented* and *ecstatic.*

When you are trying to understand an author's tone, look for adjectives that will show you the degree of intensity with which the author describes ideas and events. Many words can have the same basic meaning, but they express different degrees of intensity. Look at these words, which all share the same working definition of "not cold":

cool lukewarm warm hot boiling

LOW INTENSITY   HIGH INTENSITY

The words are arranged from least hot to most hot. Knowing what degree of intensity an author is using can help you understand the tone. Here's an example:

> Vivian was lukewarm about the proposal.

> Vivian was boiling about the proposal.

The words *lukewarm* and *boiling* here suggest certain emotional states. In the first sentence, Vivian isn't terribly enthusiastic about the proposal, but she's not totally cold toward it, either. In the second sentence, she is very angry. The first sentence suggests low intensity, the second sentence high intensity.

INTERACTION 2–26	Identifying Degrees of Intensity

Each group of words shown here has a meaning in common, stated in a working definition that begins with the word "not." (Look up the words whose meanings you don't know in a dictionary.) Number the words so that the lowest intensity word is "1," the medium intensity word is "2," and the highest intensity word is "3."

1. not dark _____ bright _____ dim _____ blinding

2. not new _____ worn out _____ decrepit _____ used

3. not young _____ prehistoric _____ vintage _____ antique

4. not dirty _____ clean _____ antiseptic _____ sanitary

5. not short _____ skyscraping _____ towering _____ tall

6. not feeling safe _____ shy _____ fearful _____ terrified

7. not silent _____ loud _____ deafening _____ audible

8. not distracted _____ engrossed _____ aware _____ attentive

9. not bored _____ enthusiastic _____ interested _____ obsessed

10. not unskilled _____ able _____ competent _____ expert

Review: Degrees of Intensity

Nouns and verbs can both carry connotative meaning, but it is the job of adjectives to state the characteristics of a person, place, thing, or idea.

- Look for adjectives to determine the author's attitude.
- Decide what degree of intensity the adjective reveals.

The larger your vocabulary becomes, the more you will be able to take advantage of degrees of intensity to understand the author's tone.

Tone Supports the Author's Purpose.

As you learned in Lesson 1, the author's general purpose might be to persuade readers, to inform readers, or to entertain readers. The tone of voice an author uses supports the purpose. (See Table 2.1.)

Subjective writing uses words with connotations and different degrees of intensity. The author's emphasis is on creating emotional states—either persuading readers to feel certain emotions or

Table 2.1 Tone Supports Purpose

General Purpose	General Tone
To inform (teach) readers	• **Objective:** The reading selection focuses on facts and ideas. Connotative language is not used much. • **Impersonal:** The author does not describe his or her point of view.
To entertain readers or to express the feelings or thoughts of the writer	• **Subjective:** The reading selection includes emotional connotations. • **Personal:** The author focuses attention on one particular point of view.
To persuade readers to believe or do something	• **Subjective:** The reading selection includes emotional connotations. • **Personal:** The author focuses attention on a particular point of view although much time may also be given to supporting that opinion with fact.

entertaining readers by revealing the emotions of the writer. However, the writing may still include facts and information.

Objective writing uses words without many connotations and with fewer degrees of intensity. The emphasis is on helping readers understand with their minds, rather than feeling emotions. Because connotations suggest the author's emotional stance, the lack of words with such meanings suggests an attempt to be objective rather than subjective.

Here are some examples of the connection between purpose and tone.

Informative purpose and objective tone

Johnny Bowden, a nutritionist, wrote a book called *The 150 Healthiest Foods on Earth.*

This sentence merely tells readers that something happened. It doesn't give the writer's thoughts or feelings about the author or the book. It just reports the facts. So it has an objective tone.

Entertainment/expressive purpose and subjective tone

Beets may be healthy, but when I see the red stains on my hands and napkin after eating them, I always look to see where I'm bleeding.

The writer expresses personal feelings about his or her own experience. The tone is subjective.

Persuasive purpose and subjective tone

You should eat the foods that will keep you the healthiest.

This sentence tells readers what the writer thinks they should do. Others might not agree. The tone is subjective.

INTERACTION 2–27 | **Determining an Author's Purpose and Tone**

While you read the following selections, underline any words that have connotations or that demonstrate a medium to high degree of intensity. Some selections won't have any.

Excerpt from *Those Who Can, Teach*

A large employer of teachers is the U.S. government. The Department of Defense operates 222 elementary and secondary schools in seven states, Puerto Rico, Guam, and twelve countries around the world. These schools enroll approximately 102,600 students and employ about 8,800 teachers. Salaries are comparable to those in the United States, but preference is given to applicants who have at least one year of successful full-time employment as a professional educator.

—Ryan & Cooper, *Those Who Can, Teach*, 12th edition

1. What is the purpose of this paragraph? _____

2. Circle the tone words that you think best describe the tone of the passage.

   objective　　or　　subjective

   factual　　or　　emotional

Excerpt from "I Can't Imagine Why Anyone Would Want to Stop Crying"

Emmett Henson, 2-month-old

Life has so many wonderful experiences to offer. Like sleep. Or ingestion and evacuation. But I find life offers few opportunities more rewarding than screaming like a maniac until your voice cracks with the strain, so that the entire universe can share in your distress. That's what life is all about, right? The sheer exhilarating thrill of nonstop crying at the top of your lungs. It's such an important part of why we are here—why would anybody ever want to do anything else?

Don't get me wrong—I like squirming, drooling, and sporadically attempting to focus on colors and shapes as much as the next guy. But of all the various activities one can choose to pursue in life, crying is tops as far as I'm concerned. In my opinion, I find nothing is more fulfilling than a good steady holler. It takes no experience to begin, and within moments, all one's needs are instantly met! It's my favorite part of the day.

—*The Onion*, April 9, 2008

3. What is the purpose of this paragraph? _____

4. Circle the tone words that you think best describe the tone of the passage.

    objective   or   subjective

    factual   or   emotional

Excerpt from a Letter to the Editor: "Will Restricting Salt Improve Health?"

It seems so obvious: the first and most important step in addressing health care in the United States is to do whatever we can to make Americans healthier so they need less care, thereby reducing the cost of the system and making more services available to all.

—Gerald J. Glasser, *New York Times*, January 16, 2010

---

5. What is the purpose of this paragraph? _____

6. Circle the tone words that you think best describe the tone of the passage.

    objective   or   subjective

    factual   or   emotional

How Rare Are Earthquakes in the Caribbean?

Earthquakes can occur anywhere there is a fault line. They are actually fairly common in the Caribbean, but they are typically much smaller—magnitude 4 or 5—and they usually occur along the eastern edge of the Caribbean plate, where it pushes against the North American plate. Last night's quake occurred along the southern edge of the plate; this particular fault has not experienced a significant earthquake since 1770.

—Jeneen Interlandi, "Thrust Faults, Slip Faults, and Aftershocks," *Newsweek* Web Exclusive, January 13, 2010

---

7. What is the purpose of this paragraph? _____

8. Circle the tone words that you think best describe the tone of the passage.

    objective   or   subjective

    factual   or   emotional

> ### Excerpt from "A Poor Prison Plan for California"
>
> Schwarzenegger has a terrific idea for a pilot program. But to suggest that such an untested and possibly dangerous experiment is the solution to our prison problems, or that it could quickly produce a dramatic drop in expenditures, is . . . irresponsible.
>
> —*Los Angeles Times,* January 17, 2010

9. What is the purpose of this paragraph? _____

10. Circle the tone words that you think best describe the tone of the passage.

   objective   or   subjective

   factual   or   emotional

Review: Tone and Purpose

Tone reflects an author's purpose.

- When the purpose is informative, the tone will be objective and factual.
- When the purpose is to entertain or express, the tone will be subjective and emotional.
- When the purpose is to persuade, the tone will be subjective and emotional.

Facts and objective information are included in all writing, so don't automatically think that writing is informative and objective because these are present.

Learn to Use More Specific Tone Words.

The words *subjective* and *objective* are very general. It is helpful to become familiar with a range of more specific words you can use to describe an author's tone, especially a subjective tone. If you want to be able to talk in class about an author's ideas, or write about them for a college assignment, you will probably need to use words like these to describe the author's tone. Here are some possibilities.

Objective Tone Words

These six words are, roughly speaking, synonyms.

balanced   fair   impartial   matter-of-fact   objective   unprejudiced

Subjective Tone Words

To give you a starting place for understanding these tone words, they are divided into broad categories with working definitions. However, the words within each category are *not* exact synonyms. When possible, words are arranged in a category by degrees of intensity, but this is not always possible.

Not happy: annoyed   angry   indignant   outraged   bitter
Not excited: apathetic   bored   cold
Not mean: thoughtful   respectful   loving   righteous
Not kind: disapproving   cynical   sarcastic   arrogant   cruel
Not sure: ambivalent   skeptical   inconclusive   wavering
Not secure: alarmed   fearful   pessimistic   appalled
Not doubtful: confident   hopeful   optimistic
Not serious: irreverent   amused   wry   humorous   flippant
               mocking   hyperbolic
Not calm: excited   celebratory   urgent   elated   sensational
Not direct: reticent   ironic   evasive
Not indirect: sincere   direct   outspoken   demanding
Not satisfied: frustrated   ambitious   nostalgic

INTERACTION 2–28	Finding the Meanings of Tone Words

With your classmates, form six groups. Each group takes one of these categories from the Subjective Tone Words list:

    not happy   not kind   not serious
    not calm   not secure   not indirect

1. **In your group,** discuss the meanings of any words in the category that you already know. Check to make sure your definitions are accurate by using a dictionary app, online dictionary, or print dictionary. Everyone in the group should write down each word and its definition. Write the definitions to make it easy to understand the differences between the meanings of the words.

- _____
- _____
- _____
- _____
- _____
- _____

2. **In your group,** each person selects one unfamiliar word from the category, looks it up in a dictionary, and shares the definition with the group. (If you have more people than words, double or triple up on a word.) Everyone in the group should write down each word and its definition. Write the definitions to make it easy to understand the differences between the meanings of the words.

- _____
- _____
- _____
- _____
- _____
- _____

3. **In your group,** talk about a situation in which you would feel each tone. Picture and hear a scene in which you would feel the emotion of the tone word you are working on. For each word, select a person or two to describe the situation or act out the scene for the class.

4. **With the whole class,** one group at a time, write your words and definitions on the board so that everyone can see them. Then each person describes the situation or acts out the scene for the class. Classmates from other groups guess which tone word fits your situation. Correct their guesses as needed by explaining the differences between the tone words.

5. **On your own,** take one of the categories not covered in class. Follow the same process on your own that you did in your group. This time, write out the scene in which you would feel the emotion that each tone word describes, and explain why you would feel that emotion.

INTERACTION 2–29	Using Specific Tone Words

Circle the best tone word for each item. Use a dictionary as needed.

1. I'm the best lawyer in this room and there is nothing you can say that will make me believe otherwise.

      reticent   arrogant   respectful

2. I may have been in the house when the robbery occurred; I can't remember.

      righteous   loving   evasive

3. You can't be serious! When you lied in court, you committed a crime yourself.

      appalled   cynical   direct

4. It doesn't matter what I say, no one is going to believe an old, broken-down wreck of a human being like me anyway.

      thoughtful   bitter   ambitious

5. You have to tell the judge right away! Maybe she will let you go with a warning.

      urgent   outraged   elated

6. They can send me to jail or let me go—whatever.

      angry   apathetic   celebratory

7. So you don't think you'd like to tell the judge what happened so you can go home tonight instead of going to jail?

      skeptical   outspoken   cruel

8. I suppose it would be best to admit I lied. Even if I have to go to jail for a few days, at least when I come back out I'll still have my self-respect.

      alarmed   amused   balanced

9. How I wish for the days before I made that terrible decision.

      sincere   matter-of-fact   nostalgic

10. Well, I can make different kinds of decisions in the future that will work out better.

      sensational   pessimistic   optimistic

The 5 keys to understanding tone are

Review: Five Points to Notice That Reveal an Author's Tone

Finding an author's tone requires paying close attention to the following aspects of the reading selection:

pay attention

- The denotative meanings of words (the dictionary definition).
- The connotative meanings of words (the emotional associations).

Determining
- Whether the author gives his or her opinions.
- What degree of intensity adjectives convey.

Deciding
- What purpose the author has for writing.

Whether the author's general tone is objective or subjective, you will be in a better position to understand the reading selection when you can identify the tone the author wants to convey.

ACTIVATE YOUR SKILLS 1
Examining the Author's Tone

Read the selections and then answer the questions that follow.

> Our soft, luxurious sheets and comforters will help you create a perfect nest for relaxing in your bedroom.

1. What is the purpose of this statement? Circle the letter of the answer.
   a. to inform readers about a new kind of bedclothes
   b. to persuade readers to purchase these bedclothes
   c. to entertain readers with a funny description of bedclothes

2. What word has connotations in this context? _____

3. What are the word's connotations? _____

4. What two words are high-intensity adjectives?

   - _____

   - _____

5. Which words best describe the tone?

> objective and factual   subjective and emotional

I believe the $7.25 per hour minimum wage should be raised to a more livable $10.25. Why? People who earn the minimum wage usually have to spend far more than 30 percent of their income on housing. (The government defines 30 percent as the highest percentage people should pay for housing and still be financially healthy.) Also, minimum-wage earners with preschool children often can't get the child care subsidies they need in order to pay for child care. What are they supposed to do with their children while they are working? Finally, think about your last trip to the supermarket. Imagine trying to feed a family of four on $7.25 an hour. Could <u>you</u> do it?

---

6. What is the purpose of this selection? Circle the letter of the answer.

   a. to persuade readers to support raising the minimum wage

   b. to entertain readers who earn far more than the minimum wage

   c. to inform readers of the benefits and disadvantages of the minimum wage

7. What two sets of words in the first sentence show that the author is giving an opinion about the minimum wage?

   • _____

   • _____

8. Which word best describes the tone?

> objective   subjective

9. Which of the following words describes the tone more specifically?

> indignant   irreverent   bored

10. Which of the following tone words describes the last question in the reading selection?

> ironic   demanding   wry

A few years back we ran a study for a wireless phone provider that was developing a prototype retail store. And we found that men and women used the place in very different ways. Women would invariably walk right up to the sales desk and ask staffers questions about the phones and the various deals being offered. Men, however, went directly to the phone displays and the signs that explained the agreements. They then took brochures and application forms and left the store—all without ever speaking to an employee. When these men returned to the store, it was to sign up. The women, though, on average required a third visit to the store, and more consultation, before they were ready to close.

—Underhill, *Why We Buy*

11. What is the purpose of this selection? Circle the letter of the answer.
    a. to entertain readers with a story about men and women shopping
    b. to inform readers about the differences in how men and women shop
    c. to persuade readers that men and women shop differently

12. How many words with connotations do you find in this selection? _____

13. How many words do you find that show the author is giving his opinion? _____

14. Which word best describes the tone?
        objective   subjective

15. Which word best describes the tone?
        factual   emotional

In my slow, painstaking, ragged handwriting, I copied into my tablet everything printed on that first page, down to the punctuation marks.

—Malcolm X, *Autobiography of Malcolm X*

16. What is the purpose of this statement? Circle the letter of the best answer.
    a. to inform readers about how to copy a page of a book
    b. to persuade readers that they, too, should copy a page of a book
    c. to entertain readers with a story that will help them understand the writer

17. What three adjectives does the author use to describe his handwriting?

    - _____

    - _____

    - _____

18. For each set of words, number them according to their degree of intensity.

"not fast"   _3_ glacial   _1_ slow   _2_ sluggish

"not careless"   _1_ careful   _2_ scrupulous   _3_ painstaking

"not smooth"   _2_ broken   _3_ ragged   _1_ uneven

19. What do the two high-intensity adjectives imply about the author's activities?
    a. he writes almost constantly
    b. he writes rarely, if ever
    c. nothing

20. Which words best describe the tone?
    dogged   ambivalent   elated

ACTIVATE YOUR SKILLS 2
Examining the Author's Tone

Decide whether each selection has an objective or a subjective tone. Then tell why you chose that tone.

1.
> I'm a volunteer firefighter and proud of it.

   objective   subjective

Why? _____

_____

2.
> Hispaniola is a wonder. The mountains and hills, the plains and the meadow lands are both fertile and beautiful. They are most suitable for planting crops and for raising cattle of all kinds, and there are good sites for building towns and villages. The harbors are incredibly fine and there are many great rivers with broad channels and the majority contain gold. . . .
> —Christopher Columbus

   objective   subjective

Why? _____

_____

3.   Ever wonder why green-tea drinkers never seem to get the "hypers" that coffee drinkers get, even when the green tea is fully caffeinated? The answer in all likelihood is a nonprotein amino acid found in tea called *theanine*.

—Bowden, *Most Effective Natural Cures on Earth*

objective   subjective

Why? _____

_____

4.   My mother, Alice, had a special talent. Anything that my father could kill with a rifle, my mother could transform into something delicious.

—Beckwith, *The Invisible Touch*

objective   subjective

Why? _____

_____

5.   Before the team physician or certified athletic trainer clears an athlete to return to his or her sport, several criteria must be met: full strength, freedom from pain, ability to perform the skills of the sport, and emotional readiness to return to competition.

—France, *Introduction to Sports Training and Athletic Medicine*

objective   subjective

Why? _____

_____

Select the best tone word for each item. Then tell why you chose it.

bored   cheerful   fearful   pessimistic   thoughtful

6.   She cowered under the bridge, praying that no one would notice her. _____

Why? _____

_____

7. The sun flooded in the window, rushing to paint the room with a bright glow.

_____

Why? _____

_____

8. He wandered around the kitchen, picking up utensils and then putting them back down on the counter. _____

Why? _____

_____

9. "I'm never going to finish this project," the woman said glumly to herself. _____

_____

Why? _____

_____

10. When Dad gets home from work, he's going to be tired and hungry. I'll make some dinner. _____

Why? _____

_____

MASTER YOUR SKILLS 1
Examining the Author's Tone

Read each paragraph of the following excerpt from *The School Days of an Indian Girl*. Then answer the questions that follow, using a dictionary when necessary.

The Cutting of My Long Hair

Zitkala-Sa

1   The first day in the land of apples was a bitter-cold one; for the snow still covered the ground, and the trees were bare. A large bell rang for breakfast, its loud metallic voice crashing through the belfry overhead and into our sensitive ears. The annoying clatter of shoes on bare floors gave us no peace. The constant clash of harsh noises, with an undercurrent of many voices murmuring an unknown tongue, made a bedlam within which I was securely tied. And though my spirit tore itself in struggling for its lost freedom, all was useless.

1. Which sense do most of the words with connotations relate to?

    sight (sound) taste feeling smell

2–5. For each high-intensity adjective that was used, write a low-intensity word that has the same basic meaning.

    - crashing _broking_
    - clatter _talking_
    - clash _loud_
    - harsh _mean_

6. What does *bedlam* mean? Look in a dictionary if needed. _confution_

7. Which of the following words best describes the author's tone?

    (overwhelmed) excited annoyed

---

2   A paleface woman, with white hair, came up after us. We were placed in a line of girls who were marching into the dining room. These were Indian girls, in stiff shoes and closely cling-ing dresses. The small girls wore sleeved aprons and shingled hair. As I walked noiselessly in my soft moccasins, I felt like sinking to the floor, for my blanket had been stripped from my shoulders. I looked hard at the Indian girls, who seemed not to care that they were even more immodestly dressed than I, in their tightly fitting clothes. While we marched in, the boys entered at an opposite door. I watched for the three young braves who came in our party. I spied them in the rear ranks, looking as uncomfortable as I felt.

8–11. What words does the author use to describe the clothing the other Indian girls are wearing?

    - _Closely clingindd dress_
    - _Stiff shoes_
    - _Sleeved aprons_
    - _tightly fitting clote_

12–13. What words does she use to describe the clothes she is wearing now and was wearing earlier?

    - _____
    - _blacket_

14. Which of the following words best describes the author's tone?

    appalled   sarcastic   uncomfortable

3   A small bell was tapped, and each of the pupils drew a chair from under the table. Supposing this act meant they were to be seated, I pulled out mine and at once slipped into it from one side. But when I turned my head, I saw that I was the only one seated, and all the rest at our table remained standing. Just as I began to rise, looking shyly around to see how chairs were to be used, a second bell was sounded. All were seated at last, and I had to crawl back into my chair again. I heard a man's voice at one end of the hall, and I looked around to see him. But all the others hung their heads over their plates. As I glanced at the long chain of tables, I caught the eyes of a paleface woman upon me. Immediately I dropped my eyes, wondering why I was so keenly watched by the strange woman. The man ceased his mutterings, and then a third bell was tapped. Every one picked up his knife and fork and began eating. I began crying instead, for by this time I was afraid to venture anything more.

15. What inference can you make (that is, what can you assume) about what the author is describing in the sentences that begin *I heard a man's voice* and end with *The man ceased his mutterings*? praying

_____

4   But this eating by formula was not the hardest trial in that first day. Late in the morning, my friend Judewin gave me a terrible warning. Judewin knew a few words of English, and she had overheard the paleface woman talk about cutting our long, heavy hair. Our mothers had taught us that only unskilled warriors who were captured had their hair shingled by the enemy. Among our people, short hair was worn by mourners, and shingled hair by cowards!

5   We discussed our fate some moments, and when Judewin said, "We have to submit, because they are strong," I rebelled.

6   "No, I will not submit! I will struggle first!" I answered.

16. What tone word best describes these paragraphs?

    hyperbolic   passionate   flippant

7   I watched my chance, and when no one noticed I disappeared. I crept up the stairs as quietly as I could in my squeaking shoes—my moccasins had been exchanged for shoes. Along the hall I passed, without knowing whither I was going. Turning aside to an open door, I found a large room with three white beds in it. The windows were covered with dark green curtains, which made the room very dim. Thankful that no one was there, I directed my steps toward the corner farthest from the door. On my hands and knees I crawled under the bed, and cuddled myself in the dark corner.

8   From my hiding place I peered out, shuddering with fear whenever I heard footsteps near by. Though in the hall loud voices were calling my name, and I knew that even Judewin was searching for me, I did not open my mouth to answer. Then the steps were quickened and the voices became excited. The sounds came nearer and nearer. Women and girls entered the room. I held my breath, and watched them open closet doors and peep behind large trunks. Some one threw up the curtains, and the room was filled with sudden light. What caused them to stoop and look under the bed I do not know. I remember being dragged out, though I resisted by kicking and scratching wildly. In spite of myself, I was carried downstairs and tied fast in a chair.

17. What emotions do you feel as you read this account? _____ frighten _____

9   I cried aloud, shaking my head all the while until I felt the cold blades of the scissors against my neck, and heard them gnaw off one of my thick braids. Then I lost my spirit. Since the day I was taken from my mother I had suffered extreme indignities. People had stared at me. I had been tossed about in the air like a wooden puppet. And now my long hair was shingled like a coward's! In my anguish I moaned for my mother, but no one came to comfort me. Not a soul reasoned quietly with me, as my own mother used to do; for now I was only one of many little animals driven by a herder.

18. The author says about the scissors that she "heard them gnaw off one of my thick braids." What associations come to mind as you think about the word *gnaw*? Who or what gnaws? _Animal_____

_____

19. The author says she was "tossed about in the air like a wooden puppet." What associations come to mind as you think about the word *puppet*? _toy with_
_string_____

20. When you think about the selection as a whole, what tone word seems best to describe it? _afraid insence_____

MASTER YOUR SKILLS 2
Examining the Author's Tone

Read each selection and then answer the questions.

Excerpt from *The Glass Castle*

Jeanette Wells

1   I was sitting in a taxi, wondering if I had overdressed for the evening, when I looked out the window and saw Mom rooting through a Dumpster. It was just after dark. A blustery March wind whipped the steam coming out of the manholes, and people hurried along the sidewalks with their collars turned up. I was stuck in traffic two blocks from the party where I was heading.

2   Mom stood fifteen feet away. She had tied rags around her shoulders to keep out the spring chill and was picking through the trash while her dog, a black-and-white terrier mix, played at her feet. Mom's gestures were all familiar—the way she tilted her head and thrust out her lower lip when studying items of potential value that she'd hoisted out of the Dumpster, the way her eyes widened with childish glee when she found something she liked. Her long hair was streaked with gray, tangled and matted, and her eyes had sunk deep into their sockets, but still she reminded me of the mom she'd been when I was a kid, swan-diving off cliffs and painting in the desert and reading Shakespeare aloud. Her cheekbones were still high and strong, but the skin was parched and ruddy from all those winters and summers exposed to the elements. To the people walking by, she probably looked like any of the thousands of homeless people in New York City.

3   It had been months since I'd laid eyes on Mom, and when she looked up I was overcome with panic that she'd see me and call out my name, and that someone on the way to the same party would spot us together and Mom would introduce herself and my secret would be out.

___ 1. This selection is from a memoir, which is an account of an author's personal experiences. What do you suppose is the author's main purpose?

    a. to persuade

    b. to inform

    c. to entertain or express

___ 2. Is the author's tone objective or subjective?

    a. objective

    b. subjective

___ 3. Reread the first sentence. This is the very first sentence of the memoir. What emotion is the author trying to get readers to feel?

    a. impatience

    b. anger

    c. surprise

    d. nostalgia

___ 4. In the last paragraph, the author says she was "overcome with panic." This phrase is:

    a. a "plain" word suggesting no special intensity

    b. a word with a medium level of intensity

    c. a high-intensity word

___ 5. What tone word best describes the author's feelings?

    a. ashamed

    b. assertive

    c. urgent

    d. arrogant

Excerpt from *Traffic*

Tom Vanderbilt

One routinely hears of "traffic problems." But what is a traffic problem? To a traffic engineer, a "traffic problem" might mean that a street is running below capacity. For a parent living on that street, a "traffic problem" could be too many cars, or cars going too fast. For the store owner on that same street, a "traffic problem" might mean there is not enough traffic. Blaise Pascal, the renowned seventeenth-century French scientist and philosopher, had perhaps the only foolproof remedy for traffic: Stay home. "I have discovered that all the unhappiness of men arises from one single fact," he wrote. "That they cannot stay quietly in their own chamber." Pascal, as it happens, is credited with inventing history's first urban bus service. He died a mere five months later. Was Parisian traffic his undoing?

___ 6. How many different possible definitions of "traffic problem" does the author list?

a. one

b. two

c. three

d. four

___ 7. How many different people's viewpoints are considered in those definitions?

a. three

b. four

c. one

d. two

___ 8. Does the author reveal his own personal feelings about "traffic problems"?

a. yes

b. no

___ 9. What is the general tone of this selection?

a. subjective and emotional

b. objective and factual

___ 10. Which of the following more specific tone words best describes this selection?

a. balanced

b. overwrought

c. sarcastic

d. joyous

Excerpt from *Open*

Andre Agassi

Please let this be over.

I'm not ready for it to be over.

___ 11. What is the general tone?

    a. objective and factual

    b. subjective and emotional

___ 12. Which more specific tone word describes this selection?

    a. flippant

    b. authoritative

    c. disapproving

    d. ambivalent

Excerpt from *A Walk in the Woods*

Bill Bryson

1   When, after much solemn consideration, I settled on a backpack—a very expensive Gregory, top-of-the-range, no-point-in-stinting here sort of thing—he said, "Now what kind of straps do you want with that?"

2   "I beg your pardon?" I said, and recognized at once that I was on the brink of a dangerous condition known as retail burnout. No more now would I blithely say, "Better give me half a dozen of those, Dave. Oh, and I'll take eight of these—what the heck, make it a dozen. You only live once, eh?" The mound of provisions that a minute ago had looked so pleasingly abundant and exciting—all new! all mine!—suddenly seemed burdensome and extravagant.

3   "Straps," Dave explained. "You know, to tie on your sleeping bag and lash things down."

4   "It doesn't come with straps?" I said in a new, level tone.

5   "Oh, no." He surveyed a wall of products and touched a finger to his nose. "You'll need a raincover, too, of course."

6   I blinked. "A raincover? Why?"

7   "To keep out the rain."

8   "The backpack's not rainproof?"

9   He grimaced as if making an exceptionally delicate distinction. "Well, not a hundred percent. . . ."

10 This was extraordinary to me. "Really? Did it not occur to the manufacturer that people might want to take their backpacks outdoors from time to time? Perhaps even go camping with them. How much is this backpack, anyway?"

11 "Two hundred and fifty dollars."

12 "Two hundred and fifty dollars! Are you shi—,?" I paused and put on a new voice. "Are you saying, Dave, that I pay $250 for a backpack and it doesn't have straps and it isn't waterproof?"

13 He nodded.

14 "Does it have a bottom in it?"

___ 13. What emotion does the author seem to be feeling in paragraph 4?

    a. aggravation, although he is trying to contain it

    b. friendliness, although he is trying to hide it

    c. sadness

    d. amusement

___ 14. What attitude does the author display in paragraph 8?

    a. happiness

    b. fear

    c. anxiety

    d. disbelief

___ 15. What kind of attitude does the author display in paragraph 10?

    a. sincere

    b. optimistic

    c. sarcastic

    d. matter-of-fact

___ 16. What kind of attitude does Dave display throughout?

    a. matter-of-fact

    b. sympathetic

    c. pessimistic

    d. angry

___ 17. What kind of emotion does the author display in paragraph 12?

    a. thoughtful

    b. indignant

      c. cruel

      d. mocking

___ 18. What attitude does the author display in paragraph 14?

      a. surprise

      b. amazement

      c. delight

      d. sarcasm

Excerpt from *Game Change*

John Heilemann and Mark Halperin

Barack Obama jerked bolt upright in bed at three o'clock in the morning. Darkness enveloped his low-rent room at the Des Moines Hampton Inn; the airport across the street was quiet in the hours before dawn. It was very late December 2007, a few days ahead of the Iowa caucuses. Obama had been sprinting flat out for president for nearly a year. Through all the nights he'd endured in cookie-cutter hotels during the months of uncertainty and angst—months of lagging by a mile in the national polls, his improbable bid for the White House written off by the Washington smart set, his self-confidence shaken by his uneven performance and the formidability of his archrival, Hillary Clinton—Obama always slept soundly, like the dead. But now he found himself awake, heart pounding, consumed by a thought at once electric and daunting—*I might win this thing.*

___ 19. What tone do the authors set up in the first sentence?

      a. everything is in order

      b. something unusual has happened

      c. nothing at all is happening

      d. something joyful has occurred

___ 20. What do the authors suggest about Obama's emotions in the last sentence?

      a. He feels as if he is having a heart attack.

      b. He feels as if he will die if he doesn't win in Iowa.

      c. He feels excited and scared about his possible victory.

      d. He feels fearful and even paranoid about becoming president.

Summary Activity: Vocabulary Development

Part 2 has discussed how to develop your vocabulary before, during, and after reading by understanding word parts, noticing context clues, and using the dictionary. It has also introduced some of the qualities of a reading you can consider as you figure out the author's tone. Fill in the Reading Guide by completing each idea on the left with information from Part 2 on the right. You can return to this guide throughout the course as a reminder of how to develop your vocabulary.

Reading Guide to Developing Your Vocabulary

Complete this idea	with information from Part 2.
Three kinds of words parts that you can use to figure out the meaning of a word are	1. _____ 2. _____ 3. _____
The main meaning of the word is carried by this word part:	4. _____
The word part that changes the meaning of the root is the	5. _____
The word part that changes the part of speech of a root is the	6. _____
Once you know the meaning of each part of a word, you may have to use _____ to understand what overall meaning they add up to.	7. _____
When you encounter a word that seems to be composed of word parts, you can use this book's ____ to find the meaning of each one.	8. _____
If you don't understand the meaning of a word based on its word parts, follow these two steps:	9. _____ 10. _____
Four kinds of context clues are	11. _____ 12. _____ 13. _____ 14. _____
The signal words *that is* and *in other words* may suggest this kind of context clue:	15. _____

Complete this idea	with information from Part 2.
The signal words *however* and *in contrast* may suggest this kind of context clue:	16. _____
The signal words *to illustrate* and *for example* suggest this kind of context clue:	17. _____
You need to take a word's context into account even if you have found its definition in the dictionary because	18. _____ _____ _____ _____
When you look up a word's meaning in a dictionary, you will find its _____ meaning.	19. _____
A word's connotations are its	20. _____
When you are trying to figure out the tone of a reading selection, look at these five factors:	21. _____ 22. _____ 23. _____ 24. _____ 25. _____
Think about what your vocabulary strategies were before you read Part 2. How did they differ from the suggestions here? Write your thoughts. _____ _____ _____	

Application: Vocabulary Development

ONLINE NEWSPAPER

● Pre-Reading the Selection

"Mistakes, I've Made a Few" appeared in *The Sporting News* on August 16, 2004. Kyle Busch, then a new race car driver, had had a few problems on the track. More recently, in the 2009 racing season, Busch earned $4.8 million in winnings.

Surveying the Reading

Survey the title of the selection and the first sentence of each paragraph. What is the general topic of the reading selection? _____

_____

Guessing the Purpose

Judging from the title, what do you suppose is the purpose of this article? _____

Predicting the Content

Based on your survey, what are three things you expect the reading selection to discuss?

- _____
- _____
- _____

Activating Your Knowledge

Think back to anything you've heard or read about NASCAR racing or Kyle Busch. Jot down at least three pieces of information, even if they seem vague.

- _____
- _____
- _____

Common Knowledge

Read these terms and their definitions to help you understand the reading selection.

Kentucky Speedway *(paragraph 4)* A 1.5-mile racetrack in Sparta, Kentucky.

Busch Series race *(paragraph 4)* NASCAR's racing series for drivers wanting to get into the Sprint Cup series. In December 2006, the series name was changed to NASCAR Nationwide Series when the Anheuser-Busch company stopped sponsoring the series and Nationwide Insurance took it over.

Points race *(paragraph 6)* Points earned throughout a racing season that determine the season winner.

● Reading with Pen in Hand

Now read the selection. Pay attention to and mark any ideas that seem important, and respond to the questions and vocabulary items in the margin.

Access the Reading CourseMate via www.cengagebrain.com/shop/ ISBN/1413033156 to hear vocabulary words from this selection and view a video about this topic.

Mistakes, I've Made a Few

Kyle Busch

1   At the beginning of the season, I told myself that as a **rookie** driver, I was going to make some mistakes. I sure haven't fallen short on that prediction.

2   I'm just lucky to have a **veteran** team behind me that catches me when I stumble and helps me get back on my feet. That has happened a couple of times lately, and I don't know where I'd be if I didn't have my crew to keep me straight.

3   Some of you might have read about what happened to us at Dover, where I hit another car when I was leaving my pit stall and damaged the fender on my car. I came back into the pits, and the team fixed me up. We had some other problems that ended up knocking us back as far as 32nd position, but thanks to my team never giving up, we came back and finished fifth.

Reading Journal

rookie Use your logic based on the rest of the sentence. Is a *rookie* driver new or experienced?

● Listen to the words Busch says to himself.

veteran The word *rookie* in the previous paragraph is an antonym to *veteran*. What does *veteran* mean?

● Make a mental movie of the ideas here and in the next two paragraphs.

Rusty Jarrett/Getty Images for NASCAR/Getty Images

highlights *Highlights* is contrasted with *biggest mistake*. What might be the definition of *highlights*?

4   My biggest mistake so far this season ended up being one of the **highlights** of my year, believe it or not. We were real fast at Kentucky Speedway in practice and ended up qualifying second for the Busch Series race there in June. The car was awesome. During final practice, I had just finished making a bunch of laps and was taking the car to the garage. I cut the motor off and started to duck down on to the apron of the track to get out of the way of some cars behind me.

● Search for a connection to your own life.

5   I was still going too fast when my tires got down on the apron, and I ended up spinning the car and hitting the wall. The car was pretty much finished, and we had to go to a backup car and start from the rear of the field. I was ticked off at myself for wrecking the car because it was completely unnecessary. All I had to do was slow down more, and everything would have been fine. It was a rookie mistake, for sure. Fortunately, everything turned out OK when we ended up taking the backup car to victory lane on Saturday night.

● Make a mental movie of these events.

missteps Use your knowledge of word parts. What is a synonym for *missteps*?
jelled Think about jelly. Using your logic, think about this context. What might *jelled* mean?

6   I wasn't so lucky at a race in Milwaukee. I used up the tires during a spin in qualifying, and I had to start the race on the old tires. I ended up going two laps down and finishing 16th. I know it could've been worse, but we lost ground in the points race.

● How can this information help you in your life?

7   While I've definitely had some **missteps**, I'm still very happy with how we've performed this season. The fact that we're in the points chase at all says a lot about how well the team has **jelled** and about how well my crew chief, Lance McGrew, and I are communicating.

We've had some tough breaks, but we've also had a lot of things go our way. We've just got to keep our eye on the prize and stay focused on the big picture, which is staying within reach of the points lead.

8   This sport is definitely a roller-coaster ride, but there's one thing I can say—the ride is never dull.

● Make a mental movie of these ideas.

● Vocabulary in New Contexts

Review the vocabulary words in the margins of the reading selection and then complete the following activities.

EASY Note Cards

Make a note card for each vocabulary word from the reading. On one side, write the word. On the other side, divide the card into four areas and label them E, A, S, and Y. Add a word or phrase in each area so that you wind up with an example sentence, an antonym, a synonym, and, finally, a definition that shows you understand the meaning of the word with your logic. Remember that a synonym or an antonym may have appeared in the reading.

Relationships Between Words

Circle the best answer. Then explain your answer.

1. Does a **rookie** or a **veteran** have more career **highlights**?   A rookie   A veteran

   Explain. _____

   _____

2. Might a **veteran** feel like a **rookie** because of **missteps**?

   Yes   No

   Why or why not? _____

   _____

3. Is it generally true that a **rookie's** habits will **jell** over time?

   Yes   No

   Why or why not? _____

   _____

Language in Your Life

Write short answers to each question. Look at vocabulary words closely before you answer.

1. What is one **misstep** you have made in the last year? _____

   _____

2. What is one **highlight** from your previous schooling? _____

   _____

3. When did your plans for college **jell**? _____

   _____

4. In what part of your life are you a **rookie**? _____

   _____

5. In what part of your life are you a **veteran**? _____

   _____

Language in Use

Select the best word to complete the meaning of each sentence.

highlights	jelled	missteps	rookie	veteran

1. Eighty-two-year-old John Gagliardi is a _____ coach of St. John's University football team.

2. At age 16, Gagliardi was a _____ when he became the coach at his high school, Holy Trinity, when the adult coach was drafted into the military to fight in World War II.

3. His ideas about how to coach _____ rapidly as he stopped asking players to do the things he had always hated to do as a player, including running sprints and doing exercises.

4. He had no real way of knowing whether this style of coaching would prove to be a _____.

5. But now he knows. Among Gagliardi's career _____ are a national NAIA championship in 1963, another in 1965, and two NCAA Division III titles in 1973 and 2003. After 600 games that he has coached, his record is 439–119–10.

Spotlight on Word Parts: *Mis-*

As you have learned, *missteps* are wrong steps. The word *missteps* is composed of three parts:

mis- means "wrong" or "bad" + step + -s means "more than one"

The word part **mis-** is used in other words.

misconduct = bad behavior

misfortune = bad luck

misspeak = speak wrongly

mislead = lead in the wrong direction

misunderstanding = failure to understand correctly

Circle the correct word in each of these sentences.

1. It was her (misfortune / misstep / misunderstanding) to find the pirates' gold before they did.

2. A (misunderstanding / misleading / misconduct) clue caused them to search on the other side of the island—away from the treasure.

3. The pirate (misbehaved / misspoke / misunderstood), and the sailor thought she was going to die.

4. The sailor was found to be guilty of (misspeaking / misconduct / misleading), and she was thrown in the ship's jail.

5. Their (misfortune / misleading / misunderstanding) led to a bigger fight later that night.

Spotlight on Inference: The Author's Tone

1. Reread the first paragraph of the reading selection on page 207. Which word expresses Busch's tone best?

   aggressive   modest   bitter

   Why do you say so? _____

2. What tone word best describes the following two sentences from the selection? *"I'm just lucky to have a veteran team behind me that catches me when I stumble and helps me get back on my feet."*
   "Thanks to my team never giving up, we came back and finished fifth."

   grateful   annoyed   cynical

Test 2: Reading Comprehension

Your instructor may ask you to take practice tests throughout the semester to help you decide which topics you need to study the most. All the tests in this book include questions about all the major reading comprehension skills after the reading selection.

● Pre-Reading the Selection

The following article comes from *Success* magazine, whose mission is to "reveal [successful people's] key ideas and strategies to help you excel in every area of your personal and professional life."

Surveying the Reading

Survey the title of the selection and the first sentence of each paragraph. What is the general topic of the reading selection? _____

_____

Guessing the Purpose

Judging from the type of publication this article appears in and its title, what do you suppose is the purpose of this article? _____

Predicting the Content

Predict three things this selection will discuss.

- _____
- _____
- _____

Activating Your Knowledge

Think back to anything you've heard or read about how to win, how to set goals, women's basketball, or Pat Summitt. Jot down at least three pieces of information, even if they seem vague.

- _____
- _____
- _____

Common Knowledge

Read this term and its definition to help you understand the reading selection.

NCAA *(paragraph 4)* National Collegiate Athletic Association, a voluntary organization through which colleges and universities govern their athletic programs.

● Reading with Pen in Hand

Now read the selection. As you read, pay attention to and mark any ideas that seem important, and respond to the questions and vocabulary items in the margin.

Access the Reading CourseMate via **www.cengagebrain.com/shop/ ISBN/1413033156** to hear vocabulary words from this selection and view a video about this topic.

Winning Every Day: Pat Summitt's Strategy Centers on Goal-Setting

Don Yaeger

Reading Journal

1   Eight times Pat Summitt's University of Tennessee women's basketball team has ended the season by lifting high the national championship trophy. Not once was that her team's goal.

● What surprises you about this information?

2   Before each of the 34 seasons that Summitt has been a head coach of some of the most accomplished teams of all time, she and her captains have committed a set of goals to writing.

● Pick out three pieces of information you didn't already know.

3   "We always make sure," Summitt says, "that our plans for the season can be achieved. Setting goals is incredibly important to success. But if you set a goal that seems impossible to achieve—if you go into a year saying your goal is to win the national championship—then you risk losing morale, self-discipline and chemistry if you **falter** early.

● Listen to what Summitt is saying as if she were talking to you.

falter Use your logic. Put a blank line in this sentence where *falter* is. Then reread the whole sentence. What other words would fit there instead of *falter*?

4   "Set a goal that stretches you, requires exceptional effort, but one that you can reach," says Summitt, the bearer of more championship jewelry than any coach in women's basketball history. "We might set a goal that we win 20 or so games, that we win a conference championship, that we make the NCAA tournament. If we do those things, the truth is we have a chance of winning the national championship. But I would never want that to be the only goal."

● Search for a connection to your own goals.

5   The numbers suggest Summitt's strategy is solid. Seven times she has been named the national coach of the year. Her 983 wins are

● What are you learning here that's new?

the most ever for a coach—more victories than Adolph Rupp, Dean Smith and Bob Knight, three **titans** of basketball. Summitt knows how to win—every day, and in every way.

6   The key to her on- and off-court success, Summitt is famous for saying, is remembering that "winners aren't born, they are self-made."

7   "And the only way to ensure you become a winner is to set goals every day, and hold yourself and your teammates accountable for reaching those goals," she says. "Setting up a system that rewards you for meeting your goals and has **penalties** for failing to hit your target is just as important as putting your goals down on paper."

8   As an example, Summitt says that if her team were to set a daily goal—reducing turnovers during scrimmages is an often-set objective—that she would let her players know that reaching the objective would result in a more relaxed shooting drill to end their practice. But failing to meet the goal meant the entire team had to run sprints.

9   "They get to choose," Summitt says about her players, "whether they run or whether they shoot. It makes the goal so much easier to keep in sight. Reward or consequence. Their choice."

titans Three examples of *titans* are named. Use your logic to figure out what *titans* are.

● Do you know anyone who is a "self-made" success?

● How can this information help you in your life?

penalties An antonym comes earlier in the sentence (but it is stated as an action, not a thing). Also, the next paragraph includes an example of a *penalty*—running sprints. What are *penalties*?

● Make a mental movie of these ideas.

● Search for a connection to your own life.

● Put each of these ideas in your own words.

unattainable A synonym in the next sentence is *pie-in-the-sky*. Is an *unattainable* goal one that can be reached or one that cannot be reached?

empowerment Use your logic. When you set your own goals and then try to achieve them, do you gain power or lose power? *Empowerment* means the act of what?

Pat Summitt on Goal-Setting

■ Set realistic goals that make your team stretch. If the goal is too big and **unattainable**, morale can suffer. Hitting the smaller goals will get you closer to that pie-in-the-sky goal anyway.

■ Small goals you set and achieve every day work best. Be personally accountable for those and help your teammates do the same.

■ Instill the idea of rewards for reaching goals, and consequences if you don't.

■ Be sure to involve everyone in goal-setting. This provides a sense of **empowerment**—and accountability.

■ Realize that others help you achieve your goal; no matter who makes the coaching decisions, nothing will get done without a strong team.

■ Commit your goals to writing.

More strategies for champions@success.com/Wooden

• Comprehension Questions

Write the letter of the answer on the line. Then explain your thinking.

Main Idea

Think of the main idea as the "point" of the paragraph or passage. To find the main idea, notice which sentence explains the author's most important point about the subject. The other sentences in the paragraph should offer explanations, examples, and details about the main idea. The details are more specific than the main idea.

___ 1. Which of the following best states the main idea of paragraph 4?

    a. "Set a goal that stretches you, requires exceptional effort, but one that you can reach," says Summitt.

    b. "We might set a goal that we win 20 or so games, that we win a conference championship, that we make the NCAA tournament.

    c. "If we do those things, the truth is we have a chance of winning the national championship.

    d. "But I would never want that to be the only goal."

WHY? What information in the selection leads you to give that answer? _____

_____

_____

_____

___ 2. Which of the following statements is the best main idea of the list at the end of the passage?

    a. To be successful, set big goals that you can achieve in one to two years.

    b. Write down your goals.

    c. Goal setting is important.

    d. Pat Summitt has a strategy for setting goals that will help you succeed.

WHY? What information in the selection leads you to give that answer? _____

_____

_____

_____

_____

Supporting Details

Think of the supporting details as the "proof" for the main idea. To locate the supporting details, find the main idea and then look for the information the author uses to explain it in more detail. Sometimes, if a main idea covers more than one paragraph, you will find the supporting details in several paragraphs.

___ 3. Which detail supports the following main idea? *The numbers suggest Summitt's strategy is solid.*

    a. Not once was that her team's goal.

    b. "We might set a goal that we win 20 or so games."

    c. Her 983 wins are the most ever for a coach.

    d. For thirty-four seasons, Summitt has been a head coach.

WHY? What information in the selection leads you to give that answer? _____

_____

_____

_____

___ 4. Based on the details given in the reading selection, what percentage of the seasons that Summitt has coached has she won the national coach of the year award?

    a. About 10 percent.

    b. About 15 percent.

    c. About 20 percent.

    d. About 25 percent.

WHY? What information in the selection leads you to give that answer? _____

_____

_____

_____

Author's Purpose

The author's general purpose may be to persuade (change the reader's mind or behavior), inform (share information with the reader), or entertain (make the reader feel a certain way, often through stories), or it may be a combination of these purposes. At specific points in a text, an author may use a variety of methods to achieve the general purpose. You should always assume that the author has a particular reason for what he or she wrote.

    5. What is the purpose of the list at the end of the passage?

      a. To entertain readers with amusing thoughts.

      b. To inform readers how they can use Summitt's strategy to be successful.

      c. To persuade readers that no matter what their skill level, they will always meet the hardest goals if they just break them into smaller goals.

      d. To persuade readers that winning depends on who the coach is.

WHY? What information in the selection leads you to give that answer? _____

_____

_____

_____

_____

    6. Why does the author tell readers at the beginning of the article how many times the University of Tennessee women's basketball team has won the national championship?

      a. To inform them that Summitt is very successful in order to persuade them that they might learn something from her.

      b. To suggest that Summitt did fairly well, but like most of us, does falter sometimes.

      c. To illustrate the idea that setting pie-in-the-sky goals makes for sky-high success rates.

      d. To inform readers that Summitt's success happened in the sport of basketball, not volleyball.

WHY? What information in the selection leads you to give that answer? _____

_____

_____

_____

Relationships

The ideas in a reading selection are related to one another in different ways. For instance, one sentence might discuss the causes of an event mentioned in a different sentence. Some relationships have to do with time, space, comparisons and contrasts, causes and effects, and so on. You may see the relationships between the ideas in different parts of one sentence, in different sentences, or even in different paragraphs. Many times, these relationships are indicated with signal words or transitions such as *but, and, however, for example,* and so on.

_____ 7. What is the relationship between the two parts of Summitt's saying, "Winners aren't born, they are self-made"?
   a. Comparison or similarity.
   b. Cause and effect.
   c. Time order.
   d. Contrast or difference.

WHY? What information in the selection leads you to give that answer? _____

_____

_____

_____

_____ 8. What is the relationship of paragraph 8 to paragraph 7?
   a. Cause and effect.
   b. Comparison or similarity.
   c. Space order.
   d. Example.

WHY? What information in the selection leads you to give that answer? _____

_____

_____

_____

Fact, Opinion, and Inference

A fact is a true statement that can be verified by using another source of information: *It is 85 degrees outside.* An opinion is a person's personal reaction: *It's too hot to play baseball.* An inference is an idea the reader gets from the other ideas that the author has stated: *That person must be from up north.* To be valid, an inference must be a logical extension of what the author has written.

___ 9. Which of the following statements is Pat Summitt's opinion?

    a. Summitt and her captains commit goals to writing.

    b. The only way to ensure you become a winner is to set goals every day.

    c. Summitt bears more championship jewelry than any other coach in women's basketball history.

    d. Summitt doesn't set the goal of winning the national championship.

WHY? What leads you to give that answer? _____

_____

_____

_____

___ 10. Which of the following statements is an opinion?

    a. When Summitt's players don't meet a daily goal, they experience a negative consequence.

    b. Summitt's players decide how hard they will try to achieve the daily goal.

    c. Summitt is a better person than Dean Smith.

    d. Setting goals plays a role in being successful.

WHY? What leads you to give that answer? _____

_____

_____

_____

_____

● Vocabulary in New Contexts

Review the vocabulary words in the margins of the reading selection and then complete the following activities.

EASY Note Cards

Make a note card for each vocabulary word from the reading. On one side, write the word. On the other side, divide the card into four areas and label them E, A, S, and Y. Add a word or phrase in each area so that you wind up with an example sentence, an antonym, a synonym, and, finally, a definition that shows you understand the meaning of the word with your logic. Remember that a synonym or an antonym may have appeared in the reading.

Relationships Between Words

Circle yes or no to answer the question. Then explain your answer.

1. Would a **titan** always find that his or her goals are **unattainable**?

    Yes   No

    Why or why not? _____

    _____

2. Does **empowerment** cause a person to **falter**?

    Yes   No

    Why or why not? _____

    _____

3. Should a person get a **penalty** for not achieving an **unattainable** goal?

    Yes   No

    Why or why not? _____

    _____

Language in Your Life

Write short answers to each question. Look at vocabulary words closely before you answer.

1. Name one goal you have that you think is **attainable**. _____

    _____

2. Name one time when you felt **empowered** to succeed. _____

    _____

3. Name one area of life in which you want to be a **titan**. _____

    _____

4. Name one time you got a **penalty** when you shouldn't have. _____

    _____

5. Name a person you know who has **faltered** but then reached a goal. _____

    _____

Language in Use

Select the best word to complete the meaning of each sentence.

> empowerment   falter   penalties   titan   unattainable

1. Many of us are raised with a belief that being rich is an _____ goal.

2. Some children in Allentown, Pennsylvania, are instead developing a sense of _____ about this goal when they attend Camp Millionaire.

3. The camp director uses games to teach kids about financial ideas, such as setting goals, saving for different purposes, and understanding interest rates and _____.

4. Many adults who are successful in other areas of life _____ when it comes to money management.

5. If they had attended Camp Millionaire, maybe they would be _____ of finance today.

Spotlight on Word Parts: *Un-*

As you have learned, *unattainable* means "not able to be reached." The word *unattainable* is composed of three parts:

un- means "not" + attain means "reach" + -able means "able to be"

When you put the three parts together, you get "not able to be reached."

The word part un- is used in many other words.

un hurried = not in a rush

un easy = not secure

un foreseen = not expected

un intended = not on purpose

un ruly = impossible to rule or control

Circle the correct word in each of these sentences.

1. Her quick decision led to (unruly / uneasy / unintended) results.

2. She walked at an (unforeseen / unhurried / uneasy) pace.

3. He got an (unintended / unhurried / uneasy) feeling in his stomach.

4. The underdog won an (unforeseen / unruly / uneasy) victory over the world champion.

5. The (uneasy / unruly / unhurried) mob charged up the steps of the courthouse.

In the movie *Monster-in-Law*, Charlie (Jennifer Lopez) asks Dr. Kevin Fields (Michael Vartan), "What color are my eyes?" He replies: "Well, at first glance your eyes are brown. But when the light hits them, they change to amber. And if you look really close around the iris, the color is pure honey. But when you look into the sun, they almost look green. That's my favorite."

MAPP for Reading Comprehension

Dr. Fields's answer reveals a man who pays attention to the details! In the movie he makes quite an impression on his love interest with his answer. This is something most (if not all) of us appreciate—a person who notices and admires the little things that make us unique. In most areas of life, not just relationships, paying attention to details makes the difference between understanding and confusion, a good job and a poor one, or success and failure.

School is no different. Knowing the details of a class, the syllabus, the textbook, or an assignment can directly impact your grade. For example, simply reading and understanding directions can make a difference between a passing test grade and a failing one. Details bring comprehension, and comprehension brings confidence.

Knowing how to identify the topic, main idea, and important details of a reading is vital to your overall success in most of your classes. The next four lessons will walk you through a reading strategy that can help you not only pay attention to details but also know which ones are key to your comprehension. When you finish Part 3, you should have a clear reading MAPP!

Find chapter-specific interactive learning tools for *Activate,* including quizzes, videos, and more, through CengageBrain.com.

Videos Related to Readings

Vocab Words on Audio

Read and Talk on Demand

Share Your Prior Knowledge

Have you ever made a simple mistake that caused a lot of problems for you that could have been avoided if you had paid attention to the details? Share the story with a classmate and explain what you learned from this experience.

Survey the Lessons

Take a moment to turn to the table of contents and survey Lessons 8 through 11 in Part 3 so you know what to expect. For each lesson, name one thing you think you already know about that topic:

Lesson 8: _____

Lesson 9: _____

Lesson 10: _____

Lesson 11: _____

What does MAPP stand for?

M: _____

A: _____

P: _____

P: _____

Name one thing you want to read more about to understand better:

_____

Read and Talk

In college, reading is just the beginning of how you will share new ideas with others in your class. So the first reading in each part of this book is meant to give you the chance to talk about reading. Read the article, and then use the four discussion questions to talk about your ideas with your classmates and your instructor. Make this an opportunity to create new friendships and knowledge through the art of listening to the ideas of others, the enjoyment of discussing your thoughts, and the fun of reading something new.

Access the Reading CourseMate via **www.cengagebrain.com/shop/ ISBN/1413033156** to hear a reading of this selection and view a video about this topic.

I Know What I Like

Charles Hoffer

1   Everyone likes at least one kind of music. Usually it is the type of music with which he or she is familiar—and it is often the only kind the person listens to. The saying *I know what I like* is true. But so is the phrase *I like what I know*. It is not surprising that people feel more comfortable and competent with the music they know. The problem with stopping at this comfort level, however, is that it usually confines them to only a tiny bit of the rich world of music.

Kevin Winter/Getty Images Entertainment/Getty Images

analogy The entire second paragraph gives an example of an analogy. What does *analogy* mean?

2   Consider this **analogy**: Suppose you had the chance to advise a person from a foreign country about what to see on a tour of the United States. You might suggest seeing the part of the country where you live, and that would be fine. But is that all a visitor should experience of the United States? What about its other great cities and natural resources? The analogy with music seems clear. There is a vast and varied world of music out there. Why confine yourself to just one small portion and miss out on other kinds of music that could enrich your life? The more people know about music, especially art music, the more quality they add to their lives.

Talking About Reading

Respond in writing to the questions here and then discuss your answers with your classmates.

1. What kind of music do you know you like? _____

_____

2. When did you first hear that kind of music? What memories does it bring up for you? _____

_____

3. If you had grown up listening to a different kind of music, do you think you would have learned to like it? Why or why not? _____

_____

4. The author says, "The more people know about music, especially art music, the more quality they add to their lives." How would knowing more about music add to the quality of life? _____

_____

MAPP: A Reading Plan

The author of "I Know What I Like" suggests that there are benefits to listening to new kinds of music you've never been exposed to before. To prove his point, he compares listening to new kinds of music to traveling to new places.

Reading is also like traveling to new places. When you read, you learn about new ideas, you think new thoughts, and you meet new people, just as you do when you travel. But both traveling and reading can be difficult if you don't know the way. You may want to see the Grand Canyon, but if you're in Miami and don't have a road map or a GPS, you won't know how to get there. The same is true of reading—you need to know how to get from here to there. In short, you need a map. The figure below shows a map for reading called a MAPP.

MAPP: A Plan for Reading

Mark = **Mark** the answers to your questions.

About = Topic: What is the reading **about**?

Point = Main Idea: What is the **point**?

Proof = Supporting Detail: What is the **proof**?

A MAPP will help you find your way through a reading selection. Using a MAPP every time you read will improve your reading comprehension. And that is one goal of Part 3 of this book: to ask you to use a MAPP until it becomes a habit.

In Part 3, we will discuss a plan for reading that will help you understand the structure of what you read. It is called MAPP. Understanding the structure of a text will help you decide which ideas are more important and which ideas are less important.

The M of MAPP Is "Mark."

In this lesson, we will discuss the "M" of MAPP, which stands for "Mark the answers to your questions." There are three steps in this process:

1. Form questions from titles and headings.

2. Read for the answer to your question.

3. Mark the answer to the question.

When you need to learn something from a reading selection, you need to ask questions about it. Searching for the answers to your questions will give you a well-defined purpose for reading. Stating your purpose for reading will motivate you to read actively and clarify (make clear) what information you are looking for.

Step 1: Form Questions from Titles and Headings.

The title at the beginning of a reading and headings within the reading usually provide powerful clues about the topic of the reading—that is, what it is about. So start by turning the title or heading into a question.

Use the 5W's and H to Form Questions

To turn the title or heading of a reading into a question, you can use the "5W's and H" listed in one of the reading selections in Lesson 1:

The 5W and H Questions

who, what, when, where, why, and how

Examples of Step 1: Turning Titles and Headings into Questions

Heading in a health textbook:	The Causes of Bulimia Nervosa
Question formed from the heading:	What causes bulimia nervosa? *or* What are the causes of bulimia nervosa?

Heading in an education textbook:	The Severe Shortage of Minority Teachers
Question formed from the heading:	How severe is the shortage of minority teachers? *or* Why is there a severe shortage of minority teachers?

Heading in a chemistry textbook:	Molecular Mass and Formula Mass
Question formed from the heading:	What are molecular mass and formula mass? *or* What is the difference between molecular mass and formula mass?

Look back at the questions. Which of the "5W and H" words do you find? Highlight them or make a list.

As you have seen, the words *what, why,* and *how* are particularly useful when forming questions from headings and titles. They are broader or more general than the other "w" words, *where, when,* and *who.* These last three words may still come in handy for specific kinds of headings, however. Here are two examples.

Heading from a sociology textbook:	Early Thinkers
Question formed from the heading:	Who were the early thinkers?

Heading from an art textbook:	Art Used Dynamically in Rituals
Question formed from the heading:	When is art used dynamically in rituals? *or* Where is art used dynamically in rituals? *or* How is art used dynamically in rituals?

INTERACTION 3–1	Forming Questions from Headings in Textbook Chapters

Form at least one question from each textbook heading.

1. Textbook heading: Strategies for Protesting Oppression

   Question: _What are the Strategies for Protesting oppression_

2. Textbook heading: Combating Delinquency and Crime at an Early Age

   Question: _How do you deal with Combating Delinquency and Crime at an early Age_

3. Textbook heading: Building Healthy Relationships

   Question: _How to build a healthy relationships_

4. Textbook heading: Socrates

   Question: _What is Socrates_

5. Textbook heading: Managing Information

   Question: _How to Managing Information_

INTERACTION 3–2	More Practice with Forming Questions from Headings and Titles

Form at least one question from each title and heading.

1. Book title: *Patterns in Prehistory: Mankind's First Three Million Years*

   Question: _What are the patterns_

2. Textbook heading: Preparing for an International Assignment

   Question: _How do I preparing_

3. Article title: "Supreme Court Puts Brake on Car Searches"

   Question: _____Why_____

   _____

4. Textbook heading: Cells Receive and Respond to Signals

   Question: _____How cells receive and respond to_____

   _____signals_____

5. Book title: *Vanished Smile: The Mysterious Theft of the Mona Lisa*

   Question: _____who stolen it_____

   _____

Sometimes, You May Ask More Than One Question

Many book titles, chapter titles, and headings have two parts: a main title and a subtitle. Others include several ideas in a single, main title. So consider forming more than one question from a title or heading to make sure you get the whole meaning.

Book title and subtitle:	*Outliers: The Story of Success*
Three questions formed from the title:	What are outliers? What is the story of success? What do outliers have to do with the story of success?
Heading in a chemistry textbook:	Water—An "Unusual" Compound
Two questions formed from the heading:	What kind of compound is water? Why is water an unusual compound?
Heading in an education textbook:	Key Events and Curriculum Trends in American Education
Two questions formed from the heading:	What key events have shaped American education? What curriculum trends have occurred in American education?

INTERACTION 3–3	Forming More than One Question from a Title or Heading

Form at least two questions from each title or heading.

1. Book title: *The Yankee Years*

   Questions: • What were the yankee years
   • When were the yankee years

2. Article title: "Parents of Seniors: Don't Sweat D-Day"

   Questions: • What is D Day
   • why are parents sweating it

3. Textbook heading: Industrial and Postindustrial Societies

   Questions: • what is the different
   • What is Industrial and Postindustrial

4. Book title: *Joker One: A Marine Platoon's Story of Courage, Leadership, and Brotherhood*

   Questions: • What is Joker one
   • How do they do all that

5. Textbook heading: Electronic Surveillance and the Fight Against Terrorism

   Questions: • How do you use Electronic
   •

Think About the Relationship Between the Minor Heading and the Major Heading

Textbook chapters often include different levels of headings. You will find a chapter title, major headings for sections of the chapter, and within each section, minor headings. When forming questions from headings, take into account their relationship to the heading at the next highest level. Here is an example from a communications textbook:

Chapter title
Interviewing
>   *Major heading for a section of the chapter*
>   Questions Used in Interviewing
>>   *Minor headings within that section*
>>   Open Versus Closed Questions
>>   Neutral Versus Leading Questions
>>   Primary Versus Secondary Questions

—Verderber, Verderber, & Sellnow, *COMM*

When you form questions for the minor headings, you can take into account your knowledge that the entire section is about questions used in interviewing.

- How are open and closed questions used in interviewing? Are they used for different purposes or at different times?

- What are the differences between neutral and leading questions when interviewing? How and when should they be used?

- What are primary questions and secondary questions? When should they be used in interviewing, and why?

In the example, also note that each minor heading has the word *versus* in it. So each heading introduces a discussion of how the two types of questions are different: open versus closed, neutral versus leading, and primary versus secondary. Thus, the questions you form should deal with differences.

INTERACTION 3–4	Forming Questions from Minor Headings in Relation to Major Headings

Form a question for each minor heading that takes into account its relation to the major heading.

1. *Major heading in a history textbook chapter*

    Expansion of Colonial Economy and Society in New England, 1700–1763

    Minor headings

    Economy   Question: Who did the economy expan

    Society   Question: How did the Society expan

Life   Question: *How did life change for the people.*

—Headings adapted from Schultz, *HIST*, Volume 1

2. Major heading in a biology textbook

The Central Nervous System

Minor headings

The Spinal Cord   Question: *What is the role of the Spinal Cord.*

Regions   Question: *What are the region of the Brain.*
of the Brain

—Starr, Evers, & Starr, *Biology: Today and Tomorrow,* 2nd edition

3. Major heading in a health textbook

The Impact of Alcohol

Minor headings

Digestive System   Question: *What does alcohol affect the digestive system*

Weight and Waists   Question: *How does it affect the weight and waists*

Breast Cancer   Question: *How does it affect breast Cancer.*

Increased Risk   Question: *How does alcohol In*
of Dying

—Hales, *An Invitation to Health,* 12th edition

4. Major heading in a criminal justice textbook

The Purposes of Criminal Law

Minor headings

Protect and Punish: Question: _What is the legal function_
The Legal Function   _of the_ _____
of the Law

Maintain and Teach: Question: _How does the social_
The Social Function   _function of_ _____
of the Law

—Gaines & Miller, *Criminal Justice in Action: The Core*, 5th edition

5. *Major heading in a sociology textbook*

Comparing Sociology with Other Social Sciences

Minor headings

Anthropology   Question: _What is the differen_
_____

Psychology   Question: _What is Psychology_
_____

Economics   Question: _____
_____

Political Science   Question: _How does Political_
_____

—Kendall, *Sociology in Our Times*, 7th edition

INTERACTION 3–5	**More Practice with Forming Questions from Minor Headings in Relation to Major Headings**

Form a question for each minor heading that takes into account its relation to the major heading.

1. *Major heading in a business textbook*

Basic Math Skills for Entrepreneurs (*Entrepreneurs* are people who start and run their own businesses.)

Minor headings

Addition and Subtraction	Question: _____
	_____
Multiplication and Division	Question: _____
	_____
Averages	Question: _____
	_____

—Greene, *Exploring Entrepreneurship and Economics*

2. ***Major heading in a chemistry textbook***

Characteristics of a Chemical Change

Minor headings

Chemical Equations	Question: _____
	_____
Energy in Chemical Change	Question: _____
	_____

—Cracolice & Peters, *Basics of Introductory Chemistry: An Active Learning Approach,* 2nd edition

3. ***Major heading in a composition handbook***

Strategies for Structuring Paragraphs

Minor headings

Give Examples	Question: _____
	_____
Define Key Terms	Question: _____
	_____
Compare and Contrast	Question: _____
	_____

—Raimes & Jerskey, *Universal Keys for Writers,* 2nd edition

4. *Major heading in a business management textbook*

Making Sense of Changing Environments

   Minor headings

   Environmental Scanning   Question: _____

   _____

   _____

   Interpreting   Question: _____
   Environmental Factors
   _____

   _____

   Acting on Threats   Question: _____
   and Opportunities
   _____

   _____

—Williams, *Management,* 4th edition

5. *Major heading in a nursing textbook*

Theories of Human Behavior and Health

   Minor headings

   Healthy Belief Model   Question: _____

   _____

   Protection Motivation   Question: _____
   Theory
   _____

—Maville & Huerta, *Health Promotion in Nursing,* 2nd edition

Review: Forming Questions from Titles and Headings

You can form questions from titles and headings to develop your active reading skills. As you form questions, keep the following ideas in mind:

- Use the 5 W's and H to form questions from headings.
- Realize that sometimes you may need to ask more than one question.
- Think about the relationship between the minor heading and the major heading.

Step 2: Read for the Answer to Your Question.

You have changed headings into questions that you can use to guide you when you read. Use these questions to focus your attention on the main points the author wants to make. In other words, read to find the answers to your questions. Note that you will probably find different parts of the answer in different places in the reading selection.

Example of Step 2: Reading for the Answer to Your Question

The following selection is taken from a health textbook. The heading for the major section in which this reading appears is already stated as a question:

Hazardous means dangerous

Is Stress Hazardous to Physical Health?

The rest of the example is one part of this major section. Read the question next to the minor heading. Then read the selection. The answers to the question are highlighted.

Stress and Digestion   Question: How is stress dangerous to digestion?

1   Do you ever get butterflies in your stomach before giving a speech or before a big game? The digestive system is, as one psychologist quips, "an important stop on the tension trail." To avoid problems, pay attention to how you eat. ==Eating on the run, gulping food, or overeating results in poorly chewed foods, an overworked stomach, and increased abdominal pressure.==

2   Some simple strategies can help you avoid stress-related stomachaches. ==Many people experience dry mouth or sweat more under stress.== By drinking plenty of water, you replenish lost fluids and prevent dehydration. Fiber-rich foods counteract ==common stress-related problems, such as cramps and constipation.== Do not skip meals. If you do, you're more likely to feel fatigued and irritable.

3   Good nutrition can help soothe a stressed-out stomach. Complex carbohydrates are an ideal anti-stress food because they boost the brain's level of the mood-enhancing chemical serotonin. Good sources include broccoli, leafy greens, potatoes, corn, cabbage, spinach, whole-grain breads and pastas, muffins, crackers, and cereals. Leafy vegetables, whole grains, nuts, and seeds also are rich in other important nutrients, including magnesium and vitamin C.

4   <mark>Be wary of overeating under stress</mark>. Some people eat more because they scarf down meals too quickly. Others reach for snacks to calm their nerves or to comfort themselves. In a study of college women, higher stress increased the risk of binge eating. Watch out for caffeine. <mark>Coffee, tea, and cola drinks can make your strained nerves jangle even more. Also avoid sugary snacks. They'll send your blood sugar levels on a roller coaster ride—up one minute, down the next.</mark>

—Hales, *An Invitation to Health*, 12th edition

You can see that the question you ask determines what you will focus on the most when you read. Here, we asked "How is stress dangerous to digestion?" All the highlighted words are parts of the answer to this question. If we had asked instead, "What can you do to lessen the danger of stress to your digestion?" we would have highlighted different words. The author seems to have two purposes here: to teach you about how stress affects digestion, and to teach you how to lessen the dangers.

INTERACTION 3–6	Reading to Answer Your Question

For questions 1 and 2, form a question from the heading. Then read for the answer.

1. Question: _What are Iformative Speeches_

Informative Speeches

When the goal of a speech is to share information with others, the speech is informative. An **informative speech** communicates knowledge about a process, an event, a person, a place, an object, or a concept, and it does so by describing, explaining, clarifying, or demonstrating information about its subject. Informative speeches are given in a wide range of situations, from informal to formal, and can vary in length depending on the situation and the audience's need.

—Griffin, *Invitation to Public Speaking*, 3rd edition

Answer to your question: _Share information with_
other

2. Question: _What are persuasive speeches_

> ## Persuasive Speeches
>
> A **persuasive speech** is one whose message attempts to change or reinforce an audience's thoughts, feelings, or actions. When we speak to persuade, we act as advocates, encouraging or discouraging certain thoughts and actions. We urge our audience to accept our views or solutions, take a particular action, buy certain products, or adopt specific proposals. When we persuade others, we defend an idea and ask our audience to agree with us rather than someone else. We seek to change or reinforce our audience's attitudes (positive or negative feelings about something), beliefs (ideas about what is real or true), or values (ideas of what is good or worthy).
>
> —Griffin, *Invitation to Public Speaking*, 3rd edition

Answer to your question: _____

_____

3. Both of these selections, "Informative Speeches" and "Persuasive Speeches," are in a section called "Types of Public Speaking." Does the author want you to focus on the similarities or the differences between these two types? _____

_____

INTERACTION 3–7 | **More Practice with Reading to Answer Your Question**

Form a question from the heading. Then read for the answer.

1. Question: _____

_____

> ## Spelling Successfully
>
> 1   If you are not spelling effectively, the problem is the way you are representing words to yourself. So what's the best strategy for spelling? The way to learn to spell is to make visual pictures that can be easily accessed at any time.

2   Take the word "Albuquerque." The best way to learn to spell it isn't to say the letters over and over again—it's to store the word as a picture in your mind. The best way to learn to spell Albuquerque is to place the word up and to your left and form a clear visual image of it.

3   At this point I need to add another concept: chunking. Generally, people can consciously process only five to nine chunks of information at once. People who learn rapidly can master even the most complex tasks because they chunk information into small steps and then reassemble them into the original whole. The way to learn to spell Albuquerque is to break it down into three smaller chunks like this: *Albu/quer/que.* I want you to write the three parts on a piece of paper, hold them above and to the left of your eyes, see *Albu,* then close your eyes and see it in your mind. Continue to do this four or five or six times until you can close your eyes and clearly see *Albu.* Next take the second chunk, *quer.* Flash on the letters faster and follow the same process with it, and then with the *que* chunk, until the entire image Albuquerque is stored in your mind. If you have a clear picture, you'll probably have a feeling (kinesthetic) that it's spelled right. Then you'll be able to see the word so clearly you can spell it not only forward but backward. Try it. Spell Albuquerque. Then spell it backward. Once you have that, you've got that word spelled forever. You can do that with any word and become a superb speller, even if you've had trouble spelling your own name in the past.

—Robbins, *Unlimited Power*

Answer to your question: _____

_____

_____

> **Review:** Reading to Find the Answer to Your Question
>
> ▪ After you form your question from the heading, focus your attention on finding the answer as you read.
>
> ▪ Different parts of the answer are likely to be found in different places in the reading selection.

Step 3: Mark the Answer to Your Question.

Now you have formed a question from the heading, and you have read for the answer. One more step will increase your comprehension even more. When you reach a point that helps to answer the question you formed from the heading, mark it in some way. Highlight it with a yellow marker, underline it, bracket it, or otherwise mark it. Be careful to mark only the ideas that directly answer the question. Don't highlight too much. If you do, you will find it difficult later to review the material for a test.

Example of Step 3: Marking the Answer to Your Question

The following selection is taken from a criminal justice textbook. Here is the heading for the major section it is a part of:

The Responsibilities of the Police

The rest of the example is one part of this major section. Read the question next to the minor heading. Then read the selection. The answers to the question are highlighted.

Providing Services

What services do police provide as part of their responsibilities?

A great deal of a police officer's time is spent providing services for the community. The motto "To Serve and Protect" has been adopted by thousands of local police departments, and the *Law Enforcement Code of Ethics* recognizes the duty "to serve the community" in its first sentence. The services that police provide are numerous—a partial list would include <mark>directing traffic, performing emergency medical procedures, counseling those involved in domestic disputes, providing directions to tourists, and finding lost children</mark>. Along with firefighters, police officers are often among the first public servants to arrive at disaster scenes to <mark>conduct search and rescue operations</mark>. This particular duty adds considerably to the dangers faced by law enforcement agents. In the aftermath of Hurricane Katrina, New Orleans police officers had to dodge snipers' bullets as they tried to <mark>restore order</mark> to the city. Police are also required to <mark>deal with the problems of the homeless and the mentally ill</mark> to a greater extent than in past decades.

Rick Wilking/Reuters/Landov

Earl Dunbar of the Louisiana State Capitol Police carries a five-day-old baby, an evacuee brought for treatment near the Superdome in downtown New Orleans.

—Adapted from Gaines & Miller, *Criminal Justice in Action: The Core*, 5th edition

You can see that each highlighted part of the selection helps to answer the question "What services do police provide as part of their responsibilities?"

| INTERACTION 3–8 | Marking the Answer to Your Question |

Form a question from each heading. Then read for the answer. Mark the parts of the answer as you find them, either by highlighting, underlining, or some other method.

Characteristics of an Effective School

Question: _what are characteristics of an effective school_

> Researchers have been looking for the characteristics or qualities of effective schools. Among the most significant characteristics they found to occur in schools with high achievement in the basic skills were (1) high expectations for student performance, (2) communication among teachers, and (3) a task orientation among the staff.

The Teachers' Expectations

Question: _What are the teachers Expectations_

> Through their attitude and regular encouragement, teachers in effective schools communicate to students their belief that the students will achieve the goals of instruction. In effect, the teachers get across to students a "can-do" attitude about learning.

Communication Among Teachers

Question: _What are Communication Among teachers_

Teachers in effective schools do not operate in a vacuum, each in his or her isolated classroom. Instead, they talk among themselves about their work. They converse about one another's students. They know the curricular materials and activities that go on in one another's classrooms, and they are helpful to one another. In short, effective schools have teachers who are good colleagues.

Task Orientation

Question: _What is Task Orientation_

The teachers at effective schools are highly task oriented. They begin instruction early in the class period and end instruction late in the period. The staff approaches its teaching responsibilities with a serious air and wastes little time in class. Whether the classes are formal or informal, underneath the surface of events lies a seriousness of purpose that is communicated to students.

—Adapted from Cooper, *Those Who Can, Teach*, 12th edition

Mark Only the Most Important Points and Details

When you are looking for the answer to your question, mark only the most important points and significant details. Long after you have read a selection, you may need to review it as you study for a test on the material. The best way to do that is to review the headings and your marks. If you mark too much material, you will have to reread much of the reading selection, which is an inefficient way to study. Mark no more than about 20 percent of a reading selection to make your highlighting the most effective.

INTERACTION 3–9	Marking the Least Amount of Text to Answer the Question

For each item, form a question from the heading, and then read to find the answer. Mark the least amount of text you can to answer the question, but do mark enough so that if you had to reread your markings, you would be able to understand them.

1. Question: _____

Foreign Language Speakers Needed at the CIA

At the CIA, we need people who speak foreign languages to aid us in gathering information around the world. If you have excellent language skills, you can contribute to our mission of protecting America. People who speak different languages conduct research, examine foreign media, and teach critical language skills to others in the CIA. It is an opportunity to put your unique skills to work in a meaningful career for the good of the nation.

—Adapted from the CIA Web site

2. Question: _____

Employers Expect a Good Attitude

Employers expect you to possess a good attitude at all times—whether you're happy or sad, feeling good or bad, or experiencing problems outside of work. A good attitude increases creativity and productivity, which leads, ultimately, to greater profits for the employers and larger raises for the employees.

A bad attitude is like a virus. It can spread quickly and affect everyone who comes in contact with it. Once a company, department, or work crew "catches" a bad attitude, it can take days, weeks, or months to recover. In the meantime, everyone's stress increases, accidents occur, morale dips, productivity slumps, and the bottom line suffers. One person with a bad attitude can infect an entire company. It's easy to see why company owners and supervisors reward employees who are positive and enthusiastic.

—Adapted from Rokes, *What Your Employer Expects*

3. Question: _____

Responsibilities of Air Traffic Controllers

1   More than 14,000 men and women work as air traffic controllers in the United States. Almost all of them are employed by the Federal Aviation Administration (FAA), an agency of the United States government. **Tower controllers** are probably the employees most people picture when they think of air traffic controllers. They work in glass towers managing air traffic between 3 and 30 miles from the airport. Tower controllers monitor all planes that travel through the airport's airspace. Their main job is to organize the flow of aircraft into and out of the airport.

2   **Radio controllers** watch aircraft on radar and communicate with the pilots when necessary, warning them about nearby planes, bad weather conditions, and other potential hazards. And **enroute controllers** work in more than 20 centers around the country, away from airports. They direct airplanes for most of their journey, controlling all air traffic above 17,000 feet.

—*The 16 Career Clusters: A Project-Based Orientation*

4. Question: _____

Effective Business Writing

Business writing is effective when individuals pay attention to and incorporate the following concepts into their writing: Clear, Concise, Correct, Courteous, Conversational, Convincing, and Complete, also known as "The Seven C's of Business Letter Writing." In business situations, your reader's time is precious. So your correspondence must be succinct and accurate to avoid creating confusion, wasting the reader's time, or failing to achieve its goal. To help eliminate confusion, use short sentences and simple words, and avoid using wordy phrases, jargon, technical terms and abbreviations, and abstract words and phrases. Use courteous language to convey professionalism and a caring, thoughtful attitude. Carefully select your words to effectively convey important points to the reader. The information you supply must be complete enough for the reader to draw correct conclusions from the message, but free of unnecessary details that may cause confusion.

—Solomon, Tyler, & Taylor, *100% Career Success*

5. Question: _____

Education for Athletic Trainers

To become an athletic trainer, a student must become competent in both the classroom and clinical settings. In the classroom and in the clinic, a student's knowledge, skill, professional behaviors, and clinical proficiencies (professional, practice-oriented outcomes) are measured. In addition to basic college courses such as human anatomy and nutrition, students must learn specific subject matter like risk management and injury/illness prevention, therapeutic exercise, and medical ethics.

—Adapted from the National Athletic Trainers Association Web site

---

INTERACTION 3–10   **More Practice Marking the Least Amount of Text to Answer the Question**

For each item, form a question from the heading, and then read to find the answer. Mark the least amount of text you can to answer the question, but do mark enough so that if you had to reread your markings, you would be able to understand them.

1. Question: _____

Artistic Creativity in the United States Today

Creativity allows us to cause some object to come into being. What that means exactly can vary from culture to culture. In the United States today, creativity is thought to have two essential ingredients. The first is innovation, or the making of something that is new. The second is self-expression, which refers to individual artists' own styles and personal concepts of the world, all of which are embedded in their unique works of art.

—Adapted from Lazzari & Schlesier, *Exploring Art,* 3rd edition

2. Question: _____

Robots Help Catch Animal Poachers

The Fish and Wildlife departments of many states now use animal robots to catch poachers. Poachers are hunters who shoot animals out of season or shoot animals that are protected by state laws. In other words, they are hunting illegally. Certain kinds of bear, moose, deer, and turkeys all have decoy robot versions to help protect them. The robotic decoys are made from molded fiberglass covered with real animal hides. They can be made to move their ears, heads, and tails because they have radio-controlled motors inside them. Wildlife management officers nearby can activate the motors to make the "animals" move. When a hunter shoots at the robotic animal, the wildlife officers can arrest them.

Birmingham News/Landov

3. Question: _____

> ### Advantages of Starting Your Own Business
>
> Entrepreneurs who start their own business get to make all the decisions. They decide where to locate the business, how many employees to hire, and what prices to charge. They are completely independent and responsible for their own future. Many entrepreneurs find great satisfaction in starting their own businesses. Many are attracted to the challenge of creating something entirely new. They also get a feeling of success when their business earns a profit.
>
> —Greene, *Exploring Entrepreneurship and Economics*

4. Question: _____

> ### Reactions to Swine Flu Outbreak
>
> In 2009, a new influenza (flu) virus called "swine flu" became a major cause for concern around the world. In Mexico, where thousands of people fell ill from the flu, about 400 people eventually died from it. In the United States, 10,000 people had died from it by the end of 2009. Reactions to the quick-spreading flu virus varied around the U.S. President Obama called the situation "serious" but asked Americans not to panic. However, hundreds of American schools closed their doors to make sure the flu would not spread among students, including 50 in New York, 26 in Texas, and 14 in California. The Centers for Disease Control and Prevention had sensible advice for individuals worried about getting the flu: wash your hands frequently, stay in good general health, and avoid close contact with people who are sick.

5. Question: _____

Principles of Democracy

Democratic governments are ones in which the people and the government are connected; in other words, the people govern themselves. The first principle of democracy is that there are elections in which the people are free to choose and reject government officials by voting. Another principle in democracy is that all the people—with all their differing opinions and values—are able to compete for attention and followers. No one group has a special claim to be heard over the others. A third factor is that the people are protected from the government. For example, the constitution of a democratic country may include protections for the freedom of speech. A fourth factor is that the people in a democratic country should be living as well as the natural and technological resources permit. So how much people earn, how well they can read, how long they typically live, and other similar measurements should reflect how wealthy the country as a whole is.

—Adapted from Grigsby, *Analyzing Politics,* 4th edition

Review: Marking the Answer to Your Question

When you read to find the parts of the answer to the question you formed from the heading, mark them.

- Highlight, underline, bracket, or use some other method to mark the answers.
- Be careful to mark only the ideas that directly answer the question.
- Mark no more than 20 percent of the selection.
- When you return to the material to study for a test, ask the questions and read the highlighted answers only—don't reread the entire selection.

ACTIVATE YOUR SKILLS 1
Asking Questions and Marking the Answers

A. What six words can you use to form questions from the titles and headings as you are reading?

   1. _who what when where why and how_

B. Form a question from each title or heading from the college textbook *Voyages in World History* by Hansen and Curtis.

   2. A Time of Upheaval, 1966–1974 _What cause the time of uphe_

   3. The Postal Relay System _what was the Postal Relay Syste_

   4. The Multiple Centers of Europe, 500–1000 _What is the_

   5. The First Hominids _What is the first hominids_

   6. The First Anatomically Modern Humans Leave Africa _When did I_

C. The following selection is from a chapter in *Voyages in World History* called "Voyage into the Twenty-First Century." Read it using the "asking questions and marking the answers" strategy you have been practicing in this chapter.

Questions of Identity

1   Questions of identity—especially multiple, overlapping identities—are frequently at the heart of Mira Nair's films. In *Mississippi Masala* (1991), Jay Patel is unable to settle down and appreciate the success his family is having in the motel business in the rural American south. Though his origins lie in India, the home he longs for is in Uganda, the country from which his family had been expelled in the 1970s, along with the entire Ugandan Indian community, by the dictator Idi Amin. Self-identifying as an African, Patel writes letter after letter trying to have his property restored.

2   Meanwhile, his daughter Mina is developing a relationship with Demetrius, an African American carpet cleaner. Their relationship is frowned on by both the Indian and African American communities, even though both of them are "colored" in the eyes of the town's white population. In these circumstances, what does it mean to be "black," "Indian," "African," or "American"? The complexity of that question was recognized by the United States Census in 2000 when, for the first time, citizens were given the option to check more than one racial box.

7. What kind of identity are the authors referring to in the heading? _____

_____

8. What movie is used to provide an example of these identities? _____

_____

9. What identities does Jay Patel have? _____

_____

10. What ethnic community is the Patel family a part of in their town? _____

_____

ACTIVATE YOUR SKILLS 2
Asking Questions and Marking the Answers

A. Change the following headings from the college textbook *COMM* by Verderber, Verderber, and Sellnow into questions.

Major Heading: The Communication Process

   1. Question: _____

   Minor Heading: Participants

   2. Question: _____

   Minor Heading: Messages

   3. Question: _____

   Minor Heading: Contexts

   4. Question: _____

B. Change the following headings from the college textbook *Cultural Anthropology* (6th edition), by Ferraro, into questions. Then read the selection for the parts of the answers and mark them.

Major Heading: Food-Producing Societies

   5. Question: _____

   Minor Heading: Horticulture

   6. Question: _____

Horticulture is the simplest type of farming, which involves the use of basic hand tools such as the hoe or digging stick rather than plows or other machinery driven by animals or engines. Because horticulturalists produce low yields, they generally do not have sufficient surpluses to allow them to develop extensive market systems. The land, which is usually cleared by hand, is neither irrigated nor enriched by the use of fertilizers. A major technique of horticultural-ists is **shifting cultivation,** sometimes called **swidden cultivation** or the **slash-and-burn method.** This technique involves clearing the land by manually cutting down the growth, burning it, and planting in the burned area. Even though the ash residue serves as a fertilizer, the land is usu-ally depleted within a year or two. The land is then allowed to lie fallow to restore its fertility, or it may be abandoned altogether. This technique of slash-and-burn cultivating can eventually destroy the environment, for if fields are not given sufficient time to lie fallow, the forests will be permanently replaced by grasslands.

7. What tools do horticulturalists use? _____

8. What is a major technique of horticulture? _____

9. What is the first step in swidden cultivation? _____

_____

10. How is the land fertilized in horticulture? _____

_____

MASTER YOUR SKILLS 1
Asking Questions and Marking the Answers

Use the strategies you have just learned for changing headings into questions and mark-ing the answers. Then answer the questions that follow.

The Role of Sleep

1   You stay up late cramming for a final. You drive through the night to visit a friend at another campus. You get up for an early class during the week but stay in bed until noon on weekends. And you wonder: "Why am I so tired?" The answer: You're not getting enough sleep.

2   Whenever we fail to get adequate sleep, we accumulate what researchers call a sleep debit. With each night of too little rest, our body's need for sleep grows until it becomes irresistible. The only solution to the sleep debit is the obvious one: paying it back. College students who extended their nightly sleep time were more alert, more productive, and less likely to have accidents. And because sleepy people tend to be irritable and edgy, those who get more rest also tend to be happier, healthier, and easier to get along with.

Why Sleep Matters

3   Sleep problems, as medical scientists now recognize, are hazardous to health. Breathing-related sleep disorders, such as chronic snoring and obstructive sleep apnea, increase the risk of high blood pressure, heart attacks, and stroke. Individuals with insomnia, the most common sleep complaint, become irritable and depressed, get into more traffic accidents, develop memory problems, and have difficulties concentrating and doing their jobs. According to recent research, inadequate sleep affects growth hormone secretion, increasing the likelihood of obesity, and impairs the body's ability to use insulin, which can lead to diabetes. Individuals chronically deprived of enough sleep may become more susceptible to certain illnesses, and researchers speculate that disturbed sleep may be the reason why individuals under stress—such as students taking exams or grieving widows and widowers—may have lower levels of certain infection-fighting cells than normal.

4   College-age individuals, who often stay up late and sleep in on weekends, may suffer from Sunday night insomnia or may develop chronic problems getting up early. A single all-nighter can lead to lapses of attention and much slower reaction times. Sleep deprivation can increase the risk of physical and psychological symptoms, including depression, in college students.

The Stages of Sleep

5   A normal night of sleep consists of several distinct stages of sleep, divided into two major types: an active state, characterized by rapid eye movement (REM) and called REM sleep (or dream sleep), and a quiet state, referred to as non-REM or NREM sleep, that consists of four stages:

- **In Stage 1,** a twilight zone between full wakefulness and sleep, the brain produces small, irregular, rapid electrical waves. The muscles of the body relax, and breathing is smooth and even.

- **In Stage 2,** brain waves are larger and punctuated with occasional sudden bursts of electrical activity. The eyes are no longer responsive to light. Bodily functions slow still more.

- **Stages 3 and 4** constitute the most profound state of unconsciousness. The brain produces slower, larger waves, and this is sometimes referred to as "delta" or slow-wave sleep.

6   After about an hour in the four stages of non-REM sleep, sleepers enter the time of vivid dreaming called REM sleep, when brain waves resemble those of waking more than those of quiet sleep. The large muscles of the torso, arms, and legs are paralyzed and cannot move—possibly to prevent sleepers from acting out their dreams. The fingers and toes may twitch; breathing is quick and shallow; blood flow through the brain speeds up; men may have partial or full erections.

Strategies for Change: How to Sleep Like a Baby

- Keep regular hours for going to bed and getting up in the morning. Stay as close as possible to this schedule on weekends as well as weekdays.

- Develop a sleep ritual—such as stretching, meditation, yoga, prayer, or reading a not-too-thrilling novel—to ease the transition from wakefulness to sleep.

- Don't drink coffee late in the day. The effects of caffeine can linger for up to eight hours. And don't smoke. Nicotine is an even more powerful stimulant—and sleep saboteur—than caffeine.

- Don't rely on alcohol to get to sleep. Alcohol disrupts normal sleep stages, so you won't sleep as deeply or as restfully as you normally would.

- Don't nap during the day if you're having problems sleeping through the night.

—Hales, *An Invitation to Health,* 12th edition

1. Question formed from the **title** of the reading selection: _____

   _____

2. Answer: _____

   _____

3. Question formed from the **first heading:** _____

   _____

4. Answer: _____

5. What problems do people with breathing-related sleep disorders experience?

_____

6. What problems do people who have insomnia experience? _____

_____

_____

7. What two major health problems may inadequate sleep eventually cause?____

_____

8. Question formed from the **second heading:** _____

_____

9. Answer: _____

10. Which stage is the twilight zone between being awake and asleep? _____

11. In what stage do the eyes become unresponsive to light? _____

12. What stages are referred to as "delta" sleep? _____

13. In which stage does vivid dreaming occur? _____

14. Going from Stage 1 to Stage 4 sleep, do brain waves speed up or slow down?

_____

15. Question formed from the **title of the box:** _____

_____

16–20. Answer to question 15: _____

_____

MASTER YOUR SKILLS 2
Asking Questions and Marking the Answers

The following selections are from the college textbook *Health Promotion in Nursing* (2nd edition), by Maville and Huerta.

A. Change each title and heading into a question that would guide you as you read. Remember to consider the relationships between titles and headings.

    Chapter title: Environmental Factors

  1. **Question:** _____

    Major heading: Problem Identification

  2. Question: _____

    Major heading: The Body's Response to Environmental Influences

  3. Question: _____

        Minor heading: Acute and Chronic Exposure

    4. Question: _____

          _____

    Major heading: Sources of Pollution Exposure

  5. Question: _____

B. Here is a part of a minor section of the chapter on environmental factors. Change the heading into a question, read for the parts to the answer, and mark them. (The question and markings count as answers 6–15.) Remember to mark the least amount of text you can, thinking ahead to when you might need to review your markings before a test.

Color and Health

1   People respond to colors. Color expresses personality. The same color may have a different influence on different people. If an individual sees a color and likes it, the whole body system relaxes. Outlook becomes more optimistic. Therefore, a color that brings about a favorable response should be incorporated into that individual's surroundings. Since biological and psychological changes can be attributed to color, it is important to be attentive to individual color preferences and their effects.

2   The goal is to achieve balance while avoiding monotony of color and overstimulation by color. Visualize a color. Place it on a continuum ranging from the lightest to the darkest shade. Limit use of the color on either extreme of the continuum or combine the extremes to achieve balance. Staying in the color midrange on the continuum also provides balance. Colors that

are too bright or too dramatic can be distracting and can cause discomfort. Adjustments can be made by increasing or reducing the intensity, the amount, or the purity of a color. Adding white to a color reduces its brightness and changes its tint to a pastel that is soothing.

3   Variety is achieved by using contrasts between bright colors that stimulate and dark colors that relax. Variety is also achieved by using warm colors that excite and cool colors that soothe. For example, the blue (cool) end of the spectrum decreases arousal. Blue, violet, and green are cool, passive, and calming. Colors on the red end of the spectrum (warm) cause increased arousal. Red and its analogous hues are warm, active, and exciting. Contrary to the theory of warm colors being stimulating, certain pink hues can have a tranquilizing effect. Bubble gum pink, called passive pink, creates an almost immediate reduction in aggressive behavior, making it particularly useful with agitated clients or prisoners. Short-term exposure to a color does not necessarily have an effect. . . .

4   In manipulating the environment through color, one must consider who will be affected and for how long, where it will be used, and why it is being used. . . . In a hospital lobby, visitors will be affected. Surroundings should be pleasant and cheerful. A variety of both warm and cool colors would be appropriate. In a maternity unit, where the client is not seriously ill, peach or rose would provide a comfortable environment. The cool tones of blues, greens, and grays would create a restful environment for chronically ill clients. Relaxation of the surgical clients could be accomplished with the use of greens and blue-greens. Certain colors should be avoided in health care institutions such as those that cast unfavorable reflections on the human complexion—yellow-greens, yellow, and lavender.

C. Answer the following questions about the selection you just read.

16. Does a particular color affect everyone the same way?   Yes   No

17. If you see a color you like, how does your body react? _____

18. What kind of colors can be distracting, causing discomfort? _____

_____

19. Colors at which end of the spectrum cause arousal? _____

20. What is the exception? _____

In Lesson 8, you learned the first step in the MAPP reading plan: changing headings into questions and marking the answers. That first step can only be taken when the reading selection has a title and headings.

The A of MAPP Is "About."

In this lesson, we will discuss another question you can ask when there are no headings. The question is "What is the reading about?" The "A" of MAPP stands for "About." What a reading is about is its **topic.** So answering this question will lead you to the topic.

The "A" of MAPP Stands for "About"

Mark = **Mark** the answers to your questions.

About = Topic: What is the reading **about**?

Point = Main Idea: What is the **point**?

Proof = Supporting Detail: What is the **proof**?

MAPP will help you find your way through a reading selection. Using a MAPP every time you read will improve your reading comprehension.

What Is the Reading About? The Topic.

Everything you read is about something—a topic, or subject. In fact, the words "subject" and "topic" are synonyms for the answer to the question, "What is the reading about?"

Think for a moment about a piece of writing you have done. First, you had to decide what you were going to write about. Reading is similar to writing. When you are reading, finding the topic is also a good place to start.

One way to find the topic is to look for repeated words throughout the passage. The other is to think about which idea in the passage is the most general.

The Topic Is Repeated.

If you are in a conversation with your friend Julia and she says, "My new apartment is so much nicer than my old one. It's a two-bedroom apartment. It's also got a dishwasher. The apartment even has a patio!" then you know that Julia's topic of conversation is her new apartment. The same is true in reading.

Spotlight on Inference: Finding the Topic by Noticing Repeated Words

Recall that **inference** is the process of noticing several bits of information and then putting them together to make meaning. Here, the bits of information you should look for are repeated words and ideas. It stands to reason that if a word is repeated several times, that word indicates what the reading selection is about: its topic.

> Extinction is a natural process. Species arise and become extinct on an ongoing basis. The rate of extinction picks up dramatically during a mass extinction, when many kinds of organisms in many different habitats all become extinct in a relatively short period.
>
> —Starr, Evers, & Starr, *Biology: Today and Tomorrow*, 3rd edition

You can infer (use your logic, or make inferences) that the paragraph is about extinction from all the times the author uses forms of the word *extinction*. Compare that to the number of times the author uses other words—*process, species, arise, basis,* and so on—and you'll see that this paragraph is clearly about extinction.

Another way to use inference in finding the topic is to notice when pronouns are used instead of the topic word:

Barack Obama is the first African-American president of the United States of America. He is the 44th president . . .

Kevin Lamarque/Reuters/Landov

The pronoun *he* is used instead of repeating President Obama's name. Other pronouns to watch out for are *I, you, she, it, we,* and *they.* When you see these pronouns, think about who or what the author is referring to. In the example, the *he* means that the author has referred to Obama twice, not once. Obama is the topic of these sentences.

The Topic Is Like a Title

A good way to think about the topic is that it is like a title. Both the topic and the title tell what a reading is about. If you are marking the text as you read, you might want to write the topic in the margin to spark your memory when you come back to review for a test. The marginal note acts as a title—it focuses your attention on the topic.

Adolescents must usually start choosing courses in school by the age of 14 or 15. By then, their gender ideologies are well formed. Gender ideologies are sets of interrelated ideas about what constitutes appropriate masculine and feminine roles and behavior. One aspect of gender ideology becomes especially important around grades 9 and 10: adolescents' ideas about whether, as adults, they will focus mainly on the home, paid work outside the home, or a combination of the two.

gender ideology

—Brym & Lee, *Sociology,* brief edition

INTERACTION 3–11   Identifying the Topic of a Group of Sentences

Read each group of sentences and decide what the topic is.

A. Ask the question "What is this about?"

B. Look for repeated words, and mark them as you read. Remember the pronouns!

C. Create a title for the sentences that shows the topic.

1. • Rio de Janeiro, Brazil, is full of fun, great food, and nightlife.

   • Brazil has many beautiful beaches.

   • Brazilians are quite friendly.

   • Brazil has a captivating history and culture.

   What is a good title? _Brazil is a beautiful place for vacation_

2. • Adoptions match prospective parents with a child who needs a family.

   • Couples interested in adoption can work with public agencies or private counselors.

   • They can also work with organizations that help people adopt children from other countries.

   • Even if you can't conceive, you can still become a parent through adoption.

   What is a good title? _How to get information for people who want to adopt_

3. • The "Bunny Ears" method is a creative strategy for teaching children to tie their own shoes.

   • First, the child should make a knot for the bunny's head. Take the shoelaces and cross them over each other to make an "X." Then, pull one lace or "ear" through the bottom of the "X" and pull it tight.

   • Have the child give her bunny ears by looping the laces.

   • Next, have the child tighten the "bunny ears" (so the bunny doesn't lose its ears). This is done by making another "X" with the "bunny ears," and then putting one "ear" under the "X" and pulling it tight.

   What is a good title? _Bunny Ears Method of tieing shoes_

4. • Physics is a tough subject.

   • Like many other subjects it takes time and dedication.

   • You need a realistic goal and consistent work to do well in a physics class.

   • However, if you approach physics with a good attitude, it can be fun and rewarding.

   What is a good title? _____ *Physics* _____

5. • Can you imagine a world without music?

   • No iPods, no CDs, no concerts, no worship services, no elevator music!

   • The world would certainly be a dreary place without music.

   • It is no surprise that music exists in every culture.

   What is a good title? _____ *Music* _____

INTERACTION 3–12   **Identifying the Topic of a Paragraph**

Read each group of sentences and decide what the topic is.

   A. Ask the question "What is this about?"
   B. Look for repeated words, and mark them as you read. Remember the pronouns!
   C. Create a title for the sentences that shows the topic.

Paragraph 1   **Speech Textbook**

> When you preview your speech, you share with your audience a brief overview of each of the main points in your speech. Previews are necessary in any introduction because they prepare your audience for listening to your speech. They communicate to your audience that you are organized and competent, setting the stage for the body of the speech. Previews help your audience organize their thoughts about what they're going to hear.
>
> —Griffin, *Invitation to Public Speaking*, 2nd edition

What is the topic? _____ *Speech Preview* _____

Paragraph 2   **Biology Textbook**

Roughly speaking, your heart is located in the center of your chest. Its structure reflects its role as a long-lasting pump. The heart is mostly cardiac muscle tissue, the myocardium. A tough, fibrous sac, the pericardium (peri = around), surrounds, protects, and lubricates it. The heart's chambers have a smooth lining (endocardium) composed of connective tissue and a layer of epithelial cells. The epithelial cell layer, known as endothelium, also lines the inside of blood vessels.

—Starr & McMillan, *Human Biology*, 8th edition

What is the topic? _The heart_

Paragraph 3   **Success Skills Textbook**

As a general rule, the amount of study time a college student needs for studying or doing schoolwork is based on the number of hours he or she attends class each week. For every hour you spend in the classroom, you should set aside in your weekly calendar at least an equal number of hours for doing homework, reviewing, practicing or studying. For example, if you are in class six hours a week, then you should allocate at least six hours of study sometime during that week. If you require more time to learn—perhaps because you are not using effective or efficient learning strategies—you may need two hours study time for each class hour. If you have a light amount of homework or are efficient at getting it done you will find yourself with unexpected free time.

—Beale, *Success Skills: Strategies for Study and Lifelong Learning*, 3rd edition

What is the topic? _Study Time_

Paragraph 4   **Health Care Textbook**

Intense fear, sometimes known as phobia, daily impacts the lives of some individuals. Three common phobias are acrophobia, claustrophobia, and agoraphobia. Acrophobia is the fear of high places, and claustrophobia is fear of being confined in any small space. Agoraphobia is a fear of public places, and usually develops after having one or more panic attacks.

—Tamparo & Lindh, *Therapeutic Communications for Health Care*, 3rd edition

What is the topic? _____ Phobia _____

Paragraph 5   **Biology Textbook**

> An estuary is a mostly enclosed coastal region where seawater mixes with nutrient-rich fresh water from rivers and streams. Water inflow continually replenishes nutrients, so estuaries have a high primary productivity. Estuaries serve as marine nurseries for many invertebrates and fishes. Migratory ducks and geese often use them as rest stops. Estuaries need a constant inflow of unpolluted, fresh water to remain healthy.
>
> —Starr, Evers, & Starr, *Biology: Today and Tomorrow,* 3rd edition

What is the topic? _____ Estuary _____

The Topic Is General.

The topic is often repeated, as we have discussed. The other main characteristic of a topic is that it is more general than the other ideas in the reading selection. So to find the topic of a reading, you need to be able to tell the difference between general and specific ideas.

Which of the following is the most general word?

grapes   apples   oranges   fruit   cherries

As you can see, there are four examples of fruit, so the topic here is "fruit." The other words are specific kinds of fruit. To show which words are general and which ones are specific, indent the more specific words:

General topic   Fruit
                        1. Grapes
Specific   2. Apples
items are   3. Oranges
indented.   4. Cherries

As you read, remember the topic will be the most general idea.

A topic needs to be distinguished from the main idea and the supporting details, which we'll talk about in Lessons 10 and 11. To distinguish the topic, look for a general concept in a paragraph that is supported by the other, more specific information. Also, remember that a topic is never a complete sentence; rather, it is only a single word or a phrase.

INTERACTION 3–13   **Choosing the Most General Word**

Circle the general category that the other, more specific items fit into.

1. fish	tuna	salmon	mahi-mahi	grouper
2. basketball	soccer	sports	golf	Ping-Pong
3. Calvin Klein	Christian Dior	Gucci	Prada	fashion designers
4. John Grisham	authors	J. K. Rowling	Stephen King	Toni Morrison
5. fork	spoon	knife	utensils	chopsticks
6. finger	thumb	hand	palm	knuckle
7. mastiff	poodle	boxer	canines	beagle
8. ring types	engagement ring	wedding ring	graduation ring	purity ring
9. Red Delicious	Granny Smith	apples	Honeycrisp	Fuji
10. mustard	condiments	ketchup	mayonnaise	barbecue sauce

Distinguishing General and Specific Activities

If you can see which idea is the broadest or most general, then you should be able to identify the topic of the material you are reading.

Mark the most general idea:

_____ Place your head on the ground near the base of a wall.

_____ Place your hands flat on the ground by either ear to provide balance.

_____ How to do a headstand.

_____ Raise one leg and use the other leg to push both legs straight.

You should have marked "how to do a headstand." Each of the other ideas is one part of doing a headstand, and thus is more specific.

INTERACTION 3–14	Selecting the Most General Activity

Put an X in the space for the topic, or most general activity.

1. _____ Hammering nails

   _____ Choosing lumber

   __✓__ Building a fence

   _____ Digging post holes

2. _____ Cutting the vegetables

   _____ Seasoning the fish

   _____ Mashing the potatoes

   _____ Cooking dinner

3. _____ Practicing good hygiene

   _____ Brushing teeth

   _____ Flossing

   _____ Bathing

4. _____ Picking a topic

   _____ Brainstorming

   _____ Writing a paper

   _____ Creating an outline

5. _____ Jacking up the car

   _____ Changing a flat tire

   _____ Removing lug nuts

   _____ Putting the new tire in place

Stating Topics in Your Own Words

Now that you have practiced finding the difference between general and specific ideas, you can state the topic of a group of ideas in your own words.

What is the topic of the following list of examples? _____

   Macy's

   Sears

JCPenney

Dillard's

These are all names of department stores, so "department stores" is the general topic. Now practice on your own.

INTERACTION 3–15	Stating the Topic in Your Own Words

State the topic of each list of items using your own words.

1. Jogging

   Yoga

   Pilates

   Weight lifting

   What is this list about? Topic: _____ *going to the gym* _____

2. Headache

   Fever

   Muscle aches

   Sore throat

   What is this list about? Topic: _____ *Flu* _____

3. The turkey must be completely thawed.

   Remove the neck and giblets.

   Have a pan ready (oven bag recommended).

   Season the turkey (stuffing optional).

   The internal temperature should be 175° in the thickest part of the breast.

   What is this list about? Topic: _____ *Cooking a turkey* _____

4. Talk about stress with friends and family.

   Exercise regularly.

   Breathe deeply, think peaceful thoughts, and relax.

   Accept things that you cannot change.

   What is this list about? Topic: _____ *releaving stress* _____

5. Have a budget.

Plan your spending in advance.

Know your long-term financial goals.

Set short-term rewards.

What is this list about? Topic: ___How to mangie your money___

Finding the Topic of a Sentence

When you are reading, you are often looking for the topic of a paragraph or longer selection. However, you also have to read one sentence at a time. So let's look at finding the topics of individual sentences. You will ask the same question for sentences as you do to find the topic at any level: "What is this about?"

Here is an example to get you started. Put a bracket around the topic:

> Michael Jackson's death on June 25, 2009, shocked the world.

The topic is Michael Jackson's death. You should have bracketed that phrase as you read the sentence. If you did not, go back now and do so. The other parts of the sentence give specific details about Jackson's death: the date he died, and how the world responded.

Notice that topics answer the question "What?" If you want to check your understanding of what the topic is, ask this question about the details:

What happened on June 25, 2009? Michael Jackson died.

What shocked the world? Michael Jackson's death.

If all the "what" questions lead to the same answer, then you know you have correctly identified the topic.

INTERACTION 3-16	Identifying the Topic of Sentences

Put brackets around the [topic] of each of the following sentences. As you read these sentences, ask yourself what the sentence is about.

1. [Lee DeWyze] won the 2010 *American Idol* competition.
2. Brushing your teeth and flossing daily are important parts of [good oral hygiene.]
3. A person interested in owning and riding a motorcycle should attend a [motorcycle rider-training course] to learn how to safely and skillfully operate a bike.
4. Apple sold more than 10 million [iPhones] in 2008.
5. [Jeans] used to be called "waist overalls" until 1960 when Levi Strauss & Co. coined the word we use today.
6. In 2007, [U.S. consumption of beef] exceeded 28 billion pounds.
7. The [border collie] is considered the smartest breed of dog.
8. [Stephenie Meyer] is the best-selling author famous for the *Twilight* series.
9. The ["poison dart" frog] got its common name because of the toxin it secretes, which is sometimes used to poison the tip of blow darts used by Indians in Central and South America.
10. [Pilates,] originally called "contrology," was created by Joseph Pilates while he was a prisoner in an internment camp during World War II to help him and his fellow prisoners stay strong and healthy.

INTERACTION 3-17	Identifying the Topic of Paragraphs

Read each paragraph and decide what the topic is.
  A. Ask "What is this about?"
  B. Mark repeated words or general ideas as you read. (Some paragraphs may not have repeated words, but each has a topic.)
  C. Write down the topic.

Paragraph 1   **Internet Sources**

The movie *Titanic,* starring Leonardo DiCaprio and Kate Winslet, is one of the most successful box office films of all time. Since its release in 1997, it has grossed almost $2 billion. In addition to its financial success, the film also won 11 Academy Awards. And it is a good thing that *Titanic* was successful; the film cost $200 million to make and almost bankrupted Paramount Pictures and 20th Century Fox.

What is this about? Topic: _____

Paragraph 2   Health Textbook

Legal in most states, gambling can take many forms: lottery, scratch cards, casino games, sports betting, Internet gambling, horse and racetrack wagering, videogame betting, and playing cards and dice. In a national survey, about eight in ten adults—and the same percentage of 12 to 17 year-olds—reported they had gambled the last year.

—Hales, *An Invitation to Health,* 12th edition

Hermes Images/PhotoLibrary

What is this about? Topic: _____

Paragraph 3   Management Textbook

Abraham Maslow's motivation theory, commonly referred to as the hierarchy of needs, is based on two key assumptions. First, different needs are active at different times, and only needs not yet satisfied can influence behavior. Second, needs are arranged in a fixed order of importance called a hierarchy, which is where the term hierarchy of needs comes from.

—Adapted from Dumler & Skinner,
A Primer for Management, 2nd edition

What is this about? Topic: _____

Paragraph 4   History Textbook

Mesopotamian civilization began around 3000 B.C.E. in Sumeria, the rich agricultural delta where the Tigris and Euphrates Rivers empty into the Persian Gulf. The Mesopotamian civilization was built on cities. Twenty principal cities such as Uruk, Kish, and Ur had populations of over 50,000 each and occupied all of the farmland close to the rivers.

—Adapted from Kidner, Bucur, Mathisen, McKee, & Weeks,
Making Europe: People, Politics and Culture

What is this about? Topic: _____

Paragraph 5   Biology Textbook

Science requires an objective mind-set, and this means that scientists can only do certain kinds of studies. No experiments can explain the "meaning of life," for example, or why each of us dies at a certain moment. Those kinds of questions have subjective answers, shaped by our experiences and beliefs. It is these reasons that limit science to the realm of objective fact.

—Adapted from Starr & McMillan, *Human Biology*, 8th edition

What is this about? Topic: _____

> ## Review: What the Reading Is About—Its Topic
>
> Find the topic of a reading selection by asking "What is this about?" You can identify the topic in two ways:
>
> - The topic is often repeated. When a word is repeated throughout a reading, it often is the topic. Sometimes, pronouns are used instead of repeating nouns.
> - The topic is general. It is more general than the specific details in the selection.
>
> Remember that the topic is what the reading is about.

Decide How Broad or Narrow the Topic Is.

You have been practicing finding the topic in a variety of situations, and you may be thinking to yourself that finding a topic isn't very difficult. It's true that at times it can be pretty easy, especially if the topic is clearly stated in the title or is mentioned multiple times in the paragraph. However, finding the topic can be tricky at times.

The main problem when choosing the topic is determining how broad or how narrow the topic actually is. If you make the topic too broad, then it can include more information than the passage you are reading has in it. If the topic is too narrow, then some of the specific details in the selection will be left out. In this case, you are probably identifying a detail, not the topic.

Here is an example:

> There are a number of wonderful makers of sports cars in the world. However, some of the best are found in Europe. In Italy, you have Lamborghini and Ferrari. In Germany, you have Porsche and BMW. In England, you have Aston Martin and Morgan.

What is the topic?_____

At first glance, you might say the topic is *makers of sports cars*. But this topic is too broad because the specific details in the rest of the paragraph are not about makers of sports cars from all around the world. Another possible topic is *makers of Italian sports cars*. This topic, however, is too narrow, since Porsche and BMW are both German, and Aston Martin and Morgan are both English. If you wrote *makers of European sports cars*, you stated the topic accurately because Italy, Germany, and England are all in Europe.

INTERACTION 3–18	Identifying the Topic That Fits the Details Best

Read each group of sentences and decide what the topic is. Start with the question "What is this about?" Decide whether each possible topic is too broad, too narrow, or just right.

Group 1   Sociology Textbook

- Sociologists distinguish two types of deviance.
- Formal deviance is behavior that breaks laws or official rules.
- Informal deviance is behavior that violates customary norms.
- Although such deviance may not be specified in law, those who uphold the society's norm see it as deviant.

—Adapted from Anderson & Taylor, *Sociology: The Essentials*, 4th edition

How sociologists view the world	✓ broad	_____ narrow	_____ just right
Formal deviance	_____ broad	✓ narrow	_____ just right
Deviance	_____ broad	_____ narrow	✓ just right

Group 2   Management Textbook

- Social responsibility is the awareness that business activities have an impact on society.
- Society expects businesses to make a profit but also to obey laws and be good corporate citizens.
- In addition to emphasizing profits, firms concerned with social responsibility voluntarily engage in activities that benefit society, such as public education.
- A socially responsible firm makes deliberate, regular efforts to increase its positive impact on society while decreasing its negative impact.

—Adapted from Dumler & Skinner, *A Primer for Management*, 2nd edition

Public education	_____ broad	_____ narrow	_____ just right
Good corporate citizens	_____ broad	_____ narrow	_____ just right
Social responsibility	_____ broad	_____ narrow	_____ just right

Group 3   **Health Textbook**

- Most people know that maintaining desired body weight can lead to a longer and healthier life.
- For this reason, many individuals try many different types of diets to lose weight.
- Research has shown that even though these diets might lead to weight loss, they usually do not allow an individual to maintain weight when the diet is no longer used.
- When individuals resume their normal eating habits, the weight they lost is quickly regained.

—Adapted from Simmers, *Diversified Health Occupations*, 7th edition

Weight loss	_____ broad	_____ narrow	_____ just right
Managing weight	_____ broad	_____ narrow	_____ just right
Normal eating habits	_____ broad	_____ narrow	_____ just right

Group 4   **Physics Textbook**

- I want to shift the way you look at and approach problem solving.
- First, we all get stuck; the question is whether you work through your confusion systematically or you get hopelessly entangled in the process.
- Second, working through a tough problem requires a clear, methodical approach.
- Third, memorizing these guidelines won't do you much good. You must train yourself to USE them as you solve problems.

—Adapted from Celesia, *Preparation for Introductory College Physics: A Guided Student Primer*

Problem solving strategy	_____ broad	_____ narrow	_____ just right
Work through your confusion	_____ broad	_____ narrow	_____ just right
Problems	_____ broad	_____ narrow	_____ just right

Group 5   **Hospitality Textbook**

- Even though Bermuda isn't part of the Caribbean, it does have much in common with its southerly neighbors: fine beaches, beach resorts, and gorgeous weather.
- Remember three things about Bermuda.
- The hotels are expensive, though less so in the winter.
- Both air and water are chilly in the winter, when the only bargains can be had.

- Most visitors have to get around in taxis or on mopeds because rental cars are not allowed.

—Adapted from Mancini, *Selling Destinations: Geography for the Travel Professional*, 4th edition

toddtaulman/iStockphoto.com

The Caribbean	_____ broad	_____ narrow	_____ just right
Bermuda	_____ broad	_____ narrow	_____ just right
Bermuda's beaches and weather	_____ broad	_____ narrow	_____ just right

INTERACTION 3–19   Stating the Topic of Paragraphs

Read each paragraph and decide what the topic is. Start with the question "What is this about?" Mark repeated words or general ideas as you read. Create a topic that is the right size to fit the paragraph's specific details.

Paragraph 1   **Health Textbook**

Your risk of divorce depends on many factors. Simply having some college education improves your odds of a happy marriage. Other factors that do the same are an income higher than $50,000, marrying at age 25 or older, not having a baby during the first seven months after the wedding, coming from an intact family, and having some religious affiliation.

—Hales, *An Invitation to Health,* 12th edition

What is the topic? _____

Paragraph 2   Political Science Textbook

> Presidential elections are decided by electoral college votes, not popular votes. The electoral college consists of a group of people who vote officially for president and vice president. To win the presidency, a candidate must receive a majority (270) of electoral college votes. The number of a state's electoral college votes equals the number of senators plus representatives in the state. The presidential candidate who wins the popular vote of a state receives all the state's electoral college votes, with the exception of Maine and Nebraska, which split electoral college votes among candidates based on each candidate's popular vote.
>
> —Grigsby, *Analyzing Politics: An Introduction to Political Science*, 4th edition

What is the topic? _____

Paragraph 3   Education Textbook

> Many students think of assessments as tests of this traditional type, given at the end of a unit. However, the more we understand about how people learn, the more we realize that an assessment is like a good instructional task and should be a part of every lesson, providing feedback to both the teacher and the students about how the students are developing their understanding of the concepts in a unit.
>
> —Koch, *So You Want to Be a Teacher: Teaching and Learning in the 21st Century*

What is the topic? _____

Paragraph 4   Finance Textbook

> Several heath-related trends are behind the rising health insurance costs. First, recent advances in medical technology have resulted in advanced prescription drugs and new treatments. Although these advances are saving more lives than ever before, they also cost more to provide. The U.S. population is also aging, resulting in growing use of healthcare services. A poor demand-and-supply distribution of healthcare facilities and services may be

> yet another factor. Administrative costs, excessive paperwork, increased regulation, and insurance fraud are also contributing to rising healthcare costs.
>
> —Gitman & Joehnk, *Personal Finance Planning,* 11th edition

What is the topic? _____

Paragraph 5   **Health Textbook**

> Regular physical activity helps maintain a healthy weight and reduces risks for several chronic diseases. While 30 minutes of moderate physical activities (such as walking at a pace of three or four miles per hour) on most days provides important benefits, exercising more often and more intensely yields additional health dividends. Many adults need up to 60 minutes of moderate to vigorous physical activity—the equivalent of 150 to 200 calories, depending on body size—daily to prevent unhealthy weight gain.
>
> —Hales, *An Invitation to Health,* 12th edition

What is the topic? _____

INTERACTION 3–20   **Stating the Topic of Paragraphs**

The following paragraphs all come from one section of a college speech textbook. The section is entitled "Speakers As Listeners: Adapting to Your Audience." However, that topic alone is too broad for each paragraph because each one gives a specific example of a type of audience. Carefully read and mark the following paragraphs to identify the specific topic of each paragraph. Complete the title of each paragraph by writing the topic on the line provided.

Radius Images/Jupiter Images

Audiences Who _____

Sometimes audience members appear to be uninterested in your speech from the start or seem to assume they already know what you will say. Address this behavior by making your introduction and first main points compelling. Genet began his speech by saying, "You say you already know. You say, 'There's nothing new here!' You might even be thinking, 'This will never happen to me,' and maybe—just maybe—you're right. But what if you're wrong? What if you're probably wrong? Are you willing to be the two out of three who didn't listen?" After this introduction, he had the full attention of the class and was able to keep their attention throughout his speech on alcohol and drug addiction.

Audiences Who _____

Some audience members may slouch, fail to make eye contact, and daydream. Others make or attend to distractions. To counter this behavior, ask questions of the entire audience or of particular members. Ask them to complete an activity related to your topic, such as making a list or jotting down what they already know about the topic. Bring particularly disruptive people into your speech. You can do this by talking or you can bring them to the front of the audience for a legitimate reason. For example, you could ask them to give a demonstration or to record discussion ideas on a white board.

Audiences Who _____

If your audience is staring at your unusual style of clothing or is straining to understand you because of differences in speech styles, take a moment to explain what the distraction means to you and why it's there. Angelique was a student with a strong accent. She shared with her audience that she was from the Dominican Republic. She explained that her husband kept trying to correct her accent but she told him, "It's my accent and I like it." Sharing this story in the introduction of her speech helped reduce the focus on her accent and enabled her audience to listen to her message instead.

Audiences Who _____

You can use a number of strategies to help audiences who appear confused by the information in your speech. You can slow down, explain with more detail, reduce your number of main points, or alter your language. Even if you had not planned to use visual aids, use an overhead projector or board, or ask someone from the audience to demonstrate your ideas. For example, Marilyn saw her audience looking confused, so she outlined her main points on the board and jotted down key words and phrases. The audience responded by saying that her speech was much easier to follow with a visual map.

Audiences Who _____

Sometimes certain audience members appear to be planning their responses to you during your speech. Acknowledge their eagerness to participate, and recognize it as a positive sign of interest. Doing so can bring a listener into your speech and help everyone feel they can express themselves. Hallie watched a member of her audience react with a frown to one of her claims and then fidget and sit on the edge of his seat. She acknowledged his desire to respond by saying, "I see I've struck a chord with some of you. If you'll hang on to your questions and hear me out, I'd love to hear your reactions at the end of the speech." He relaxed a bit and was able to put his opposition aside enough to listen to her full arguments and reasons. The conversation at the end of the speech was lively and dynamic, and both Hallie and the audience member benefited from it.

—Griffin, *Invitation to Public Speaking,* 2nd edition

Review: Topics That Fit the Specific Details

State the topic of a reading selection at the right size, or level of generality.

- The topic should not be so broad that it requires more information to support it than is given in the passage.
- The topic should not be so narrow that it can't include all the information given in the passage.
- The topic should be just broad enough to fit all the specifics the author has given.

ACTIVATE YOUR SKILLS 1
Finding the Topic or Subject of a Sentence

As you read these sentences, ask yourself "What is the sentence about?" Put brackets around the [topic] of each of the following sentences.

1. Hindu death rituals have followed a consistent and common arrangement throughout most of India for thousands of years.

2. Postpartum depression is an extreme form of "baby blues" that can last anywhere from a few months to a year.

3. There are three important actions that promote multicultural communication.

4. Stress is a part of life, no matter what stage of life people find themselves in.

5. It is rare to find a family that has not been impacted in some negative way by substance abuse.

6. Professionals have identified three categories of rape.

7. Courses in music have increased dramatically on the college and university level for several reasons.

8. Dr. Dre, whose real name is Andre Romelle Young, is a famous record producer and executive, rapper, and actor.

9. Think of France, and you think of Paris.

10. Registered nurses enjoy one of the hottest careers with more than one million job offerings over the next 10 years.

ACTIVATE YOUR SKILLS 2
Finding the Topic in Groups of Sentences and Paragraphs

A. Determine the topics for the following groups of sentences.

1. Topic: _____

   - Have a job. (It can pay an average income.)

   - Have a plan. (It's called a budget.)

   - Live on less than you make. (Avoid debt.)

   - Save and invest. (Compound interest, baby.)

   - Following this basic financial advice does lead to financial success.

2. Topic: _____

- The following issues can cause divorce:

- Poor communication

- Financial issues, such as debt or different spending habits

- Having differing views on core values, such as religion

- Lack of commitment to partner

- Differing priorities

3. Topic: _____

- Exercise can help you maintain a healthy weight.

- Exercise can improve your mood.

- Exercise increases your energy.

- Exercise deepens your breathing, which helps with stress management.

- Exercise improves your self-esteem.

4. Topic: _____

- Understand the teacher's homework policies.

- Explain the importance of homework to your child.

- Help your child be organized by making a homework calendar.

- Establish a consistent time and place to do homework.

- Turn off the TV and put away the phone.

- Check homework for completion and understanding.

- Reward your child for good work habits and grades.

- Encourage and model reading for fun.

5. Topic: _____

- Provide role models in the form of highly qualified women or minority instructors, and also introduce historical figures who were mathematicians or scientists.

- Get a group of students to talk about a math problem before using numbers, mathematical symbols, or equations. Show that even wrong answers can be useful in helping other people look at the problem.

- Find a way to visualize a math problem in more concrete terms, perhaps using real-life questions of size, distance, time, or money.

- Discuss the quantitative problem in terms of ordinary words or pictures.

- Translate the problem into the formal English of mathematics.

- Translate the formal description of the problem into mathematical terms and only then try to solve the mathematical equation.

—Diverse: Issues in Higher Education Web site

B. Identify the topic of the following paragraphs. Mark any repeated ideas as you read.

6. Topic: _____

An academic calendar is made up of twelve monthly calendars, typically from September to August. It is meant to be used by people going to school or taking training courses. Whether your school runs on a quarterly, trimester, or yearly schedule, an academic calendar is flexible enough to accommodate everyone.

—Beale, *Success Skills,* 3rd edition

7. Topic: _____

Setting goals is great, but just making a goal is not enough. You need to make sure your goal is SMART, which stands for:

- **Specific** (What is your goal?)
- **Measurable** (How will you know when you've achieved it?)
- **Active** (What are you going to do?)
- **Realistic** (Can you reach it?)
- **Timely** (When will you reach it?)

Making your goals SMART will increase your chances of reaching them.

8. Topic: _____

There are many fun words in English. And while each person might have a different opinion of what "fun" means, you might agree that at least one of the following two words are fun.

Argle-bargle is a made-up word combining "argue" and "haggle" for *argle,* and then *bargle* is added just because it rhymes with *argle.* This fun word refers to bickering or arguing. I like to yell at my kids, "Stop argle-bargleing before I come in there and smacky-whacky you!" (They never take me seriously, though.) Another fun word is **canoodle.** This word means to make out. Now admittedly, making out is fun, but doesn't it sound like even more fun to canoodle?

9. Topic: _____

The manner in which crimes are classified depends on their seriousness. Federal, state, and local legislation has provided for the classification and punishment of hundreds of thousands of different criminal acts, ranging from jaywalking to first-degree murder. For general purposes, we can group criminal behavior into six categories: violent crime, property crime, public order crime, white-collar crime, organized crime, and high-tech crime.

—Gaines & Miller, *Criminal Justice in Action,* 5th edition

10. Topic: _____

Beyoncé, Bono, Bruce Springsteen, John Mayer, Justin Timberlake, Lady Gaga, Madonna, and Wyclef Jean, a native of Haiti, were just a few of the musical celebrities who helped raise money for Haiti after a 7.0 magnitude earthquake struck on January 12, 2010. In one telethon, celebrities raised more than $166 million. And movie stars did their part, too. Sandra Bullock, Leonardo DiCaprio, Brangelina, and George Clooney each personally gave $1 million to help with relief efforts. Sports celebrities lent a helping hand as well. Tiger Woods donated $3 million, and Lance Armstrong donated $250,000.

MASTER YOUR SKILLS 1
Finding the Topic of Paragraphs

Identify the topic of the following passages. Mark any repeated ideas as you read.

1. Topic: How to achieve _____

In the past, to achieve stardom, you had to "beat the pavement" for years. If you were in music, you had to do endless road tours in unknown cities in places of questionable reputation. If you were in TV, you had to be in a hemorrhoid commercial or in a role that compromised your artistic or moral values so you could "make it." If you were lucky, the years of hard work and embarrassing roles would pay off and make you a superstar. Today, it is different. Any yahoo with a video camera can upload a video to YouTube and become an overnight sensation. Any "average joe" with a few dance moves or a decent voice can win a reality show and achieve instant stardom.

2. Topic: _____Labrador retriever_____

The gentle, intelligent, and family-friendly Labrador retriever is the most popular breed in the United States for the 18th consecutive year, according to American Kennel Club registration statistics. Because of their aptitude to please their masters, Labradors excel as guide dogs for the blind, as part of search-and-rescue teams, and in narcotics detection with law enforcement.

—AKC MEET THE BREEDS®: Labrador Retriever. © The American Kennel Club, Inc.

3. Topic: _____Hypothermia_____

Very low body temperatures are indicative of abnormal conditions. Hypothermia is what happens when body temperature drops below 95° (35° C). Causes of hypothermia are starvation or fasting, sleep, decreased muscle activity, mouth breathing, exposure to cold temperatures, and certain diseases. Death usually occurs if body temperature drops below 93° (33.9° C) for a period of time.

—Adapted from Simmers, Simmers-Nartker, & Simmers-Kobelak,
Diversified Health Occupations, 7th edition

4. Topic: _____Disease_____

In a pandemic, a disease breaks out and spreads worldwide. AIDS is a pandemic that has no end in sight. A 2002–2003 outbreak of SARS (severe acute respiratory syndrome) was a brief pandemic. It began in China, and travelers quickly carried it to thirty countries around the world. Before government-ordered quarantines (isolation of those infected) halted its spread, about 8,000 people were sickened. About 10 percent of them died.

—Starr, Evers, & Starr, *Biology: Today and Tomorrow,* 3rd edition

5. Topic: _____Stuck at Prom_____

1   Have you ever considered making your prom dress or suit out of duct tape? No? How about for $3,000?

2   Duck brand Duct Tape has been organizing the "Stuck at Prom" competition for 10 straight years, challenging students to create original prom costumes using as much duct tape as possible. Competitors' costumes are judged according to the following criteria: workmanship, originality, use of color, accessories, and amount of duct tape used. The 10 best costumes are subjected to an online vote.

3   First-place winners of "Stuck at Prom" receive a $3,000 scholarship, second place gets $2,000, third place $1,000, and runners up receive $500. It may not seem like much, but in these troubled times any penny counts. And plus, you get to wear a cheap prom costume that will definitely catch everyone's eyes.

—Reprinted with permission from Oddity Central.
Copyright © Oddity Central. www.odditycentral.com

(CB/WNJ/WENN.com/Newscom

6. Topic: _____ *Allergies* _____

1   Do you have allergies? Maybe it is where you live that is making you sniffle! When it comes to spring allergies, the amount of Kleenex one goes through varies year to year, often depending on Mother Nature, personal triggers, and where you live.

2   What is the worst place for sufferers? Tulsa, Okla. That's according to a report out from the Asthma and Allergy Foundation of America. A not-for-profit organization that provides information, community-based services, and a support network, it has culled 2006 data and ranked the worst cities for spring allergies based on three factors: pollen counts, medication usage by allergy patients, and the number of board-certified allergists per patient. Dallas–Fort Worth came in second. The trigger for all the top allergy cities seemed to be the same thing—mild winters.

—Adapted from *Forbes* Web site

7. Topic: _____ *The media* _____

To make a profit, the media have to be responsive to the people. They present the news they think the people want. Because they believe the majority desire entertainment, or at least diversion, rather than education, they structure the news toward this goal. For the majority who want entertainment, national and local television and radio provide it. For the minority who want education, the better newspapers and magazines provide it. Public radio, with its morning and evening newscasts, and public television, with its nightly newscast, also provide quality coverage. In addition, Internet websites provide news on demand. The media offer something for everyone.

—Welch, Gruhl, Comer, & Rigdon, *Understanding American Government: The Essentials*

8. Topic: _____ *Women in poverty* _____

Many poor women worldwide do not have access to commercial credit and have trained only in traditionally female skills that produce low wages. These factors have contributed to the global feminization of poverty, whereby women around the world tend to be more impoverished than men. Despite the fact that women have made some gains in terms of well-being, the income gap between men and women continues to grow wider in the low-income, developing nations as well as in the high-income, developed nations such as the United States.

—Kendall, *Sociology in Our Times*, 7th edition

9. Topic: _____Benin_____

The kingdom of Benin already had a long history of political and cultural achievement before the arrival of the first Europeans in the sixteenth century. Descendants of Oduduwa (oh-doo-doo-wah), ancestor of all Yoruba kings, Benin's rulers, the *obas,* were associated with great spiritual powers. The artists of Benin were organized into a guild by the Benin king in the fourteenth century, and began producing magnificent brass sculptures of royalty. Their achievement became known for its technical and artistic qualities. The Benin bronzes were known for their naturalism, a quality that made them highly attractive to European collectors.

—Adapted from Hansen & Curtis, *Voyages in World History*

10. Topic: _____Be an active Reader_____

Read, reread, re-reread, drill, train, practice, work things out without looking at the answers, ask yourself questions, work in groups, ask your instructor questions, work with classmates, read other resources—in other words, do whatever it takes to be an active learner. The following elements are fundamental to any effective and efficient study routine. Discipline yourself to implement the plan and you will reap the benefits.

1. **Pre-read** material to be covered in class. Then reread as needed.
2. Keep a **study journal**—include anything that you aren't totally clear on, big or small.
3. Get your **questions answered.** Then check off the question in your journal.
4. Create **summaries.**
5. **Practice regularly.** An absolute minimum of 15 minutes a day. (It makes a bigger difference than most people realize.)
6. **Talk** about the material with others on a regular basis—an absolute must do.
7. Consciously implement **memorization techniques.**

—Celesia, *Preparation for Introductory College Physics: A Guided Student Primer*

MASTER YOUR SKILLS 2
Finding the Topic in Paragraphs and Lists

A. Identify the topic of the following passages. Mark any repeated ideas as you read.

1. Topic: _____

One of the most important elements of financial planning is understanding the difference between gross and net income. Gross income is your income before taxes, insurance costs, and other deductions are taken out. Net income is your income after deductions are made from it—it is the amount you actually take home. Although employers quote the gross salary (amount before taxes) as your wages, the amount you actually receive is less because of federal, state and local taxes and insurance costs that are deducted from the gross salary. As a result, it is important to plan your finances based on your net, versus your gross, income.

—Solomon, Tyler, & Taylor, *100% Career Success*

2. Topic: _____

If your credit score is not as high as you would like, there are some strategies you can implement to improve it over time.

- Always pay your bills on time. Late payments play a major role in driving down your score.

- If you have past-due bills now, get current and stay that way.

- Contact your creditors as soon as you know you will have a problem paying bills on time. Try to work out a payment arrangement and negotiate with them to keep at least a portion of the late notations off of your credit reports.

- Keep your credit card balances low. High debt-to-credit-limit ratios drive your scores down.

- Pay off debt, don't move it around. Owing the same amounts, but having fewer open accounts, can lower your score if you max out the accounts involved.

- Don't close unused accounts, because zero balance might help your score.

While all of these tips may help improve your credit score, remember that it does take time, so be patient and responsible.

—About.com: *Home Buying/Selling* Web site

3. Topic: _____

The cost to business due to employees surfing the Web during work hours exceeds one billion dollars annually. Although choosing not to abuse the Internet can be an ethical decision made by individual employees, many employees use the Internet for nonbusiness reasons during work nonetheless, and employers have had to take action in order to diminish the high cost of this misuse. Approximately 80% of employers use some type of monitoring system to track employees' use of the Internet and e-mail.

—Solomon, Tyler, & Taylor, *100% Career Success*

4. Topic: _____

What is cashmere? Cashmere is the underdown shed annually by goats living in the high, dry plateaus surrounding the Gobi Desert, which stretch from Northern China into Mongolia. These goats have a coarse outer hair that repels the weather. Under that outer coat lies a much finer fiber, cashmere, which insulates these animals from the bitter cold.

Why is cashmere so expensive? The harsh geography of this area of the Gobi Desert supports a very limited number of goats. It takes one of these rare goats four years to grow enough cashmere for one sweater. Each goat is combed by hand every spring. Then the fleece is collected and sorted by hand. Cashmere sweaters are usually knit on hand-operated machines. Therefore, the scarcity of the fiber and the handwork required to convert that fiber into a luxurious garment both contribute to cashmere's price.

—*Ben Silver: Classic Style* Web site

5. Topic: _____

Teens and young adults are more likely in their free time to check their Facebook page than read a book.

And they are dumber for it.

That is Mark Bauerlein's contention in *The Dumbest Generation: How the Digital Age Stupefies Young Americans and Jeopardizes Our Future (Or, Don't Trust Anyone Under 30)*, recently released in paperback (Tarcher/Penguin, 236 pp.).

Bauerlein, an English professor at Emory University in Atlanta, says Generation Y, ages 16–29, has been shaped by exposure to computer technology since elementary school.

The cost, he says, outweighs the convenience. Kids are writing more than ever online or in text messages, but it's not the kind of narrative skill needed as adults, he says. "Those forms groove bad habits, so when it comes time to produce an academic paper . . . or when they enter the workplace, their capacity breaks down."

Social networking sites can give young users "the sense of them being the center of the universe," Bauerlein says.

That gives them a distorted understanding of how the world works, he says. "If you go into a room of strangers, you don't know how to relate. You can't replicate your IM habits," he says. "It closes people off from a wider engagement with the world."

Parents must do more to pull their teens away from technology, including being role models in developing intellectual pursuits: "Talk with your kids. Kids can't do this by themselves."

—*USA Today* Web site, June 3, 2009

6. Topic: _____

NBC said on the eve of Sunday's Super Bowl that it has sold the last two of the 69 advertising spots for the game, pushing total ad revenue for the event to a record $206 million.

The network said its total of $261 million in ad revenue for all of Super Bowl day also is a record, calling it an especially impressive feat in the middle of the economy's steep downturn.

The Super Bowl is the premier advertising event with a U.S. audience of 100 million viewers, many of whom watch closely during game breaks for the debut of entertaining, big-budget commercials. The ads have sold for between $2.4 million and $3 million per 30-second slot this year.

"These advertising milestones show the power of the NFL brand and the strength of the Super Bowl as a TV property in this economic climate," said Jeff Zucker, president and CEO of NBC Universal, a unit of General Electric Co. "The Super Bowl has become one of our country's biggest holidays, a uniquely American day, and advertisers recognized the value in being a part of it."

Thirty-two advertisers in all will showcase their products during Super Bowl coverage.

—*NBC Sports* Web site, January 31, 2009

7. Topic: _____

Fluoride exists naturally in water sources and is derived from fluorine, the thirteenth most common element in the Earth's crust. It is well known that fluoride helps prevent and even reverse the early stages of tooth decay. Fluoride combats tooth decay in two ways. It is incorporated into the structure of developing teeth when it is ingested and also works when it comes in contact with the surface of the teeth. Fluoride prevents the acid produced by the bacteria in plaque from dissolving, or demineralizing, tooth enamel, the hard and shiny substance that protects the teeth. Fluoride also allows teeth damaged by acid to repair, or remineralize, themselves. Fluoride cannot repair cavities, but it can reverse low levels of tooth decay and thus prevent new cavities from forming.

—*Kids Health* Web site

8. Topic: _____

One basic way to categorize religions is by the number of gods or goddesses they worship. Monotheism is the worship of a single god. Christianity, Judaism, and Islam are monotheistic in that they all believe in a single god. Monotheistic religions typically define god as omnipotent (all-powerful) and omniscient (all-knowing). Polytheism is the worship of more than one deity.

Hinduism, for example, is extraordinarily complex with millions of gods, demons, sages, and heroes—all overlapping and entangled in religious mythology; within Hinduism, the universe is seen as so vast that it is believed to be beyond the grasp of a single individual, even a powerful god.

—Adapted from Anderson & Taylor, *Sociology: The Essentials*, 4th edition

B. Create a title for the following lists, marking repeated words as you read.

9. Title: _____

1. Use attentive body language—an attentive listener will lean forward, make eye contact, and face a customer squarely. Actions speak louder than words.

2. Focus—when listening to a customer, try not to be distracted by other thoughts you may have or other visual distractions.

3. Listen more than you speak—you have two ears and one mouth for a reason. If you are speaking you can't hear what the customer is saying and thus you are defeating the purpose of listening.

4. Have an open mind—just because you may dislike what a customer is saying doesn't give you the right to ignore it. Try to be open to all ideas and views that a customer may be expressing. After all, your view may not be the right one either.

5. Don't jump to conclusions—don't judge customers by their race, religion, or anything else. Every customer deserves respect. Customers should not be interrupted by you or have to contend with you completing their sentences—it is rude and inconsiderate.

6. Show understanding—if a customer is speaking to you, make sure to acknowledge that you are hearing him or her. No one wants to speak to a wall. You should provide encouraging responses where needed, reflect the customer's feelings, and summarize that you understand what the customer has expressed.

—Adapted from *Ezine Articles: Effective Listening Skills* Web site

10. Title: _____

1. Communications Skills (listening, verbal, written). By far, the one skill mentioned most often by employers is the ability to listen, write, and speak effectively. Successful communication is critical in business.

2. Analytical/Research Skills. Employers value your ability to assess a situation, seek multiple perspectives, gather more information if necessary, and identify key issues that need to be addressed.

3. Computer/Technical Literacy. Almost all jobs now require some basic understanding of computer hardware and software, especially word processing, spreadsheets, and email.

4. Flexibility/Adaptability/Managing Multiple Priorities. Employers value your ability to manage multiple assignments and tasks, set priorities, and adapt to changing conditions and work assignments.

5. Interpersonal Abilities. The ability to relate to your co-workers, inspire others to participate, and mitigate conflict with co-workers is essential given the amount of time spent at work each day.

6. Leadership/Management Skills. While there is some debate about whether leadership is something people are born with, these skills deal with your ability to take charge and manage your co-workers.

7. Multicultural Sensitivity/Awareness. There is possibly no bigger issue in the workplace than diversity, and job-seekers must demonstrate a sensitivity and awareness to other people and cultures.

8. Planning/Organizing. Employers value your ability to design, plan, organize, and implement projects and tasks within an allotted timeframe. Planning also involves goal-setting.

9. Problem-Solving/Reasoning/Creativity. This set of abilities involves the ability to find solutions to problems using your creativity, reasoning, and past experiences, along with the available information and resources.

10. Teamwork. Because so many jobs involve working in one or more work-groups, you must have the ability to work with others in a professional manner while attempting to achieve a common goal.

—From *Quintcareers.com*

In Lesson 8, you learned the first step in the MAPP reading plan: changing headings into questions and marking the answers. That first step can only be taken when the reading selection has a title and headings. In Lesson 9, you learned a question you can ask to find the topic when a reading selection doesn't have a title or headings: "What is the reading about?"

The First P of MAPP Is "Point."

In this lesson, you will learn about the first "P" of MAPP—the point. The point is the main idea, and you can find it by asking the question, "What is the point?"

The First "P" of MAPP Stands for "Point"

Mark = **Mark** the answers to your questions.

About = Topic: What is the reading **about**?

Point = Main Idea: What is the **point**?

Proof = Supporting Detail: What is the **proof**?

MAPP will help you find your way through a reading selection. Using MAPP every time you read will improve your reading comprehension.

What Is the Point? The Main Idea.

The most important skill you can develop in order to understand what you read at the college level is finding and understanding the main idea. The **main idea** is the point the author is trying to get across to you. The main idea limits the topic to the one important idea about that topic that the author wants to discuss.

Suppose the topic of a reading is "healthy foods." This is a very broad topic. An author could explore many different main ideas about healthy foods. For example, an author might want to make one of the following points:

> **About:** Healthy foods
> **Point:** can help keep your eyes sharp, your heart healthy, and your immune system strong.
> **Point:** don't have to be expensive.
> **Point:** are easy to tell apart from unhealthy foods.

The details the author would select to support each point would be different. For example, a paragraph with the main idea that says healthy foods are easy to tell apart from unhealthy foods would probably include details about what both healthy and unhealthy foods look like and taste like. A different set of details would be used to support the main idea that healthy foods don't have to be expensive—for example, a list of cheap healthy foods.

INTERACTION 3–21	Making Points About Topics

Work in groups of three or four. Select three topics from the list below. For each topic, each person should make a point about the topic that is different from everyone else's.

1. Couples
2. Rainy days
3. Best friends
4. Jobs that pay well
5. Singers who win awards
6. What clothing reveals about a person
7. How to name babies
8. Going to the doctor
9. Traveling away from home
10. Being successful

INTERACTION 3–22	Predicting the Kinds of Details You'll Find

Select one of the points you made about a topic in Interaction 3–21. Based on your point, what kinds of details can you think of to support it so that a listener would understand your point of view?

Topics and Main Ideas in the Topic Sentence

When the topic and main idea are stated in the same sentence in a paragraph, that sentence is called the **topic sentence.** Use this simple formula as a memory aid:

$$T \quad + \quad MI \quad = \quad TS$$
Topic + Main Idea = Topic Sentence

Let's look at a few examples of topic sentences that include the topic "healthy food" and the main ideas from above. In the first topic sentence, the [topic] is in brackets and the <u>main idea</u> is underlined. You can do the same in the remaining sentences. Throughout this chapter, you will be asked to use these annotations as you read.

[Healthy foods] <u>can help keep your eyes sharp, your heart healthy, and your immune system strong.</u>

Healthy foods don't have to be expensive.

Healthy foods can be distinguished from unhealthy foods.

INTERACTION 3–23	**Identifying the Topic and Main Idea in a Topic Sentence**

In the following topic sentences, put brackets around the [topic] and underline the <u>main idea</u>.

1. Marriage has many health benefits.

2. Cell phones have changed the way we communicate.

3. Afghanistan has a long and interesting history.

4. Mallika Sherawat is one of the most popular actresses in Bollywood today.

5. The Ducati is the undisputed "king" of street bikes.

Courtesy of Ducati

The Location of the Main Idea in the Topic Sentence

The topic and the main idea can be expressed in different orders in a topic sentence. The order isn't important. What is important is that the main idea limits the topic to just one area that the author will discuss.

> There are <u>129 foods that have made</u> [a list of "The World's Healthiest Foods."]
>
> You can <u>eat</u> [healthy food] <u>without having to pay a hefty price.</u>
>
> A survey revealed that <u>teenage girls eat less</u> [healthy food] <u>than any other group</u>.
>
> Online, <u>you can get lists</u> of [healthy foods] <u>to take grocery shopping with you.</u>

INTERACTION 3–24	Identifying the Topic and Main Idea in a Topic Sentence

In the following topic sentences, put brackets around the [topic] and underline the <u>main idea</u>.

1. There was a famous singer in the 1990s known as Selena, the "Queen of Tejano Music."

2. Consider three different methods for cleaning your apartment.

3. A study showed that many obese children watch commercials on television.

4. On exhibit in the Museum of Broken Relationships is a Champagne bottle bought for a first anniversary that never happened.

5. A good example of contemporary bluegrass bands is The HillBenders.

Finding the Topic Sentence in a Group of Sentences

When you read, you will usually encounter the topic sentence among other sentences in a paragraph, so it's important that you learn to differentiate the main idea from both the topic and the supporting details. We have just discussed how to distinguish the main idea from the topic.

Supporting details will be discussed (in great detail!) in Lesson 11, but you need to know now that the main idea is more general than the details. The details support, or give more specific information about, the main idea. Keep this in mind when you are trying to decide which sentence among other sentences contains the main idea.

Let's look at two examples.

[Marriage] <u>has many health benefits</u>.

The topic is *marriage,* which is a very broad and general idea. The main idea is that marriage *has many health benefits,* which is a little more specific than the topic. However, we do not know what the health benefits might be. There are no details, no specifics, no examples, only the general statement about many health benefits.

Compare that sentence to these sentences:

Studies show that married couples are sick less frequently than unmarried couples.

Also, married couples report less depression and greater happiness.

These sentences are supporting details. The details tare the actual benefits of being married, so these sentences are more specific than the general statement about marriage having many health benefits. Noticing the difference between specific details and more general statements can help you identify the author's point.

Here is another example that shows the levels of general and specific ideas by indenting the more specific ideas the most.

About: Cell phones

Point: have changed the way we communicate.

Proof: 1. They have made getting in touch with friends and family more convenient.

2. Not only can you call them from almost anywhere, you can also text, e-mail, or tweet them.

3. If you are stranded with a flat tire, you can use your cell phone to call for help, and when you are at the grocery store and forget what you are supposed to get, you can just pull out your cell phone to call and ask.

Each sentence of proof is a supporting detail that is more specific than the topic sentence.

INTERACTION 3–25 | **Finding the Topic Sentence in a Group of Sentences**

A. Write TS next to the topic sentence of each group.

B. In the topic sentence, put brackets around the [topic] and underline the <u>main idea</u>.

C. If a sentence is a detail, write D in front of it and bracket the topic (if it is repeated).

Group 1

Bettmann/CORBIS

_____ 1. Many claim that Michael Jordan is the greatest basketball player of all time.

_____ 2. Michael Jordan led the Chicago Bulls to a total of six NBA championships.

_____ 3. Michael Jordan earned the nickname "Air Jordan" due to his ability to do slam dunks jumping from the free throw line.

_____ 4. He has also been hailed as one of the great defensive players of basketball.

Group 2

_____ 1. Purchasing a reusable water bottle is a great way to decrease the 70 million plastic bottles going into landfills each day.

_____ 2. Taking your own bags to the grocery store is another great recycling idea.

_____ 3. There are many easy ways to recycle.

_____ 4. Instead of throwing away that old T-shirt, why not cut it up and recycle it as a rag for household cleaning.

Group 3

_____ 1. Heather Rigdon's song "Table for Two" was featured in the movie _Trust the Man_ (2005), starring David Duchovny and Julianne Moore.

_____ 2. Her debut CD _Young and Naïve_, released in 2007, received positive reviews.

_____ 3. Heather's voice has been compared to contemporary Melody Gardot and classic artist Peggy Lee.

_____ 4. Heather Rigdon is a new-on-the-scene contemporary jazz singer with promise.

Group 4

_____ 1. Six Flags over Texas is located in Arlington, Texas, and opened in 1961.

_____ 2. The Texas location was the first of the Six Flags properties to open.

_____ 3. When the park opened, admission for adults was $2.75; today an adult ticket costs $51.99.

_____ 4. The property sits on 212 acres and boasts more than 50 rides.

Group 5

_____ 1. Have you ever heard of a "superfood"?

_____ 2. Superfoods are foods packed with nutrients and health benefits.

_____ 3. Blueberries often top the list of superfoods, offering antioxidants, potassium, and vitamin C.

_____ 4. Omega-3s, which can help your heart, joints, and possibly your brain, are found in salmon and walnuts, both superfoods.

INTERACTION 3–26 Finding the Topic Sentence in a Paragraph

As you read the following paragraphs, put brackets around the [topic] and underline the <u>main idea</u>. Then answer the questions that follow.

Paragraph A   Forensics Textbook

AP Photo/Damian Dovarganes

¹In 1961, Thomas Noguchi emigrated from Japan and was hired as a medical examiner with Los Angeles County. ²Just a year into the job, he performed the autopsy on Marilyn Monroe. ³Fame and fortune have followed him ever since. ⁴He did the autopsy on Robert F. Kennedy, Sharon Tate, Natalie Wood, and John Belushi. ⁵If a case seemed particularly important or perplexing, Dr. Noguchi was called. ⁶Before the age of big forensic labs, Dr. Noguchi was a forensic investigator, going over every crime scene with a fine-toothed comb.

—From Bertino, *Forensic Science: Fundamentals and Investigations*

1. What is the paragraph about? Topic: _____

2. What is the point of this paragraph? Main idea: _____

_____

3. Which sentence is the topic sentence? T + MI = TS: _____

Paragraph B   Anthropology Textbook

¹The smallest family unit is known as the nuclear family. ²The nuclear family is a group consisting of one or two parents and dependent offspring,

which may include a stepparent, stepsiblings, and adopted children. [3]Until recently, the term nuclear family referred solely to the mother, father and child(ren) unit. [4]In the United States father/mother/child(ren) nuclear family households reached their highest frequency around 1950, when 60 percent of all households conformed to this model. [5]Today such families comprise only 24 percent of U.S. households.

—Adapted from Haviland, Prins, Walrath, & McBride,
The Essence of Anthropology

4. What is the paragraph about? Topic: _____

5. What is the point of this paragraph? Main idea: _____

_____

6. Which sentence is the topic sentence? T + MI = TS: _____

Paragraph C   Nursing Textbook

[1]People see only when there is enough light, touch only when contact is made with someone or something, and hear only sounds that are loud enough. [2]But with every breath, the sense of smell is active. [3]Smell is the mute sense, one without words. [4]Smells are usually described in terms of other things such as smoke, fruit, flowers, and citrus or by the feelings they inspire as in disgusted, delighted, sickened, hypnotized, or intoxicated.

—Maville & Huerta, *Health Promotion in Nursing,* 2nd edition

7. What is the paragraph about? Topic: _____

8. What is the point of this paragraph? Main idea: _____

_____

9. Which sentence is the topic sentence? T + MI = TS: _____

Paragraph D   Media Textbook

[1]Today, the Internet delivers all types of media—print, broadcast, movies and recordings—using a single delivery system without barriers. [2]You can

receive all types of media just about anywhere you want. [3]This media is delivered by many different types of companies, carried on invisible electronic signals you can't see. [4]The Internet has caused the emergence of new media products and new competition in the media business that were impossible to foresee when the Internet first emerged 30 years ago. [5]The Internet was originally designed by a group of scientists who were simply hoping to share information.

—Adapted from Biagi, *Media Impact:
An Introduction to Mass Media*, 8th edition

10. What is the paragraph about? Topic: _____

11. What is the point of this paragraph? Main idea: _____

_____

12. Which sentence is the topic sentence? T + MI = TS: _____

Paragraph E   **Personal Finance**

[1]Do you live in an apartment, condo, or house where you are paying rent to a landlord? [2]If so, listen up. [3]The building you live in is probably insured. [4]However, your belongings are not. [5]If something were to happen, like fire or water damage, your possessions would not be covered. [6]You need to make sure you have renter's insurance. [7]This way you will have peace of mind that if anything unforeseen happens, you have coverage to replace your valuables.

13. What is the paragraph about? Topic: _____

14. What is the point of this paragraph? Main idea: _____

_____

15. Which sentence is the topic sentence? T + MI = TS: _____

The Location of the Topic Sentence in a Paragraph

Have you noticed that the topic sentence can appear in different places within each paragraph? In one paragraph the topic sentence is the first sentence. In another paragraph it can come last. And you can find a topic sentence anywhere in between. The rule about topic sentences is simple: they can be anywhere in a paragraph. It is not the location of the topic sentence that is important; it is the relationships between the ideas in the paragraph that matter.

Think about this analogy. Some of you may live in cities, states, or even countries far away from the rest of your family. Let's say, just for example, that you live in Florida, your sister lives in California, your uncle and his family live in New York, and your grandparents are in South Korea. Are you still family? Of course! Silly question, right? That is because it is the relationship between you and your family that matters, not your location.

In a paragraph, it is the same for the topic, main idea, and supporting details. It does not matter where they are located because their relationship is always the same.

So when you are searching for the topic sentence of a paragraph, look for the relationships among the ideas—which ideas are the broadest, narrower, and narrowest—rather than expecting to find the topic sentence in a particular location.

INTERACTION 3–27   Understanding the Relationships Among Sentences

Read each group of sentences. Label each sentence within the group:

TB = Too broad; it will introduce the topic but not include the main idea.
TS = Topic sentence
D = Detail

Group 1

_TB_ There are many types of trees that can be used for bonsai.

_TS_ One of the most popular bonsai trees is the Chinese Elm.

_D_ The Chinese Elm makes a great bonsai tree because it is versatile.

_D_ It is also a sturdy tree.

Group 2

_D_ *Star Wars,* another cult film, was the next blockbuster in the summer of 1977.

_TB_ Summer is the time for blockbuster movies.

_T_ Some of America's most culturally influential films helped establish the summer blockbuster phenomenon.

D *Jaws* (the film that puts fear in all our hearts) is credited with starting the "blockbuster" in the summer of 1975.

Group 3

TS One such company is S.C. Johnson & Son, and the new "green" product it is touting is Windex.

IP The trend to become green has caused quite a few large companies to make changes in their most popular products.

D The company claims it has removed most of the harsh chemicals that pollute the environment from the familiar blue cleaner while increasing its cleaning power by 30 percent.

D As a result of this move to "green," S.C. Johnson has brought in more of the other type of green.

Group 4

_____ Despite this nomination, several established rap artists, like Snoop Dogg and Ice-T, have been critical of Soulja Boy's style.

_____ He is probably best known for his song "Crank That (Soulja Boy)," which was nominated for a Grammy in 2008.

_____ Soulja Boy is an American rapper, whose real name is DeAndre Ramone Way.

_____ Rap artists offer diverse contributions to a popular genre of music.

Group 5

_____ The company Naked and Famous Denim has a line of jeans called The Hank-Dyed Line.

_____ Jeans are made by many companies and come in many shapes, sizes, and prices.

_____ What do you get for this high price tag? Every pair is handmade from beginning to end as well as signed and numbered.

_____ It is the one of the most expensive jeans in the world, at $777 a pair.

INTERACTION 3–28 Finding the Location of the Topic Sentence in a Paragraph

As you read the following paragraphs, put brackets around the [topic] and underline the main idea. Then answer the questions that follow.

Paragraph 1   **Political Science Textbook**

> [1]The White Rose was a resistance movement against the Nazis. [2]It was organized in Munich by a small group consisting primarily of university students. [3]The White Rose operated in 1942–1943. [4]Its members wrote pamphlets calling on their fellow German citizens to carry out "passive resistance" to the fascist government. [5]They copied their papers and left them in public places within Munich as well as other cities. [6]The members of The White Rose knew they were in danger from the Nazis but showed bravery by standing for their convictions, even though it cost them their lives.
>
> —Adapted from Grigsby, *Analyzing Politics*, 4th edition

1. What is the paragraph about? Topic: _____

2. What is the point of this paragraph? Main idea: _____

_____

3. Which sentence is the topic sentence? T + MI = TS: _____

Paragraph 2   **Student Success Textbook**

> [1]Psychologist Richard Logan has found the secret to success. [2]He has studied people who have gone through difficult experiences. [3]For example, he has studied survivors of concentration camps and explorers lost in the frozen Arctic. [4]He found that all of these victims shared a common belief. [5]They saw themselves as personally responsible for the outcomes and experiences of their lives. [6]Personal responsibility is the foundation for success.
>
> —Adapted from Downing, *On Course*, 5th edition

4. What is the paragraph about? Topic: _____

5. What is the point of this paragraph? Main idea: _____

_____

6. Which sentence is the topic sentence? T + MI = TS: _____

Paragraph 3   Sociology Textbook

[1]The media routinely drive home two points to the viewer: that violent crime is frequent and increasing, and that it is random and constantly around us. [2]However, this is contradicted by research. [3]The truth about criminal violence shows a different story. [4]Criminal violence is actually decreasing. [5]In addition, criminal violence is not random, but patterned and even predictable.

—Adapted from Anderson & Taylor,
Sociology: The Essentials, 4th edition

7. What is the paragraph about? Topic: _____

8. What is the point of this paragraph? Main idea: _____

_____

9. Which sentence is the topic sentence? T + MI = TS: _____

Paragraph 4   Sports Medicine Textbook

[1]Television, radio, and newsprint all contain the newest quick-fix remedy. [2]Billions of dollars are spent each year on a variety of products. [3]Each claims to be the newest breakthrough to lose weight, gain weight, gain muscle, or improve other areas of the body. [4]A licensed nutritionalist plays a vital role in ensuring a correct diet and properly instructing athletes on supplements and dietary aids. [5]Whether the athlete is involved in running marathons or playing football, a nutritionalist can help.

—Adapted from France, *Introduction to Sports Medicine
and Athletic Training*

10. What is the paragraph about? Topic: _____

11. What is the point of this paragraph? Main idea: _____

_____

12. Which sentence is the topic sentence? T + MI = TS: _____

Paragraph 5   **Human Development Textbook**

> ¹The divorce rate in the United States is one of the highest in the world. ²It has become a national concern. ³As a result, our society has taken several approaches to help make marriage more successful. ⁴Some of these approaches include mandatory premarital counseling, cooling-off periods, and the abolition of no-fault divorce. ⁵These are all being tried, with varying degrees of success. ⁶In 1997 Louisiana adopted a different and controversial approach. ⁷When couples get married, they choose between a "no-fault marriage" and a "covenant marriage." ⁸The no-fault marriage only requires a separation of 6 months. ⁹The covenant marriage requires a two-year separation, proof of an affair or some type of abuse, as well as mandatory counseling. ¹⁰There are several other states that have also adopted these approaches.
>
> —Adapted from Kail & Cavanaugh, *Human Development: A Life-Span View,* 4th edition

13. What is the paragraph about? Topic: _____

_____

14. What is the point of this paragraph? Main idea: _____

_____

15. Which sentence is the topic sentence? T + MI = TS: _____

Review: Identifying the Author's Point

Keep the following points in mind when you are identifying the author's point.

- The main idea is the author's point. It limits the topic to just one idea the author wants to discuss about the topic.

- The topic sentence is the sentence where the topic and main idea are found together: T + MI = TS

- The topic sentence can be found anywhere within a paragraph.

The Main Idea Isn't Always Stated.

So far we have been talking about main ideas found in topic sentences. These are stated main ideas. However, not all main ideas are stated. Some are implied. An **implied main idea** is not stated directly; rather, it is suggested. The author suggests the main idea by giving details. The reader then infers (makes an educated guess about) the main idea from the details. In a sense, it becomes your job to create a topic sentence. Another way to say this is that you summarize the details of the passage in one sentence in order to draw a conclusion about the author's meaning.

Implied Main Ideas in Cartoons

Cartoons are a good beginning point for figuring out implied main ideas because cartoonists rarely state their ideas directly. Instead, they expect readers to look at the details of the picture and words to supply the main idea themselves. Look at the following cartoon.

"I'm looking for something in a teen to English dictionary."

Mark Anderson

What details do you notice?

The woman is in a bookstore.

The text says "teen to English dictionary."

What does the second detail imply, or suggest? It suggests that the woman doesn't understand what a teenager is saying; she needs a dictionary in order to translate the teen's language into her own. Even though the cartoon does not say so, you could guess that this woman is a mother who has a teenaged child.

Once you have considered these clues, you can ask, "What is the implied main idea of the cartoon?" Your answer should be phrased in a complete sentence, as if you were creating a topic sentence. Here is an example:

This mother does not understand what her teen is talking about.

How do we know this is true? She is trying to buy a "teen to English dictionary"!

Spotlight on Inference: Using Inductive Reasoning to Find an Implied Main Idea

"Inductive reasoning" is the formal name for the process of using details to make a generalization, or general statement. You use inductive reasoning every day. Here is an example:

You see Chris.

Chris is wearing a brown uniform.

Chris is exiting a boxy, brown truck.

Chris is carrying a package.

What is Chris's job? _____

Do you see how the details helped you? Each detail is a clue that adds a piece to the puzzle; each clue leads to the same job.

A Process for Finding the Implied Main Idea

You can use this five-step process for finding an implied main idea:

1. Identify the topic. (What is this about?)

2. Look for the details. (What is the proof?)

3. Ask yourself what general idea all the details have in common, or what point they add up to. This is the main idea. (What is the point?)

4. Combine your answer with the topic to create a topic sentence (T + MI = TS).

5. Double-check the main idea by turning your topic sentence into a question to see if the details answer it.

INTERACTION 3–29   Finding the Implied Main Idea

A. Use the five-step process for finding the implied main idea of these details.

- Distance learning has the extra cost of technology, such as a computer with the latest versions of hardware and software, Internet access, and video capability.
- Distance learning requires you to manage your time efficiently.
- Distance courses often require more time and effort than a face-to-face class.

1. What is the topic? _____

2. What are the details?

- _____

- _____

- _____

3. What general idea do the details have in common, or add up to? _____

_____

4. Combine the topic and the general idea to make a topic sentence: _____

_____

5. Double-check your topic sentence by turning it into a question: _____

_____

Do the details answer the question?   Yes   No

B. Use the five-step process for finding the implied main idea of this cartoon.

Roz Chast/Cartoonbank.com

6. What is the topic? _____

7. What are the details?

   • _____

   • _____

   • _____

8. What general idea do the details have in common, or add up to? _____

   _____

9. Combine the topic and the general idea to make a topic sentence: _____

   _____

10. If you wrote a paragraph based on this topic sentence, what two details might you want to include? _____

   _____

INTERACTION 3–30   **Deciding What General Idea the Details Have in Common**

For each group of ideas, state what they add up to or what they have in common.

1. General idea: _____Winter Sport_____

Downhill skiing	Speedskating
Half-pipe	Ice dancing

2. General idea: _____Spanish Speaking Country_____

Mexico	Spain
Colombia	Bolivia

3. General idea: _____TV Sit Com_____

Family Guy	*30 Rock*
The Cosby Show	*The Office*

4. General idea: _____

Google	Wikipedia
Yahoo!	Ask.com

5. General idea: _____Vacation_____

   Lie on the beach or look for shells.   Go to see relatives.

   Visit a different city where friends live.   Go camping in a state park.

6. General idea: _____Kinds of bread_____

   Whole wheat   Rye

   Potato   Pumpernickel

7. General idea: _____lay out of the bedroom_____

   To the left is the dresser.   To the right is the bed.

   Above the dresser is the window.   Straight ahead is the closet.

8. General idea: _____How to prepar your kid for em_____

   First, tape emergency numbers next to the phone; also put them on speed dial.

   Second, teach children what to say if they have to call in an emergency.

   Third, talk children through various scenarios such as fires and break-ins.

9. General idea: _____how to make food healthy_____

   French fries can be roasted instead of fried.

   You can take the skin off chicken.

   Bacon can be laid on a paper towel to remove excess fat.

10. General idea: _____People who live in city can still go fishing_____

    In San Francisco Bay, people fish for striped bass.

    In Brooklyn, New York, charters are available to go fishing for tuna.

    In Chicago, fishers catch largemouth bass in Lake Michigan.

INTERACTION 3–31   **Finding the Implied Main Idea from a Group of Details**

   A. Look for the [topic] of each group and put brackets around it.

   B. Pay attention to the details and ask yourself, "What do the details have in common?" The answer will be the main idea.

   C. Answer the questions that follow.

Group 1   Accounting

- A used car is less expensive than a new car of the same make and model.

- A used car will not depreciate as quickly.

- Buyers of a used car do not need to have a down payment as large as they might to finance a new car.

1. What is the reading about? _____

2. What are the details? _____

   _____

3. What do the details add up to or have in common? _____

   _____

4. Form a topic sentence using your main idea. _____

   _____

Group 2   Psychology

- One strategy for falling asleep is to read a book for about 15 minutes before you retire.

- If you can't fall asleep, another strategy you might try is to engage in an activity that relaxes you, like listening to music.

- If those strategies don't help, you can always revert to counting sheep.

5. What is the reading about? _____

6. What are the clues? _____

   _____

7. What do the clues or details have in common? _____

   _____

8. Form a topic sentence using your main idea. _____

   _____

Group 3   Human Development

- If your friend talks about committing suicide, pay attention.

- People who threaten to end their own lives frequently do commit suicide.

- Another indicator is obvious changes in personality.

- An abnormal focus on death can also be an indicator of suicide.

9. What is the reading about? _____

10. What are the details? _____

_____

11. What do the details have in common? _____

_____

12. Form a topic sentence using your main idea. _____

_____

Group 4   Speech

- When creating a PowerPoint presentation you should use images when you can.
- Images often help you express an idea more powerfully than your words.
- Stories also help make a boring PowerPoint slide, like a graph or chart, more interesting.
- Maintaining eye contact as well as using energy and enthusiasm in your voice will help keep your listener's interest in your presentation.

13. What is the reading about? _____

14. What are the details? _____

_____

15. What do the details have in common? _____

_____

16. Form a topic sentence using your main idea. _____

_____

Group 5   Health

- Gardening helps to increase your strength.
- It can also improve your flexibility.
- Gardening is fun and can help reduce stress and increase energy.

17. What is the reading about? _____

18. What are the clues? _____

_____

19. What do the clues or details have in common? _____

_____

20. Form a topic sentence using your main idea. _____

_____

INTERACTION 3–32   **Finding the Implied Main Idea in a Paragraph**

A. Look for the [topic] of each group and put brackets around it.

B. Pay attention to the details and ask yourself, "What do the details have in common?" The answer will be the main idea.

C. Answer the questions that follow.

Paragraph 1   **Education**

> Organizing activities, putting together needed materials, keeping records, managing the classroom, and delivering instruction are just a part of an instructor's daily ritual. An instructor may have 150 or more students each day. Each student requires attention, attendance taken, grades recorded, and feedback on work completed. Sometimes instructors need to meet with a student outside the classroom to discuss an issue or to give extra help with a problem. In addition, instructors are often required to be members of committees.

1. What is the reading about? ___*Instructors*___

2. What are the clues? ___*Organizing activities putting*___

_____

3. What do the clues or details have in common? This is the main idea: _____
___*Teachers have a lot of responsible*___

4. Form a topic sentence using your main idea (T + MI = TS): _____
___*Instructors have a lot of responsible*___

Paragraph 2   **Student Success**

> Tablet PC's typically have the full functionality of a notebook, as well as some added features including handwriting recognition (you can take notes directly on your screen and it will convert it to text), speech recognition, and a rotating screen. For students, this means you can take your tablet to class with you and take notes directly onto the screen and then save them into a folder created for each class. And lastly, if you get tired of writing, you can type, or vice-versa.
>
> —Adapted from Beale, *Success Skills: Strategies for Study and Lifelong Learning,* 3rd edition

5. What is the reading about? _____

6. What are the details? _____

_____

7. What do the clues or details have in common? This is the main idea: _____

_____

8. Form a topic sentence using your main idea (T + MI = TS): _____

_____

Paragraph 3   Health

How do you separate fitness fiction from fitness fact? There are probably more wrong ideas about fitness than there are correct ones floating around out there. Here are a few of the common fictional fitness claims along with the facts about them. *No pain, no gain.* Some muscle soreness when you start or intensify your workout program is okay, but you do not have to push yourself to tears to get results. Exercise should never hurt. If it does, stop. *Women who work with weights will get bulky.* Women do not have enough testosterone—the hormone that develops bulky muscles in men—to start looking like bodybuilders. *Crunches can flatten your stomach.* While this exercise certainly will add strength to your stomach muscles, the only thing that will help you lose that pot belly is to eat fewer calories!

—Adapted from Hales, *An Invitation to Health,* 12th edition

9. What is the reading about? _____

10. What are the details? _____

_____

11. What do the details have in common? This is the main idea: _____

_____

12. Form a topic sentence using your main idea (T + MI = TS): *There are probely more wrong idea about fitness*

Paragraph 4   Nursing

First, the term refers to the distinct second step in the nursing process, diagnosis. Next, "nursing diagnosis" refers to the label. Finally, a nursing diagnosis refers to one of many diagnoses in the classification system established and approved by NANDA.

—Adapted from Seaback, *Nursing Process: Concepts and Applications,* 2nd edition

13. What is the reading about? _Nursing diagnosis_

14. What are the details? _second step in nursing process_

15. What do the details have in common? This is the main idea: _____

16. Form a topic sentence using your main idea (T + MI = TS): _The term nursing diagnosis has three meaning_

Paragraph 5   **Personal Safety**

> Never leave your keys in your ignition, but this is a "no-brainer." You should always lock your car and hide your valuables. It also helps to park in a well-lit and populated area. In addition, you can install car alarms and wheel or steering wheel locks. If you want to be really cautious, you could remove your battery cables every time you leave your car. However, this might be a little extreme.

17. What is the reading about? _thing to do to not get your car stolen_

18. What are the details? _never leave your keys_

19. What do the details have in common? This is the main idea: _Serval was to stop your car from stolen_

20. Form a topic sentence using your main idea (T + MI = TS): _____

Review: Using Inference to Find an Implied Main Idea

You can ask these questions when you need to identify an implied main idea:

- What is the reading about?
- What details lead me to the author's point?
- What do the details have in common?

The main idea you create should be supported by the details you find in the paragraph or longer passage.

ACTIVATE YOUR SKILLS 1
Identifying the Topic and Main Idea

A. In the following topic sentences, put brackets around the [topic] and underline the main idea.

1. Caffeine is a hard habit to kick.

2. If you can afford it, Hawaii is one of the best vacation destinations you can travel to.

3. Ikebana is the art of Japanese flower arranging.

4. The success of Disney's first animated film *Snow White* helped begin what is referred to as the "golden age of animation" for Walt Disney.

5. The first permanent English settlement in America was established in 1607 at Jamestown.

B. Identify the topic sentence of each group. Label each sentence:

TB = Too broad to be the topic sentence; does not include the main idea

TS = Topic sentence

D = Detail

Group 1

_____ Our world is filled with many amazing sites.

_____ The Grand Canyon in Arizona is first on that list.

_____ However, only a handful of these sites make the list of "Seven Natural Wonders of the World."

_____ Some other sites are the Great Barrier Reef in Australia, Mount Everest in Nepal, and Victoria Falls in Africa.

Group 2

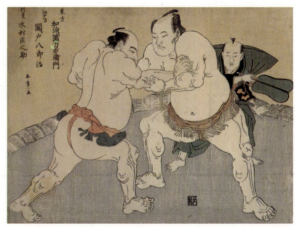

_____ While the actual beginnings of Sumo are unknown, ancient Japanese writings record that the first fight was held in 23 B.C.

_____ By request of the emperor, Taima no Kehaya (the bad guy) fought Nomi no Sukune (the good guy).

_____ Nomi no Sukune, a potter, won this first bout and is considered the "Father of Sumo."

Apic/Getty Images

_____ Sumo wrestling has a long history.

Group 3

_____ People usually think that winning the lottery will end all their troubles.

_____ But what often happens is that their troubles simply multiply.

_____ Most people are not prepared to handle the sudden infusion of cash.

_____ They overspend, get taken advantage of, and often end up with nothing to show for their winnings in just a few short years.

Group 4

_____ In England, Mrs. Goss advises the government on the speech development of children.

_____ Last week, she issued a stark warning about the effect that television and electronic media communication are having in limiting children's vocabulary development.

_____ "We need to help today's teenagers understand the difference between their textspeak and the formal language they need to succeed in life—800 words will not get you a job."

_____ Teenagers should have developed a broad vocabulary of 40,000 words by the time they reach 16. However, linguists have found that while they may understand thousands of words, many teens limit their use to as little as 800 words per day.

—Adapted from Salkeld, "The Teens Who Can
Barely Talk," *Daily Mail,* January 10, 2010

Group 5

_____ Celebrations for mothers date back to the time of the Greeks.

_____ In America, though, "Mother's Day" has been official only for about 100 years.

_____ Thanks to the work of Anna Jarvis, President Woodrow Wilson signed a bill making Mother's Day an official holiday in 1914.

_____ Mother's Day is now celebrated the second Sunday of May, which has become the most popular day for eating out in America.

ACTIVATE YOUR SKILLS 2
Finding the Topic Sentence

As you read the following paragraphs, put brackets around the [topic] and underline the main idea. Then answer the questions that follow.

Paragraph 1   Sociology

[1] The constant presence of cell phones has changed how we communicate, and, unfortunately, not all of the changes are good ones. [2] First, there is "Spontaneity over Planning." [3] Some people don't make specific plans and others do not stick to the plans/appointments they do make. [4] They change their minds on the fly when something better comes up. [5] Next, there is "Can You Help Me?" [6] Cell phones will get you out of jams, but they also encourage you to not bother avoiding getting into jams. [7] It's so easy just to make a call. [8] In some cases we have become over-dependent on the "bailout call." [9] Third, there is "Voice Mail Suspicion." [10] If you can't reach someone on their cell phone, not only are you indignant, but you become suspicious. [11] Is the person filtering you out, ignoring you, or with someone else? [12] Finally, cell phones are all about "Me, Me, Me." [13] One of the great things about cell phones is they let you fill up time that would otherwise be wasted: taxicab rides, running errands, and so forth. [14] Still, whatever happened to looking up at the world around you, and enjoying being where you are or who you are with?

—Adapted from Tim Hanrahan and Jason Fry, "Fingers do the Stumbling."

The Wall Street Journal Online, February 14, 2005

1. What is the paragraph about? Topic: _____

2. What is the point of this paragraph? Main idea: _____

_____

3. Which sentence is the topic sentence? T + MI = TS: _____

Paragraph 2   Health

[1] You may not know it, but you and I are junkies. [2] Our drug comes in three forms: pure, crystal, or powder, though you have your preference, as I have mine. [3] It is more addicting than cigarettes; however, there is no minimum age requirement to buy it. [4] It can seem as addictive as heroin, but it is not illegal, and we definitely have easier access to it. [5] This substance is in almost everything we eat. [6] It gives a fast high but causes us to crash quickly, craving more. [7] What is our drug of choice? [8] It is sugar, and it is a hard habit to break.

4. What is the paragraph about? Topic: _____

5. What is the point of this paragraph? Main idea: _____

_____

6. Which sentence is the topic sentence? T + MI = TS: _____

Paragraph 3   **Environmental Studies**

[1]Our landfills are accumulating waste at a rate of 2 to 5 pounds of trash per person per day. [2]Over our lifetime, the total would be staggering. [3]But we can help to reduce this waste by reusing and recycling certain items. [4]It's a very small, virtually no-cost way of doing our part and helping our environment. [5]Take a day and really look at what you throw out. [6]You will be amazed at what could be recycled or reused.

—From Mifflin, "Recycling Made Easy and How to Get Started," About.com

7. What is the paragraph about? Topic: _____

8. What is the point of this paragraph? Main idea: _____

_____

9. Which sentence is the topic sentence? T + MI = TS: _____

Paragraph 4   **Biology**

[1]The world's great forests influence life in profound ways. [2]They take up carbon dioxide from the air and release oxygen into it. [3]At the same time, the forests act like giant sponges absorbing water from the rains, then releasing it slowly. [4]By sucking up water and holding soil in place, forests prevent erosion, flooding, and sedimentation that can disrupt rivers, lakes, and reservoirs. [5]Strip forests away, and exposed soil can wash away or lose nutrients.

—From Starr, Evers, & Starr, *Biology: Today and Tomorrow*, 3rd edition

10. What is the paragraph about? Topic: _____

11. What is the point of this paragraph? Main idea: _____

_____

12. Which sentence is the topic sentence? T + MI = TS: _____

Paragraph 5   **Human Development**

¹Do babies who are quiet and easygoing grow up to be quiet and easygoing adults? ²What about babies who are active and antsy? ³Do they grow up to be the same as adults? ⁴While emotional temperaments do tend to be predisposed, there are other influential factors involved as well. ⁵For example, parents can play a big role in emotional development. ⁶If a parent has a baby that has an easygoing personality, they may tend to do more a laid back activity like reading with the child. ⁷Whereas if an infant has a more active disposition, then the parent may be more likely to play a physical game.

—Adapted from Kail & Cavanaugh, *Human Development: A Life-Span View*, 4th edition

13. What is the paragraph about? Topic: _____

14. What is the point of this paragraph? Main idea: _____

    _____

15. Which sentence is the topic sentence? T + MI = TS: _____

MASTER YOUR SKILLS 1
Finding Stated Main Ideas

As you read the following paragraphs, put brackets around the [topic] and underline the *main idea*. Then answer the questions that follow.

Paragraph 1   **Biology**

¹The praying mantis has remarkable camouflage, acute hearing, and keen vision. ²The praying mantis can detect prey as far as 60 feet away while staying hidden itself. ³The mantis's menu consists mainly of other insects, sometimes including other mantises. ⁴It is usually the female that will eat the male, which can make mating a challenge. ⁵However, the male has the ability to mate successfully even while being eaten! ⁶The praying mantis is one amazing bug.

ahnhuynh/Used under license from Shutterstock.com

1. What is the paragraph about? Topic: _The praying mantis_

2. What is the point of this paragraph? Main idea: _s2_

_____

3. Which sentence is the topic sentence? T + MI = TS: _The praying mantis_ _one amazing bug_

Paragraph 2   **Human Development**

¹When couples pledge their love to each other "in sickness and in health," most envision the sickness part to be no worse than an illness lasting a few weeks. ²That may be the case for many couples, but for some their pledge of love is severely tested by the illness they experience. ³Francine and Ron are such a couple. ⁴After 42 years of mainly good times together, Ron was diagnosed as having Alzheimer's disease. ⁵"At times it's very hard," said Francine. ⁶"Especially when he looks at me and has no idea who I am. ⁷But I love him and I know he would do the same for me."

—Adapted from Kail & Cavanaugh, *Human Development: A Life-Span View,* 4th edition

4. What is the paragraph about? Topic: _How couple pledge their love_

5. What is the point of this paragraph? Main idea: _relationships are_ _tested by illness_

6. Which sentence is the topic sentence? T + MI = TS: _For some couple their_ _pledge of love for each other_

Paragraph 3   **Media**

¹Ever wondered what the top sites were for Internet traffic? ²The top five websites by volume are household names and receive millions or even billions of hits per day. ³Every day almost 43% of all Internet users worldwide go to Google. ⁴This translates to 1.5 billion hits every day! ⁵Almost 31% of Internet users "Facebook" on a daily basis. ⁶Coming in third is Yahoo, with about 27% of all worldwide users clicking to that webpage. ⁷YouTube gets about 24%, and Windows Live comes in fifth with 17%.

—Data from Alexa.com

7. What is the paragraph about? Topic: _Top five website_

8. What is the point of this paragraph? Main idea: _The get mpilion or bellion of hits ever dow_

9. Which sentence is the topic sentence? T + MI = TS: _The five website by volume are household name_

Paragraph 4   **Sociology**

[1]People can understand each other not just because of spoken language, but also because of [nonverbal cues]. [2]Body language is an important part of our communication. [3]In fact, it is involved in about 50 percent of our communication. [4]Body language can communicate many emotions and behaviors. [5]Some of these include aggression, boredom, anger, attraction, and lying.

10. What is the paragraph about? Topic: _Body lo_

11. What is the point of this paragraph? Main idea: _Important part of Communication_

12. Which sentence is the topic sentence? T + MI = TS: _Body language is an important part of communication_

Paragraph 5   **Media Studies**

[1]Avijit Halder was born into a brothel in the Indian city of Calcutta, but his life has undergone a dramatic transformation. [2]The 20-year-old is currently pursuing a degree at one of the top film schools in the U.S. [3]It all started with the filming of an Oscar-winning documentary, *Born into Brothels*, which dealt with the lives of the children of Indian sex workers. [4]Avijit Halder was one of eight children of sex workers who was featured in the 2004 documentary film, co-directed by Zana Briski and Ross Kauffman.

—Rizvi, "From a Calcutta Brothel to a New York University,"
BBC News, February 7, 2010

13. What is the paragraph about? Topic: _Avijit Halder_

14. What is the point of this paragraph? Main idea: _He went through a dramit transformation_

15. Which sentence is the topic sentence? T + MI = TS: _____

MASTER YOUR SKILLS 2
Finding the Implied Main Idea

A. Look for the [topic] and put brackets around it.
B. Pay attention to the details and ask yourself, "What do the details have in common?" The answer will be the main idea.
C. Answer the questions that follow each group of sentences.

Group 1   Criminal Justice

- Community corrections focuses on reintegration, which helps rebuild an offender's ties with the community.

- Community corrections also employs a strategy called diversion, which tries to keep shrinking jail and prison spaces for the most dangerous criminals.

- As a general rule, community corrections is less expensive than incarceration.

—Adapted from Gaines & Miller, *Criminal Justice In Action,* 5th edition

1. What is the reading about? _Community Corrections_
2. What are the details? _focuses on reintegration shrinking jail_
3. What do the details have in common? _____
4. Form a topic sentence. _There are three goal of Community Corrections_

Group 2   History

- "Genghis Khan," as most Americans call him, was actually named Temujin by his parents.

- When he was a teenager, Temujin's father was killed, and he used this as an opportunity to build alliances and begin a systematic expansion of power.

- At age 39, Temujin gained leadership of the Mongol people.

- In recognition of his leadership, the Mongols gave him the title Chinggis Khan , which literally means "oceanic leader."

- Chinggis Khan ruled Mongolia for 21 years and expanded its kingdom greatly.

1. What is the reading about? _Chinggis Khan_

2. What are the details? _____

_____

3. What do the details have in common? _____

4. Form a topic sentence. _Over the life of Chinggis Khan and how he become a Mongols leadership_

Group 3   **Popular Culture**

- Keira Knightley supposedly moved from the U.K. to the U.S. because of multiple stalkers.

- Paula Abdul had a female stalker who apparently committed suicide just a few feet from Paula's home.

- Janet Jackson was stalked by a man for nine years and finally received a restraining order after he showed up at a taping armed.

- Madonna, Brad Pitt, Steven Spielberg, and John Lennon (who was killed by a crazed fan) have all been threatened by stalkers.

1. What is the reading about? _Stalker_

2. What are the details? _name of Celbrete_

_____

3. What do the details have in common? _c_

4. Form a topic sentence. _The more famous you are the more likly you are to have a stalkers_

Group 4   **Student Success**

- One way to find success in school is to commit to attending every class from the beginning of a semester to the end.

- Another way to be successful in school is to do your best on all homework assignments.

- Finally, you should participate actively in your classes by doing your work, listening, taking notes, and discussing ideas.

—Adapted from Downing, *On Course,* 5th edition

1. What is the reading about? _____

2. What are the details? _____

_____

3. What do the details have in common? _____

4. Form a topic sentence. _____

Group 5   Personal Finance

- Create a realistic financial budget and live within it.

- Become debt free by paying off unsecured debts from smallest to largest.

- Create an emergency fund of 3–6 months' living expenses.

- Save for retirement (about 15% of your monthly income).

- Save for college expenses.

- Pay off the house early.

- Build wealth and give as you can to help others.

—Adapted from Ramsey, "The 7 Baby Steps," Daveramsey.com

1. What is the reading about? _____

2. What are the details? _____

_____

3. What do the details have in common? _____

4. Form a topic sentence. _____

Paragraph 6   Speech

Whether the culture comes from our nationality, race, ethnicity, religion, work environment, peer group, family, or even gender, we can't ignore its effect on communication. When we give or listen to speeches, we bring our cultural styles of communication with us. For example, a person from an oral culture like is found in Africa would probably rely on the use of storytelling in their speech. A person from an Arab society might include poetry, which is highly revered in that culture. In western culture, speakers tend to speak directly and use specific examples and logical reasoning because that is the expected style of communication.

—Adapted from Griffin, *Invitation to Public Speaking*, 3rd edition

1. What is the reading about? _____

2. What are the details? _____

_____

3. What do the details have in common? _____

4. Form a topic sentence. _____

Paragraph 7   History

Mardi Gras originated in the time of the ancient Greeks. It evolved from a pagan festival to include Christian themes. It has been celebrated in France since the Middle Ages. Since 1699, Mardi Gras has been part of New Orleans's history. Today, Mardi Gras, or Fat Tuesday, is always celebrated 46 days before Easter. Mardi Gras is a time to let go and be wild before the beginning of Catholic Lent, which starts on Ash Wednesday (the day after Fat Tuesday) and is a 40-day period of repentance and sacrifice.

1. What is the reading about? _____

2. What are the details? _____

_____

3. What do the details have in common? _____

4. Form a topic sentence. _____

Paragraph 8   Travel

Puerto Rico is an island in the Caribbean. If you are traveling from America, it is easy to get to, fairly inexpensive, and fun with lots to do and see. For starters, Puerto Rico has wonderful beaches. It also has a huge rain forest—El Yunque—that boasts many beautiful plants and exotic wildlife. The town of Old San Juan has a great ambiance and history with the ruins of El Morro fort. Last but certainly not least are the many casinos, clubs, and fantastic restaurants.

Nik Wheeler/Alamy

1. What is the reading about? _____

2. What are the details? _____

_____

3. What do the details have in common? _____

4. Form a topic sentence. _____

Paragraph 9   Health

First, focus on friendship when you fight. If a committed relationship is not built on a strong friendship, it may be difficult to stay connected over time, especially during fights. Second, remember what you loved and admired in your partner in the first place. Focusing on these qualities can foster a much more positive attitude toward him or her and maybe cause you to be more civil during a fight. Next, show respect, especially during a disagreement. Your partner deserves the same courtesy and civility that your colleagues do. Without respect, love cannot survive. You also need to compliment what your partner does right. Noticing the positive can change how both of you feel about each other. Finally, forgive each other. When your partner hurts your feelings in an argument or fight but then reaches out, don't reject his or her attempts to make things better.

—Adapted from Hales, *An Invitation to Health,* 12th edition

1. What is the reading about? _____

2. What are the details? _____

_____

3. What do the details have in common? _____

4. Form a topic sentence. _____

_____

Paragraph 10   Careers

Air traffic controllers work in glass towers managing air traffic between 3 to 30 miles from the airport. They monitor all planes that travel through the airport's airspace, but their main job is to organize the flow of aircraft into and out of the airport. Air traffic controllers help maintain the flow of air traffic in a safe and orderly manner. They also help prevent aircraft collisions. Every day, air traffic controllers protect almost 2 million air passengers. In the U.S. alone, they safely direct over 60 million aircraft to their destinations each year.

—Adapted from *The 16 Career Clusters: A Project-Based Orientation*

1. What is the reading about? _____

2. What are the details? _____

_____

3. What do the details have in common? _____

4. Form a topic sentence. _____

Recall that MAPP is the reading plan that will help you achieve better reading comprehension. In the last three lessons, you have worked on marking answers to the questions you formed from headings (Lesson 8), searched for what readings are about (Lesson 9), and found the point the author wants to make (Lesson 10).

The Second P of MAPP Is "Proof."

In this lesson we will focus on the second P—Proof.

The Second "P" of MAPP Stands for Proof

Mark = **Mark** the answers to your questions.

About = Topic: What is the reading **about**?

Point = Main Idea: What is the **point**?

Proof = Supporting Detail: What is the **proof**?

What Is the Proof for the Author's Point? The Supporting Details.

Every paragraph has a main idea. Recall that when the main idea is in the same sentence as the topic, the sentence is called the topic sentence (T + MI = TS). Once you have located the main idea or the topic sentence, you know what the author's point is.

Asking "What is the proof?" leads you to the **supporting details** that explain that point. The details are called "supporting" because they give support—evidence or proof for the author's point. The support might consist of examples, statistics, facts, anecdotes, or expert opinion. Let's look at the proof in a sample paragraph.

"Designer dogs"—hybrids created from interbreeding two different types of dogs—are becoming popular. One kind of designer dog is the "puggle," a mix of a pug and a beagle. Another kind is the Maltepoo, which combines the Maltese and the poodle. A third type is the Chipin, a cross between a Chihuahua and a pinscher. Yet another is the Labradoodle, a Labrador-poodle mix.

Mary E. Cioffi/Used under license from Shutterstock.com

A puggle

To find the supporting details in a paragraph, turn the topic sentence into a question and look for the answers.

Turn the Topic Sentence into a Question

What "designer dogs" are becoming popular?

Each answer should be a supporting detail.

Proof—The Supporting Details

1. The "puggle"
2. The Maltepoo
3. The Chipin
4. The Labradoodle

You may have noticed that each sentence with a supporting detail began with a clue that it would state another type of designer dog:

One kind of designer dog . . .

Another kind . . .

A third type . . .

Yet another . . .

Supporting details are often arranged in patterns like this, although sometimes the pattern won't be quite this obvious. We'll talk about patterns of organization in detail in Lessons 12 and 13.

INTERACTION 3–33   **Mapping the Supporting Details**

As you read the following paragraphs, put brackets around the [topic] and underline the main idea. Then form a question from the topic sentence and list the supporting details that answer the question.

A.

> Making a healthy vegetable omelet is easy. First, chop the ingredients you'd like to put in the omelet aside from the eggs, such as red peppers, mushrooms, onions, or spinach. Heat two teaspoons of olive oil in a frying pan until it moves around and is fragrant. Add the vegetables. While the vegetables are cooking, break two eggs into a bowl, season with salt and pepper, and stir quickly until the eggs are foamy. When the vegetables are cooked but still brightly colored, pour the eggs on top of them. As the bottom of the eggs cooks, lift a side of them with a spatula and let the uncooked eggs run underneath. Keep doing this around the edge until the eggs are cooked through. Finally, fold one half of the omelet over the other, slide onto a plate, and grab a fork. Bon appetit!

Question formed from the topic sentence: _____

Proof—the supporting details:

1. _____

2. _____

3. _____

4. _____

5. _____

_____

6. _____

B.

Ashtanga yoga, also known as power yoga, is a fast-paced practice that improves strength and flexibility and provides numerous other benefits. Its active stretching restores the natural range of motion in joints and muscles. Its weight-bearing poses create stronger, denser bones. The practice enhances circulation, lowers blood pressure, and lowers cortisol, the stress hormone.

Compassionate Eye Foundation/
Stockbyte/Jupiter Images

Question formed from the topic sentence: _____

Proof—the supporting details:

1. _____

2. _____

3. _____

   _____

C.

> Michael Phelps has won 14 Olympic gold medals for swimming, more than any other Olympic athlete. He also holds seven world records in swimming. Phelps's incredible motivation and intense training are two reasons for his success, but his physique also plays a role. First, his arms act as paddles, extending 6 feet 7 inches, a wider span than most people his height have. Second, his torso is long and thin, which reduces drag in the water. Third, his large feet and hyperextensible ankles allow him to move his feet like fins.

Question formed from the topic sentence: _____

_____

Proof—the supporting details:

1. _____

2. _____

3. _____

D.

> "Commitment contracts" are one way to help people quit smoking. Yale economist Dean Karlan spearheaded a test program in the Philippines in which smokers who wanted to quit deposited the money they would have spent on cigarettes into a special bank account. After six months those who had succeeded got their money back, while those who had failed lost it. Such a program could be run here by public-health clinics and offer greater incentives, such as letting winners divvy up the money forfeited by losers. Even without such an enhancement, says Karlan, "Filipino participants were 39 percent more likely to quit than those who were not offered the option."
>
> —Willett & Underwood, "Crimes of the Heart," *Newsweek*, February 5, 2010

Question formed from the topic sentence: _____

_____

Proof—the supporting details:

1. _____

_____

2. _____

_____

3. _____

_____

4. _____

_____

E.

> The cameras available today for under $300 are very different from those available in 2001. Back in 2001, every camera on the market had an eye-piece viewfinder; today, almost none do. Then, all $300 cameras ran on AA batteries; today, all use rechargeables. Then, you got a whopping 1.3 or 2.2 megapixels; now, 12 or 14 is standard. Then, some cameras could actually zoom—wow!—up to 2X. Now, pocket cams with 10X or 12X zooms aren't unusual.
>
> —Adapted from Pogue, "Best Cameras for $300 or Less,"
> *New York Times*, February 4, 2010

Question formed from the topic sentence: _____

_____

Proof—the supporting details:

1. _____

2. _____

3. _____

4. _____

_____

INTERACTION 3–34 | **More Practice Mapping the Supporting Details**

Mark the topic and the main idea in the paragraph itself. As you read the following paragraphs, put brackets around the [topic] and underline the main idea. Then form a question from the topic sentence and list the supporting details that answer the question.

A.

Developed first as a comic book character, Superman has since been heard and seen in many different media. From 1939 to 1966, Superman appeared in a daily newspaper comic strip written by his original creators, Jerry Siegel and Joe Shuster. A radio program called *The Adventures of Superman* followed, lasting for 11 years, until 1951. Superman's next media appearance was in a television series that was broadcast for most of the 1950s. In 1966, a Superman movie was made. It was called *It's a Bird, It's a Plane . . . It's Superman!* Superman has also appeared in a variety of movies, among them *Superman* starring Christopher Reeve in 1978, as well as its sequels *Superman II*, *Superman III*, and *Superman IV*.

Pictorial Press Ltd/Alamy

Question formed from the topic sentence: _____

_____

Proof—the supporting details:

1. _____

2. _____

3. _____

4. _____

5. _____

B.

> According to Tuckman's 1965 model of group development, work groups tend to move through stages of development. These stages are forming, storming, norming, performing, and adjourning. **Forming** is the initial stage, during which people come to feel valued and accepted so that they identify with the group. **Storming** is the stage of group development in which the group clarifies its goals and determines the role each member will have in the power structure. **Norming** is the stage during which the group solidifies its rules for behavior, especially those for how conflict will be managed. **Performing** is the stage when the skills, knowledge, and abilities of all the group members are combined to overcome obstacles and meet goals successfully. Finally, **adjourning** is the stage in which members assign meaning to what they have done and determine how to end or maintain interpersonal relations they have developed.
>
> —Adapted from Verderber, Verderber, & Sellnow, *COMM*

Question formed from the topic sentence: _____

_____

Proof—the supporting details:

1. _____

_____

2. _____

_____

3. _____

_____

4. _____

_____

5. _____

_____

C.

> Thanks to new products and programs, it may be easier than ever before to become an ex-smoker. Joining a support group, such as those run by the American Cancer Society or the American Lung Association, doubles your chances of quitting for good. Going to a stop-smoking class can be helpful;

> these are often available through science departments and student health services on many campuses. Smokers who use one of the several forms of Nicotine Replacement Therapy (NRT) are 1.5 to 2 times more likely to quit.
>
> —Adapted from Hales, *An Invitation to Health,* 12th edition

Question formed from the topic sentence: _____

_____

Proof—the supporting details:

1. _____
2. _____
3. _____

D.

> Most Americans take it for granted that individuals guilty of identical crimes should face identical punishments. From an economic perspective, however, this emphasis on equality renders our system decidedly unequal. Take two citizens, one a millionaire investment banker and the other a checkout clerk earning the minimum wage. Driving home from work one afternoon, each is caught by a traffic officer doing 80 miles per hour in a 55-mile-per-hour zone. The fine for this offense is $150. This amount, though equal for both, has different consequences. It represents mere pocket change for the investment banker, but a significant chunk out of the checkout clerk's weekly paycheck.
>
> —Gaines & Miller, *Criminal Justice in Action:*
> *The Core,* 5th edition

Question formed from the topic sentence: _____

_____

Proof—the supporting details:

1. _____
2. _____
3. _____

E.

> One way to avoid this inequality is the "day-fine," as practiced in Sweden and several other European countries. In this system, the fine amount is linked to the offender's daily income. Depending on the seriousness of the crime, a Swedish wrongdoer must pay the equivalent of between 30 and 150 days' pay or, as combined punishment for multiple crimes, up to 200 days' pay. Each day, the offender is required to pay the equivalent of one-third of her or his daily discretionary income to the court. Thus, the day-fine system reflects the seriousness of the crime and also ensures that the economic burden will be equal for those offenders with different incomes.
>
> —Gaines & Miller, *Criminal Justice in Action:*
> *The Core*, 5th edition

Question formed from the topic sentence: _____

_____

Proof—the supporting details:

1. _____
2. _____
3. _____
4. _____
5. _____

Review: Identifying Supporting Details

To decide whether you understand or agree with the author's point, you'll need to identify the supporting details. To find the major supporting details, take the following steps:

- Find the sentence that includes the topic and main idea.
- Turn it into a question.
- Search for the answers, which are the major supporting details.

Major Details Are Different from Minor Details.

There are two types of supporting details: major and minor. The **major details** provide the direct proof for the main idea. They also give organizational structure to the paragraph. The **minor details** give readers extra information about the major details.

The topic is bracketed and the main idea is underlined in this example.

Men and women are a lot more alike than you may think. [The time men and women put in caring for family and doing housework, their reactions to work-family conflict, the ways they want to structure work around family]—all are growing more similar.

- **More men than women plan to provide care for elderly relatives.** A survey of 1,015 Americans by the National Partnership for Women and Families, previously the Women's Legal Defense Fund, shows 56% of men and 53% of women expect to do so in the next 10 years.

- **Men are doing more housework.** The amount of time that employed, married men spend on cooking, repairs, laundry, bill-paying and other housework has risen nearly an hour per workday since 1977, regardless of whether they have working wives. The time that employed, married women spend fell by a half-hour, leaving only about a 45-minute daily gap between men's and women's chore time, the Workforce study shows. The gap in 1977 was three times that.

- **Men drink alcohol and get depressed just as often as women when work and family clash.** That's the conclusion of a four-year study by Michael Frone of the Research Institute on Addictions in Buffalo, N.Y., and others. The sexes are also equally prone to high blood pressure.

- **Men want the freedom to join women in "sequencing" their careers.** They want to be able to slow their job progress during family-focused stages of life, and then speed up again without prejudice from employers. A Catalyst study of 852 partners in dual-earning households found 65% of men want to do so, compared with 72% of women.

—Adapted from Shellenbarger, *Work and Family*

Each sentence printed in bold is a major detail. Notice how the major details directly support the main idea. (They answer the question formed from the topic sentence.) They are all ways that men have become more similar to women in how they think and act about home and work. The minor details give extra information about the major details. In this passage, the minor details give the particular percentages or other numbers that support the major detail.

To put this in the context of MAPP, if we were going to map major and minor details in the second "P" section, we would indent minor details more than the major details. This would show that they support the major details rather than directly supporting the main idea. Here's an example using one of the major supporting details from above.

Proof

1. Major supporting detail: Men want the freedom to join women in "sequencing" their careers.

> *Minor supporting detail:* They want to be able to slow their job progress during family-focused stages of life, and then speed up again without prejudice from employers.

> *Minor supporting detail:* A Catalyst study of 852 partners in dual-earning households found 65% of men want to do so, compared with 72% of women.

INTERACTION 3–35	Mapping the Minor Details

Read each paragraph. As you read the following paragraphs, put brackets around the [topic] and underline the main idea. Number each major supporting detail. Then answer the questions that follow.

A.

Some people learn best by reading and writing—the traditional approach taken in schools. But researchers have identified other basic learning styles as well. *Auditory learners* learn best through verbal lectures, discussions, talking things through, and listening to what others have to say. For these people, written information may have little meaning until it is heard. Such learners often benefit from reading text aloud and using a tape recorder. *Visual learners* need to see the teacher's body language and facial expressions to fully understand the content of a lesson. They may think in pictures and learn best from visual displays, including diagrams, illustrated textbooks, overhead transparencies, videos, flipcharts, and handouts. *Kinesthetic learners* learn best through a hands-on approach, actively exploring the physical

> world around them. They may find it hard to sit still for long periods and may
> become distracted by their need for activity and exploration.
>
> —Adapted from Koch, *So You Want to Be a Teacher: Teaching*
> *and Learning in the 21st Century*

1. What three clues could you use to figure out which ideas are the major supporting
   details?

   - Auditory (listen)
   - Visual (have to see)
   - Kinesthetic (hands on)

2. For each type of learner, which of the five senses is predominant?

   - _____
   - _____
   - _____

B.

> Despite the wide variety of lifestyles developed by the pre-Columbian
> peoples, there are some broad general similarities among the tribes in North
> America during the late 1400s. Most of the tribes, for instance, were based
> on a clan system, in which a tribe was divided into a number of large family
> groups. They were also mostly matrilineal, meaning that children typically
> followed the clan of their mother and that a man, when married, moved into
> the clan of his wife. Matrilineal societies usually develop when agriculture is
> the primary food source for a society. In these societies women are in charge
> of farming (Europeans were universally surprised to see women working
> in the fields). Thus Indian women maintained the tribe's social institutions
> while men were hunting, fishing, or off to war. This system was not univer-
> sal in Native North America, but it does signify a level of sexual equality

absent from Europe at the time. Land was customarily held in common as well. Enslavement (usually of captured enemies) was also relatively common. Indian enslavement varied in severity, and it is unlikely that enslavement was inherited. In other words, the children of slaves were not themselves automatically slaves.

—Schultz, *HIST,* Volume 1

1. What clues could you use to figure out which ideas are the major supporting details?

   • _Clan system_____

   • _Matrilineal society_____

   _____

2. Fill in the minor supporting details in this "Proof" section of MAPP.

   Major supporting detail: They were also mostly matrilineal, meaning that children typically followed the clan of their mother and that a man, when married, moved into the clan of his wife.

   Minor supporting detail: _agriculture (woman farming)_

   _____

   Minor supporting detail: _Maintained Social Institution_

   _____

   Minor supporting detail: _Equality of the Sexes_

   _____

   Minor supporting detail: _new to europeans_

   _____

C.

   In order to provide culturally sensitive health care, health care professionals must understand and take into consideration the cultural differences of their clients. The first step is to learn more about clients' cultures by reading and viewing material about their cultures. Begin by making a list of the cultures served and conduct a systematic study of each. Libraries contain autobiographies, biographies, novels, and essays related to various cultures. The Internet is another useful resource. Television provides travel documentary programs that are both interesting and informative. A second step is to immerse yourself in the food of a culture. Enjoy a restaurant meal with a different cultural cuisine. Consider involving staff in a culture-of-the-month study. At the end of the month, an in-house luncheon could be shared, with each staff member bringing a food contribution representing that culture. Sharing the knowledge learned broadens the base for each staff member and builds a comfort level for interacting with clients of that culture.

—Adapted from Tamparo & Lindh, *Therapeutic Communications for Health Care*,
3rd edition

1. Fill in the minor supporting details in this "Proof" section of MAPP.

   Major supporting detail: The first step is to learn more about clients' cultures by reading and viewing material about their cultures.

   Minor supporting detail: _____

   _____

   Minor supporting detail: _____

   _____

   Minor supporting detail: _____

   _____

   Minor supporting detail: _____

   _____

2. Fill in the minor supporting details in this "Proof" section of MAPP.

> **Major supporting detail:** A second step is to immerse yourself in the food of a culture.
>
> *Minor supporting detail:* _____
>
> _____
>
> *Minor supporting detail:* _____
>
> _____
>
> _____
>
> *Minor supporting detail:* _____
>
> _____

Review: The Difference Between Major and Minor Supporting Details

Learning to distinguish (tell apart) major and minor supporting details will improve your reading comprehension.

- Major details directly support the topic sentence.
- Minor details provide extra details about major supporting details.

ACTIVATE YOUR SKILLS 1
Recognizing Supporting Details

A. As you read the following paragraphs, put brackets around the [topic] and underline the main idea.
B. Mentally turn the main idea into a question to help you identify the major supporting details.
C. Number each major detail.

1.

> Egypt was divided into three parts: Lower Egypt (the Delta region north of present-day Cairo), Upper Egypt (which ran from the First Cataract to the Delta), and Nubia (sometimes called Kush), south of the First Cataract.
>
> —Hansen & Curtis, *Voyages in World History*

2.

> Teams help businesses increase customer satisfaction in several ways. One way is to create work teams that are trained to meet the needs of specific customer groups. Businesses also create problem-solving teams and employee involvement teams to improve overall customer satisfaction and make recommendations for improvements. Teams like these typically meet on a weekly or monthly basis.
>
> —Adapted from Williams, *Management,* 4th edition

3.

> Books on study skills offer a number of suggestions on how to take good-quality lecture notes, two of which are summarized here:
> - Extracting information from lectures requires *active listening.* Focus full attention on the speaker. Try to anticipate what's coming and search for deeper meanings.
> - When course material is especially complex, it is a good idea to prepare for the lecture by *reading ahead* on the scheduled subject in your text. Then you have less brand-new information to digest.
>
> —Adapted from Weiten, *Psychology,* 7th edition

4.

> A person's handwriting exhibits unique characteristics that make it distinguishable from other samples. Handwriting experts examine 12 major categories of exemplars. These 12 characteristics are functions of letter form, line form, and formatting. Letter form includes the shape of letters, curve of letters, the angle or slant of letters, the proportional size of letters, and the use and appearance of connecting lines between letters. Line form includes the smoothness of letters and the darkness of the lines on the upward compared to the downward stroke. Formatting includes the spacing between letters, the spacing between words and lines, the placement of words on a line, and the margins a writer leaves empty on a page.
>
> —Bertino, *Forensic Science*

5.

Planning is one of the best ways to improve performance. It encourages people to work harder, to work hard for extended periods, to engage in behaviors directly related to goal accomplishment, and to think of better ways to do their jobs. But most importantly, companies that plan have larger profits and faster growth than companies that don't plan.

—Williams, *Management*, 4th edition

6.

Leaders are frequently classified as one of three types based on how they perform. The *democratic leader* encourages the participation of all individuals in decisions that have to be made or problems that have to be solved. The *laissez-faire leader* will strive for only minimal rules or regulations, and will allow the individuals in a group to function in an independent manner with little or no direction. An *autocratic leader,* on the other hand, maintains total control, makes all of the decisions, and has difficulty delegating or sharing duties.

—Adapted from Simmers, Simmers-Nartker, & Simmers-Kobelak,
Diversified Health Occupations, 7th edition

7.

Arrest warrants are not always required, and in fact, most arrests are made on the scene without a warrant. A law enforcement officer may make a warrantless arrest if the offense is committed in the presence of the officer. An officer may also make a warrantless arrest if the officer has knowledge that a crime has been committed and probable cause to believe the crime was committed by a particular suspect.

—Adapted from Gaines & Miller, *Criminal Justice in Action:
The Core*, 5th edition

8.

I have polled thousands of college instructors, and they consistently identify three behaviors that their most successful students demonstrate. These rules apply just as well to creating great outcomes in other life roles such as your career and relationships. Consider, then, these three rules as the foundation of your personal code of conduct. "I show up." Commit to attending every class from beginning to end. Makes sense, doesn't it? How can you be successful at something if you're not there? "I do my best work." Commit to doing your best work on all assignments, including turning them in on time. You'd be amazed at how many sloppy assignments instructors see. "I participate actively." Commit to getting involved. College, like life, isn't a spectator sport. Come to class prepared. Listen attentively. Take notes. Think deeply about what's being said. Ask yourself how you can apply your course work to achieve your dreams and goals. If you participate at this high level of involvement, you can't keep yourself from learning even if you wanted to.

—Adapted from Downing, *On Course,* 5th edition

9.

Although much of traditional Navajo culture remains intact, the People Diné, as the Navajos call themselves, also welcome new ideas and change. Their scholarship funds enable hundreds of young people to attend colleges and universities around the country, including their own Navajo Community College on the reservation. A battery of attorneys and a Natural Resources Committee keep watch on the mining leases and lumber operations. The Navajos also operate motels, restaurants, banks, and shopping centers, and they encourage small industries to establish themselves on the reservation. Some Navajos jet to administrative and development conferences in Washington, DC; others speak no English and herd sheep on horseback or on foot miles from the nearest paved road.

—Titon, ed., *Worlds of Music,* Shorter 3rd edition

10.

Archaeologists work with three types of material remains: artifacts, features, and ecofacts. **Artifacts** are objects that have been made or modified by humans and that can be removed from the site and taken to the laboratory for further analysis. Tools, arrowheads, and fragments of pottery are examples of artifacts. **Features,** like artifacts, are made or modified by people, but they cannot be readily carried away from the dig site. Archaeological features include such things as house foundations, fireplaces, and postholes. **Ecofacts** include objects found in the natural environment (such as bones, seeds, and wood) that were not made or altered by humans but were used by them. Ecofacts provide archaeologists with important data concerning the environment and how people used natural resources.

—Ferraro, *Cultural Anthropology,* 6th edition

ACTIVATE YOUR SKILLS 2
Recognizing Supporting Details

I. The topic and main idea are given after each paragraph. Fill in the major and minor supporting details as indicated by the indented lines.

A.

Photography has different meanings in different cultures. Even though cameras can be useful for documenting cultural features, they must be used with caution. In addition to being an invasion of privacy—as may be true in our own society—there are additional reasons why East Africans are reluctant to have their pictures taken. For example, because some East Africans (particularly in the coastal region) are Islamic, they feel strongly about not violating the Koranic prohibition against making images of the human form. Moreover, people who do not understand the nature of photography may believe that having one's picture taken involves the entrapment of their souls in the camera. In those societies where witchcraft is practiced, the prospect of having one's soul captured, particularly by a witch, can be terrifying.

—Ferraro, *Cultural Anthropology,* 6th edition

About: East Africans are reluctant to get their pictures taken

   Point: for reasons in addition to it being an invasion of privacy.

     Proof: 1. _____

               _____

           2. _____

               _____

a. _____

_____

B.

> The best research on the subject shows that by itself, IQ [intelligence quotient] contributes to academic success and to economic success later in life. However, a number of background factors also influence success. One set of background factors derives from the home environment. Your success in school and your economic success later in life depends directly on how much money your parents earn, how many years of education they have, how much they encourage your creativity and studying, how many siblings you have, and so forth. In general, having encouraging parents with more education and higher income, and having fewer siblings, gives a person the greatest chance of success. A second set of background factors influencing success derives from the community environment. As we have already suggested, your academic and economic success depend directly on the percentage of disadvantaged students in your school, the dropout rate in your school, which part of the country you come from, and so forth. These home and community background factors bestow privileges and disadvantages on people independent of IQ.
>
> —Adapted from Brym & Lie, *Sociology,* 3rd edition

About: In addition to IQ, a number of background factors

Point: influence academic and economic success.

Proof: 1. _____

_____

a. _____

b. _____

c. _____

d. _____

2. _____

_____

a. _____

b. _____

c. _____

C.

> The signs of public speaking apprehension vary from individual to individual, and symptoms range from mild to debilitating. Symptoms include physical, emotional, and cognitive reactions. Physical signs may be stomach upset (or butterflies), flushed skin, sweating, shaking, light-headedness, rapid or heavy heartbeats, and verbal disfluencies including stuttering and vocalized pauses ("like," "you know," "ah," "um," and so on). Emotional symptoms include feeling anxious, worried, or upset. Symptoms can also include specific negative cognitions or thought patterns. For example, a highly apprehensive person might dwell on thoughts such as "I'm going to make a fool of myself," or "I just know that I'll blow it."
>
> —Verderber, Verderber, & Sellnow, *COMM*

About: The signs of public speaking apprehension

Point: include physical, emotional, and cognitive reactions.

Proof: 1. _____

     a. _____

     b. _____

     c. _____

     d. _____

     e. _____

     f. _____

     g. _____

  2. _____

     a. _____

     b. _____

     c. _____

  3. _____

     a. _____

     b. _____

II. Provide the type of detail indicated by the indented lines.

D. **About:** Drivers

Point: sometimes feel angry with other drivers.

Proof: 1. _____

_____

2. _____

_____

E. **About:** My favorite place

Point: _____

Proof: 1. _____

2. _____

3. _____

MASTER YOUR SKILLS 1
Recognizing Supporting Details

Use the MAPP reading system to read each selection. Then fill out the major and minor details in the APP after the selection.

A.

Strategies for Your Walt Disney World Visit

To make the most of the time you have at Disney World, follow these tips. First, make your dining reservations and purchase your park tickets before you leave home. Second, plan to arrive at the parks at least 30 minutes ahead of the published opening times, so that you can use the lockers, rent strollers, and otherwise take care of business before everyone else. Third, see the three-star attractions either first thing in the morning, at the end of the day, during a parade, or with a FASTPASS appointment.

—Adapted from Fodor's *Walt Disney World,*
Universal Orlando, and Central Florida

About: The time you have at Disney World

Point: Make the most of it by following these tips.

Proof: 1. *Make dinning reservation and purchase your Dork ticket before you leave home*

2. *arrive 30 mins before opening so you could use the locker and get a rental stroller*

3. *See the three star attraction in the morning at the end of the day during the parade.*

B.

Hallucinogens

1   Hallucinogens are often derived from plants. Hallucinogens derived from plants include mescaline from a cactus (peyote), marijuana, and extracts from certain mushrooms. Other hallucinogens such as LSD, MDMA (the amphetamine ecstacy), and PCP (angel dust), are chemically manufactured.

2   Hallucinogens affect the user's perceptions, thinking, self-awareness, and emotions. LSD is one of the most potent mood-changing chemicals. LSD was originally found in 1938 in a fungus that grows on rye and other grains. It is odorless, colorless, and tasteless and is sold in tablets or on absorbent paper divided into small decorative squares. PCP was first developed as an anesthetic, but it is no longer used because it induces hallucinations. In the illicit drug market, PCP is available in a number of forms. It may be a pure, white, crystal-like powder, a tablet, or a capsule. It can be sniffed, swallowed, smoked, or injected. Mescaline is smoked or swallowed in the form of capsules or tablets. Marijuana leaves (cannabis) may be smoked or refined, concentrated, and sold as hashish. Hashish is made from resin found on ripe flowers, which are rolled into balls and smoked.

—Adapted from Bertino, *Forensic Science*

Paragraph 1

About: Hallucinogens

Point: are often derived from plants.

Proof: 1. *Hallucinogens derived from plants include mescaline from a cactus, Marijuana*

2. *Hall*

Paragraph 2

About: Hallucinogens

Point: affect the user's perceptions, thinking, self-awareness, and emotions.

Proof: 1. _LSD is one of the most potent mood-changing chemical_

   a. _It was found in 1938 on a fungus that grows on rye and other grain_

   b. _it is odorless, colorless and tasteless_

2. _PCP was first developed as an anesthetic, b_

   a. _____

   b. _____

   c. _____

3. _Mescaline is smoked or swallowed_

4. _Marijuana leaves may be smoked or refined/concentrated and sold as hash_

   a. _Hashis is made from resin found_

C.

> The first settlers came to southern Mesopotamia from the eastern Mediterranean and western Turkey. They found the environment harsh. Each year not enough rain fell to support farming, and no wild grain grew naturally in the marshlands. In addition,

the Tigris and Euphrates Rivers tended to flood in the late summer, when crops were ripening, and the floodwaters often washed away the settlers' homes.

2   The settlers responded by developing techniques for draining the water. They settled along the shore of the Euphrates, which flowed less rapidly than the Tigris, and dug channels for the floodwater from the Euphrates. They discovered that they could use these channels to move the water to fields far from the river. Using irrigation, these early farmers permanently settled the lower Mesopotamian plain between 6000 and 5000 B.C.E.

—Hansen & Curtis, *Voyages in World History*

Paragraph 1

About: The first settlers to southern Mesopotamia

Point: found the environment harsh.

Proof: 1. Each year not enough rain to support their farming no wild grain grow

2. The Rivers tended to flood in the summer, when crops were ripening, and the floodwaters

Paragraph 2

About: The settlers

Point: responded by developing techniques for draining the water.

Proof: 1. They settled along the shore of the Euphrates

2. They

3. dug channels for the flood water from the Euphrates.

MASTER YOUR SKILLS 2
Recognizing Supporting Details

Read the following selection from an American government textbook. Then answer the questions that follow.

Economic and Demographic Diversity

1   Diversity involves more than differences in people's race, national origin, and religious affiliation. What people do for a living, how much they earn, where they live, and how old they are all are potential bases for political differences, and over time these factors are probably more important than their national origin or religious affiliation.

2   Economic diversity especially is important. Some prefer to think of America as a country without social classes (or without any classes except a middle class), but we do have a range of social classes, from the lower class to the middle class to the upper class, and with multiple levels in each one.

3   Many like to think of America as a land of opportunity, but opportunity knocks harder and louder for those who are better off. Most of those who are born poor stay poor. Although our society is not as class conscious as many others, our personal economic situations play an important part in shaping our views toward politics and our roles in the political process. Most people who are poor, for example, do not vote, but those who do vote tend to vote Democratic. Most people who are well-off do vote, and they are more likely to vote Republican than Democratic.

4   Regional and residential differences also are important. The sharpest split historically has been between the North and the South, as a result of the division over the right of the southern states to secede from the Union in order to maintain a regional economic system rooted in slavery and the Civil War that resulted from this division. Other regional differences exist as well. People on the East Coast and West Coast tend to have different views than those in the middle of the country. Residential differences shape politics too. City dwellers have different views than rural residents, and suburbanites may have different views than either.

5   Age differences also can affect political orientation. The needs and interests of older citizens are substantially different from those of young adults. Older citizens vote at higher rates, and their interest groups are among the most powerful in the country. This fact has made economic security and health care for senior citizens high-priority policy issues, even while the number of children living in poverty is increasing.

—Welch, Gruhl, Comer, & Rigdon, *Understanding American Government: The Essentials*

1. People often think of diversity as being about differences in race, origin, and religion. What other factors are involved?

- What do people do for a living
- How much they earn
- Where they live
- How old they are

2. Of the following factors, which one is the most important in determining how people view politics?

____ National origin

____ Religious affiliation

_✓_ Economic diversity

3. Does America have different social classes?   Yes   No

4. Do the authors suggest that people from upper classes have more opportunities than people from lower classes?   Yes   No

5. When poor people vote, whom do they usually vote for?   Republicans   Democrats

6. When well-off people vote, whom do they usually vote for? Republicans Democrats

7. What supporting details do the authors give to support this part of one of their main ideas? *Regional differences are also important.*

- The sharpest split historically has been between the north and the south as a result of the division over the right Southern
- State

8. What supporting details do the authors give to support this part of one of their main ideas? *Residential differences are also important.*

- City dwellers have different views than rural resident, and suburbanites may have different views than either

9. MAPP the final paragraph of this selection.

   About: _About ege different ___ versity_

   Point: _____

   Proof: 1. _the needs of older peple are different from young people_

   2. _the old people intrest rate are higher than the yound_

   3. _health care for senior citizerp high-priority policy issues, even while the number of children leving in poverty_

10. Which of the main ideas in this selection is supported by details in two paragraphs rather than just one paragraph?

   ___✓ Economic diversity is important in political differences.

   _____ Regional and residential diversity is important in political differences.

   _____ Age diversity is important in political differences.

Summary Activity: MAPP for Reading Comprehension

Part 3 has discussed how to use MAPP to improve your reading comprehension. Fill in the Reading Guide by completing each idea on the left with information from Part 3 on the right. You can return to this guide throughout the course as a reminder of how to use this process when you are reading articles or textbook chapters.

Reading Guide to Using MAPP

Complete this idea	with information from Part 3.
State the meaning of each letter of MAPP.	1. _____ 2. _____ 3. _____ 4. _____
The reason for using the MAPP system is	5. _____
Three steps you can take to improve your reading comprehension when a reading selection has a title and/or headings are:	6. _____ 7. _____ 8. _____
When you ask the question "What is the reading about?" you are trying to identify _____.	9. _____
Two things you can look for to help you identify the topic of a reading selection are:	10. _____ 11. _____
You'll know that you have stated the topic at the right level of generality if	12. _____
When you ask the question "What is the point?" you are trying to identify	13. _____
You can identify the main idea by these features:	14. It is _____ than the topic. 15. It is _____ than the supporting details. 16. It often appears in a sentence with the _____ .

Complete this idea	with information from Part 3.
The main idea is	17. _____ _____
The statement T + MI = TS means	18. _____
The topic sentence of a paragraph can be located	19. _____
When the main idea of a reading selection is not stated, you need to _____ in order to understand what it is.	20. _____ _____
When you ask the question "What is the proof?" you are trying to identify	21. _____
In a paragraph, the supporting details function to	22. _____
To help you find the supporting details, you can take the topic sentence (or main idea) and	23. _____
What is the next step?	24. _____
The difference between major and minor details is that	25. _____ _____

Think about what your reading habits were before you read Part 3. How did they differ from the reading suggestions here? Write your thoughts. _____

_____

_____

Application: MAPP for Reading Comprehension

SPEECH

● Pre-Reading the Selection

Sting (British rock musician Gordon Sumner) gave the commencement address at Berklee School of Music on May 15, 1994. The following reading, "The Mystery of Music," is part of that speech.

Surveying the Reading

What parts of the reading selection should you survey? _____

_____ *to entertain* _____

Go ahead and survey the reading that begins on page 365.

Guessing the Purpose

Based on the occasion for which Sting gave his speech and the title of the reading, what do you suppose the speaker's purpose is: to persuade, inform, or entertain? _____

_____

Predicting the Content

Based on your survey, what are three things you expect the reading selection to discuss?

- *why musician is not good role models*
- *why is music*
- _____

Activating Your Knowledge

Search your memory for knowledge you have about any of the following topics: musicians, melodies, metaphors, silence, songwriting, meditation, or religious rites. Write down three of these pieces of prior knowledge, even if what you know seems vague.

- _____
- _____
- _____

● Reading with Pen in Hand

Now read the selection. Pay attention to and mark any ideas that seem important, and respond to the questions and vocabulary items in the margin.

Access the Reading CourseMate via **www.cengagebrain.com/ shop/ISBN/1413033156** to hear vocabulary words from this selection and view a video about this topic.

The Mystery of Music

Sting

Reading Journal

1   Musicians aren't particularly good role models in society. We really don't have a very good reputation. Philanderers, alcoholics, addicts, **alimony-jumpers**, tax-evaders. And I'm not just talking about rock musicians. Classical musicians have just as bad a reputation. And jazz musicians . . . forget it!

2   But when you watch a musician play—when he enters that private musical world—you often see a child at play, innocent and curious, full of wonder at what can only be adequately described as a mystery—a sacred mystery even. Something deep. Something strange. Both joyous and sad. Something impossible to explain in words. I mean what could possibly keep us playing scales and arpeggios hour after hour, day after day, year after year? Is it some vague promise of glory, money, or fame? Or is it something deeper?

3   Our instruments connect us to this mystery and a musician will maintain this sense of wonder 'til the day he or she dies. I had the privilege of spending some time with the great arranger Gil Evans in the last year of his life. He was still listening, still open to new ideas, still open to the wonder of music. Still a curious child.

4   So we stand here in our robes with our diplomas, our degrees of excellence. Some are merely **honorary**, some diligently worked for. We have mastered the laws of harmony and the rules of counterpoint, the skills of arranging and orchestrating, of developing themes and rhythmic motifs. But do any of us really know what music is? Is it merely physics? Mathematics? The stuff of romance? Commerce? Why is it so important to us? What is its essence?

5   I can't even pretend to know. I've written hundreds of songs, had them published, had them in the charts. Grammys and enough written proof that I'm a **bona fide**, successful songwriter. Still, if

● Picture what the author is saying.

alimony-jumpers Who pays alimony to whom? What do you guess it means to "jump" alimony?

● Who is the author using as an example of a musician's sense of wonder?

● Imagine the scene the author is describing.

● Does any information here surprise you? Why? Make a brief note.

honorary Look for the antonym in the next part of the sentence. What words are the antonym? What does *honorary* mean?

bona fide The examples in the first part of this sentence explain what these words mean. Guess the meaning.

Mirrorpix/Trinity Mirror/Alamy

a paradox is a contretton

metaphor The context does not give any clue about the meaning of *metaphor*, so use a dictionary to look it up.

● Are any ideas here new to you? Which ones?

paradoxically The end of the sentence—"the importance of silence in music"—gives an example of a possible *paradox*, which is the root of *paradoxically*. What do you think a *paradox* is?

● Search for connections. Have you ever found silence awkward or frightening?

somebody asks me how I write songs, I have to say, "I don't really know." I don't really know where they come from. A melody is always a gift from somewhere else. You just have to learn to be grateful and pray that you will be blessed again some other time. It's the same with the lyrics. You can't write a song without a **metaphor**. You can mechanically construct verses, choruses, bridges, middle eights, but without a central metaphor, you ain't got nothing.

6   I often wonder: where do melodies and metaphors come from? If you could buy them in a store I'd be first in line, believe me. I spend most of my time searching for these mysterious commodities, searching for inspiration.

7   **Paradoxically**, I'm coming to believe in the importance of silence in music. The power of silence after a phrase of music for example; the dramatic silence after the first four notes of Beethoven's Fifth Symphony, or the space between the notes of a Miles Davis solo. There is something very specific about a rest in music. You take your foot off the pedal and pay attention. I'm wondering whether, as musicians, the most important thing we do is merely to provide a frame for silence. I'm wondering if silence itself is perhaps the mystery at the heart of music? And is silence the most perfect music of all?

8   Songwriting is the only form of meditation that I know. And it is only in silence that the gifts of melody and metaphor are offered. To people in the modern world, true silence is something we rarely

experience. It is almost as if we conspire to avoid it. Three minutes of silence seems like a very long time. It forces us to pay attention to ideas and emotions that we rarely make any time for. There are some people who find this awkward, or even frightening.

9   Silence is disturbing. It is disturbing because it is the wavelength of the soul. If we leave no space in our music—and I'm as guilty as anyone else in this regard—then we rob the sound we make of a defining context. It is often music born from anxiety to create more anxiety. It's as if we're afraid of leaving space. Great music's as much about the space between the notes as it is about the notes themselves. A bar's rest is as important and significant as the bar of demi-, semi-quavers that precedes it. What I'm trying to say here is that if ever I'm asked if I'm religious I always reply, "Yes, I'm a **devout** musician." Music puts me in touch with something beyond the intellect, something otherworldly, something sacred.

- Can you think of any examples of songs that seem to create anxiety? Make a note.

devout A synonym for *devout* is given in the sentence before this one. What is the synonym?

10   How is it that some music can move us to tears? Why is some music indescribably beautiful? I never tire of hearing Samuel Barber's "Adagio for Strings" or Faure's "Pavane" or Otis Redding's "Dock of the Bay." These pieces speak to me in the only religious language I understand. They **induce** in me a state of deep meditation, of wonder. They make me silent.

- Search for connections. What songs have moved you to tears? Write down the titles.

induce The sentence after this one gives a synonym for *induce*. What is the synonym?

11   It's very hard to talk about music in words. Words are superfluous to the abstract power of music. We can fashion words into poetry so that they are understood the way music is understood, but they only **aspire** to the condition where music already exists.

aspire to The end of the sentence contrasts with *aspire to*. What contrasting idea is given? What does *aspire to* mean?

12   Music is probably the oldest religious rite. Our ancestors used melody and rhythm to co-opt the spirit world to their purposes—to try and make sense of the universe. The first priests were probably musicians. The first prayers were probably songs.

13   So what I'm getting round to saying is that as musicians, whether we're successful, playing to thousands of people every night, or not so successful, playing in bars or small clubs, or not successful at all, just playing alone in your apartment to the cat, we are doing something that can heal souls, that can mend us when our spirits are broken. Whether you make a million dollars or not one cent, music and silence are priceless gifts. May you always possess them. May they always possess you.

- Picture each musician the author discusses: the successful, the not so successful, and the not successful at all.

● A MAPP of the Selection

1. What question did you form from the title? _What is the Mystry of music._

2. Go back and reread the reading. Look for the various parts of the answer to that question. For each paragraph listed below, make a note about the part of the answer contained in that paragraph. Don't list a lot of information; write a single sentence.

   1. Paragraph 2: _____

      _____

   2. Paragraph 3: _____

   3. Paragraph 4: _____

      _____

   4. Paragraph 5: _____

      _____

   5. Paragraph 6: _____

   6. Paragraph 7: _____

   7. Paragraph 8: _____

   8. Paragraph 9: _____

      _____

   9. Paragraph 10: _____

   10. Paragraph 11: _____

      _____

   11. Paragraph 12: _____

   12. Paragraph 13: _____

      _____

● MAPPs of Individual Paragraphs

Fill in the missing elements of each MAPP.

13. Paragraph 1

   About: _____

    Point: _____

       Proof: 1. We really don't have a very good reputation.

a. Philanderers, alcoholics, addicts, alimony-jumpers, tax-evaders.

2. And I'm not just talking about rock musicians.

3. Classical musicians have just as bad a reputation.

4. And jazz musicians . . . forget it!

14. Paragraph 2

About: Watching a musician entering that private musical world

Point: _____

Proof: 1. A musician is innocent and curious, full of wonder at what can only be adequately described as a mystery—a sacred mystery even.

2. Something deep. Something strange. Both joyous and sad. Something impossible to explain in words.

3. I mean what could possibly keep us playing scales and arpeggios hour after hour, day after day, year after year?

a. Is it some vague promise of glory, money, or fame?

b. Or is it something deeper?

15. Paragraph 3

About: _____

Point: _____

Proof: 1. I had the privilege of spending some time with the great arranger Gil Evans in the last year of his life.

2. He was still listening, still open to new ideas, still open to the wonder of music.

3. Still a curious child.

16. Paragraph 5

About: _____

Point: _____

Proof: 1. I don't really know where they come from.

2. A melody is always a gift from somewhere else.

3. You just have to learn to be grateful and pray that you will be blessed again some other time.

17. Paragraph 7

   About: Silence in music

   Point: _____

   Proof: 1. _____

   a. The dramatic silence after the first four notes of Beethoven's Fifth Symphony.

   b. The space between the notes of a Miles Davis solo.

   2. _____

   3. _____

   4. _____

   _____

18. Paragraph 12

   About: _____

   Point: _____

   Proof: 1. _____

   _____

   2. _____

   3. _____

Spotlight on Inference: The Speaker's Purpose

When you are reading, keep in mind that the author has a purpose for writing, or in this case, speaking. The speech you have read is Sting speaking to musicians who are just graduating from college. Keep this larger purpose in mind when you are trying to figure out the author's purpose in different parts of the selection.

19. Paragraph 1 doesn't seem to have anything to do with the mystery of music. Reread it and the second paragraph. Why do you think the speaker included Paragraph 1? _____

   _____

   _____

20. Paragraph 13 ends the speech. Why do you think Sting includes the detail about different degrees of success? Draw on your prior knowledge and logic. _____

   _____

   _____

Test 3: Reading Comprehension

ONLINE NEWSPAPER ARTICLE

Your instructor may ask you to take practice tests throughout the semester to help you decide which topics you need to study the most. All the tests in this book include questions about all the major reading comprehension skills after the reading selection.

● Pre-Reading the Selection

The following selection, "The Power of Music," was printed in the October 29, 2007, issue of Boston.com, the online version of the *Boston Globe* newspaper.

Surveying the Reading

What parts of the reading should you survey? _____

_____

Go ahead and survey the reading that begins on page 373.

Guessing the Purpose

Based on the title of the article and the place of publication, do you think the author's purpose is to persuade, inform, or entertain? _____

Predicting the Content

Based on your survey, what are three things you expect the reading selection to discuss?

- _____

- _____

- _____

Activating Your Knowledge

Search your memory for knowledge you have about any of the following topics: cerebral palsy, computerized music, human sensitivity to music, strokes, and pain reduction. Write down three of these pieces of prior knowledge, even if what you know seems vague.

- _____

- _____

- _____

Common Knowledge

Read these terms and their definitions to help you understand the reading selection.

cerebral palsy *(paragraph 2)* A disorder that causes reduced ability to use muscles and poor coordination; sometimes it also causes speech and learning difficulties.

evolution *(paragraph 5)* A gradual process that occurs over generations of a species, causing the species to change and become better adapted to its environment.

stroke *(paragraph 9)* A sudden loss of brain function caused by the rupturing or blockage of a blood vessel in the brain.

● Reading with Pen in Hand

Now read the selection. As you read, pay attention to and mark any ideas that seem important, and respond to the questions and vocabulary items in the margin.

Access the Reading CourseMate via **www.cengagebrain.com/ shop/ISBN/1413033156** to hear vocabulary words from this selection and view a video about this topic.

The Power of Music

Judy Foreman

Reading Journal

1   Dan Ellsey, 33, was sitting in his wheelchair in a soulless room at Tewksbury Hospital, his virtually useless arms and weak torso strapped to the chair for safety. Suddenly, as soon as we were introduced, he arched his back, grinned broadly, and aimed the riveting power of his dark brown eyes at me, as if eye contact were his only means of **transcending** the prison of his body.

● Picture Dan Ellsey in the hospital room using the details supplied by the author.

transcending Look at the words starting with "as if" to guess what *transcending* means.

2   But it isn't. In the last few years, Ellsey, who was born with cerebral palsy, has discovered another, almost miraculous, way of expressing himself: music. Not just listening to country and soft rock, as he has done for years, but composing music himself with a special computerized system called Hyperscore, developed by composer-inventor Tod Machover, professor of music and media and director of the Opera of the Future group at the MIT Media Lab.

● You should have formed a question from the title of this article. What is one answer to it, based on this paragraph?

3   I stand there, awed, as we listen to Ellsey's music, which on the computer has an abstract, eerie sound that swells and recedes like ocean waves. As we listen, we watch on the computer screen as the "score"—colored lines on a graph that represent different instruments—unfolds before our eyes.

"score" Dan's "score" is defined inside the dashes after "score." The quotation marks indicate that the word is not being used in its usual sense. What is a musical *score,* usually?

Pat Greenhouse/Boston Globe/Landov

4   A look of pure bliss crosses his face. For Ellsey, as for most human beings, music has almost inexplicable power—to rouse armies to battle, to soothe babies, to communicate peaks of joy and depths of sorrow that mere words cannot.

5   Just why evolution would have endowed our brains with the **neural** machinery to make music is a mystery.

6   "It's unclear why humans are so uniquely sensitive to music—certainly music shares many features with spoken language, and our brains are particularly developed to process the rapid tones and segments of sound that are common to both," said Dr. Oliver Sacks, the neurologist whose latest book, *Musicophilia,* is about the brain's sensitivity to music. Some researchers, he added in an e-mail interview, believe that in primitive cultures, music and speech were not **distinct**. Other researchers debate which came first in evolution, speech or song.

7   What is clear is that the brain is abundantly wired to process music.

8   Scientists at the Montreal Neurological Institute, for instance, have found dramatic evidence on brain scans that the "chills," or a visceral feeling of awe, that people report listening to their favorite music are real. Music that a person likes—but not music that is

● What are three other answers to the question you formed from the title?

neural The *-al* ending here shows that this word is an adjective. The related noun is *neuron.* A *neuron* is a particular kind of cell. Find out what kind of cell it is.

● What expert is being cited here? What is the title of his book?

distinct This sentence starts "Some researchers believe." The next one starts "Other researchers debate." The author has set up a contrast between the two sentences. Guess what *distinct* means.

● What is another answer to the question you formed from the title?

disliked—activates both the higher, thinking centers in the brain's cortex, and, perhaps more important, also the "ancient circuitry, the motivation and reward system," said experimental psychologist Robert Zatorre, a member of the team. It's this ancient part of the brain that, often through the neurotransmitter dopamine, also governs basic drives such as for food, water, and sex, suggesting the tantalizing idea that the brain may consider music **on a par with** these crucial drives.

9   But music has the power not just to awe but to heal. If a person has a stroke on the left side of the brain, where the speech centers are located in most people, that "wipes out a major part of communication," said Dr. Gottfried Schlaug, chief of the Cerebrovascular Disorder Division and Stroke-Recovery Laboratory at Beth Israel Deaconess Medical Center.

10   But if the right side, where a lot of music is processed, is intact, some stroke patients can use "melodic intonation therapy," which involves singing using two tones (relatively close in pitch) to communicate. Schlaug's research suggests that with intense therapy some patients can even move from this two-tone singing back to actual speech.

11   Stroke patients with **gait** problems also profit from neurologically based music therapy. At the Center for Biomedical Research in Music at Colorado State University in Ft. Collins, director Michael Thaut and his team have shown that people partially paralyzed on one side can **retrain** to walk faster and in a more coordinated way if they practice walking rhythmically, cued by music or a metronome. Combining rhythmic training with physical therapy also helps stroke patients recover gait faster, he said in an e-mail.

12   "Music helps us organize our movement," said Kathleen Howland, who has a PhD in music and cognition and teaches at Lesley University in Cambridge. Twenty years ago, she said, therapists tried to get stroke patients to walk better by flashing lights at them. But music, especially rhythm, works much better, she said.

13   A number of studies show that music therapy—the use of music for medical goals—can reduce pain. In a 2001 study on burn patients, whose burns must be frequently scraped to reduce dead tissue, researchers found that music therapy significantly reduced the **excruciating** pain. Patients undergoing colonoscopy also seem

---

on a par with The author says that music activates the ancient part of the brain that governs the drive to find food, water, and sex. What does *on a par with* probably mean?

● What is another answer to the question you formed from the title?

● Imagine hearing what this change from two tone singing to speech might sound like.

gait The rest of this paragraph suggests the meaning of *gait*. What does it mean?

retrain This word is composed of *re* + *train*. What does it mean?

● Picture the people described in paragraphs 11 and 12. What quality of music do they find helpful?

excruciating Imagine that you have burns on your body that need to be scraped. Is *excruciating* pain more like a harmless ache or a terrible pain?

● What power of music do paragraphs 13 and 14 discuss?

14 to feel less pain and need fewer sedative drugs if they listen to music during the procedure, according to several studies.

But not all studies have been so clear-cut. One 2007 review by the Cochrane Collaboration, a nonprofit, international organization that evaluates medical research, involved pooling data from 51 pain studies; it showed that listening to music can reduce the intensity of pain and the need for narcotic drugs, but cautioned that, overall, the benefit was small.

● What three kinds of people may be helped by music?

15 Music therapy may also improve mental state and functioning in people with schizophrenia, according to a 2007 Cochrane review. Premature infants who listen to lullabies learn to suck better and gain more weight than those who don't get music therapy. And Deforia Lane, director of music therapy at the University Hospitals Ireland Cancer Center in Cleveland, has found an improvement in **immune** response among hospitalized children who played, sang, and created music compared to children who did not get music therapy.

immune A related word is *immunization*. If you get an *immunization* against measles, can you get measles later? What does *immune* probably mean?

16 Indeed, the list of potential benefits from music therapy seems almost endless (check out the website of the American Music Therapy Association, musictherapy.org). For some people, like Dan Ellsey, they can be nothing short of liberating.

● Imagine you are in Dan's situation. What would it feel like to be able to say what is reported here and in paragraph 18?

17 As the sound of Ellsey's music faded away the other day, I asked him what message he would like to tell people through his music. **Painstakingly**, he tapped out his answer, aiming a laser device on his forehead to highlight pictures and letters on his computer. "I am smart," he wrote, arching his back, joy beaming from his eyes. "I have a good personality."

painstakingly This word is composed of *pains + taking + ly*. It means "taking great pains with something." If you take great pains with something, do you do it carelessly or carefully?

18 Anything else? Eyes alight, he tapped: "I am a musician."

● Comprehension Questions

Write the letter of the answer on the line. Then explain your thinking.

Main Idea

_____ 1. Which of these sentences best expresses the main idea of this passage?

a. The brain is sensitive to music.

b. Music has almost inexplicable power.

c. Music can heal people.

d. Music helps organize our movement.

WHY? What information in the selection leads you to give that answer? _____

_____

_____

_____

_____ 2. What is the main idea of paragraph 2?

a. Ellsey has discovered an almost miraculous way of expressing himself: music.

b. Ellsey was born with cerebral palsy.

c. He uses a computerized system called Hyperscore to compose music.

d. Hyerscore was developed by Tod Machover.

WHY? What information in the selection leads you to give that answer? _____

_____

_____

_____

Supporting Details

_____ 3. What detail supports the following idea? *Music has the power not just to awe but to heal.*

a. Music rouses armies to battle.

b. Scientists have found dramatic evidence that the "chills" people get while listening to their favorite music are real.

c. Music can communicate deep emotion.

d. Music can help stroke victims learn how to communicate again.

WHY? What information in the selection leads you to give that answer? _____

_____

_____

_____

_____ 4. In paragraph 13, which sentences are the supporting details?

a. Sentences 1 and 2.

b. Sentences 2 and 3.

      c. Sentences 1 and 3.

      d. None of them.

WHY? What information in the selection leads you to give that answer? _____

_____

_____

_____

Author's Purpose

____ 5. Why does the author begin and end this article with Dan Ellsey's story?

      a. Ellsey's story demonstrates the sad state of music education.

      b. Ellsey's story is an example of a miracle cure for cerebral palsy.

      c. Ellsey's story helps readers become interested in the power of music.

      d. Ellsey's story is taken from Dr. Oliver Sacks's book *Musicophilia*.

WHY? What information in the selection leads you to give that answer? _____

_____

_____

_____

____ 6. What is the author's main purpose in this reading selection?

      a. To inform readers about the diverse ways music affects people.

      b. To persuade readers that Dan Ellsey represents people of the future, who will use laser beams to work on their computers.

      c. To help readers feel pity and rage at Dan Ellsey's situation.

      d. To inform readers about the effects of evolution on the ancient part of the brain.

WHY? What information in the selection leads you to give that answer? _____

_____

_____

_____

Relationships

_____ 7. In paragraph 2, what does the word *but* suggest about the relationship between paragraph 1 and paragraph 2?

    a. A contrast or difference between the paragraphs.

    b. A similarity or comparison between the two paragraphs.

    c. A definition was given in paragraph 1 and an example of it in paragraph 2.

    d. A cause was given in paragraph 1 and its effect was given in paragraph 2.

WHY? What information in the selection leads you to give that answer? _____

_____

_____

_____

_____ 8. What is the relationship between the phrase "music therapy" and the words inside the dashes? *A number of studies show that music therapy—the use of music for medical goals—can reduce pain.*

    a. The words inside the dashes are an example of music therapy.

    b. The words inside the dashes explain how music therapy developed.

    c. The words inside the dashes don't have a relationship to music therapy.

    d. The words inside the dashes are the definition of music therapy.

WHY? What information in the selection leads you to give that answer? _____

_____

_____

_____

Fact, Opinion, and Inference

_____ 9. Which researcher does the author name to support the idea that the brain is "abundantly wired to process music"?

    a. Dr. Gottfried Schlaug

    b. Deforia Lane

    c. Tod Machover

    d. Robert Zatorre

WHY? What information in the selection leads you to give that answer? _____

_____

_____

_____

_____ 10. The following words were all used in this article: *neural, neurologist, neurological, neurotransmitter, neurologically.* Based on their use in this article, what do these words probably relate to?

a. The emotions experienced when music is played.

b. The brain and other parts of the nervous system.

c. The legs of premature infants.

d. A person's self-worth.

WHY? What information in the selection leads you to give that answer? _____

_____

_____

_____

● Vocabulary in New Contexts

Review the vocabulary words in the margins of the reading selection and then complete the following activities.

EASY Note Cards

Make a note card for each vocabulary word from the reading. On one side, write the word. On the other side, divide the card into four areas and label them E, A, S, and Y. Add a word or phrase in each area so that you wind up with an example sentence, an antonym, a synonym, and, finally, a definition that shows you understand the meaning of the word with your logic. Remember that a synonym or an antonym may have appeared in the reading.

Relationships Between Words

Circle yes or no to answer the question. Then explain your answer.

1. Do some people have **distinct gaits**?

   Yes   No

   Why or why not? _____

2. Would you respect a person who had **transcended excruciating** pain?

   Yes   No

   Why or why not? _____

3. Is receiving a vaccination **on a par with** having **immunity**?

   Yes   No

   Why or why not? _____

Language in Your Life

Write short answers to each question. Look at vocabulary words closely before you answer.

1. Name one problem in your life that you have had to **transcend**. _____

   _____

2. Name one person you know who has **retrained** for a new job. _____

   _____

3. Name one thing in your life that's **on a par with** taking a vacation. _____

   _____

4. Name one situation in which you are **painstaking**. _____

   _____

5. Name one person whom it's a **distinct** pleasure to know. _____

   _____

Language in Use

Select the best word to complete the meaning of each sentence.

> **distinct   excruciating   gait   immunity   neural**
> **on a par with   painstakingly   score   transcending**

1. Some people might say that climbing a huge mountain like Mount Everest or K2 is _____ exploring the deep sea bed, but others would say that climbing is far more difficult and dangerous.

2. Both adventures require _____ preparations, including getting into extremely good physical shape, purchasing all kinds of specialized gear, and mapping the best routes.

3. However, no amount of preparation can grant _____ to the dangers of extreme mountain climbing, which include frostbite, lung problems, and death.

4. Beck Weathers, a famous mountaineer, suffered an _____ case of frostbite when he got caught in a sudden blizzard high on Mount Everest in May 1996. (Once he got off the mountain, his fingers and nose had to be amputated.)

5. _____ the problem of being utterly snowblind, he somehow made it back to camp, but his _____ was severely affected by not being able to feel his toes.

6. While each mountain climber has his or her own _____ challenges, a research finding that applies to all climbers is that the more time spent above 20,000 feet, the more damaged the brain becomes.

7. Perhaps the _____ pathways in the brain become damaged by repeated exposure to high altitude. Scuba diving at extreme depths or in very cold water also impairs mental functioning.

Spotlight on Word Parts: *Trans-*

As you have learned, *transcend* means "to rise above." The word *transcend* is composed of two parts:

trans- means "across, through, beyond" **+** scend means "climb"

When you put the two parts together, you get "climb beyond."

The word part trans- is used in many other words.

transplant = plant across

transfer = carry across

transmit = send across

translucent = shine through

transfix = pierce (cut) through

Circle the correct word in each of these sentences.

1. The stained glass window in the church was (transplant / transmit / translucent).

2. The cell phone tower (transplants / transmits / translucent) signals.

3. She was a (transmit / transfix / transplant) from urban New York City to rural Vermont.

4. The snake's unblinking eyes (transfixed / transplanted / transferred) the rabbit, causing it to freeze.

5. The bank will (transfer / translucent / transfix) money from one account to another.

PART 4

"It's a funny thing about comin' home. Looks the same, smells the same, feels the same. You'll realize what's changed is you."

Brad Pitt said this as Benjamin Button in *The Curious Case of Benjamin Button.*

Find chapter-specific interactive learning tools for *Activate,* including quizzes, videos, and more, through CengageBrain.com.

Videos Related to Readings

Vocab Words on Audio

Read and Talk on Demand

Paramount Pictures/Warner Bros. Pictures/
The Kobal Collection/Picture Desk

Reading Textbooks

Have you ever returned home after a long absence to find that it seems the same as when you left it, yet at the same time realize that you yourself have changed? This experience isn't uncommon; most people leave and come back to friends or family numerous times through the years.

Benjamin Button contrasts, or emphasizes differences, when he says that home stays the same while he changes. People often contrast one thing with another to make each one clearer to a viewer, listener, or reader. Contrast is one of the basic methods we use to understand and describe the world. A few other methods are defining things, giving examples, and explaining how one event causes another.

Authors use these same basic thought patterns to help readers understand the relationships between ideas in a paragraph. When you are reading, identifying the patterns helps you comprehend the author's ideas more quickly than if you did not understand these relationships. Knowing what signal words to look for can help you sort through complex ideas more easily.

. . . .

Share Your Prior Knowledge

Talk with a classmate about how someone or something from your past has changed, either for better or worse. For example, you might describe a friend from childhood or the town in which you grew up.

Survey the Lessons

Take a moment to turn to the table of contents and survey the headings in Lessons 12 and 13 in Part 4 so you know what patterns to expect. See if you have the prior knowledge to define each pattern we will explore. If you are not sure what the pattern is, then leave the line blank. You will learn about it soon.

Time order: _____

Space order: _____

Definition: _____

Examples: _____

Cause and effect: _____

Comparison and contrast: _____

Classification: _____

Now turn to the headings in Lesson 14. Which of these techniques do you use when reading textbooks? Which are entirely new to you?

Already use: _____

_____

Entirely new: _____

_____

Read and Talk

FORENSICS TEXTBOOK

In college, reading is just the beginning of how you will share new ideas with others in your class. So the first reading in each part of this book is meant to give you the chance to talk about reading. Read the article, and then use the four discussion questions to talk about your ideas with your classmates and your instructor. Make this an opportunity to create new friendships and knowledge through the art of listening to the ideas of others, the enjoyment of discussing your thoughts, and the fun of reading something new.

Access the Reading CourseMate via **www.cengagebrain.com/shop/ ISBN/1413033156** to hear a reading of this selection and view a video about this topic.

The Romanovs (1918)

1   On July 16, 1918, the last royal family of Russia died at the hands of a firing squad (Figure 4.1). The royal family consisted of Tsar Nicholas II, his wife Alexandra, four daughters, one son, and their servants. Bolshevik Jacob Yurosky commanded the death squad. He boasted that the world would never know what had happened to the royal family.

2   That was true for the next 75 years. Then a team of specialists including Michael Baden, William Maples, and **forensic** dentist

forensic Use your prior knowledge of TV crime shows to think about what the word *forensic* means.

Bettmann/Corbis

Figure 4.1 The last royal family of Russia.

Lowell Levine examined the skeletons discovered in a shallow grave outside of Ekaterinburg, Russia (Figure 4.2). The team was able to determine the age and sex of all nine skeletons. Five were identified as females and four as males. The skulls had all been crushed. This made identification difficult.

Figure 4.2 Location of bones from the mass grave of the Romanovs.

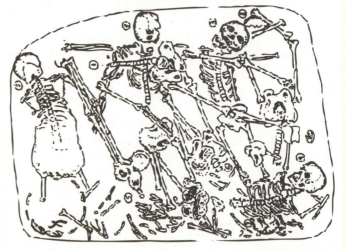

© Cengage Learning, 2009

3

calcification The body includes a mineral called calcium. Think about word parts. What does *calcification* probably mean?

The bones and teeth helped. One female had poor dental work and **calcification** of knee joints. This indicated a person who had spent time scrubbing floors and doing manual labor. One male skeleton was mature, probably the remains of the royal family physician, Dr. Botkin. The recovered dental plate and skull similarities to a photograph provided evidence to the doctor's identity. Expensive dental repairs and dental records identified the rest of the royal party. Because some of the leg bones were crushed, height estimations were calculated using arm length. The remains of Anastasia and Alexei, who were 17 and 14, **respectively**, were not found.

respectively Notice that this word refers to two people mentioned previously. What does *respectively* probably mean?

—Adapted from Bertino, *Forensic Science: Fundamentals and Investigations*

Talking About Reading

Respond in writing to the questions below and then discuss your answers with your classmates.

1. Do you have any prior knowledge of the Romanovs? If so, share your knowledge.

   _____

   _____

2. Do you find it interesting that science can help uncover a 75-year-old mystery? Why or why not? _____

   _____

3. Can you imagine the horror of the night this family was murdered? Discuss what the emotions might have been for both the family and the soldiers who committed the crime. _____

   _____

4. What do you think happened to Anastasia and Alexei? Do you think they survived or were buried somewhere else? _____

   _____

Reading Textbooks for Maximum Comprehension

The story of the Romanovs is told in time order. When the scientists found the shallow graves, they classified the skeletons; that is, they divided the skeletons into male and female and lower class and upper class, based on calcification or expensive dental work. Not only did patterns help tell the story, but they helped scientists solve a mystery. As you learn to recognize and use patterns, they too can help you understand stories, solve comprehension mysteries, and more.

Different kinds of writing, such as romance novels, mystery novels, short stories, magazine articles, and others use the patterns of organization you'll learn about in the next two lessons. Textbook writers also tend to use these patterns in easy-to-recognize ways, and if you read for patterns in your textbooks, you'll understand more about the relationships between ideas than if you don't. In Lesson 14, you can add to this textbook reading comprehension strategy with several other strategies.

Lesson 12

In Part 3, you studied MAPP. MAPPing is a system of structuring your reading so that you understand the main idea of a paragraph or longer passage and the details the author provides as support. In this lesson, we are going to study how the major details of a paragraph are organized into patterns. Understanding patterns is a significant help in making sense of what you read.

Major Details Are Often Organized in Patterns.

The major details of a paragraph or longer passage are often organized according to a certain pattern. For example, a recipe is organized by the steps in a process that you have to follow to make the dish. A story is often organized by when things happen, in time order. Identifying the pattern of organization can help you distinguish the major supporting details the author uses to make his or her point from the less important, minor details.

You Can Predict Paragraph Patterns—Sometimes

You have been turning titles, headings, and topic sentences into questions in order to predict what a reading selection is going to be about. For example, you might read the heading "The Causes of the Civil War" in an American history textbook and form the question, "What are the causes of the Civil War?" This prepares you to search for the parts of the answer to the question, which are the main ideas.

In addition to predicting content, you may also be able to predict the **structure** or **pattern** of the information that you will be reading. The question "What are the causes of the Civil War?" will lead you to search for these causes while you read. As another example, suppose you read the following sentence:

Achieving an ethnic identity seems to occur in three phases. (A *phase* is a stage or step.)

First, you can turn the sentence into a question:

> What three phases are involved in achieving an ethnic identity?

Second, you can mentally prepare a structure for the answers to this question, which you are about to learn by reading the paragraph. Your mental structure might look like this:

> Phase 1: ?
>
> Phase 2: ?
>
> Phase 3: ?

You don't know yet what the phases are, but you have prepared yourself to pick them out from all the other details in the passage. As you read, you will mentally fill in phases 1, 2, and 3.

INTERACTION 4–1	Fill in the Structure with Information

Read the following paragraphs to find out what the three phases of forming an ethnic identity are. After you read, fill in the blanks on page 392 with the three phases.

1   Roughly one third of the adolescents (that, is teenagers) and young adults living in the United States are members of ethnic minority groups, including African Americans, Asian Americans, Latino Americans, and Native Americans. These individuals typically develop an **ethnic identity:** They feel a part of their ethnic group and learn the special customs and traditions of their group's culture and identity.

2   Achieving an ethnic identity seems to occur in three phases. **At first,** adolescents have not examined their ethnic roots. A teenage African American girl in this phase remarked, "Why do I need to learn about who was the first Black woman to do this or that? I'm just not too interested." **In the second phase,** adolescents begin to explore the personal impact of their ethnic heritage. The curiosity and questioning that is characteristic of this stage is captured in the comments of a teenage Mexican American girl who said, "I want to know what we do and how our culture is different from others." **In the third phase,** individuals achieve a distinct ethnic self-concept. One Asian American adolescent explained his ethnic identification like this: "I have been born Filipino and am born to be

> Filipino. . . . I'm here in America, and people of many different cultures are here, too. So I don't consider myself only Filipino, but also American."
>
> —Adapted from Kail & Cavanaugh, *Human Development: A Life-Span View,* 4th edition

Phase 1: _____

Phase 2: _____

Phase 3: _____

Remember: Noticing the paragraph pattern will help you grasp which details are more important to the author's main idea. In the second paragraph in Interaction 4–1, each major supporting detail—phase 1, 2, and 3—was supported by a quotation from a teenager. These quotations make the paragraph more lively and interesting, but it's important to keep in mind that they are <u>minor</u> supporting details. Focus mostly on the <u>main idea and the major details</u> in order to comprehend what you read.

You Can Search for Signal Words to Find Paragraph Patterns

Sometimes the main idea of a paragraph will not tell you which pattern of organization a paragraph uses. In these cases, you can search for signal words as you read. (Signal words are also called "transitions.") For example, if you see the words *when, then, tonight,* and *tomorrow,* you might realize the paragraph is organized in time order.

In this lesson and in Lesson 13, you will study seven patterns of organization, and for each one, a list of signal words is given. Also, on page 426, a master list of signal words is provided in alphabetical order. You can search for a word on this list while you are reading to see which pattern of organization it signals.

Each Pattern Answers a Question

Each pattern of organization answers a general question that corresponds to the 5 W's and H words you learned in Lesson 1. The question and the signal words naturally go together.

Question	Sample Signal Words	Pattern of Organization
When did that happen?	then, now, a week ago	time order
Where are things located?	above, below, on the left	space order
What does this mean?	means, is, namely	definition
What are examples of this general idea?	for example, to illustrate	examples
What made this happen? What does this lead to?	reasons, because, consequences	cause and effect
How are these the same? How do they differ?	similar, alike, in contrast, however	comparison and contrast
What kinds are there?	types, kinds, forms	classification

Review: Patterns of Details

Pay attention to patterns when you are reading. Patterns can help you decide which details are major and which are minor.

- Sometimes you can predict the pattern of a paragraph by turning the topic sentence into a question and forming a mental structure for the answers. Then as you read you can put the answers into the structure.

- You can search for signal words to help you find patterns.

Time Order: When Did That Happen?

Time order tells readers when things happen, and in what order: first, second, third, and so on. Words that signal time include *before, after, during, meanwhile,* and *later*. Two kinds of writing often use time order: narrative writing and process writing.

Reading Narrative Writing

One kind of time order is called **narration** (also called "story"). In narrative writing, the author uses time order to show what events a person or character experiences. The Harry Potter series happens in time order. Each book takes place during a different school year at Hogwarts School of Witchcraft and Wizardry.

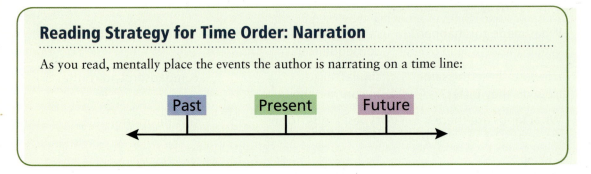

Reading Strategy for Time Order: Narration

As you read, mentally place the events the author is narrating on a time line:

Past   Present   Future

Time Order: Narrative Paragraph   **Novel**

Use the reading strategy for time order as you read the following paragraph. Then go back and read the highlighted words and the annotations that explain their function in the narration pattern. A list of signal words for narration follows the paragraph.

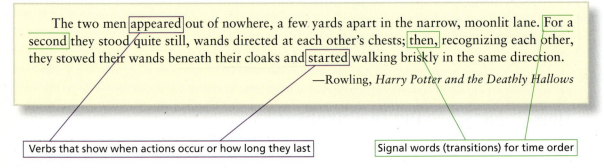

The two men appeared out of nowhere, a few yards apart in the narrow, moonlit lane. For a second they stood quite still, wands directed at each other's chests; then, recognizing each other, they stowed their wands beneath their cloaks and started walking briskly in the same direction.

—Rowling, *Harry Potter and the Deathly Hallows*

Verbs that show when actions occur or how long they last

Signal words (transitions) for time order

Signal Words (Transitions) for Time Order

When you are reading, look for phrases that will help you figure out when things have occurred. Here are some examples.

- before, during, after
- first, second, third
- next, then, later

- preceding, following, afterward
- as soon as, when, while, until, since
- days, dates, and times, such as Monday through Friday; on March 17, 2010; since 2009; during the week

INTERACTION 4–2	Recognizing the Features of Narration

Circle any words that signal time order in the following paragraph. (Consult the signal words list as needed.)

> Everything changed when Alice was laid off, after her company was sold. First she grieved. Then she picked up the pieces and went into job-search mode.... She ended up taking a job, but the price was a $20,000 salary cut, one-third of her former earnings. The PR job didn't work out, but it did teach her about her psychological makeup. When her supervisor let her go, "it was, like, 'Fine, I'm on unemployment, don't bother me for a while. I need to think, about what I want and what I need.'" So she did a little networking, made some contacts, and began freelancing for an advertising company.
>
> —Schor, *The Overspent American*

Reading Process Writing

A second kind of time order is called **process.** In process writing, the author tells readers what steps need to occur to achieve a goal, and in what order. Sometimes words like *first step, second phase, next stage,* and *finally* are used to show the main steps. The second paragraph on page 391 about forming an ethnic identity is an example of process writing.

Reading Strategy for Time Order: Process

To keep the order of events clear as you read, mentally fill in the events on a generalized time line:

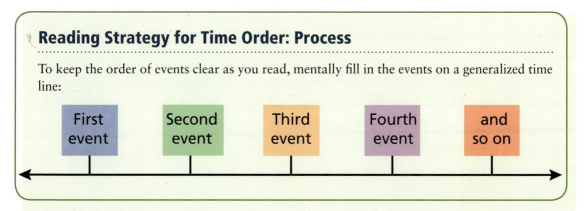

First event   Second event   Third event   Fourth event   and so on

Time Order: Process Paragraph   Forensic Science Textbook

Use the reading strategy for process writing as you read the following paragraph. Then go back and read the highlighted words and the annotations that explain their function in the process pattern. A list of signal words for process writing follows the paragraph.

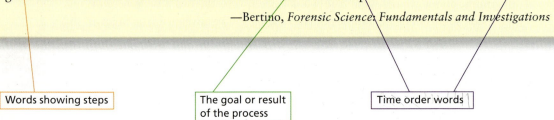

Crime-Scene Investigation of Blood

In an attempt to hide evidence of a violent crime, a perpetrator may try to remove blood evidence by cleaning the area. Although a room may look perfectly clean and totally free of blood after a thorough washing of the walls and floor, blood evidence still remains. Red blood cells contain hemoglobin, the iron-bearing protein that carries oxygen. To detect hemoglobin, an investigator's first step is to mix Luminol powder with hydrogen peroxide in a spray bottle. The mixture is then sprayed on the area to be examined for blood. The iron from the hemoglobin, acting as a catalyst, speeds up the reaction between the peroxide and the Luminol. As the reaction progresses, light is generated for about 30 seconds on the surface of the blood sample.

—Bertino, *Forensic Science: Fundamentals and Investigations*

Words showing steps

The goal or result of the process

Time order words

Signal Words (Transitions) for Process Writing

When you are reading, look for phrases that will help you figure out in what order steps have to occur in order to achieve the desired result.

- first step, second step, third step; first stage, second stage; first phase, second phase
- first, next, then, eventually, last
- start, continue, end
- any of the words from the Signal Words for Time Order list on page 393

INTERACTION 4–3   **Recognizing the Features of Process Writing**

Circle the words that signal the stages of a process in the following paragraph. (Consult the signal words list as needed.) Underline any other words that indicate time order.

> Once found, there are several steps used in processing a bloodstain, and each can provide a different kind of critical information. The first step is to confirm the stain is blood. Could ketchup, ink, or any other red substance cause the red stain? Before trying to collect the blood, it is necessary to confirm that the evidence is blood, either by using the Kastle-Meyer test or the Leukomalachite green test. If the substance proves to be blood, the second step is to confirm that the blood is human. One test that can be used to determine this is the ELISA test. The third step is to determine the blood type. Depending on the circumstances, blood typing may not be done at all, just DNA analysis.
>
> —Adapted from Bertino, *Forensic Science: Fundamentals and Investigations*

Space Order: Where Are Things Located?

Space order shows readers where things are located in space. Some signal words for space order are *above, below, behind, in front of,* and *near.* Space order is often used in **descriptions.** In a description, the author asks the reader to use sight, hearing, and feeling to imagine experiencing the events or items the author has written about.

Reading Strategy for Space Order

As you read, mentally use your senses, especially your sense of sight, to recreate the scene the author is describing.

Space Order Paragraph   **Novel**

Use the reading strategy for space order as you read the following paragraph. Then go back and read the highlighted words and the annotations that explain their function in the description pattern. A list of signal words for space order follows the paragraph.

Located on a hill with open views in the middle of the city, the dormitory compound sat on a large quadrangle surrounded by a concrete wall. A huge, towering zelkova tree stood just inside the front gate. People said it was at least a hundred and fifty years old. Standing at its base, you could look up and see nothing of the sky through its dense cover of green leaves.

—Murakami, *Norwegian Wood*

Descriptive details

Signal words (transitions) for space order

Signal Words (Transitions) for Space Order

When you are reading, look for words that signal how the author wants you to picture the scene, and how the elements of the scene are arranged.

- on the left, in the middle, on the right

- in front of, in back of

- above, below, underneath, behind, forward

- off in the distance, beyond, up close, near, far

- at, in, on (as in *at the store, in the wilderness, on the table*)

- inside, outside, inward, outward

INTERACTION 4–4	Recognizing the Features of Space Order

Circle any words that signal space order in the following paragraph. (Consult the signal words list as needed.)

The tide is going out. Near the shore the water is flat, metal-colored, although out past Longway Rock, it's starting to get choppy; there's even a whitecap or two. Lobster buoys down in the cove bob slightly, and seagulls circle the wharf near the marina. The sky is still blue, but off to the northeast, the horizon is lined with a rising cloud bank, and the tops of the pine trees are bending, over there on Diamond Island.

—Strout, *Olive Kitteridge*

Definition: What Does This Mean?

Definition tells what a word or idea means—what it is. Definitions include the term being taught and a description of its meaning. Often, examples are given to illustrate the meaning of the term. Sometimes, illustrations of what the term does *not* include are also provided.

Reading Strategy for Definition

As you read a definition, mentally slot the various parts of the definition into these categories:

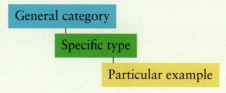

General category

Specific type

Particular example

Definition Paragraph   Health Textbook

Use the reading strategy for definition as you read the following paragraph. Then go back and read the highlighted words and the annotations that explain their function in the definition pattern. A list of signal words for definition follows the paragraph.

> By simplest definition, health means being sound in body, mind, and spirit. The World Health Organization defines health as "not merely the absence of disease or infirmity," but "a state of complete physical, mental, and social well-being," Health is the process of discovering, using, and protecting all the resources within our bodies, minds, spirits, families, communities, and environments.
>
> —Hales, *An Invitation to Health*, 12th edition

Word to be defined

Definition signal word

General term

Specific detail

Signal Words (Transitions) for Definitions

As you read, look for words that suggest definitions are being used.

- is, that is
- is called, can be understood as
- means, has come to mean
- defined as
- consists of
- is not (used to show what a term does not mean)

INTERACTION 4–5	Recognizing the Features of Definition Writing

Circle the words that signal definition in the following paragraph. (Consult the signal words list as needed.) Then underline the definitions themselves.

> Wellness can be defined as purposeful, enjoyable living, or, more specifically, a deliberate lifestyle choice characterized by personal responsibility and optimal enhancement of physical, mental, and spiritual health. John Travis, MD, author of *The Wellness Workbook*, notes that "The 'well' person is not necessarily the strong, the brave, the successful, the young, the whole, or even the illness-free being. No matter what your current state of health, you can begin to appreciate yourself as a growing, changing person and allow yourself to move toward a happier life and positive health."
>
> —Adapted from Hales, *An Invitation to Health*, 12th edition

Examples: What Are Examples of This General Idea?

Examples give the specific, down-to-earth details that help readers understand the general statements a writer is making. Examples are often provided for definitions as well. Examples help make general statements come alive.

Reading Strategy for Examples

As you read, create a mental list of examples the author is providing.

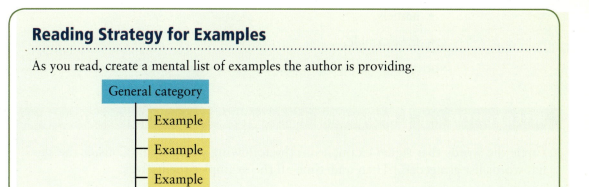

Example Paragraph   **Nonfiction Book**

Use the reading strategy for examples as you read the following paragraph. Then go back and read the highlighted words and the annotations that explain their function in the example pattern. A list of signal words for examples follows the paragraph.

Body Posture

Body posture is an important influence on one's state. For example, most people would probably find it very difficult to learn effectively with their heads down and their shoulders hunched forward. If you put yourself into that physiology, you will find it's going to be difficult to be inspired. When people are visualizing, for instance, they often tend to be in an erect posture. When people are listening, they tend to lean back a bit with their arms folded or heads tilted. When people are having feelings, they tend to lean forward and breathe more deeply. These cues won't necessarily tell you if the feeling is positive or negative, only that an individual is accessing feelings. So somebody might be feeling very relaxed and have the same general posture as somebody who's feeling depressed.

—Dilts, *Effective Presentation Skills*

General idea   Example signal words   Examples

Signal Words (Transitions) for Examples

- for instance,
- to illustrate,

- namely,

- for example,

Notice that example phrases are often followed by a comma.

INTERACTION 4–6   **Recognizing the Features of Writing That Uses Examples**

Circle the words that signal examples in the following paragraph. (Consult the signal words list as needed.) Then underline all the examples themselves.

> Anger typically emerges between 4 and 6 months. Infants will become angry, for example, if a favorite food or toy is taken away. Reflecting their growing understanding of goal-directed behavior, infants also become angry when their attempts to achieve a goal are frustrated. For example, if a parent restrains an infant trying to pick up a toy, the guaranteed result is a very angry baby.
>
> —Kail & Cavanaugh, *Human Development*, 4th edition

Review: Four Patterns of Organization

Recognize the features of four patterns of organization as you read.

- **Time order:** Time order describes when things occur in relation to one another—*last Friday, this minute, later tonight, first this happens, then that happens.*

- **Space order:** Space order describes where things are in relation to one another—*above, below, beyond.*

- **Definition:** Definition provides the meanings of words by telling what general category a term belongs in and then what makes it different from others of its kind. Words such as *means* and *defined as* are used.

- **Examples:** Examples provide specific instances of a general concept, sometimes introduced by phrases such as *for example* and *to illustrate.*

ACTIVATE YOUR SKILLS 1
Recognizing Patterns of Organization

A. Predict the pattern of organization that each topic sentence in questions 1–5 introduces. Then list three signal words you might find in the paragraph that the sentence comes from.

| Definition | Example | Space order | Time order (narration) | Time order (process) |

1. Building a yurt should take about three days if you have a building kit from a yurt manufacturer and a couple of friends to help you.

    Pattern: _____ Time _____

    Possible signal words: _____ about three day _____

AP Photo/John Heilprin

2. Around the inside walls of a 32-foot diameter yurt in California were couches with curved backs designed to fit the space.

    Pattern: _____ Space _____

    Possible signal words: _____ around, inside _____

3. A yurt is a round, tent-like structure that has lattice walls (imagine baby gates tied together) and a cone-shaped roof supported by rafters that meet in a center ring.

    Pattern: _____ difinition _____

    Possible signal words: _____ means _____

4. Yurts can be found in many parts of the country.

Pattern: _____ *eg* _____

Possible signal words: _____ *O for eg* _____

5. Nomadic tribes in Europe and Asia have lived in yurts for thousands of years.

Pattern: _____ *Time order* _____

Possible signal words: _____ *before* _____

B. Read the following paragraph. Bracket the [topic], underline the main idea, and number each major supporting detail. ① ② ③ ④

[Persuasion], the act of influencing people's thinking, feelings, or behavior, is so common that few of us could go through a day without encountering some sort of persuasive communication. For example, as you drive to school in the morning, a radio advertisement tries to convince you that you'll have the time of your life if you attend an upcoming concert. Before lunch, you try to convince your friends to eat at the campus cafeteria because it's cheaper than eating at a restaurant off campus. And in the evening, your roommate tries to convince you to go out to a campus demonstration even though you have to get up early for work the next morning.

—Griffin, *Invitation to Public Speaking*, 3rd edition

6. Which word in the paragraph is defined? _____ *Per* _____

7. What definition is given? _____

8. How many examples of persuasive communication are given? _____ *3* _____

9. What pattern is used to organize these examples? _____ *Time Order (Process)* _____

10. List the signal words that led you to your answer for question 9.

   • _____ *for eg* _____
   • _____ *before* _____
   • _____ *In the evening* _____

ACTIVATE YOUR SKILLS 2
Recognizing Patterns of Organization

Read each paragraph and answer the questions that follow.

A.

Siege Warfare

An enemy attacking a castle would make a formal demand for the people inside to surrender. If this was rejected, he would try to take the castle by siege. There were two methods. The first was to surround the castle, keep the people from leaving or going in, and starve the defenders into submission. The second was to use force. Attackers could tunnel under the wall and come up inside, or undermine the wall and bring it down. Alternatively, the attackers could try to break the walls down with catapults, or, from the 14th century on, cannon. They could also try to get over the wall using scaling ladders or a moving tower fitted with a drawbridge that could be let down on the top of the wall.

—Gravett, *Knight: Noble Warrior of England, 1200–1600*

_b_ 1. What is the main purpose of this paragraph?

    a. To persuade readers about the best way to lay siege to a castle.

    b. To inform readers about the process by which an enemy could attack a castle.

    c. To entertain readers with stories of individual people who attacked castles.

_b_ 2. If you had to label one of the following sentences as the "second step" of attacking a castle, which sentence would you choose?

    a. Sentence 1

    b. Sentence 2

    c. Sentence 3

    d. Sentence 4

_c_ 3. What three sets of words are signals for the two methods the author discusses?

    a. Would try, surround the castle, starve the defenders

    b. If, or, alternatively

    c. Two methods, the first, the second

    d. Would, could, was to use

4. What are the three steps of method 1 of laying siege to a castle?

- <u>sourr the</u>
- <u>Keeppen</u>
- <u>Shorv</u>

5. Using signal words for space order, describe how invaders could use force to get into a castle.

- <u>Tun wal</u>
- <u>under mind the</u>
- <u>brok the wall down</u>
- <u>get the wall down</u>

B.

The Worst Trek of All

Tony Steinhardt/Author's Image/Jupiter Images

We marched for three successive days without coming to tents. Then we saw in the distance a great column of smoke rising into the sky. We wondered if it came from a chimney or a burning house, but when we got near we saw it was the steam rising from hot springs. We were soon gazing at a scene of great natural beauty. A number of springs bubbled out of the ground, and in the middle of the cloud of steam shot up a splendid little geyser fifteen feet high. Our next thought was to have a bath. . . . The water was boiling when it came out of the ground, but it was quickly cooled to a bearable temperature by the frosty air. We hurriedly turned one of the pools into a comfortable bathtub. What a joy it was! Since we had left the hot springs at Kyirong we had not been able to wash or bathe, and our hair and beards were frozen stiff.

—Harrer, *Seven Years in Tibet*

d 6. What two patterns do you find in this paragraph?

    a. Time order (process), example

    b. Example, space order

    c. Space order, definition

    d. Time order (narration), space order

c 7. Which pattern do these signal words—*when, soon, since*—used in the selection indicate?

    a. Definition

    b. Example

    c. Time order

    d. Space order

a 8. Which pattern do these signal words—*in the distance, out of the ground, in the middle*—used in the selection indicate?

    a. Space order

    b. Definition

    c. Example

    d. Time order

a 9. Of the following events mentioned in this paragraph, which came first in time?

    a. The men marched for three days.

    b. The men saw smoke.

    c. The men found hot springs and a geyser.

    d. The men bathed at the hot springs at Kyirong.

10. Which of the following places is the most likely setting for this paragraph?

a. The seacoast of Italy.

b. The mountains of Tibet.

c. The plains of Africa.

d. The desert of Arizona.

MASTER YOUR SKILLS 1 *Home work*
Recognizing Patterns of Organization

Decide which patterns of organization are used in each paragraph in Selections A–E. **Hint:** Two paragraphs use more than one pattern. Choose from these patterns of organization:

| Definition | Example | Space order | Time order (narration) | Time order (process) |

Selection A   Public Speaking Textbook

Idioms are especially difficult for people of other cultures to understand. An **idiom** is a fixed, distinctive expression whose meaning is not indicated by its individual words. "I was in stitches" and "they kept me in the dark" are examples of English idioms.

—Griffin, *Invitation to Public Speaking*, 3rd edition

Pattern(s): _Definition_

Selection B   College Success Textbook

Twenty-three years after dropping out of high school, I finally enrolled in college. In between, I got married, worked as a waitress, had three children, and adopted a fourth. My first baby got cancer and had three serious operations between the ages of two and five. What she and the other kids at the hospital went through touched my heart, and I knew I wanted to help kids who were dealing with serious illnesses. I had always thought that school was useless and that I didn't have the smarts to finish, but I started to see that the only way I was going to make something of myself was to go to college. When I was in my thirties, I got my GED and became a certified nursing assistant. A few years later, I took the big step and came to college.

—Donna Ludwick in Downing, *On Course*, 5th edition

Pattern(s): _Time order (narration)_

Selection C   American Government Textbook

Cases normally start in a district court. Individuals who lose then have a right to have their case decided by one higher court to determine whether there was a miscarriage of justice. They normally appeal to a court of appeals. Individuals who lose at this level have no further right to have their case decided by another court, but they can appeal to the Supreme Court. However, the Court can exercise almost unlimited discretion in choosing cases to review. No matter how important or urgent an issue seems, the Court doesn't have to hear it.

—Welch, Gruhl, Comer, & Rigdon, *Understanding American Government: The Essentials*

Pattern(s): _Time Order (Process)_

Selection D   Psychology Textbook

The word *stress* has been used in different ways by different theorists. We'll define **stress** as any circumstances that threaten or are perceived to threaten one's well-being and that thereby tax one's coping abilities. The threat may be to immediate physical safety, long-range security, self-esteem, reputation, peace of mind, or many other things that one values.

—Weiten, *Psychology*, 7th edition

Pattern(s): _____

Selection E   Anthropology Textbook

In Standard American English, we find large numbers of words that refer to technological gadgetry (such as *tractor, microchip,* and *intake valve*) and occupational specialties (such as *teacher, plumber, CPA,* and *pediatrician*) for the simple reason that technology and occupation are points of cultural emphasis in our culture. Thus, the English language helps North Americans adapt effectively to their culture by providing a vocabulary well suited for that culture. Other cultures have other areas of emphasis.

—Adapted from Ferraro, *Cultural Anthropology*

Pattern(s): _____

MASTER YOUR SKILLS 2   Hw
Recognizing Patterns of Organization

A. Write the letter of the pattern of organization each signal word indicates.

_c_   1. between   a. Definition

_e_   2. next stage   b. Example

_a_   3. can be understood as   c. Space order

_c_   4. in front of   d. Time order (narration)

_d_   5. later   e. Time order (process)

_b_   6. on Monday

_a_   7. means

_b_   8. to illustrate

_e_   9. fourth step

_b_   10. namely

B. For each main idea in questions 11–15, select a reading strategy that you would use to read a paragraph containing that main idea.

a.   Past   Present   Future

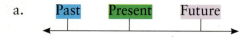

b.   First event   Second event   Third event   Fourth event   and so on

c. Mentally recreate the scene the author describes using your senses, especially your sense of sight.

d. General category

    Specific type

        Particular example

e. General statement

   ├─Example

   ├─Example

   ├─Example

_E_ 11. Three cities are outstanding places to live in the United States.

_b_ 12. To develop a strong résumé, you should consider your skills, use strong verbs to describe your experiences, and take care to proofread the résumé carefully.

_C_ 13. The iPod was sleek and colorful.

_A_ 14. The gift basket arrived on Tuesday, March 19, three weeks late.

_d_ 15. A morpheme is the smallest unit of meaning in a language.

C. Read the following selection from a psychology textbook, then answer questions 16–20.

Frustration

I had a wonderful relationship with a nice man for three months. One day when we planned to spend the entire day together, he called and said he wouldn't be meeting me and that he had decided to stop seeing me. I cried all morning. The grief was like losing someone through death. I still hurt, and I wonder if I'll ever get over him.

This scenario illustrates frustration. As psychologists use the term, frustration occurs in any situation in which the pursuit of some goal is thwarted. In essence, you experience frustration when you want something and you can't have it. Everyone has to deal with frustration virtually every day. Traffic jams, difficult daily commutes, and annoying drivers, for instance, are a routine source of frustration that can elicit anger and aggression. Fortunately, most frustrations are brief and insignificant. You may be quite upset when you go to a repair shop to pick up your ailing DVD player and find that it hasn't been fixed as promised. However, a week later you'll probably have your DVD player back, and the frustration will be forgotten.

—Weiten, *Psychology*, 7th edition

16. What organizational pattern do you find in the first, italicized paragraph? _____
    _____Time Ord_____

17. What relationship does that first paragraph have with the term *frustration*? _____
    _____Example_____

18. What definition is given for the topic of the selection? _____
    _____

19. What pattern of organization supports the following idea? *Everyone has to deal with frustration virtually every day.* _____

20. What two patterns are at work in supporting the following idea? *Most frustrations are brief and insignificant.* _____

In Lesson 12 you learned that the major details of a paragraph (or longer selection) are often arranged in a particular pattern of organization. Sometimes you can predict the pattern from the topic sentence. You can also look for signal words to find paragraph patterns. In that lesson you also studied four patterns: time order, space order, definition, and example. In this lesson you will learn three more: cause and effect, comparison and contrast, and classification.

Cause and Effect: What Made This Happen? What Does This Lead To?

Cause-and-effect paragraphs may focus on the causes of an event, in which case they answer a question such as "What made this happen?" or "What's the reason this occurred?" When they focus on the effects that came about because of something else that happened, a cause-and-effect paragraph answers a question like "What does this lead to?" or "What is the result of this action?"

A cause-and-effect paragraph may describe how a single cause leads to multiple effects, or how multiple causes create a single effect. A piece of writing may even describe how one cause leads to an effect, which then becomes the cause of a second effect, which then becomes the cause of yet another effect, and so on. Think of dominoes falling. The first one knocks over the second one, and when the second one falls, it knocks over the third one, and so on. This last type is called a *causal chain*.

Reading Strategy for Cause and Effect

As you read, visualize the causes that lead to effects as arrows:

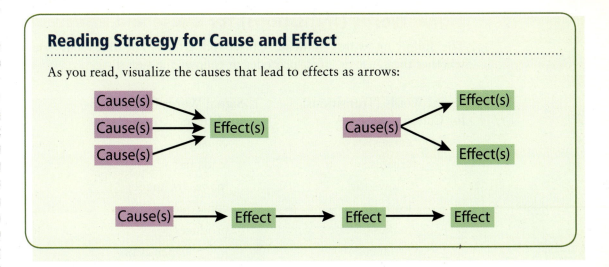

Cause-and-Effect Paragraph

Blog Posting

Use the reading strategy for cause and effect as you read the following paragraph. Then go back and read the highlighted words and the annotation that explains their function in the cause-and-effect pattern. A list of signal words for cause and effect follows the paragraph.

Medical Bills Cause Most Bankruptcies

Nearly two out of three bankruptcies stem from medical bills, and even people with health insurance face financial disaster if they experience a serious illness, a new study shows. The study data, published online Thursday in *The American Journal of Medicine*, likely understate the full scope of the problem because the data were collected before the current economic crisis. In 2007, medical problems contributed to 62.1 percent of all bankruptcies. Between 2001 and 2007, the proportion of all bankruptcies caused by medical problems rose by about 50 percent.

—Adapted from Parker-Pope, Well Blog, *New York Times*, June 4, 2009

Signal words showing cause or effect

Signal Words (Transitions) for Cause and Effect

The following words indicate cause and effect. The lines tell you whether the cause or effect precedes or follows the signal word.

Signal Words (Transitions) for Causes

_____ causes

_____ creates

_____ allows for

_____ leads to

_____ makes

_____ produces

are due to _____

because _____

reason is _____

Signal Words (Transitions) for Effects

causes _____

leads to _____

makes (or made) _____

consequences are _____

produces _____

_____ depends on

_____ were the effects

_____ is the result

INTERACTION 4–7	Recognizing the Features of Cause-and-Effect Writing

Circle the words that signal causes and effects in the following paragraph. (Consult the signal words list as needed.) Then underline all the causes and effects.

Staying Healthy Longer

The unexercised body—though free of the symptoms of illness—will rust out long before it could ever wear out. Inactivity can make anyone old before his or her time. Just as inactivity accelerates aging, activity slows it down. The effects of ongoing activity are so profound that gerontologists sometimes refer to exercise as "the closest thing to an antiaging pill." Exercise slows many changes associated with advancing age, such as loss of lean mus-

webphotographeer/iStockphoto.com

cle tissue, increase in body fat, and decreased work capacity. The bottom line: What you *don't* do may matter more than what you *do* do.

—Hales, *An Invitation to Health,* 12th edition

Comparison and Contrast: How Are These the Same? How Do They Differ?

Comparisons show how two things are similar. Contrasts show how they are different. Sometimes the word *comparison* is used more generally to indicate both of these moves.

Reading Strategy for Comparison and Contrast

Mentally or on paper, form two lists, one for each item being compared or contrasted. As the author gives each piece of information for an item, place it in the appropriate list.

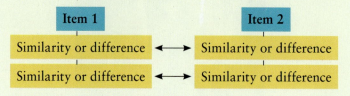

Comparison Paragraph   **Health Textbook**

Use the reading strategy for comparison as you read the following paragraph. Then go back and read the highlighted words and the annotations that explain their function in the comparison pattern. A list of signal words for comparison follows the paragraph.

Protecting Yourself

There is a great deal of overlap between **prevention** and **protection**. Some people might think of immunizations as a way of preventing illness; others see them as a form of protection against dangerous diseases. In many ways, protection picks up where prevention leaves off. You can prevent sexually transmitted infections or unwanted pregnancy by abstaining from sex. But if you decide to engage in potentially risky sexual activities, you can protect yourself with condoms and spermicides. Similarly, you can prevent many automobile accidents by not driving when road conditions are hazardous. But if you do have to drive, you can protect yourself by wearing a seat belt and using defensive driving techniques.

—Hales, *An Invitation to Health,* 12th edition

Words that signal sameness

Signal Words (Transitions) for Comparisons

As you read, check for words that signal the comparison pattern of organization.

- the same, identical

- similar, similarly, a similarity
- alike, like, likewise
- both
- not only . . . but also

| INTERACTION 4–8 | Recognizing the Features of Comparison Writing |

Circle the words that signal comparison or similarity in the following paragraph. (Consult the signal words list as needed.) Then underline the comparisons themselves.

> Despite their obvious differences, books and movies can both affect the reader or moviegoer profoundly. The reader can "overhear" the inner voice of a character in a book. Reading this internal dialogue helps the reader understand and feel the emotions of that character in a way that is not usually available in real life. Similarly, the moviegoer sees a rich visual landscape that suggests the emotional context of the character's life. The creators of books and movies alike do their best to help readers and viewers identify with the main character. Then they will be able to relate to the character's problems, since they will feel them as their own.

Contrast Paragraph   ## Nonfiction Book

Use the reading strategy for contrast as you read the following passage. Then go back and read the highlighted words and the annotations that explain their function in the contrast pattern. A list of signal words for contrast follows the paragraph.

> It's revealing to take a look at the animal kingdom and notice the relationship between creatures' eating patterns and their body "types." At one end of the spectrum are animals that load up on large amounts of food at one "meal," then go for days, weeks, or even months without

Words that signal differences   The ideas the paragraph contrasts

eating at all. Bears are a prime example of this type of infrequent feeder. They're what I call bingers. They have huge body-fat storage compartments to stockpile the fuel they'll need to carry them from one feeding to the next. At the other end of the eating-pattern spectrum are the frequent feeders: animals that eat almost constantly but in far lesser amounts. Horses, buffalo, elk—I call these *grazers*. Relatively speaking, they have very low body fat and lots of lean muscle.

—Phillips, *Body for Life*

The ideas the paragraph contrasts

Words that signal differences

Signal Words (Transitions) for Contrast

When you are reading, look for phrases that will help you figure out which ideas the author is contrasting.

- differs from, differs by, a difference
- contrasts with, in contrast, to the contrary
- on the one hand . . . on the other hand
- however, although, but, while
- instead, rather

INTERACTION 4–9 | **Recognizing the Features of Contrast Writing**

Circle the words that signal contrast in the following paragraph. (Consult the signal words list as needed.) Then underline the pairs of ideas being contrasted.

> Dictionaries define the calendar almost as if it were a machine: "a system for fixing the beginning, length, and divisions of the civil year." But in every society calendars are much more than that. People experience time as both linear and circular. On the one hand, it marches remorselessly from birth to death, a vector with fixed endpoints and a constant velocity. On the other hand, time is cyclical, with the wheel of the seasons endlessly spinning, and no clear end or beginning. Calendars are records of a culture's attempt to weight and reconcile these different visions.
>
> —Mann, *1491: New Revelations of the Americas Before Columbus*

Classification: What Kinds Are There?

Classification answers the question "What kinds are there?" Suppose someone asked you, "What kinds of music do you like?" You might answer, "I like country, folk, and bluegrass." These are categories, or kinds, of music. In other words, a general topic, music, has been divided up into different types.

Reading Strategy for Classification

As you read, mentally slot the details into the following categories:

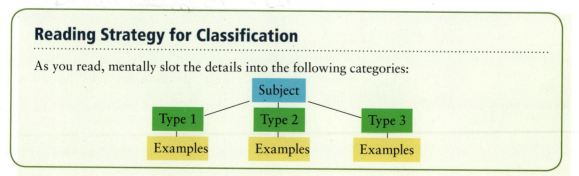

Classification Paragraph   Business Management Textbook

Use the reading strategy for classification as you read the following paragraph. Then go back and read the highlighted words and the annotations that explain their function in the classification pattern. A list of signal words for classification follows the paragraph.

Companies have four different types of social responsibility or duties. The first duty of a company is to be profitable, and this is called its economic responsibility. The company also has a duty to obey laws and regulations; that is, it has a legal responsibility. Third, companies have an ethical responsibility to abide by accepted principles of right and wrong. Finally, companies can choose what social roles they will play—they have discretionary responsibility.

—Adapted from Williams, *Management*, 4th edition

Words that indicate division into kinds

Description of each type

Signal Words (Transitions) for Classification

When you are reading, look for phrases that signal classification into types.

- several kinds
- certain forms
- three patterns
- four types
- different groups
- separate categories

Other kinds of words that indicate classification are verbs that show the action of dividing up:

- divided into
- classified by
- split up

INTERACTION 4–10	Recognizing the Features of Classification Writing

Circle any words that signal classification in the following paragraph. (Consult the signal words list as needed.) Then underline the classes themselves.

Dmitriy Shironosov/Used under license from Shutterstock.com

Leaders choose one of four kinds of leadership styles depending on how much they think they need to emphasize task behavior (that is, concern for production) and relationship behavior (concern for people). A *telling* leadership style is based on one-way communication, in which followers are told what, how, when, and where to do particular tasks. For instance, someone using a telling leadership style would identify all the steps in a project and give explicit instructions on exactly how to execute each one. A *selling* leadership style involves two-way communication and psychological support to encourage followers to "own" or "buy into" particular ways of doing things. A *participating* style is based on two-way communication and shared decision making. Someone using a participating leadership style might solicit ideas from a subordinate about a project, let the subordinate get started, but ask to review progress along the way. A *delegating* style is used when leaders basically let workers "run their own show" and make their own decisions.

—Adapted from Williams, *Management*, 4th edition

INTERACTION 4–11	Predicting the Pattern of Organization

Predict the pattern of organization that each topic sentence in questions 1–4 introduces. Then list three signal words you might find in the paragraph that the sentence comes from.

Cause and effect   Comparison   Contrast   Classification

1. There are several kinds of personal computers, or PCs, that you can choose from.

Pattern: _____

Possible signal words: _____

2. A desktop system is usually less expensive than a laptop.

Pattern: _____

Possible signal words: _____

3. A PDA is similar to a handheld computer.

Pattern: _____

Possible signal words: _____

4. Which PC to select depends on where and how you intend to use it.

Pattern: _____

Possible signal words: _____

INTERACTION 4–12   **Applying Your Knowledge of Patterns**

Circle the signal words in each paragraph in Selections A–E. If the signal words relate to the major details, use this information to determine which paragraph pattern is being used. You will also need to think about the APP of each selection: What's it about? What's the point? What's the proof? *Hint:* One pattern will be used twice.

Choose from these paragraph patterns:

Cause and effect   Comparison   Contrast   Classification

Selection A   **Online Source**

1   Tornado conditions are caused when different temperatures and humidity meet to form thunderclouds. In the United States, warm, wet winds from the Gulf of Mexico move northward in spring and summer, meeting colder, dry Canadian winds moving southward. The place where these two winds meet is called a dry line. High, dry air coming from the

Jeff Smith/iStockphoto.com

north piles on top of low-moving, moist Gulf air at a height of over 10,000 feet. The warm southern winds try to rise, but the cold northern air blocks them. This clash causes the warm, trapped air to rotate horizontally between the two air masses. At the same time, the sun heats the earth below, warming more air that continues to try and rise. Finally, the rising warm wind becomes strong enough to force itself up through the colder air layer.

2   When this occurs, the cold air on top begins to sink, sending the rising warm wind spinning upward. The warm winds rotate faster and faster in a high column. When the updraft is strong, the column can rise to heights of 10 miles or more, twisting at speeds of up to 100 miles an hour. The rotating winds produce strong storm clouds about 70,000 feet high, sometimes spreading 10 miles wide.

—Oracle Education Foundation, "Forces of Nature," ThinkQuest 2000

Pattern: _____

Selection B   **Health Textbook**

There are four levels of anxiety: mild, moderate, severe, and panic. The first level, mild anxiety, is healthy, as it increases perception. During **mild anxiety**, a person's body functions well. It is stimulated by the increased production of adrenaline, which enables us to think clearly and focus on details. A person who is experiencing **moderate anxiety**, the second level, has decreased perception. His or her focus is on a particular task or problem rather than on the overall circumstance. Concentration will be focused on one challenge at a time. In the third level of anxiety, **severe anxiety**, a person can't focus on details. Abstract thinking is lost. Because of the inability to concentrate, these individuals will be very indecisive. In the fourth level, **panic anxiety**, a person is consumed with escape. Attention is focused on a minute detail that is often blown out of proportion. Speech is usually incoherent and communication is ineffective.

—Adapted from Tamparo & Lindh, *Therapeutic Communications for Health Care*, 3rd edition

Pattern: _____

Selection C   **Sociology Textbook**

Before considering differences in crime rates by males and females, three similarities should be noted. First, the three most common arrest categories for both men and women are driving under the influence of alcohol or drugs (DUI), larceny, and minor or criminal mischief types of offenses. These three categories account for about 47 percent of all male arrests and about 49 percent of all female arrests. Second, liquor law violations (such as underage drinking), simple assault, and disorderly conduct are middle-range offenses for both men and women. Third, the rate of arrests for murder, arson, and embezzlement is relatively low for both men and women.

—Adapted from Kendall, *Sociology in Our Times*, 6th edition

Pattern: _____

Selection D   **American Government Textbook**

> Dividing the country into red states (for Republicans) and blue states (for Democrats) provides an interesting story line for journalists and pundits. It reduces the election outcome to a simple and intriguing explanation and one that is easily grasped by average Americans. Conservative red America has been described as religious, moralistic, patriotic, white, masculine, and less educated. In contrast, liberal blue America has been depicted as secular, relativistic, internationalist, multicultural, feminine, and college educated. Reds are seen as supporting guns, the death penalty, and the Iraq War, while blues are seen as supporting abortion and the environment. According to the stereotypes, in red America Saturday's pastime is NASCAR; Sunday is church. In blue America, Saturday is for the farmer's market, and Sunday is for reading the *New York Times*.
>
> —Adapted from Welch, Gruhl, Comer, & Rigdon,
> *Understanding American Government*

Pattern: _____

Selection E   **Nonfiction Book**

> Temperature and wind cause the internal seiche. Water is most dense at 40 degrees. When summer air warms Lake Champlain, it creates a layer of higher-temperature, less dense water on the surface, while the water 40 to 80 feet below forms a fairly cohesive, cooler thermocline layer. In summer and fall, strong southerly winds actually push the warmer, less dense surface water to the north end of the lake. Since the surface of the lake remains level, the weight of this piled-up water depresses the denser, cooler thermocline down, sending it south. In a north wind the reverse happens. This sets up a huge underwater rocking motion, called the internal seiche, which reverses itself roughly every four days.
>
> —Adapted from Frank & Holden, *A Kayaker's Guide to Lake Champlain*

Pattern: _____

Signal Words and the Patterns They Indicate

The following chart lists signal words that point to the different patterns of organization you have learned about in Lessons 12 and 13. You may want to consult the chart when you are trying to determine how a reading is organized.

Signal Words	Organizational Patterns
above	space order
after, afterward	time order
agree	comparison
alike	comparison
allows for	cause and effect
although	contrast
are called	definition
as	time order
as soon as	time order
at	space order
because	cause and effect
before	time order
behind	space order
below	space order
beyond	space order
both	comparison
brought about by	cause and effect
but	contrast
can be understood as	definition
categories	classification
cause, causes	cause and effect
closer	space order

Signal Words	Organizational Patterns
consequences are	effect
consists of	definition
continue	time order
contrasts with	contrast
creates	cause and effect
defined as	definition
depends on	cause and effect
difference	contrast
different groups	classification
differs by, differs from	contrast
due to	cause and effect
during, during that time	time order
effect	effect
end	time order
eventually	time order
ever since	time order
factors	causes
farther away	space order
first (or second, third, fourth, etc.)	time order, example
first stage, first step	time order (process)
first type	classification
following	time order
for example	example
for instance	example
forms (used as a noun)	classification
forward	space order

Signal Words	Organizational Patterns
here	space order
however	contrast
identical	comparison
if . . . then . . .	cause and effect
immediately	time order
in	space order, time order
in addition	example
in back of, in the background	space order
in contrast	contrast
in front of, in the foreground	space order
in the middle	space order
inside	space order
instead	contrast
is	definition
kinds	classification
last	time order
later	time order
leads to	cause and effect
like, likewise	comparison
makes, made	cause and effect
means, has come to mean	definition
meantime, meanwhile	time order
namely	definition
near, nearby	space order
next	time order
not only . . . but also	comparison

Signal Words	Organizational Patterns
off in the distance	space order
on	space order, time order
on the one hand . . . on the other hand	contrast
outside, outward	space order
phases	process, classification
preceding	time order
rather	contrast
reason is	cause
result is	effect
second; second stage or step; second type	time order, example
share	comparison
similar, similarity, similarly	comparison
since	time order
start	time order
still	time order
subsequently	time order
that is	definition
the same	comparison
then	time order
there	space order
third; third stage or step; third type	time order, example
through	space order, time order
to illustrate	example
to the contrary	contrast
types	classification
under, underneath	space order

Signal Words	Organizational Patterns
until	time order
up close	space order
when	time order, cause
while	time order, contrast

Review: Four More Patterns of Organization

Recognize the features of four patterns of organization as you read.

- **Cause and effect:** Cause and effect describes what made something happen and what it leads to. Signal words such as *because*, *leads to*, *due to*, *causes*, and *consequences* are used.

- **Comparison:** Comparison shows how things are similar to each other. Signal words such as *like*, *similar*, and *same* are used.

- **Contrast:** Contrast shows how things are different from each other. Signal words such as *different*, *in contrast*, and *however* are used.

- **Classification:** Classification describes the different kinds or types of a larger idea or event. Signal words include *types*, *kinds*, and *groups*.

ACTIVATE YOUR SKILLS 1
Recognizing More Patterns of Organization

A. Name the pattern of organization used in each paragraph in questions 1–4.

Cause and effect   Comparison   Contrast   Classification

1.
Cuts from different types of saws can be distinguished by forensic anthropologists. Cuts made by a stryker show circular areas with a short radius. Cuts made by a band saw are very smooth. Cuts made by a table saw show parallel, curved striations.

--Adapted from Bertino, *Forensic Science: Fundamentals and Investigations*

Pattern: _____Classification_____

2.

> A storm off the coast of Brazil caused a ship carrying sixty-four people to keel over and sink in just half an hour. High school and college students were in class on the *SV Concordia* when a "microburst," a sudden burst of wind moving at the speed of a tornado, turned the boat on its side. The leaning of the ship caused an automatic beacon to start signaling that the ship was in trouble, but rescue didn't occur until the third day. All sixty-four people survived in good shape.

Pattern: _____Cause and effect_____

3.

> The Kallawaya people, who live on the eastern slope of the Andes in Bolivia, live at different altitudes in the Charazani Valley—from 9,000 to 16,000 feet above sea level. Those at the lower elevations speak Quechua and cultivate potatoes, barley, and beans, while those at the upper elevations speak Aymara and keep llamas, alpaca, and sheep.
>
> —Adapted from Titon, ed., *Worlds of Music*, Shorter 3rd edition

Pattern: _____Contrast_____

4.

> James Cameron has produced, written, and directed several extraordinary movies, among them *Titanic* (1997) and the long-awaited *Avatar* (2009). In both films, fairly standard story lines are enacted in richly detailed settings that make the stories feel real and important. Of course, *Titanic* does tell a real story, although Cameron adds a pair of fictional lovers to give us someone to identify with. The most important similarity between the two movies, however, is Cameron's use of technology to recreate, in *Titanic*, the sinking of a great ship, and to create for the first time, in *Avatar*, 3-D characters from a far-in-the-future moon who move us every bit as much as—no, more than—the humans in the story.

Pattern: _____Comparison_____

B. Indicate which paragraph from questions 1–4 you would read using the given reading strategy.

5. Paragraph __2__

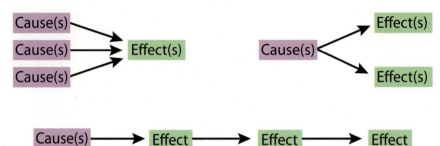

6. Paragraph __4__

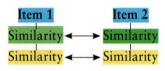

7. Paragraph __3__

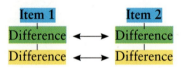

8. Paragraph __1__

Subject

Type 1   Type 2   Type 3

Examples Examples Examples

C. Compare and contrast your current home with either (1) your previous home or (2) the home of a friend. Include at least three different points of comparison. Fill in the following comparison and contrast chart with the details.

My current home	My previous home OR a friend's home
1.	1.
2.	2.
3.	3.
4.	4.

ACTIVATE YOUR SKILLS 2
Recognizing More Patterns of Organization

A. Name the pattern of organization used in each sentence in questions 1–5. Then list three signal words that a paragraph organized by that pattern might use.

Cause and effect	Comparison	Contrast	Classification

1. Because clinics in poor countries, such as Malawi, cannot afford to test children for malaria, many children wind up taking anti-malarial drugs when they actually have a different health problem.

   Pattern: _Cause and Effect_

   Signal words: _because when_

2. Although some of the French defenders managed to escape the carnage, 132 soldiers and civilians were killed in the fighting in the small fort.

   —Davis, *America's Hidden History*

   Pattern: _Contrast_

   Signal words: _Although however but_

3. Ferdinand and Isabella aimed to unite Spain and took the field—both of them literally went off to battle—with Isabella proving her mettle as both a military organizer and strategist.

   —Davis, *America's Hidden History*

   Pattern: _Comparison_

   Signal words: _and with both like_

4. Jeremiah Creedon writes in the *Utne Reader* that there are 19 kinds of friends.

   Pattern: _Classification_

   Signal words: _kind different_

5. Canada and the United States are similar in terms of culture.

   Pattern: _Comparison_

   Signal words: _like similar_

B. For each paragraph in questions 6–10, bracket the [topic], underline the <u>main idea</u>, and number each major supporting detail. ① ② ③ ④ Then answer the questions that follow.

6.

> Interest groups can be distinguished by their goals. <u>One kind is the private inter-est group, which seeks economic benefits for its members or clients.</u> An example is the American Federation of Labor–Congress of Industrial Organizations (AFL–CIO), a labor union with 9 million members. The second type is the public interest group, which lobbies for political and social causes rather than financial gain for its members. An example of this second type is Amnesty International, which lobbies for the rights of political prisoners around the world.
>
> —Adapted from Welch, Gruhl, Comer, & Rigdon, *Understanding American Government*

a. What pattern organizes this paragraph's major supporting details? _Class_ _Secon time Kind_

b. What signal words point to that pattern in the major details? _7_ _Example_

c. What pattern is used for the minor supporting details? _Interest group_

d. What signal words point to the pattern in the minor details? _____

7.

> Two interest groups are involved in the debate over abortion rights. On the one hand, pro-life groups, such as the National Right to Life Committee, want a con-stitutional amendment banning all abortions. Because this is unlikely, they have pushed for federal and state laws restricting the availability of abortions, such as laws requiring waiting periods and parental notification or consent for minors. On the other hand, pro-choice groups, such as the National Abortion Rights Action League (NARAL), want to maintain a woman's right to choose.
>
> —Adapted from Welch, Gruhl, Comer, & Rigdon, *Understanding American Government*

a. What pattern organizes this paragraph's major supporting details? ___*contra*___

_____

b. What signal words point to that pattern in the major details? ___*on the*___
___*other hand*___

c. What pattern is used in the one minor supporting detail? _____

___*because this is unlikely, they have*___

d. What signal word points to the pattern in the minor detail? _____

___*such as   cause and effect*___

8.

When you want to convince your audience that something is true, good, or appropriate, you will be more successful if you use evidence that is *specific* rather than *general*. Your evidence should support your claims as explicitly as possible. For example, in a speech persuading her audience not to smoke, Shannan used the following evidence to describe the toxic ingredients in cigarettes:

> You want to make a cigarette? According to Dr. Roger Morrisette of Farmington State College, a single cigarette contains over 4,000 chemicals. If you want the recipe, well, this is what you'll need. You'll need some carcinogens, or cancer-causing agents; some form-aldehyde, or embalming fluid; some acetone, which is paint stripper or nail polish remover; benzene or arsenic; pesticides such as fungi-cides, herbicides, and insecticides; and toxins like hydrogen cyanide, ammonia, and nicotine.

In contrast, Shannan could have argued "Cigarettes are toxic and contain thou-sands of poisonous chemicals," but that is far less specific than her list of ingredients. She is more persuasive because she uses specific evidence rather than simply making a general claim.

—Griffin, *Invitation to Public Speaking*, 3rd edition

a. What pattern organizes this paragraph's major supporting details? _____2_____

_____Contrast_____

b. What signal words point to that pattern in the major details? _____

_____In Contract_____

c. What pattern is used in the one minor supporting detail? _____

_____

d. What signal words point to the pattern in the minor details? _____

_____

9.

> Effective speeches and essays have much in common. Both have a thesis, or main claim, that the speaker or writer is trying to make. In both the speech and the essay, the author uses enough supporting examples, stories, and other details to help the audience understand, appreciate, and perhaps even agree with the thesis. Excellent speeches and essays also share a sense of style that make the work interesting and even enjoyable to hear or read.

a. What pattern organizes this paragraph's major supporting details? _____

_____Comparison_____

b. What signal words point to that pattern in the major details? _____

_____these, use enough datial to support the_____

10.

> There are three types of prints found by investigators at a crime scene. **Patent fingerprints,** or visible prints, are left on a smooth surface when blood, ink, or some other liquid comes in contact with the hands and is then transferred to that surface. **Plastic fingerprints** are actual indentations left in some soft material such as clay, putty, or wax. **Latent fingerprints,** or hidden prints, are caused by the transfer of oils and other body secretions onto a surface. They can be made visible by dusting with powders or making the fingerprints in some way more visible by using a chemical reaction.
>
> —Bertino, *Forensic Science: Fundamentals and Investigations*

a. What pattern organizes this paragraph's major supporting details? _____

_____ Classification _____

b. What signal words point to that pattern in the major details? _____

_____ Topses _____

MASTER YOUR SKILLS 1 *HW*
Recognizing More Patterns of Organization

A. Write the letter of the pattern of organization each signal word indicates.

a. Cause and effect	b. Comparison	c. Contrast	d. Classification

C 1. difference   d 5. groups   b 8. alike

b 2. similarly   c 6. in contrast A 9. results in

A 3. as a consequence A 7. leads to   b 10. but

d 4. types

B. Identify the pattern of organization in each sentence from the textbook *Cultural Anthropology,* 6th edition, by Gary Ferraro.

> **a. Cause and effect**   **b. Comparison**   **c. Contrast**   **d. Classification**

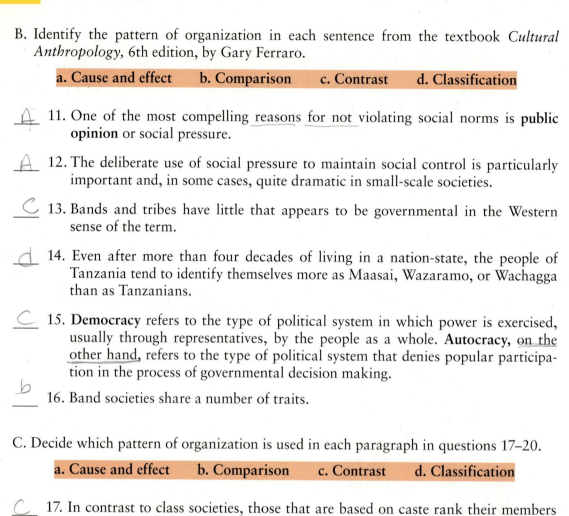

A 11. One of the most compelling reasons for not violating social norms is **public opinion** or social pressure.

A 12. The deliberate use of social pressure to maintain social control is particularly important and, in some cases, quite dramatic in small-scale societies.

C 13. Bands and tribes have little that appears to be governmental in the Western sense of the term.

d 14. Even after more than four decades of living in a nation-state, the people of Tanzania tend to identify themselves more as Maasai, Wazaramo, or Wachagga than as Tanzanians.

C 15. **Democracy** refers to the type of political system in which power is exercised, usually through representatives, by the people as a whole. **Autocracy,** on the other hand, refers to the type of political system that denies popular participation in the process of governmental decision making.

b 16. Band societies share a number of traits.

C. Decide which pattern of organization is used in each paragraph in questions 17–20.

> **a. Cause and effect**   **b. Comparison**   **c. Contrast**   **d. Classification**

C 17. In contrast to class societies, those that are based on caste rank their members according to birth. Membership in castes is unchangeable, people in different castes are segregated from one another, social mobility is virtually nonexistent, and marriage between members of different castes is strictly prohibited.

d 18. Caste societies can be found in a number of regions of the world, such as among the Rwandans in Central Africa, but the best-known—and certainly the best-described—example of the caste system is in Hindu India. Hinduism's sacred Sanskrit texts rank all people into four categories, called **varnas,** which are associated with certain occupations. The highest caste, the Brahmins, were priests and scholars. The Kshatriyas were warriors. The Vaishyas were tradesmen. The Shudras were cultivators and servants.

_b_ 19. Members of the same social class share not only similar economic levels but also similar experiences, educational backgrounds, political views, memberships in organizations, occupations, and values. In addition, studies of social class have shown, not surprisingly, that members of a social class tend to associate more often with one another than with people in other classes. In other words, a person's life chances, though not determined, are very much influenced by social class.

_A_ 20. Ethnic groups exist because of their shared social experiences over time. To illustrate, during the first several decades of the twentieth century, hundreds of thousands of Italians immigrated to New York City through Ellis Island. Coming, as they did, from all over Italy, they had identified themselves before leaving Italy with their town, village, or city, and with their extended family networks. Upon arrival in the new world, however, they shared a number of common experiences, including living in the lower east side of Manhattan, reading Italian-language newspapers, competing with other groups for jobs and resources, and buying ricotta cheese by the pound rather than in little plastic containers. These shared experiences over time forged a new ethnic identity as Italian-Americans, an identity which to some degree still exists today.

MASTER YOUR SKILLS 2 _Hw_
Recognizing More Patterns of Organization

Read the following selection and answer the questions that follow.

The "Wedding Cake" Model of Criminal Justice

1   Some people believe that the current informal approach to criminal justice creates a situation in which cases are not treated equally. As evidence, they point to a landmark case in the American criminal justice system—the highly publicized O. J. Simpson trial of 1994. In this case, the wealthy, famous defendant had an experience far different from that of most double-murder suspects. To describe this effect, criminal justice researchers Lawrence M. Friedman and Robert V. Percival came up with a "wedding cake" model of criminal justice. Like any

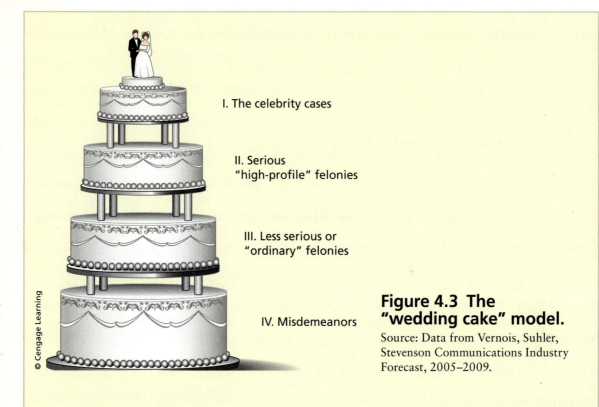

I. The celebrity cases

II. Serious "high-profile" felonies

III. Less serious or "ordinary" felonies

IV. Misdemeanors

© Cengage Learning

Figure 4.3 The "wedding cake" model.
Source: Data from Vernois, Suhler, Stevenson Communications Industry Forecast, 2005–2009.

wedding cake, Friedman and Percival's model has the smallest layer at the top and the largest at the bottom. (See Figure 4.3.)

1. The "top" layer consists of a handful of "celebrity" cases that attract the most attention and publicity. Recent examples of top-level cases include the trials of former FBI agent John Connolly, connected to the mob-related death of a Miami gambling executive; Mark Jensen, convicted of killing his ex-wife by poisoning her with antifreeze in Wisconsin; and O. J. Simpson, again, who was found guilty on twelve counts of kidnapping and armed robbery following a violent dispute in a Las Vegas hotel room.

2. The second layer consists of "high-profile" felonies. A *felony* is a serious crime such as murder, rape, or burglary. This layer includes crimes committed by persons with criminal records, crimes in which the victim was seriously injured, and crimes in which a weapon was used, as well as crimes in which the offender and the victim were strangers. These types of felonies are considered "high profile" because they usually draw a certain amount of public attention, which puts pressure on prosecutors to bring such a case to trial instead of accepting a guilty plea for a lesser sentence.

3. The third layer consists of "ordinary" felonies, which include less violent crimes such as burglaries and thefts or robberies in which no weapon was used. Because of the low profile of the accused—usually a first-time offender who has had a prior relationship with his or her victim—these "ordinary" felonies often do not receive the full, formal process of a trial.

4. Finally, the fourth layer consists of misdemeanors, or crimes less serious than felonies. *Misdemeanors* include petty offenses such as shoplifting, disturbing the peace, and violations of local ordinances. More than three-quarters of all arrests made by police are for misdemeanors.

2   The cases on the top level come closest to meeting our standards of ideal criminal justice. In these celebrity trials, we get to see committed (and expensive) attorneys argue minute technicalities of the law, sometimes for days on end. The further one moves down the layers of the cake, the more informal the process becomes. Though many of the cases in the second layer are brought to trial, only rarely does this occur for the less serious felonies in the third level of the wedding cake. By the fourth level, cases are dealt with almost completely informally, and the end goal appears to be speed rather than what can be called "justice."

3   Public fascination with celebrity cases obscures a truth of the informal criminal justice process. Trial by jury is relatively rare (only about 5 percent of those arrested for felonies go to trial). Most cases are disposed of with an eye more toward convenience than ideals of justice or fairness. Consequently, the summary of the criminal justice system provided by the wedding cake model is much more realistic than the impression many Americans have obtained from the media.

—Adapted from Gaines & Miller, *Criminal Justice in Action: The Core*, 5th edition

 1. What paragraph pattern organizes most of this selection?

    a. Cause and effect

    b. Comparison

    c. Contrast

    d. Classification

 2. Does the largest layer of the wedding cake represent the most talked-about cases or the least talked-about cases?

    a. Most

    b. Least

C   3. At which levels do you find people who have committed felonies?

a. 1 and 2

b. 1 and 4

c. 1, 2, and 3

d. 2, 3, and 4

d   4. In the first sentence, what pattern do you find?

a. Cause and effect

b. Comparison

c. Contrast

d. Classification

A   5. In the sentence right before the numbered list starts, what pattern do you find?

a. Cause and effect

b. Comparison

c. Contrast

d. Classification

C   6. What pattern is used for the minor details in paragraph 1?

a. Definition

b. Space order

c. Example

d. Process

d   7. What pattern is used for the minor details in paragraph 2?

a. Cause and effect

b. Comparison

c. Contrast

d. Classification

A   8. What pattern is used in the first sentence of paragraph 3?

a. Cause and effect

b. Comparison

c. Contrast

d. Classification

_d_ 9. In the wedding cake model, which layer represents the least formal processes of the criminal justice system?

   a. 1

   b. 2

   c. 3

   d. 4

_A_ 10. What is the relationship between the last two sentences in the selection?

   a. Cause and effect

   b. Comparison

   c. Contrast

   d. Classification

As you learned in Lesson 1, there is a process for reading, and as you have probably already figured out, college requires a lot of reading! In fact, most classes have a required textbook, and sometimes what you are assigned to read will not be discussed in class. Yet you will still be responsible for knowing all of the material. Your ability to effectively navigate through your textbooks directly impacts your academic success. This lesson will help you improve your textbook reading strategies.

Make Sense of the "Text" in Your Textbook.

These four strategies will help make reading your textbooks a more efficient and productive activity:

1. **Use the reading process to your advantage.** Refer to the Reading Guide you created in Part 1 (pp. 65–66) to remind yourself of how to read actively.

2. **Understand that textbooks are often hierarchical in the way they present content.** Textbooks usually move from general or broad ideas to more specific or narrow ideas within a chapter and within a section. Refer to the Reading Guide you created in Part 3 (pp. 360–361) to refresh your mind on the hierarchy of topic, main idea, major details, and minor details.

3. **Take notes as you read.** Highlighting, making brief notes in the margins of your textbooks, and using the MAPP strategy to take longer notes in a notebook are all effective ways to increase your comprehension. Paying attention to the pattern of organization and signal words can also help you stay on track (as you learned in Lessons 12 and 13).

4. **Use the learning aids in your textbooks during each stage of the reading process.** Textbooks are put together in a way to help make your reading and learning process easier. They often include helpful aids such as a table of contents, chapter summaries, study questions, and visuals, which are covered later in this lesson.

Learn Useful Note-Taking Strategies.

Let's look at some strategies to improve your textbook reading comprehension and help you remember what you have read:

- Annotating—that is, highlighting and writing in the margin of the text.
- Using a double-column system in your notebook.
- Using the MAPP reading strategy to "decode" your textbook.
- Creating summaries from your annotations and MAPP.

Annotating

The purpose of annotating while you read is to leave a record for yourself of what you have learned. Later, when you are preparing to take a test and want to study the ideas in your textbook, you don't want to have to reread a whole chapter or chapters. Instead, you should be able to go back and read only your annotations.

Your annotations should be complete enough to include the topic, main idea, and major details. However, if you mark too much, you will have to reread more than you should while you are studying. While each situation is a little different, in general you should mark no more than about 20 percent of a selection. To achieve this, you can mark just the key words of the topic, main idea, and major details.

To create a good annotation, you can follow the "APP" of the MAPP reading plan—something you have been practicing. You have marked answers to the questions you formed from headings (Lesson 8), searched for what readings are about (Lesson 9), found the point the author wants to make (Lesson 10), and understood the proof the author uses to support the point (Lesson 11).

Here is a breakdown of the process in a little more detail.

About: Finding the Topic

- Ask, "Who or what is the reading about?"
- Look for a title or heading.
- Look for repeated words or phrases within the reading.
- Mark the answer to your question by highlighting or putting a bracket around the [topic]. To avoid highlighting too much, mark

the topic only where it appears in the topic sentence, or only in one place if there is no topic sentence.

Point: Finding the Main Idea

- Ask, "What is the point?"

- Look for the idea that limits the topic the author wants to discuss.

- The main idea, together with the topic, is often found in a sentence called the topic sentence: T + MI = TS.

- Mark the answer to your question by highlighting or underlining the *main idea*. To avoid highlighting too much, don't mark words like "the" and "and"; only mark words that carry meaning.

Proof: Finding the Major Details

- Ask, "What is the proof?"

- Pay attention to signal words to help you find the pattern of the details.

- Double-check that the details do support the main idea.

- Mark the answer to your question by highlighting or labeling the major details with numbers: ① ② ③ ④. If you are highlighting, mark only the words that carry the key ideas.

Examples of Annotating

Let's look at some examples. For each of the following paragraphs, decide whether the amount of highlighting is too little, too much, or just right. Let two questions guide you:

- Are the key words in the topic, main idea, and major details highlighted?

- Is about 20 percent of the reading highlighted?

The paragraphs used in the examples come from Gitman & Joehnk, *Personal Finance Planning,* 11th edition.

Example A

Many people choose to rent rather than buy their home. Young adults usually rent for one or more of the following reasons: They don't have the funds for a down payment and closing costs. They are unsettled in their jobs and family status. They don't want the additional responsibilities associated with home ownership. They believe they can afford a nicer home later by renting now because housing market conditions or mortgage rates are currently unattractive.

Kseniya Ragozina/istockphoto.com

Too little   Too much   Just right

Why do you give that answer? _____

_____

Example B

Many people choose to rent rather than buy their home. Young adults usually rent for one or more of the following reasons: They don't have the funds for a down payment and closing costs. They are unsettled in their jobs and family status. They don't want the additional responsibilities associated with home ownership. They believe they can afford a nicer home later by renting now because housing market conditions or mortgage rates are currently unattractive.

Too little   Too much   Just right

Why do you give that answer? _____

_____

Example C

> Many people choose to <mark>rent rather than buy</mark> their home. <mark>Young adults</mark> usually <mark>rent for</mark> one or more of the following <mark>reasons</mark>: They <mark>don't have the funds</mark> for a down payment and closing costs. They <mark>are unsettled</mark> in their jobs and family status. They <mark>don't want the additional responsibilities</mark> associated with home ownership. They <mark>believe they can afford a nicer home later</mark> by renting now because housing market conditions or mortgage rates are currently unattractive.

Too little   Too much   Just right

Why do you give that answer? _____

_____

Symbols and Abbreviations

Using symbols can help eliminate highlighting clutter. Table 4.1 provides some basic suggestions if you choose to use symbols and abbreviations.

Table 4.1 Use Symbols and Abbreviations to Point Out Important Ideas

Use this symbol or abbreviation	to indicate . . .
main (or) key (or) * point	A main idea or important point
① ② ③	List of details or steps in a sequence
def	Definition of a key term
circle	Key words or words you do not know
imp ex	An important example
! (or) ?	Personal reactions to the material
Exam	Possible exam question

It may be easiest to understand your markings later if you combine the methods we have been discussing. For example, writing a big star and the word "Point" in the margin next to the main idea will help you focus on that main idea first when you go back to review the book. If you further note something about the topic and pattern of organization, the note will help jog your memory later about the major details. Whatever you decide to use, make sure that the markings you create make sense to you, so you can effectively use them.

Many people choose to rent rather than buy their home. Young adults usually rent for one or more of the following reasons: ① They don't have the funds for a down payment and closing costs. ② They are unsettled in their jobs and family status. ③ They don't want the additional responsibilities associated with home ownership. ④ They believe they can afford a nicer home later by renting now because housing market conditions or mortgage rates are currently unattractive.

—Adapted from Gitman & Joehnk, *Personal Finance Planning,* 11th edition

*Point—young people's causes for renting

INTERACTION 4–13	Annotating the Paragraphs You Read

Apply your reading strategy to the following paragraphs from college textbooks. Mark your answers as you find them. You have several choices for annotation.

- You can highlight the key words in the topic, main idea, and major details.

- You can bracket the topic, underline the main idea, and number the major details.

- You can use the symbols and abbreviations from Table 4.1.

- You can combine these methods in any way that works best for you.

1. **Paragraph from a sociology textbook**

   Question that leads you to the topic: _____

*Point—
_____
_____

Class is a structural phenomenon; it cannot be directly observed. Because sociologists cannot isolate and measure social class directly, they use other indicators to serve as measures of class. A prominent indicator of class is income; other common indicators are education, occupation, and place of residence. These indicators alone do not define class, but they are often accurate measures of the class standing of a person or group. These indicators tend to be linked. A good income, for example, makes it possible to afford a house in a nice neighborhood and provide a private education for one's children.

—Adapted from Andersen & Taylor, *Sociology: The Essentials,* 4th edition

2. Paragraphs from a mass media textbook

   Question that leads you to the topic: _____

*Point—
_____
_____

To understand mass communication in the digital age, first it is important to understand the process of communication. Communication is the act of sending messages, ideas and opinions from one person to another. Writing and talking to each other are only two ways human beings communicate. We also communicate when we gesture, move our bodies or roll our eyes.

Three ways to describe how people communicate are:

- Intrapersonal communication
- Interpersonal communication
- Mass communication

Each form of communication involves different numbers of people in specific ways. If you are in a market and you silently debate with yourself whether to buy a package of double-chunk chocolate chip cookies, you are using what scholars call *intra*personal communication—communication within one person. To communicate with each other, people rely on their five senses—sight, hearing, touch, smell, and taste. Scholars call this direct sharing of experience between two people *inter*personal communication. Mass communication is communication from one person or group of persons through a transmitting device (a medium) to large audiences or markets.

> —Biagi, *Media Impact: An Introduction to Mass Media*, 8th edition

3. Paragraph from a success skills textbook

  Question that leads you to the topic: _____

Learning is much more than just memorizing. It is acquiring knowledge through systematic, methodical study, or in simpler terms, by frequent review. To learn new information, two things are needed, repetition and time. In fact, there are 4 levels of memory that illustrate this. Level 1 is your shortest short-term memory. It lasts for only about five to eight seconds. This type of memory is jokingly referred to as "in one ear and out the other." Level 2 is cramming. This is where you haven't really studied and try to "cram" a lot of information into your head just before you take a test. This type of memory is not very reliable, and is usually done under stressful conditions (last minute) and ineffective at best. Level 3 is our effective recall level, where you can recall studied information in a variety of ways. At this level, you can understand and apply what you have been learning on a test or in conversation. This level requires time, repetition and your being active in your learning. Level 4 is your long-term memory. This is where your permanent memory is stored, and it becomes prior or background knowledge. This can only happen with continual active learning and frequent review.

*Point—

_____

_____

> —Adapted from Beale, *Success Skills: Strategies for Study and Lifelong Learning*, 3rd edition

4. Paragraph from an anthropology textbook

Question that leads you to the topic: _____

*Point—

_____

_____

> One important type of ritual is the rite of passage. Rites of passage mark important stages in an individual's life cycle. In one of anthropology's classic works, French folklorist Arnold van Gennep analyzed the rites of passage that help individuals through the crucial crisis or major social transitions in their lives, such as birth, puberty, marriage, parenthood, advancement to a higher class, occupational specialization, and death. He found it useful to divide ceremonies for all of these life crises into three stages: separation, transition, and incorporation—first ritual removal of the individual from everyday society, followed by a period of isolation, and, finally, formal return and readmission back into society in his or her new status.
>
> —Haviland, Prins, Walrath, & McBride, _The Essence of Anthropology_

5. Paragraph from a health textbook

Question that leads you to the topic: _____

*Point—

_____

_____

> Researchers have known for years that one's self concept has several effects on their behavior. If an individual devalues himself or herself and sees themselves as helpless and certain of failure, then this perception will almost guarantee failure. This has been referred to as the _self-fulfilling prophecy_. Conversely, if you see your self as succeeding, your chances of success will be greatly enhanced. Self-perception also has its effect on hostility. People with low self-esteem are more vulnerable to interpersonal insult than those with high self-esteem. In addition, those with low self-esteem become angrier if they do not get an apology than those with high self-esteem.
>
> —Girdano, Dusek, & Everly, Jr., _Controlling Stress and Tension_, 7th edition

Double-Column Note Taking

Once you have asked the questions and marked the answers of a reading, you can use a notebook to take notes on the main points and key details you want to remember. A popular and helpful system for doing so is called double-column note taking. The system is also called the Cornell note-taking system; it is named for the university at which Walter Pauk, the creator of the system, taught. You can use this system by making two columns in your notebook, as the following sample paragraph and double-column note-taking entry illustrate.

Sample Paragraph

[The Qing Empire] (1644–1796) brought [stability] to the world's largest state for more than 130 years. This [stability] brought great economic growth. The ① production of luxury goods like silk, pottery, and glass was the main source of economic growth. Of the three, silk was the main financial contributor. Women played a central role in the highly profitable silk weaving process, which improved their value in society. It may also have led to a decrease in the practice of female infanticide, since women were increasingly seen as a blessing rather than a burden as they had in previous generations due to their role in silk. While the production of luxury goods had a great impact on the economics of the Qing Empire, there were other industries too. ② The growth and export of cash crops such as tobacco and cotton crops also contributed to the economic expansion of the Qing Empire. ③ Coal-mining industries as a whole also helped China maintain and grow the strongest economy in the world.

—Adapted from Hansen & Curtis, *Voyages in World History*

Sample Double-Column Note Taking Entry

About = The stability of the Qing Empire (1644–1796)	**Proof** = 1. Production of luxury items
	a. Silk—main financial contributor
Point = brought great economic growth.	b. Pottery
	c. Glass-blowing
Note: You can shorten the AP above:	2. Growth and export of cash crops
	a. Tobacco
Qing Empire's stability → economic growth.	b. Cotton
	3. Coal-mining industries

In the left column, write a heading or a few key words that summarize a main idea. In the right column, take more detailed notes. You can use the MAPP strategy, short outlines, or lists to write down the major supporting details. *Hints:*

- Use words or images that will help you remember the pattern of relationship between the ideas. Ideas are easier to remember when you understand their relationship.

- Number lists. After you have reviewed your notes several times, you will remember how many points there are in a particular answer. You can use that knowledge as a check to see whether you are remembering all the points.

- Abbreviate as you like. Develop a system of abbreviations you can use in all your classes to make note-taking more efficient.

INTERACTION 4–14   Building Your Note-Taking Skills

A. For paragraphs A–E, mark the answers to the APP questions from the MAPP reading plan. Bracket the [topic], underline the main idea, and number the major details ① ② ③ ④.

B. Change your annotations into double-column notes, and then answer the questions that follow.

Paragraph A   **Sociology Textbook**

Question that leads you to the topic: _____

Are you a doodler? Have you filled up the margins of your school notebooks with flowers, shapes, funny little faces, hearts broken and whole, and many other unidentifiable miniature pieces of art? Have your teachers and classmates thought you were wasting your time and not really learning? Well, maybe they were mistaken! Studies seem to prove that there might be some benefits to doodling. It seems to improve memory. In one study, listeners who also doodled remembered 29% more of a long phone conversation. Doodling is also supposed to help relax the mind and lower stress. And the benefits may not stop there. Doodling may have an impact on reducing cravings. Stay tuned to find out more, and in the meantime, doodle on!

About = _Doodling_

Point = _May have some bene[fit]_

Shorter version of **AP:**

Effect of doodling

Proof =

1. _improve Memory_
2. _help relax the mind_
3. _reduce Craving_

1. Based on the relationships shown in the double-entry notebook, what is the pattern of organization in this paragraph? _Cause and effect_

2. What word in the topic sentence points out this pattern? _benifits_

Paragraph B   **American Government Textbook**

Question that leads you to the topic: _Children political party_

> Children's political party identification is shaped by their family in a number of ways. Families are particularly important in shaping the opinions of children because of strong emotional ties and exclusive control during early years. Parents share opinions directly with children, who often imitate and adopt these opinions. In addition, the family partly shapes the personality of the child. A child encouraged to speak up at home will be more likely to speak out in public. Children also inherit their social and economic positions from their parents, which influence how they view not only themselves and the world at large but also how they think the world views them. For example, a child from a wealthy family has a perception quite different from a child from a poor family.
>
> —Adapted from Welch, Gruhl, Comer, & Rigdon,
> *Understanding American Government*

About = _political party_

Identification

Point = _shape by family_

Proof =

1. _Share opinions with childr[en]_
2. _Shape your personality_
3. _your view of the world_

3. Based on the relationships shown in the double-entry notebook, what is the pattern of organization in this paragraph? _Cause and effect_

4. What word in the topic sentence points out this pattern? _____

Paragraph C   Public Speaking Textbook

Question that leads you to the topic: ___*What is it about*___

> Commemorative speeches praise, honor, recognize, or pay tribute to a person, an event, an idea, or an institution. The two most common types of commemorative speeches are speeches of tribute and speeches of award. A speech of tribute is given to honor someone. A speech of award is given to present a specific award and describe why that person is receiving the award. Both highlight a person's exceptional value, qualities, contributions, or accomplishments.
>
> —Griffin, *Invitation to Public Speaking,* 3rd edition

About = *Commem*	Proof =
	1. *Speeches of tribute*
Point = *Two main type*	2. *Speeche of award*
Shorter version of **AP:**	

Andres Peiro Palmer/istockphoto.com

5. Based on the relationships shown in the double-entry notebook, what is the pattern of organization in this paragraph? *Cla__*

6. What word in the topic sentence points out this pattern? _____

Paragraph D   Media Textbook

Question that leads you to the topic: _____

> 1   Just how quickly consumers adopt new technologies is predictable, according to Paul Saffo, the director of the Institute for the Future in Menlo Park, California. Saffo theorizes that for the past five centuries the pace of change has always been 30 years, or about 3 decades, from the introduction of a new technology to its complete adoption by a culture.
>
> 2   Saffo calls his theory the **30-year rule** , which he has divided into three stages, each stage lasting about 10 years. In the first stage, he says, there is "lots of excitement, lots of puzzlement, not a lot of penetration." In the second, there is "lots of flux, penetration of the product into society is beginning." In the third stage, the reaction to technology is, "Oh,

so what?" Just a standard technology and everybody has it." By Saffo's standard, American society is approaching the end of the second stage of acceptance of online technology because use of the Internet by consumers began in 1988, when less than one-half of 1 percent of the U.S. population was on the Internet.

—Biagi, *Media Impact: An Introduction to Mass Media*, 8th edition

About =	Proof =
	1.
Point =	
	2.
Shorter version of **AP:**	
	3.

Andres Peiro Palmer/istockphoto.com

7. Based on the relationships shown in the double-entry notebook, what is the pattern of organization in this paragraph? _____

8. What word in the topic sentence points out this pattern? _____

Paragraph E   Anthropology Textbook

Question that leads you to the topic: _____

Unflattering stereotypes about foreigners are deeply rooted in cultural traditions everywhere. For example, many Japanese believe Koreans are stingy, crude, and aggressive, while many Koreans see the Japanese as cold and arrogant; similarly, we all have in mind some image, perhaps not well defined, of the typical citizen of Russia or India or England. And your image of a culture will probably be different from mine if we are from different cultures. Essentially, these are simply stereotypes. We might well ask however, if these stereotypes have any basis in fact. In reality, does such a thing as national character exist? Or are they perpetuated by mistaken cultural traditions?

—Adapted from Haviland, Prins, Walrath, & McBride, *The Essence of Anthropology*

About = _____   Proof = _____

_____   1. _____

Point = _____

_____   2. _____

_____

_____   3. _____

_____

_____   4. _____

_____

Andres Peiro Palmer/istockphoto.com

9. Based on the relationships shown in the double-entry notebook, what is the pattern of organization in this paragraph? _____

10. What words in the paragraph point out this pattern? _____

Using a MAPP to "Decode" a Section of a Textbook Chapter

You have learned that there is a hierarchy of topic, main idea, and supporting details (About, Point, and Proof) in a single paragraph. The same kind of hierarchy exists in each section of a textbook chapter.

- The **topic** for the whole section can be found in the heading, and it is often repeated throughout the rest of the section (just like a topic is often repeated throughout a paragraph). Remember to turn the heading into a question to find the main idea.

- The **main idea** is now an idea that covers the information found in several paragraphs, not just one. The main idea of a section is likely to be a bigger or more general idea than you might find in a single paragraph and is found in a sentence called a **thesis statement**. A thesis statement controls more than one paragraph, whereas a topic sentence controls a single paragraph. This is also a good time to point out that the main idea can be stated directly or implied. Remember to turn the main idea into a question to find the major details.

- The **major supporting details** for this bigger main idea are the topic sentences of each individual paragraph. When the section includes subheadings, remember these divide the main topic into subtopics that offer more detailed information about the main topic. Remember to turn the subheadings into questions to find the key details needed to fully understand what you are reading.

In the following example from a biology textbook, the most important parts are labeled.

Blood Pressure (This is the topic of the whole section.)

Blood pressure is a fluid pressure that blood exerts against vessel walls. Blood pressure is highest in the aorta; then it drops along the systemic circuit. The pressure is typically measured when a person is at rest. For an adult, the National Heart, Lung, and Blood Institute has established blood pressure values under 120/80 as the healthiest (see Table 4.2). The first number, *systolic pressure,* is the peak of the pressure in the aorta while the left ventricle contracts and pushes blood into the aorta. The second number, *diastolic pressure,* measures the lowest blood pressure in the aorta, when blood is flowing out of it and the heart is relaxed. [Values for systolic and diastolic pressure] provide important information about cardiovascular health risks.

def

Main idea for entire section found in the thesis statement

Table 4.2 Blood Pressure Values (mm of Hg)

	Systolic	Diastolic
Normal	100–119	60–79
Hypotension	Less than 100	Less than 60
Prehypertension	120–139	80–139
Hypertension	140 and up	90 and up

Hypertension (This is the topic of the first major detail.)

Chronically high blood pressure is called *hypertension.* It can be associated with a variety of illnesses. [Hypertension] is a "silent killer" that can lead to stroke or heart attack. Each year 180,000 Americans, many of whom may not have had outward symptoms, die from hypertension. Roughly 40 million people in the United States are unaware that they have hypertension. There are several factors that increase your risk of hypertension. These influences include smoking, obesity, a sedentary life, chronic stress, a diet low in fruits and vegetables, and high salt intake.

def Main idea of paragraph and major supporting detail of whole section

def
Main idea of
paragraph and
major supporting
detail of whole
section

Hypotension (This is the topic of the second major detail.)

Hypotension is abnormally *low* blood pressure. [This condition] can develop when for some reason there is not enough water in blood plasma—for instance, if there are not enough proteins in the blood to "pull" water in by osmosis. A large blood loss also can cause blood pressure to plummet. Such a drastic decrease is one sign of a dangerous condition called ***circulatory shock.***

—Adapted from Starr & McMillan, *Human Biology,* 8th edition

Once you have read and annotated a textbook section, you can transfer your annotations into a double-column notebook entry. Here is a double-column notebook entry that accurately reflects the biology textbook section.

About = Blood pressure values

Point = provide important information about cardio- vascular health risks.

Proof =

1. Hypertension (too-high blood pressure): Systolic = 140 and up; diastolic = 90 and up

   a. Effects: Stroke or heart attack

   b. Causes: Smoking, obesity, sedentary life, chronic stress, diet low in fruits and vegetables, high salt intake

2. Hypotension (too-low blood pressure): Systolic = less than 100; diastolic = less than 60

   a. Cause: Not enough water in blood plasma

      —Not enough proteins in blood

      —Large blood loss

Andres Peiro Palmer/istockphoto.com

Completing this process allows you to work through the information twice so you can commit it to memory. By the time you take your test, you will have read, annotated, and taken notes. You will have both studied and reviewed. As always when reading, pay attention to the pattern of organization, whether signal words are used or not. In this textbook section, the headings and subheadings let you know that the pattern of organization is classification.

> Blood pressure
>> First type of risk: Hypertension
>> Second type of risk: Hypotension

INTERACTION 4–15 | **Creating a MAPP from Textbook Sections**

Read the following selections from textbook chapters. Mark while you read. After each selection, make a double-column notebook entry based on the APP.

Selection A

Book Industry Has Five Major Markets

1 Books fall into five major categories. These classifications once described the publishing houses that produced different types of books. A company that was called a textbook publisher produced only textbooks, for example. Today, one publishing house often publishes several different kinds of books, although they may have separate divisions for different types of books and markets.

Trade Books

2 Usually sold through bookstores and to libraries, trade books are designed for the general public. These books include hardbound books and trade (or "quality") paperbound books for adults and children. Typical trade books include hardcover fiction, current nonfiction, biography, literary classics, cookbooks, travel books, art books, and books on sports, music, poetry, and drama. Many college classes use trade books as well as textbooks. Juvenile trade books can be anything from picture books for children who can't read yet to novels for young adults.

Textbooks

3 Textbooks are published for elementary and secondary school students (called the "el-hi" market) as well as for college students. Most college texts are paid for by the students but are chosen by their professors.

4 Very little difference exists between some college texts and some trade books. The only real difference between many textbooks and trade books is that texts include what publishers call *apparatus*—test questions, chapter summaries, and CDs with extra assignments. The difference may be

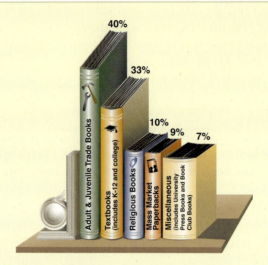

40%

33%

10%
9%
7%

Adult & Juvenile Trade Books

Textbooks
(includes K–12 and college)

Religious Books

Mass Market
Paperbacks

Miscellaneous
(includes University
Press Books and Book
Club Books)

How do publishers make money?

Most of the books people buy are trade books, but Kindergarten–12 and college text-books account for a substantial percentage of the book market.

Data from Vernois, Suhler, Stevenson Communications Industry Forecast, 2005–2009.

difficult to discern, so the Association of American Publishers classifies these two types of books according to where they are sold the most. A book that is sold mainly through college bookstores, for example, is called a textbook.

Religious Books

5   Hymnals, Bibles, and prayer books fall into the religious books category. Recently, religious publishers have begun to issue books about social issues from a religious point of view, but these books are considered trade books, not religious books.

Mass Market Paperbacks

6   Here, definitions get tricky. These books are defined not by their subjects but by where they are sold. Although you also can find them in bookstores, mass market books are mainly distributed through "mass" channels—newsstands, chain stores, drugstores, and supermarkets—and usually are "rack-sized." Many are reprints of hardcover trade books;

others are originally published as mass market paperbacks. Generally, they're made from cheaper paper and cost less than trade paperbacks.

University Press Books and Book Clubs

7   University presses publish a small number of books every year and are defined solely by who publishes them. A university press book is one that a university press publishes. Most university presses are nonprofit and are connected to a university, museum, or research institution. These presses produce mainly scholarly materials in hardcover or softcover. Most university press books are sold through direct mail and in college bookstores.

8   Book clubs publish and sell books directly to a select audience. Although they were once very popular, book clubs today represent a small portion of the book market.

—Biagi, *Media Impact: An Introduction to Mass Media,* 8th edition

Create an entry for a double-column notebook that accurately reflects this section of a textbook chapter.

About = Book industry	Proof =
	1. Trad book
Point = Five major market	sold in bookstore and library
	2. Textbook
Shorter version of AP =	elementary and High school
The five major	3. Religious books
market in the books	Hymnals, bible
Industry	4. Mass Market paperbeck z
	newstand Chain stor...
	and are rock sized
	5. University Press Book and book clu
	sell directly to a select
	audience.

Selection B

The Classroom Setting

1   Before you can select an appropriate and interesting topic for your assigned speech, you must consider the requirements of your assignments. Assigned speeches usually have several constraints because they are given in a classroom setting.

Preselected Purpose

2   An instructor usually tells you to give a particular type of speech, such as a speech to inform or persuade. You do not have the freedom to select your speech purpose, and you must select a topic compatible with the purpose.

Time Limits

3   Class size determines speech length—your instructor wants to make sure everyone in the class has time to give their speeches. Classroom speeches often only last a few minutes, and you may be penalized for going over time. You must select and narrow your topic to satisfy the assignment's time limits.

Highly Structured Assignment

4   You're usually asked to incorporate several specific speech components. You may be required to cite a specific number of outside sources, use visual aids, incorporate a specific style of language, or use a particular organizational pattern. The structure of an assigned speech often influences topic selection.

Instructor as an Audience

5   You give your classroom speeches to an instructor who is already a skilled public speaker. You must select a stimulating topic that your instructor, who has listened to many other speeches, will appreciate.

Class Members as an Audience

6   Your classmates may become the best audience for you as a beginning public speaker. They're also learning the ropes of public speaking, and they'll appreciate your diligent efforts. But they can also be a challenge

because they may be interested in topics your instructor doesn't want to hear about. Additionally, they're also searching for interesting topics, so try to avoid commonly used topics.

7   So how do you select a manageable, interesting, and dynamic topic for your required speeches? The process takes a bit of planning and effort, but you will discover that you have a wealth of usable ideas once you organize your thoughts about who you are, what you know, and what issues and events capture your own attention.

—Adapted from Griffin, *Invitation to Public Speaking*, 2nd edition

Create an entry for a double-column notebook that accurately reflects this section of a textbook chapter.

About =	Proof =
	1.
Point =	2.
	3.
	4.
	5.

Andres Peiro Palmer/istockphoto.com

Writing a Summary

The last note-taking strategy for improving your reading comprehension is to create a summary from your annotations and MAPP. It is a good way to rehearse the information you have read in a textbook. To create a summary, you boil down the information into the most important points and write it in sentences. The length of the summary depends on the length of the original text. If you are summarizing a paragraph, you might write a sentence. If you are summarizing a section of a textbook chapter, you might write a paragraph. You can even summarize a whole book using just a few paragraphs.

To write a good summary, you need to understand the relationships between the topic, the main idea, and the major supporting details. You will apply all that you have learned about MAPPing to writing a summary. In fact, it's only the final outcome that is different from what you have already been practicing. Instead of ending up with a double-column notebook entry or a MAPP outline, you write out the ideas in sentences.

Using What You Know to Write a Summary

Apply your MAPP strategy to create a good summary. As you read, mark the answers to the APP questions: Who or what is this about? What is the point? What is the proof? You can then go back and build a summary from your MAPP.

A summary = topic + main idea + major details, written in sentences

(S = T + MI + MDs)

While a good summary will consist of the T + MI + MDs, the end product can vary, depending on several things:

- The length of the material you are summarizing. (Are you summarizing a single concept or an entire section?)

- How complicated the information is. (A complicated concept might require the addition of minor details to fully explain it.)

- The pattern of organization. (Some relationships require more explanation.)

- Your prior knowledge. (You might be able to combine or simplify information based on what you already know.)

Examine this example before you try writing a summary on your own.

Paragraph from a history textbook

Question that leads you to the topic: _____

[Newton's theory] bound earth to the heavens, describing both as operating under laws that made motion as natural as rest. In Newton's view, the universe seemed to function like a huge self-regulating clock. ①After being wound up, clocks ticked away in an orderly fashion, following the laws governing their construction. The universe, he proposed, operated in the same way. ②And as a clock requires a clock maker, so the universe requires a universe maker.

—Kidener, Bucur, Mathisen, McKee, & Weeks,
Making Europe: People, Politics, and Culture

Summary: Newton believed that the universe was orderly, following laws, like a clock that acts the way its maker built it to function. Clocks are built by clock makers, so the universe must have had a creator, too.

As you can see, the summary was created by combining the topic, main idea, and major details.

INTERACTION 4–16   **Creating Summaries from an Annotated Paragraph**

For each paragraph, mark the answers to the APP questions from the MAPP reading plan. Bracket the [topic], underline the main idea, and number the major details ① ② ③ ④. Then write a summary.

1. Paragraph from a forensic science textbook

Question that leads you to the topic: Fibers

> main idea
>
> Fibers are used in forensic science to create a link between crime and suspect. For example, a thief may own a jacket made of a material that happens to match the type of fiber found at the crime scene. It does not mean he was there, but a jacket like his was. If a jacket fiber, sock fiber, and shirt fiber all from items the thief owns are found at the crime scene, then the chances that the suspect was actually there are high or increased.
>
> —Bertino, *Forensic Science: Fundamentals and Investigations*

Summary: Fibers are in forensic Science if the thief has one jacket made from the material doesnot mean you were there but if they found mulpp clothes that meck you were there.

2. Paragraph from a business textbook

Question that leads you to the topic: _What is this about_

> Let me explain how motivation works by sharing a personal story. My son, who at the time was 4, had gotten ahold of his sister's bead set, and he somehow got one of them stuck up his nose. He tried to get it out, and the thing kept getting higher up his nose. I got him in the car to take him to the emergency room, and right as I was getting ready to park I said to him, "Andrew, Daddy loves you a lot. We've got to get this thing out. If we go to the emergency room, this is going to cost Dad about $150. But here's the deal: If you can figure out a way to blow that out of your nose, first, we'll go to Blockbuster and you can buy any tape you want. And second, we'll go to Bakers Square, and you and I will split a French silk pie." Well, he blew the thing out, and it almost cracked my windshield.
>
> —Adapted from a story by Harry M. Jansen Kraemer, Jr., chairman and CEO of Baxter Intl. (a bioscience company)

Summary: _____

_____

_____

3. Paragraph from a student success textbook

Question that leads you to the topic: _____

> Before seeing a movie, don't you want to know what the movie is about? Before going to a concert, don't you want to know what kind of music the band will play? Before taking a test, wouldn't you want to know what kind of test you will be given? Since knowledge can be tested in different ways, you should know how you will be responsible for what you are studying. Here are some of the most common types of tests. One type is an objective test. These tests require correct answers and include multiple-choice, matching, true-false, and fill-in-the-blank questions. Another type is the subjective test. These include short answer and essay questions. These tests are set up to demonstrate not only whether you know the correct answer, but also what your opinion is and how you communicate your ideas in writing. The last

type of test is the performance test. These measure how well you can execute, or perform, a certain task or activity.

—Adapted from Beale, *Success Skills*, 3rd edition

Summary: _____

_____

_____

4. **Paragraph on a business management topic**

Question that leads you to the topic: _____

Human resource managers have several duties that follow a cycle of sorts. First, they must develop or follow a staffing plan that fits the needs of their company. Then, they are in charge of the hiring process, which involves recruiting and selecting the best employee for their staffing plan. There are also the details of competitive compensation and benefit packages to be negotiated. In addition, they must conduct training and employee evaluation of those hired. Finally, it is the human resource manager who deals with an employee who is leaving or did not work out as planned and must be fired.

Summary: _____

_____

_____

5. **Paragraph on a psychology topic**

Question that leads you to the topic: _____

There are a lot of opinions as to why Michael Jackson's face changed so dramatically through the years. Many seem to be based on nothing more than spiteful gossip. However, one theory that seems to be a good possibility is that Michael may have suffered from a disease known as Body Dysmorphic Disorder (BDD). This condition causes one to despise some part of his or her body and see it in a distorted and unrealistic way. Michael may have seen his nose as being ugly or fat. His BDD caused him to view his nose in an extremely unrealistic and unhealthy way.

Frank Edwards/Archive Photos/Getty Images

Michael Mariant-Pool/Getty Images

Summary: _____

_____

_____

| INTERACTION 4–17 | Creating a Summary from Multiple-Paragraph Annotations |

For the following passage from a health textbook, mark the answers to the APP questions from the MAPP reading plan. Bracket the [topic], underline the <u>main idea</u>, and number the major details ① ② ③ ④. Then write two summaries as directed.

Question that leads you to the topic: _____

1   Alcohol can have a similar effect on your body whether you drink a lot or a little; in general, it can help you feel up. However, alcohol has differing effects on your brain and behavior depending on the amount you drink.

2   In low dosages, alcohol affects the regions of the brain that inhibit or control behavior, so you feel looser and act in ways you might not otherwise. However, you also experience losses of concentration, memory, judgment, and fine motor control, and you may have mood swings and emotional outbursts.

3   Moderate amounts of alcohol can have disturbing effects on perception and judgment, including the following:

4   Impaired perceptions. You're less able to adjust your eyes to bright lights because glare bothers you more. Although you can still hear sounds, you can't distinguish between them or judge their direction well.

5   Dulled smell and taste. Alcohol itself may cause some vitamin deficiencies, and the poor eating habits of heavier drinkers results in further nutrition issues.

6   Diminished sensation. On a freezing winter night, you may walk outside without a coat and not feel cold.

7   Altered sense of space. You may not realize, for instance, that you have been in one place for several hours.

8   Impaired motor skills. Writing, typing, driving, and other abilities involving your muscles are impaired. This is why law enforcement officers sometimes ask suspected drunk drivers to touch their nose with a finger or to walk a straight line. Drinking large amounts of alcohol impairs reaction time, speed, accuracy, and consistency, as well as judgment.

9   In addition to lowering the immune system, heavy alcohol use may pose special dangers to the brains of drinkers at both ends of the age spectrum. Adolescents who drink regularly show impairments in their neurological and cognitive functioning. Elderly people who drink heavily appear to have more brain shrinkage, or atrophy, than those who drink lightly or not at all.

—Adapted from Hales, *An Invitation to Health*, 12th edition

1. Create a summary that only includes the topic, main idea, and major details.

Summary: _____

_____

2. Create a summary that includes the topic, main idea, major details, and relevant minor details.

Summary: _____

_____

_____

_____

Review: Useful Note-Taking Strategies

There are four useful note-taking strategies you can employ when studying a textbook:

- **Annotate.** Highlight no more than about 20 percent of a selection and create consistent symbols and abbreviations that make sense to you.

- **Use a double-column system.** Write a heading or a few key words in the left column and more detailed notes in the right column.

- **Use MAPP.** Remember that topic, main idea, and supporting details have a hierarchy and a pattern that can help you organize key information to improve your retention of ideas.

- **Create summaries.** A summary = topic + main idea + major details, written in sentences (S = T + MI + MDs).

Use the Chapter Resources to Improve Your Comprehension.

Textbooks are created to help you understand the material you are studying. Authors create a variety of resources in textbooks to help you be successful. Table 4.3 looks at the most common resources you will find in your textbooks.

Table 4.3 Textbook Resources from Front to Back

Resource	Description	Study Tip
Preface	The preface explains the purpose of the book, the features it contains, and, sometimes, tips on how to work through the book.	Read the preface! It shows you the big picture of what you can expect from your text.

Resource	Description	Study Tip
Table of Contents	The table of contents may be shown in two versions. 1. The brief contents shows all the chapter numbers and titles. 2. The detailed contents also lists the major headings within each chapter.	Get an overview of the book from the brief contents. Use the detailed contents to understand what is found in each chapter. It will help you quickly find what you need when you are given assignments or when you want to review information for a test.
Chapter Openers	The chapter opener often provides an overview of the key ideas of the chapter, sometimes in question form or outline form.	Use these to get a preview of the skills, concepts, or objectives of the chapter. Chapter openers can help you connect with what you already know, as well as be aware of what concepts you need to understand better.
Boxed Material or Sidebars	Boxes usually expand on an idea from the chapter. They may be stories, examples, or research studies to connect the textbook information to real-world situations.	Take the time to question and understand how the material relates to the chapter. Understand which concepts they illustrate, and how.
Key Terms	A list of key terms or concepts can be found at the beginning or end of a chapter.	Study these words to make sure you understand what they mean. Practice defining and explaining them.
Visual Aids	Visuals provide illustrations or examples of concepts, give specific statistical data to support a general idea in the text, or simplify large amounts of data.	Identify the point of the visual. Understand the relationships between any rows or colors used. Think critically about how the visual supports the text. See pages 475–489.
Review Questions, Self-Quizzes, or Critical Thinking Activities	These activities are designed to help you determine whether you have understood and learned the key material.	Work through these. If you find you cannot answer them, go back into the chapter and review the material. Later, retest yourself.

Resource	Description	Study Tip
Chapter Summaries	The chapter summary may be a bulleted list or brief text that pulls together the main ideas of the chapter. Sometimes it is a list of questions and answers.	Read the chapter summary before and after you read the chapter. This gives you a preview of the key ideas, and then a check on your comprehension afterward.
Appendix	An appendix usually gives further information about a key idea, concept, or process.	Use the appendix to find additional information on a topic you are studying.
Bibliography	The bibliography credits the work of others. The textbook author may discuss ideas from researchers or other scholars, and this list provides complete publication information about the sources. This resource can be divided into chapters or kept whole at the book's end. It is usually alphabetical.	Start with the bibliography if you have to do a research project on a concept discussed in your textbook. You can arm yourself with authors' names and titles to go online or to the library to begin your project.
Glossary	The glossary is an alphabetical list of all the key terms or concepts found in the book. This is a dictionary specific to the textbook it is in.	Use the glossary as a dictionary to quickly review or find the meaning of key terms or concepts.
Index	The index is a master list of key ideas, concepts, and names with the page number listed. It's in the back of the book.	Turn to the index to see where to find the discussion of a particular idea.

Anytime you purchase a textbook for a class, look for each of the elements listed in Table 4.3. These elements are designed to help you understand the course material, so know where they are and use them as you do the required reading.

Interpret the Meaning of Visuals.

Visuals in textbooks may provide

- Examples of the ideas being talked about.
- Specific numerical data to support the general statements in the text.
- A way to more easily compare large amounts of information.

In college textbooks, sometimes visuals include information that you must understand in order to comprehend the chapter completely. Other times the visuals are less important for comprehension but still interesting to look at. For example, the picture of the Romanov family from the Read and Talk section at the beginning of Part 4 (pp. 385–386) gives you a sense of the topic, and the visual of the bones provides an illustration of why the identity of the family members was so hard to determine.

In the rest of this lesson we will discuss several major types of visual material, such as tables, pie charts, line graphs, bar graphs, and photographs. The following points, with some adaptations, apply to reading most of these different kinds of visuals.

1. **Read the title of the table or graphic carefully.** The title often provides a summary of important information you need in order to understand the graphic. The title may function as the topic. Captions that appear under photographs are similarly important. Often, the caption functions as the main idea or the topic sentence of the graphic. It can also indicate the purpose of the visual.

2. **Read the headings of rows and columns or the labels on *x*- and *y*-axes carefully.** In a table, you should read the column headings

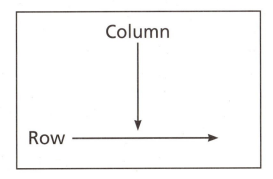

so that you will know which groups are being compared. The information in the rows often is the point of comparison between the groups listed in the columns.

When you are reading graphics, the *y*-axis is the vertical line and the *x*-axis is the horizontal line along the bottom of the figure. Read the labels carefully to make sure you understand how the information is set up.

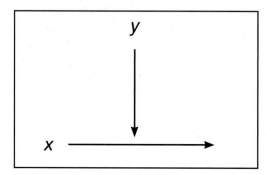

3. **Notice the meaning of each color used.** In some figures, the colors that different parts are printed in have specific meanings. Look for a key to tell you what the colors mean.

4. **Think critically about the implications of the headings, the numbers, and the way the information is presented.** Remember that graphics and tables summarize large amounts of data. In the process of reading so much information, sometimes it's easy to lose track of potential problems or questions that should be asked. Throughout the practices we'll draw your attention to questions you might want to ask about specific graphics.

Interpret Tables

A table is an arrangement of information in rows and columns. Tables condense a lot of information into a small space, and they make pieces of information easy to compare. Tables may be composed of information reported in words or in numbers.

INTERACTION 4–18   Analyzing a Table from a Sports Medicine Textbook

Read the following passage, which includes a table, and answer the questions that follow. Remember to follow these four steps:

1. Read the title of the table or graphic carefully.

2. Read the headings of rows and columns or the labels on *x*- and *y*-axes carefully.

3. Notice the meaning of each color used.

4. Think critically about the implications of the headings, the numbers, and the way the information is presented.

>   There are charts and different indexes to calculate the proper weight for people of all ages. One way is to calculate the body mass index (BMI). BMI is a reliable indicator of total body fat, which is related to the risk of disease and death. The score is valid for both men and women, but it does have some limits:
>
> - It may overestimate body fat in athletes and others who have a muscular build
>
> - It may underestimate body fat in older persons and others who have lost muscle mass
>
>   To determine BMI, weight in pounds is divided by height in inches, then divided again by height in inches and multiplied by 703.
>
>   BMI = weight in pounds ÷ height in inches ÷ height in inches × 703
>
>   Example: a person weighing 210 pounds who is 6 feet tall would calculate BMI as follows: 210 ÷ 72 inches ÷ 72 inches × 703 = 28.5.

HW

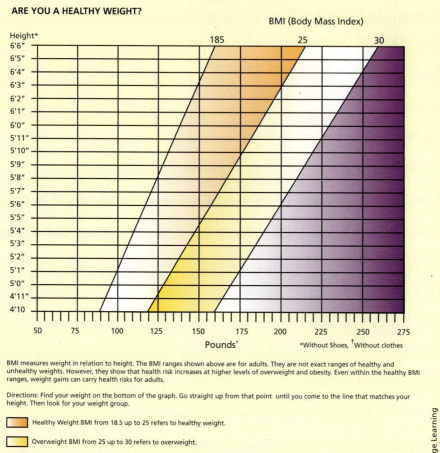

Body Mass Index

ARE YOU A HEALTHY WEIGHT?

BMI (Body Mass Index)

Height*

185   25   30

6'6"
6'5"
6'4"
6'3"
6'2"
6'1"
6'0"
5'11"
5'10"
5'9"
5'8"
5'7"
5'6"
5'5"
5'4"
5'3"
5'2"
5'1"
5'0"
4'11"
4'10

50   75   100   125   150   175   200   225   250   275

Pounds†   *Without Shoes, †Without clothes

BMI measures weight in relation to height. The BMI ranges shown above are for adults. They are not exact ranges of healthy and unhealthy weights. However, they show that health risk increases at higher levels of overweight and obesity. Even within the healthy BMI ranges, weight gains can carry health risks for adults.

Directions: Find your weight on the bottom of the graph. Go straight up from that point until you come to the line that matches your height. Then look for your weight group.

Healthy Weight BMI from 18.5 up to 25 refers to healthy weight.

Overweight BMI from 25 up to 30 refers to overweight.

Obese BMI 30 or higher refers to obesity: Obese persons are also overweight.

Source: *Report of the Dietary Guidelines Advisory Committee on the Dietary Guidelines for Americans*, 2000

© Cengage Learning

—Adapted from France, *Introduction to Sports Medicine and Athletic Training*

1. What is the purpose of this table? _____ Inform _____

_____

2. What does BMI stand for? _____ Body Mass Index _____

3. What is the *y*-axis measuring? _____

4. What is the *x*-axis measuring? _____

5. What do the colors stand for?
   a. ~~Green:~~ *Orange* Healthy weight _____
   b. ~~Orange:~~ *Yellow* Overweight _____
   c. Purple: Obese is 30 high _____

6. What is your BMI? _____

7. Are you at a healthy weight? _____ no _____

8. Is height on this scale measured with or without shoes? *without* How do you know? *It tell you to measured without shoes*

9. What is the effect of weight gain for adults? *Health risk*

10. What could cause the BMI to not be accurate? _____

_____

Interpret Pie Charts

A pie chart shows how a whole pie—100 percent of something—is divided up. Pie charts help readers compare the percentages or proportions of different components of a whole.

INTERACTION 4–19	Analyzing a Pie Chart from a Sociology Textbook

Read the following passage, which includes a pie chart, and answer the questions that follow. Remember to follow these four steps:

1. Read the title of the graphic carefully.

2. Read the headings of categories carefully.

3. Notice the meaning of each color used.

4. Think critically about the implications of the headings, the numbers, and the way the information is presented.

H W

The proportion of singles varies significantly by racial and ethnic group, as shown in Figure 4.4. Among persons age 18 and over, 40.6 percent of African Americans have never married, compared with 31.3 percent of Latinos/as, 24.8 percent of Asian and Pacific Islander Americans, and 22.3 percent of whites. Among women age 20 and over, the difference is even more pronounced; almost twice as many African American women in this age category have never married compared with U.S. women of the same age in general (U.S. Census Bureau, 2007).

Figure 4.4 Marital status of U.S. population age 18 and over by race/ethnicity.

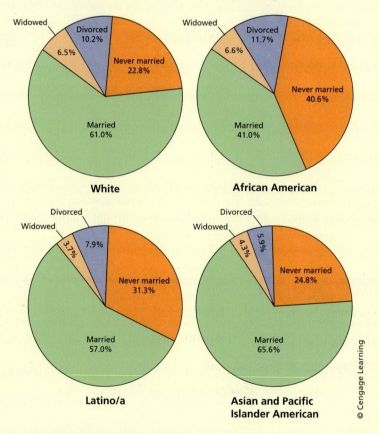

Source: U.S. Census Bureau, 2007.

—Kendall, *Sociology in Our Times*, 7th edition

HW

1. What is the purpose of the pie charts? _____ Classifitcation _____

_____

2. What pattern of organization is shown in the pie charts? Classificotion

3. What is the significance of each color? _____

4. Which group has the most unmarried adults? African American

5. Which group has the most married adults? Asian and Pacific Islande

6. Would this information be considered current? _____

7. What are some possible reasons the percentages of married adults vary among

   ethnicities? Asian and Pacific Stick to their kind

_____

Interpret Line Graphs

Line graphs are used to show how a condition or behavior changes over time. The number of people engaging in a behavior is often plotted on the *y*-axis (the vertical line). The units of time, such as years, are plotted on the *x*-axis, or horizontal line. Line graphs help make it easy to see trends in data.

| INTERACTION 4–20 | Analyzing a Line Graph from a Government Textbook |

Read the following passage, which includes a line graph, and answer the questions that follow. Remember to follow these four steps:

1. Read the title of the table or graphic carefully.

2. Read the headings of rows and columns or the labels on *x*- and *y*-axes carefully.

3. Notice the meaning of each color used.

4. Think critically about the implications of the headings, the numbers, and the way the information is presented.

> As people experience one personal president (a president perceived to have a lot of personal power) after another, they become disillusioned. Their

HW

unrealistic assumptions about presidential power, which prod the presidential candidates to make unrealistic promises, set the presidents up for failure in the eyes of the people. When the presidents can't deliver, the people lose faith. And, all along, the media exposure and scrutiny take a toll. Presidents' novelty wears off and their flaws appear. Few presidents can withstand the media microscope without losing their public esteem. Most presidents suffer a decline in popularity as they continue in office. (See Figure 4.5.)

Figure 4.5 Presidential popularity.

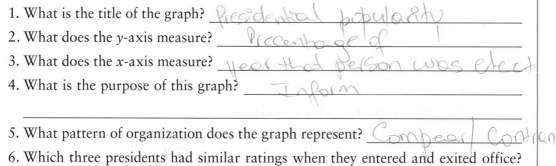

Presidential Popularity Since the end of World War II, presidential popularity has usually declined over time. Only three presidents—Eisenhower, Reagan, and Clinton—left office with ratings at a level comparable to those when they entered.

SOURCE: Adapted with permission from Gallup Inc., Presidential Job Approval Center, Historical Trend. http://www.gallup.com/poll/124922/Presidential-Job-Approval-Center.aspx. The question asked is "Do you approve or disapprove of the way (named president) is handling his job as president?" Copyright © 2010 Gallup, Inc. All rights reserved. The 2006 approval rating for G. W. Bush is from CBS News/New York Times poll data.

© Cengage Learning

—Welch, Gruhl, Comer, & Rigdon, *Understanding American Government*

1. What is the title of the graph? _Presidential popularity_
2. What does the *y*-axis measure? _Precentage of_
3. What does the *x*-axis measure? _year that person was elect_
4. What is the purpose of this graph? _Inform_

5. What pattern of organization does the graph represent? _Compear/Contranel_
6. Which three presidents had similar ratings when they entered and exited office? _Eisenhower, Reagan, Clinton_

7. Which president had the lowest approval rating exiting office? *Bush*

8. What factors impact popularity? *they can deleive*

Interpret Bar Graphs

Bar graphs help readers compare differences between groups. A graph can show the relationship between two sets of numbers, such as the number of people doing something over a certain number of years.

INTERACTION 4–21	Analyzing a Bar Graph from a Biology Textbook

Read the following passage, which includes a bar graph, and answer the questions that follow. Remember to follow these four steps:

1. Read the title of the table or graphic carefully.

2. Read the headings of rows and columns or the labels on *x*- and *y*-axes carefully.

3. Notice the meaning of each color used.

4. Think critically about the implications of the headings, the numbers, and the way the information is presented.

> 1   Most corn is grown intensively in vast swaths, which means farmers who grow it use fertilizers and pesticides, both of which are typically made from fossil fuels. Corn is an annual plant, and yearly harvests tend to cause runoff that depletes soil and pollutes rivers.
>
> 2   In 2006, David Tilman and his colleagues published the results of a 10-year study comparing the net energy output of various biofuels. The researchers grew a mixture of native perennial grasses without irrigation, fertilizer, pesticides or herbicides, in sandy soil that was so depleted by intensive agriculture that it had been abandoned. They measured the usable energy in biofuels made from the grasses, from corn, and from

H W

soy. They also measured the energy it took to grow and produce each kind of biofuel (Figure 4.6).

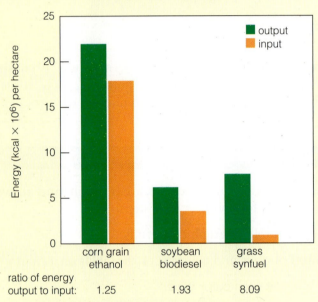

Figure 4.6 Energy efficiency of biofuel production from corn, soy, and prairie grass.

ratio of energy output to input: 1.25   1.93   8.09

Energy inputs and outputs of biofuels from corn and soy grown on fertile farmland, and grassland plants grown in infertile soil. One hectare is about 2.5 acres.

—Adapted from Starr, Evers, & Starr, *Biology: Today and Tomorrow*, 3rd edition

1. Define the term *biofuels*. are made gross corn and soy

2. Define the term *hectare*.

3. What is the *y*-axis measuring?

4. What is the *x*-axis measuring? ratio of energy output

[handwritten at top: 1+w]

5. What do the colors represent? _green output orange input_

6. About how much energy did ethanol produce from one hectare of corn? Give both the number and the unit of measure. _23 Kcal_

7. How much energy did it take to grow and produce the corn ethanol? _17_

8. Which biofuel tested had the highest ratio of energy output to energy input? ____ _grass switch grass_

Which had the lowest? _Corn grain ethanol_

9. Why might the color green have been chosen to represent the energy output of the biofuels? _because it is healthy_

Interpret Flow Charts

Flow charts, also called process charts, show how different stages in a process are connected. You should read flow charts from left to right and from top to bottom. Flow charts can become quite technical, with different box colors representing different aspects of the process.

| INTERACTION 4–22 | Analyzing a Flow Chart from a Criminal Justice Textbook |

Read the text that accompanies the flow chart in Figure 4.7, and answer the questions that follow. Remember to follow these four steps:

1. Read the title carefully.

2. Read the headings carefully.

3. Notice the flow of the boxes.

4. Think critically about the implications of the headings, the flow of the boxes, and the way the information is presented.

_Hw_

Figure 4.7

The Stages of Social Disorganization Theory

Social disorganization theory holds that crime is related to the environmental pressures that exist in certain communities or neighborhoods. These areas are marked by the desire of many of their inhabitants to "get out" at the first possible opportunity. Consequently, residents tend to ignore the important institutions in the community, such as businesses and education, causing further erosion and an increase in the conditions that lead to crime.

The Problem: Poverty
The Consequences:
Formation of isolated impoverished areas , racial and ethnic discrimination, lack of legitimate economic opportunities.

Leads to

The Problem:
Social Disorganization
The Consequences:
Breakdown of institutions such as school and the family.

Leads to

The Problem:
Breakdown of Social Control
The Consequences:
Peer groups replace family and educators as primary influences on youth; formation of gangs.

Leads to

The Problem:
Criminal Careers
The Consequences:
The majority of youths "age out" of crime, start families , and, if they can, leave the neighborhood. Those who remain still adhere to values of the impoverished-area culture and become career criminals.

Leads to

The Problem:
Cultural Transmission
The Consequences:
The younger juveniles inherit the values of delinquency and crime from their older siblings and friends, establishing a deep-rooted impoverished-area culture.

Leads to

The Problem:
Criminal Areas
The Consequences:
Rise of crime in poverty stricken neighborhood; delinquent behavior becomes socially acceptable for youths. Outside investment and support shun the area.

Source: Adapted from Larry J. Siegel, *Criminology*, 10th ed. (Belmont, CA: Thomson/Wadsworth, 2008), 180.

© Cengage Learning

1. What pattern of organization is represented in this flow chart? _Co   effect_
2. Explain what the colors within each box indicate in this flow chart. _____

_____

_____

3. Define social disorganization theory. _____

_____ _Crimers more_ _____

4. How many stages are there in social disorganization theory? _____

5. What does poverty lead to? _____ _6_

6. What does *cultural transmission* mean? _Social disorganization_

_____

7. Which age group is most at risk? Support your answer with information from the figure. ___Youth each boxes say youth___

_____

_____

Interpret Photographs

Photographs are used in textbooks to illustrate the ideas being discussed. A photograph's caption connects the photo to the idea being illustrated and should be read just as carefully as the title of a pie chart or bar graph.

Read the following passage, which includes a photo, and answer the questions that follow. Remember to follow these four steps:

1. Read the title carefully.

2. Read the caption carefully.

3. Notice the relationships within the image as well as between the image and the text.

4. Think critically about the implications of the headings and the way the information is presented.

> Ethanol is really hard on the liver. For one thing, breaking it down produces molecules that directly damage liver cells, so the more you drink, the fewer liver cells you have left to do the breaking down. Ethanol also interferes with normal processes of metabolism that keep the remaining liver cells—and the rest of the body—alive. For example, oxygen that would normally take part in breaking down fatty acids is diverted to breaking down ethanol, so fats tend to accumulate as large globules in the tissues of heavy drinkers. A

Hw

common outcome of such processes is alcoholic hepatitis, a disease characterized by inflammation and destruction of liver tissue. Alcoholic cirrhosis (see
Figure 4.8), another possibility, leaves the liver permanently scarred. (The
word *cirrhosis* is from the Greek word *kirros,* or orange-colored, after the
abnormal skin color of the people with the disease.) Eventually the liver of a
heavy drinker just quits working with dire health consequences.

Figure 4.8 Alcoholic liver disease.

Left, a normal human liver. *Right,* the enlarged, cirrhotic liver of an alcoholic. As few as
two alcoholic drinks per day can cause liver disease.

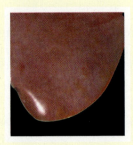

Science Photo Library/
Custom Medical Stock Photo

Biophoto Associates/
Photo Researchers, Inc.

—Adapted from Starr, Evers, & Starr, *Biology: Today and Tomorrow,* 3rd edition

1. What is the purpose of the photos in Figure 4.8? ___Inform___

_____

2. What pattern of organization do the photos illustrate? ___contrace___

3. Where would one look for the definition of "cirrhotic liver," a term found in the
   caption of the photo? ___text, dic___

4. How is ethanol hard on the liver?

   • ___Breaking it down___

   • ___enterter___

   • ___the liver of a heavy drinker just stop working___

5. Where does the word *cirrhosis* come from? _Orange_

_____

6. How many drinks per day can cause liver disease? _2 drink a day_

7. How does seeing these photos affect you? _don't drink_

Review: Interpreting the Meaning of Visuals

Depending on what type of visual is presented—table, line graph, pie chart, bar graph, flow chart, or photograph—you will need to follow steps similar to these:

- Read the title of the table, chart, or graphic carefully.
- Carefully read the captions, categories, or headings of rows and columns, or the labels on *x*- and *y*-axes.
- Notice the meaning of each color used.
- Think critically about the implications of the headings, the numbers, and the way the information is presented.

ACTIVATE YOUR SKILLS 1
MAPPing a Textbook Section   _HW_

Create a question to lead you to the topic. As you read, highlight the topic, main idea, and major supporting details. Answer the questions that follow.

1. Question that leads you to the topic: _____

1   Listen for cues in how your instructor presents material. The way instructors deliver content in the classroom and the clothes they wear can provide clues to their preferred teaching and learning styles. As you read the following descriptions, try to think of examples of past and current professors and try to guess their style.

2   Sequential-preferred instructors generally deliver content in a lecture format in a very specific order. They probably use a lot of outlined notes, detailed PowerPoint slides and/or handouts, and they rarely deviate from their established outlines. Because they are more likely to

view fun and play as wasteful, they probably use very little humor in the classroom. These instructors may have a serious, formal tone. They always stick to the topic and make clear connections to relevant topics and do not allow the class to wander very far off topic. A Sequential's clothing tends to match their teaching style. They are more likely to wear muted colors and dress in outfits or sets, which usually do not get mixed or matched. They looked organized, put together and professional.

3   Random-preferred instructors tell stories; use metaphors, analogies and humor; and allow for "wanderings" during a lecture. During a computer lesson, they might tell the "story of computers" and describe and develop its characters. Such lessons may sound more like conversation than a lecture. A Random still looks put together in their clothing, but like their teaching style, their clothing tends to be more relaxed, colorful, and casual. When they do dress up, Random men tend to choose colorful ties and Random women dangling jewelry and bold colors.

4   Instructors who are balanced in their learning preferences tend to use both styles of delivery. However, since most of the teaching models in traditional education are sequential, balanced instructors may lean in that direction. Their clothing as well will switch back and forth. They may dress up on the days they are feeling sequential and dress down on a random day.

—Adapted from Beale, *Success Skills*, 3rd edition

Question for Paragraph 1

2. Which sentence is the topic sentence? _The way instructors deliver content_

Questions for Paragraph 2

3. What is this paragraph about? _Sequential Instructor_

4. What is the point? _____

5. What does *sequential* mean? _____

6. Describe the clothing of a Sequential professor. _Match the teaching_

_____

Questions for Paragraph 3

7. What is this paragraph about? _R_____

8. What is the point? _____

_____

9. Describe the clothing of a Random professor. _more relax_

Questions for Paragraph 4

10. Who or what is this paragraph about? _Balanced Instructor_

11. What is the point? _____

12. Describe the clothing of a Balanced professor. _____

_____

13. What is the overall pattern of organization for this reading? _Classification_

Questions for Entire Selection

14–18. Create a double-column notebook entry of the entire selection.

About = _Topic_	Proof =
	1.
Point = _main idea_	
	2. _Random_
	3. _Balanced_

19–20. Decide which of the following instructors is sequential-preferred and which is random-preferred. Write a label under each photograph.

Mark Scott/ Photographer's Choice/Getty Images

Dmitriy Shironosov/Used under license from Shutterstock.com

19. _Random_

20. _Sequential_

ACTIVATE YOUR SKILLS 2   *HW*
Double-Column Note Taking

Ask your questions from the APP reading plan and mark your answers as you find them. Bracket the [topic], underline the <u>main idea</u>, and number the major details:① ② ③ ④. Then compile your annotations into double-column notes.

Paragraph 1   **Psychology**

Sheena Iyengar is a social psychologist, researcher, author, and decision-making expert. Her new book *The Art of Choosing* discusses the problem of having too many options. Most of us think choice is a good thing, but Iyengar's studies indicate just the opposite. She has shown that toddlers withdraw if they have too many toys to play with, whereas toddlers given a few toys play happily. Adults are similar. When we face too many choices, we tend to shut down. <u>In order to avoid shutting down, Iyengar offers two solutions</u>. One solution is to create limits for our choices. For example, you might choose to follow the advice of someone older or wiser that you respect. Another solution is to classify choices. For instance, if you are trying to choose a type of

Topic → (*sentence*)

cereal among the many choices found in the grocery aisle, you can lump them into categories of cereals with flakes, with holes, with marshmallows or without, with fruit or without, with fruit and nuts, granola, and so on. Putting the cereals in groups helps you narrow down your options to a manageable number.

1. Pattern of organization of the major supporting details: ___Cast one effect___

_____

2–5. Double-column notes:

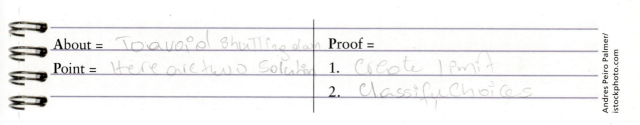

About = To avoid shutting down | Proof =
Point = Here are two solution | 1. Create limit
| 2. Classify Choices

Andres Peiro Palmer/
istockphoto.com

Paragraph 2   Health

If you are with someone who is choking and cannot cough, speak, or breathe, you might need to do the Heimlich maneuver. Even though you hope to never be in this situation, it is a good idea to know how the maneuver works, just in case. First, get the person to stand if they are not already. Next, stand behind the choking person and put your arms around his or her waist. Make a fist with one hand with your thumb pressed into the choking person's stomach between the belly button and the sternum, and then grab your fist with your other hand. Make several sharp thrusts into the person's stomach. Perform and repeat the Heimlich maneuver until the object the person is choking on is released. One word of caution: the choking person can lose consciousness and fall to the ground if the Heimlich maneuver does not dislodge the item so keep a strong grip on him or her throughout the whole process.

6. Pattern of organization: ___Time order process___

7–14. Double-column notes:

About = Heimlich menouer	Proof =
Point = How to do the	1. *sto*
	2. put your arm around them
	3. make a fist
	4. make a
	5. prform and repeat
	6.

Paragraph 3   **Biology Textbook**

Hemostasis is the name of a process that stops bleeding and so helps prevent the excessive loss of blood. In this process, an affected blood vessel constricts, platelets plug up the tear, and blood coagulates or clots. Although hemostasis can only seal tears or punctures in relatively small blood vessels, most cuts and punctures fall into this category.

—Starr & McMillan, *Human Biology*, 8th edition

15. Pattern of organization: *definition*

16–20. Double-column notes:

About = Hemostasis	Proof =
Point = How to stop bleeding	1. blood vessels constricts
	2. platelets plug up the tear
	3. blood coagulates or clots

Andres Peiro Palmer/istockphoto.com

Andres Peiro Palmer/istockphoto.com

MASTER YOUR SKILLS 1
Understanding Textbooks

Use MAPP to annotate each of the following passages. You may choose to either highlight or bracket, underline, and number. Then answer the questions that follow.

Passage A   Speech Textbook

1. Question that leads you to the topic: _What is this about_

1   Humor is perhaps one of the most complicated communication phenomena. What is funny to one person isn't always funny to another. You might tell a joke or story to two people and only one laughs. Then there are times when you tell a joke in the right environment and everyone thinks it's funny. If you repeat that joke in the wrong context, no one will find it the least bit amusing. And if subjectivity and context weren't enough to consider, delivery is also a tricky matter. If you rearrange the wording of a joke just a bit or forget to tell a line, no one will understand what is supposed to be so funny. Predicting what will make people laugh is a bit like predicting the weather—we're often wrong. However, research tells us that what makes something funny is a combination of three elements.

2   **Timing** is the way you use pauses and delivery for maximum effect. Research suggests that timing is a critical element in humor. Personal experiences also tell us that timing is integral to how a joke is received and understood. Pauses to set a mood, before punch lines, or before key phrases can make the difference between a successful joke and one that falls flat. In a now famous joke, Barbara Bush, in her 1990 speech to the graduating class of Wellesley College, told her audience, "Who knows, somewhere out in this audience may even be someone who will one day follow in my footsteps and preside over the White House as the president's spouse." She paused and added, "I wish him well."

3   The second aspect of successful humor is the objective of the joke. Appropriate jokes for speeches to entertain should strive to make light of something, remind us of our humanity, highlight the silly or the bizarre, tease others playfully, and even relieve tension in difficult times. Humor can also be used to make fun of others and put them down. Avoid this type of negative humor, as it will likely offend audience members. Appropriate humor stands a greater chance of truly entertaining the audience.

4   The third component of successful humor is the audience. Of course, no two audiences will respond to the same joke in the same way. Still, when you know your audience well, you should have a better sense of what your listeners will find funny. Remember, one of the most common reasons a joke backfires is that a speaker may have failed to consider the group memberships as well as the individual or collective experiences of the audience. This can lead to you telling a joke that "isn't funny" or that "goes too far" for the members of your audience. So before you select the amusing stories and jokes for your speeches to entertain, consider the standpoints, values, and background of your audience carefully.

—Griffin, *Invitation to Public Speaking*, 3rd edition

hw

Questions for Paragraph 1

2. What is the topic of this paragraph? __Humor__

3. What is the main idea of this paragraph? *A Combination of three elemen*

4. Which sentence is the topic sentence of this paragraph? *a funny person con make punchline*

Question for Paragraph 2

5. Explain the importance of *timing*. *It's a critical element*

_____

Question for Paragraph 3

6. Explain what the author would agree is *appropriate humor*. _____

making fun of other people

Questions for Paragraph 4

7. Explain why the author feels *audience* is important in regards to humor. _____

The topic have to be aprotote for the audience

8. What is the pattern of organization? *Cause and effect or Example*

9. List the signal words that helped you make that decision: *reson, leave*

Questions for the Entire Selection

10–14. Create a MAPP of the entire selection.

About: __Humor__

   Point: _____

      Proof: 1. __Teming__

            2. __objective of the joke__

            3. __Audience__

15. Write a summary of the selection using your MAPP as the basis. _____

_____

_____

_____

Passage B   Government Textbook

16. Question that leads you to the topic: _____ What is this about_____

1   It may seem paradoxical that as the budget deficit grows, Congress spends more and more on small projects targeted to local constituencies. But the fact that members of Congress are elected by local constituencies builds a bias for local over national needs into the budget process. Nothing gives senators and representatives more opportunity to prove to their states and districts that they are serving local needs and getting money earmarked for use at home.

2   An **earmark** is a specific amount of money designated—or set aside—at the request of a member of Congress, for a favored project, usually in his or her district. In 2006, Congress approved 13,012 earmarks at a cost of $167 billion.

3   Many of these earmarks, or *set asides* as they are also called, qualify as what are popularly known as *pork-barrel projects*. The projects may benefit a special interest, create jobs, or help the local economy in some other way, but they are not in any sense priorities, at least not outside the district. And the special interest they benefit may be big campaign contributors (see Figure 4.9).

Figure 4.9

Number of earmarks

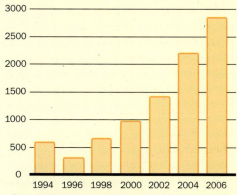

Earmarks Have Increased Dramatically
In recent years, the number of earmarks have increased dramatically. Shown here are the earmarks in defense bills.
Source: Congressional Research Service.

—Welch, Gruhl, Comer, & Rigdon, *Understanding American Government*

17. Who or what is the reading about? _earmark_

18. What are the patterns of organization of this passage? _Defeinction escomle_

19. In Figure 4.9, what is the *y*-axis measuring? _number of earmork_

20. What is the purpose of Figure 4.9? _It show you the_

MASTER YOUR SKILLS 2 _Hw_
Using Annotations and MAPPs to Create Summaries

Use MAPP to annotate each of the following passages. You may choose to either highlight or bracket, underline, and number. Then answer the questions that follow.

Passage A   Health Textbook

1. Question that leads you to the topic: _What is this about_

1   In recent years, the world has experienced terror-related disasters unparalleled in history. It has been reported that there were 12,216 individual terrorist bombings in the United States in the 10 years between 1980 and 1990, with each year becoming more destructive.

2   On April 19, 1995, the Alfred P. Murrah Federal Building, a U.S. government office complex in downtown Oklahoma City, Oklahoma, was destroyed, killing 168 people. This event was considered the largest domestic terrorist attack in the history of the United States and the largest terrorist attack of any kind in the nation's history until September 11, 2001.

3   On September 11, 2001, terrorists attacked the United States by flying two hijacked planes into the Twin Towers of the World Trade Centers in New York City, resulting in 2,752 deaths, while a third plane flown into the Pentagon killed 189 people and another 44 were killed when a fourth hijacked jet crashed into a field in Pennsylvania.

4   On July 7, 2005, a series of coordinated suicide bombings struck London's public transport system during the morning rush hour. The bombing killed 52 civilians and injured over 700 people.

—Maville & Huerta, *Health Promotion in Nursing*, 2nd edition

2. Which sentence is the thesis statement? _1_

3. What is the pattern of organization? _Time order no_

4. List the signal words that led you to the pattern: *years*

5–9. Create a MAPP of the reading selection.

    About: *Terror-related disasters*

    Point: *unparalleled*

    Proof: 1. *April 19 1995 Oklahoma City*
    kill 168 people

    2. *September 11 2001*
    2,752 people

    3. *July 7 2005 Suicide bombing*
    struck London's

10. Create a summary of the reading selection. *There are three*
Importance dates in recent history where
unparalleled

Passage B   **Management Textbook**

11. Question that leads you to the topic: *What is this about*

1   There are four basic components of goal-setting theory. **Goal**
    specificity is the extent to which goals are detailed, exact, and
    unambiguous. Specific goals, such as "I'm going to have a 3.0 aver-
    age this semester," are more motivating than general goals, such as
    "I'm going to get better grades this semester."

2   **Goal difficulty** is the extent to which a goal is hard or challeng-
    ing to accomplish. Difficult goals, such as "I'm going to have a 3.5
    average and make the Dean's List this semester," are more motivat-
    ing than easy goals, such as "I'm going to have a 2.0 average this
    semester."

3   **Goal acceptance** is the extent to which people consciously under-
    stand and agree to goals. Accepted goals, such as "I really want
    to get a 3.5 average this semester to show my parents how much
    I've improved," are more motivating than unaccepted goals, such as

About: _____

Point: _____

H W

> "My parents really want me to get a 3.5 average this semester, but there's so much more I'd rather do on campus than study!"
>
> 4   **Performance feedback** is information about the quality or quantity of past performance and indicates whether progress is being made toward the accomplishment of a goal. Performance feedback, such as "My prof said I need a 92 on the final to get an 'A' in that class," is more motivating than no feedback, "I have no idea what my grade is in that class." In short, goal-setting theory says that people will be motivated to the extent to which they accept specific, challenging goals and receive feedback that indicates their progress toward goal achievement.
>
> —Adapted from Williams, *Management*, 4th edition

12. Which sentence is the thesis statement? _____ 1 _____

_____

13. What is the overall pattern of organization for this selection? *Classification*

14–19. Create a MAPP for the reading selection.

    About: *Goal setting*

     Point: *that is has four specific component*

      Proof: 1. *Goal specific*

            2. *Goal difficulty*

            3. *Goal acceptance.*

            4. *Performance feedback.*

20. Create a summary of the reading selection. *There are four setting in the goal*

Summary Activity: Reading Textbooks

Part 4 has discussed how paragraphs are arranged according to different patterns of organization, how to annotate and take notes from textbooks, the resources used in a textbook to help you get more out of your reading, and, finally, how to interpret visuals. Fill in the Reading Guide by completing each idea on the left with information from Part 4 on the right. You can return to this guide throughout the course as a reminder of how to make the most of your textbooks.

Reading Guide to Reading Textbooks

Complete this idea	with information from Part 4.
Major details are often organized in	1.
Each pattern of organization answers a question that corresponds to	2.
Signal words are also called	3.
These signal words—*first, then, in the summer of 1912*—indicate	4.
These signal words—*called, means, can be understood as*—indicate	5.
These signal words—*consequences are . . . , leads to . . . , creates . . .*—indicate	6.
These signal words—*in front of, behind, to the side*—indicate	7.
These signal words—*first step, second step, third step*—indicate	8.
These signal words—*one type, another kind*—indicate	9.
These signal words—*the same as, different from*—indicate	10.
These signal words—*because of, due to*—indicate	11.

Complete this idea	with information from Part 4.
These signal words—*to illustrate, for instance*—indicate	12. _____
Four things that will help make reading your textbooks a more efficient and productive activity are:	13. _____ 14. _____ 15. _____ 16. _____
When you highlight, you need to be cautious of	17. _____
You should highlight approximately	18. _____
The symbols and abbreviations you create should be	19. _____
In double-column note taking, in the left column you put	20. _____
In double-column note taking, in the right column you put	21. _____
A summary usually includes	22. _____
What a summary ends up looking like can depend on:	23. _____ 24. _____ 25. _____ 26. _____
The two types of tables of contents are	27. _____
The purpose of an appendix is	28. _____ _____
In an index you find	29. _____ _____

Complete this idea	with information from Part 4.
The four actions you take to understand how a visual is organized are:	30. _____ 31. _____ _____ 32. _____ 33. _____ _____

Think about how you created and used an outline or summary before you read Part 4. How did your methods differ from the suggestions here? Write your thoughts.

_____

_____

_____

Application: Reading Textbooks

FORENSICS TEXTBOOK

● Pre-Reading the Selection

The following selection, "William Bass, the Body Farmer," is taken from a forensics text-book, *Forensic Science: Fundamentals and Investigations,* by Anthony J. Bertino. Read to find out about the unique job William Bass had.

Surveying the Reading

Survey the title of the selection and the first sentence of each paragraph, reading quickly. What is the general topic of the reading selection? _____

_____

Guessing the Purpose

Based on the title of the selection and the type of publication it is in, what do you suppose is the section's main purpose—to persuade, inform, or entertain? _____

Predicting the Content

Predict three things this selection will discuss.

- ● _____
- ● _____
- ● _____

Activating Your Knowledge

What prior knowledge do you have about forensics, dead bodies, anthropology, or Patricia Cornwell?

- ● _____
- ● _____
- ● _____

Common Knowledge

Read this term and its definition to help you understand the reading selection.

FBI *(paragraph 3)* FBI is the acronym for the Federal Bureau of Investigation, a division of the Department of Justice. It is an investigative agency responsible for solving certain categories of crime, such as kidnapping, counterfeiting, and counterterrorism.

● Reading with Pen in Hand

Now read the selection. Pay attention to and mark any ideas that seem important, and respond to the questions and vocabulary items in the margin.

Access the Reading CourseMate via **www.cengagebrain.com/shop/ISBN/1413033156** to hear vocabulary words from this selection and view a video about this topic.

William Bass, the Body Farmer

Reading Journal

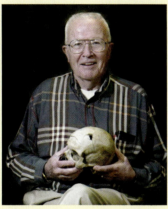

AP Photo/Wade Payne

1   William Bass was studying psychology. For fun, he enrolled in an **elective** anthropology course studying the behavior and culture of humans. His professor, a specialist in skeletal remains, was asked to come to the scene of a terrible accident. A collision on the highway resulted in a fire. Three people had died, and one body was burned so badly that identification was difficult and the professor was asked to help. The professor asked Bill for a ride to the crime scene and asked the young psychology student to join him. Bill decided right then and there to switch his studies and his career from psychology to anthropology. He learned all about the human body, skeletal remains, and what they can tell us about the life and death of a person.

2   While at the University of Tennessee, Bill spent many years examining bodies as a forensic expert assisting in solving crimes. In particular he specialized in digging up skeletal remains and learning

elective Notice that the sentence started with "For fun . . . ." What do you think *elective* means?

● Which do you think you would rather study—psychology or anthropology?

● If you were a forensics student, what question might you have about the decomposition of the human body?

utmost This word describes "importance." What might *utmost* mean?

decomposition Use context and word parts to figure out what *decomposition* means. (If you need to, see the Word Parts Glossary on pages 105–107.)

• Picture what it must be like to work at this facility.

vast The next sentence gives some examples to explain *vast array*. What does *vast* mean?

• Have you ever read *The Body Farm* or any other crime or mystery book that included forensics? If not, have you seen any TV shows about forensics?

donated A synonym is used later in this sentence. What does *donated* mean?

their secrets, to answer a question of **utmost** importance in forensic cases, "How long ago did they die?" When Bill started, little information existed to link the physical characteristics of a rotting corpse to a specific time of death. Bill saw a need—and a solution—and in 1971 he approached his university to ask for a small piece of land to do research on decomposition of the human body. His request was granted, and his research on dead bodies has never stopped. Today it is one of the few facilities dedicated to human **decomposition**. At first, the questions Bill and his team asked were pretty simple, such as, "How long does it take for a limb to fall off of a corpse?" Since then the depth and breadth of the questions being explored has exploded.

3   At any given time, there are about 40 dead bodies on the three acres of the Anthropology Research Facility. They are rotting away in different circumstances, such as in water, in the shade, in the sun, in shallow burials, and in the trunks of cars. All changes in decomposition are carefully recorded over time. The researchers ask all types of specific questions about the chemical changes in different parts of the body during decomposition, as well as the details of insect growth, and each are catalogued. The collection of skeletons is, in fact, the largest of its kind in the world and is used to provide a **vast** array of information about a person from his or her remains. For example, from skeletal comparisons, it is possible to use the length of the thighbone to determine the person's gender, race, and height. The research facility is also used to train FBI personnel. Bodies are buried with evidence planted, and the FBI is sent in to find the body and recover the evidence.

4   In 1994, Patricia Cornwell, a mystery novel author, wrote a book based on the research facility. She called her book *The Body Farm*. The name has stuck. The bodies on the body farm are not grown, however. Most bodies are **donated**, either by families of the dead or given in a will. Hundreds of people have given their remains to the cause of improving forensic science.

5   Bill Bass, the body farmer, is now retired, but he is still involved in his facility and spends a lot of time communicating forensic science to the public. His work and the body farm are featured in documentaries and books, including *Death's Acre,* which Bass wrote.

A. Recognizing Patterns of Organization

Identify the pattern and signal word(s) used in each of the following sentences. Choose from the following patterns:

Time order (narration)	Time order (process)	Space order	Definition
Example	Cause and effect	Compare and contrast	Classification

Bill Bass, the body farmer, is now retired, but he is still involved in his facility and spends a lot of time communicating forensic science to the public.

1. Pattern: _____

2. Signal word: _____

In 1994, Patricia Cornwell, a mystery novel author, wrote a book based on the research facility.

3. Pattern: _____

4. Signal words: _____

A collision on the highway resulted in a fire.

5. Pattern: _____

6. Signal word: _____

The questions Bill and his team asked were pretty simple, such as, "How long does it take for a limb to fall off of a corpse?"

7. Pattern: _____

8. Signal words: _____

The researchers ask all types of specific questions about the chemical changes in different parts of the body during decomposition, as well as the details of insect growth, and each are catalogued.

9. Pattern: _____

10. Signal word: _____

It is possible to use the length of the thighbone to determine the person's gender, race, and height.

11. Pattern: _____

12. Signal word: _____

There are usually about 40 dead bodies on the three acres of the Anthropology Research Facility owned by the University of Tennessee in Knoxville.

13. Pattern: _____

14. Signal words: _____

Bodies are buried with evidence planted, and then the FBI is sent in to find the body and recover the evidence.

15. Pattern: _____

16. Signal word: _____

17. What is the overall pattern of organization of this passage? _____

18. What is the purpose of the photograph included in this selection? _____

_____

B. Annotating and Summarizing a Textbook Reading Selection

Reread the selection on William Bass. Your reading purpose is to note the contributions William Bass has made to the field of anthropology.

19. Summarize your findings. _____

_____

_____

_____

_____

_____

Spotlight on Inference: Implied Main Idea

Being able to determine an implied main idea is an important inference skill.

Stating an Implied Main Idea

- Identify the topic.
- Find the major details and how they are organized.
- Ask, "What do all these details have in common?"
- Combine this answer with the topic to make a topic sentence.

20. Using this inference strategy, your annotations, and your summary, what is the implied main idea of this passage? _____

_____

Test 4: Reading Comprehension

FORENSICS TEXTBOOK

Your instructor may ask you to take practice tests throughout the semester to help you decide which topics you need to study the most. All the tests in this book include questions about all the major reading comprehension skills after the reading selection.

● Pre-Reading the Selection

The following excerpt, "What Bones Can Tell Us," is taken from the forensics textbook *Forensic Science: Fundamentals and Investigations,* by Anthony J. Bertino. Read to find out about some of the information bones provide forensic scientists.

Surveying the Reading

What parts of the reading should you survey? _____

_____

Go ahead and survey the reading that begins on page 511.

Guessing the Purpose

Based on your survey, what main purpose do you believe the writer has: to persuade, inform, or entertain? _____

Predicting the Content

Based on your survey, what are three things you expect the reading selection to discuss?

- _____
- _____
- _____

Activating Your Knowledge

Search your memory for knowledge you have about bones, whether your knowledge is vague or specific. Ask yourself questions like, "Do I know the differences in bones between males and females? Can I name any bones? Have I watched any crime shows that dealt with bones?"

- _____
- _____
- _____

Common Knowledge

Read these terms and their definitions to help you understand the reading selection.

osteoporosis *(paragraph 4)* A bone disease in which bones become fragile and break. This disease is common in older people, especially women after menopause.

calcium *(paragraph 4)* A mineral the body needs to build and keep strong bones and teeth.

forensic scientists *(paragraph 5)* Forensics is the application of science to solving crime. So a forensic scientist is a scientist who helps identify and solve the mystery of skeletal remains.

hormones *(paragraph 6)* Chemicals created and released by the body. Two commonly known hormones are testosterone and estrogen. Hormones impact the body by helping to control metabolism, bringing the onset of puberty or menopause, and controlling the sex drive and reproduction cycles.

● Reading with Pen in Hand

Now read the selection. As you read, pay attention to and mark any ideas that seem important, and respond to the questions and vocabulary items in the margin.

Access the Reading CourseMate via www.cengagebrain.com/ shop/ISBN/1413033156 to hear vocabulary words from this selection and view a video about this topic.

What Bones Can Tell Us

Reading Journal

Number of Bones

1   How many bones are in the human body? Most medical students will tell you 206. That answer is only partially correct. An adult has 206 bones after all bones have become fully developed. A baby has 450 bones!

● How many bones do you probably have?

How Bones Connect

2   A joint is the location where bones meet (articulate). Joints contain basically three kinds of connective tissue:

● Have you ever hurt a ligament or pulled a tendon?

- Cartilage. Wraps the ends of the bones for protection and keeps them from scraping against one another (Figure 4.10).

- Ligaments. Bands of tissue connecting together two or more bones (Figure 4.11).
- Tendons. Connect muscle to bone (Figure 4.12).

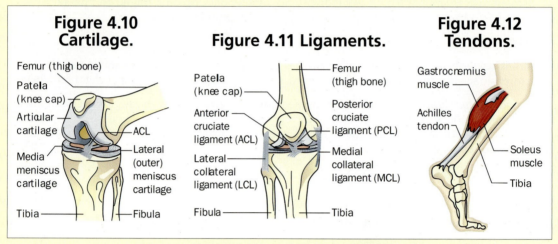

Figure 4.10 Cartilage.

- Femur (thigh bone)
- Patela (knee cap)
- Articular cartilage
- Media meniscus cartilage
- Tibia
- ACL
- Lateral (outer) meniscus cartilage
- Fibula

Figure 4.11 Ligaments.

- Patela (knee cap)
- Anterior cruciate ligament (ACL)
- Lateral collateral ligament (LCL)
- Fibula
- Femur (thigh bone)
- Posterior cruciate ligament (PCL)
- Medial collateral ligament (MCL)
- Tibia

Figure 4.12 Tendons.

- Gastrocnemius muscle
- Achilles tendon
- Soleus muscle
- Tibia

—Bertino, *Forensic Science: Fundamentals and Investigations*, 2009

Aging of Bone

● Visualize some exercises that would be good for strengthening your bones.

deteriorate At the end of the second sentence is a synonym for this word. What does *deteriorate* mean?

3   Throughout our lifetime, bones are being produced and being broken down. Children build more bones at a faster rate than the rate of bones being broken down. As a result, bones increase in size. After 30 years, the process begins to reverse; bones deteriorate faster than they are built. This deterioration can be slowed with exercise. Without exercise, bones can become frail and less dense and are easily broken later in life.

hunched Use your logic to determine the meaning. What does *hunched* mean?

● Can you visualize what a hunched elderly person looks like?

4   People with osteoporosis are at risk of breaking bones because their bones have lost calcium and tend to be porous. As the vertebrae lose calcium, they begin to collapse and can give someone a hunched appearance. Some elderly people do, in fact, shrink; the loss of height is caused by the vertebrae collapsing. The number of bones and their condition can tell an investigator about a person's age, health, and whether they had enough calcium in their food.

What Bones Reveal

● What story would your bones tell about you?

5   So much about a person is revealed by examination of his or her bones (Figure 4.13). The term **osteobiography** literally translates as the story of a life told by the bones. Bones contain a record of

the physical life. Forensic scientists know that analyzing the bones reveals clues to one's age, sex, race, approximate height, and health. For example, a loss of bone density, poor teeth, or signs of arthritis can point to a nutritionally **deficient** diet and disease. The bones of a right-handed person's arm would be slightly larger than the bones of the left arm. If someone lifted heavy objects regularly, the bones would be denser than someone who did not work physically hard. The type of sports one plays could be detected by the extra wear and tear on different joints and the sizes of the bones in general. An X ray of the bones taken during an autopsy would show previous fractures, artificial joints, and pins.

deficient Several examples of the effects of a nutritionally *deficient* diet are given. What do they suggest *deficient* means?

Figure 4.13 Our skeletons reveal information about us.

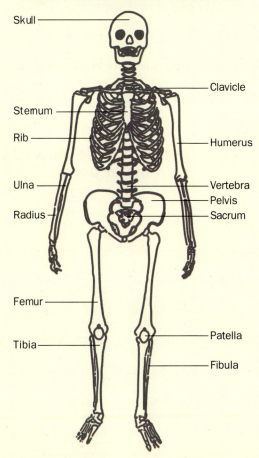

Skull
Clavicle
Stemum
Rib
Humerus
Ulna
Vertebra
Pelvis
Radius
Sacrum
Femur
Patella
Tibia
Fibula

—Bertino, *Forensic Science: Fundamentals and Investigations,* 2009

How to Distinguish Males from Females

● For the next paragraphs, picture what the author is describing.

differentiate Notice the question in the previous sentence asks about whether the bones belong to a male or female. What does *differentiate* mean?

6   Often, a detective's first question to a forensic anthropologist is whether the skeleton belongs to a male or female. How can one **differentiate** sex from bone fragments? The overall appearance of the female's skeleton tends to be much smoother (gracile) and less knobby than that of a male's skeleton (robust). A man's skeleton is usually thicker, rougher, and appears quite bumpy. Because of male hormones, muscles are more developed in the male. When muscles are larger, they require a stronger attachment site on the bones. To accommodate the larger muscles and their tendons, the surface of the bone where a muscle and tendon attach is thicker, creating the appearance of a rough or bumpy area. One place this is especially noticeable is in the knees, because the bones of the knees are more obvious than other areas of the body.

Skull

massive Use your prior knowledge and look at Figure 4.16. What difference might a male skull have that would be described as *massive*?

7   Generally, the male skull is more **massive** and bumpier than the female skull. There are many specific differences, but the first step is to review Figures 4.14 and 4.15 depicting the major bones of the skull.

Figure 4.14 Front view of skull with major bones labeled.

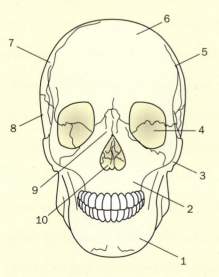

Figure 4.15 Side view of skull with major bones labeled.

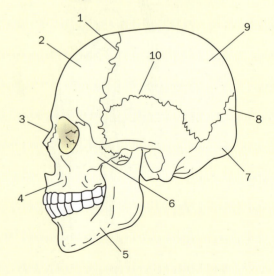

—Bertino, *Forensic Science: Fundamentals and Investigations*, 2009

Figure 4.14

Number	Name of Bone
1	Mandible
2	Maxilla
3	Zygomatic
4	Orbits of the eye; Sphenoid
5	Coronal suture
6	Frontal
7	Parietal
8	Temporal
9	Nasal
10	Vomer

Figure 4.15

Number	Name of Bone or Suture
1	Coronal suture
2	Frontal bone
3	Nasal bone
4	Maxilla
5	Mandible
6	Zygomatic complex
7	Occipital protuberance
8	Lambdoidal suture
9	Parietal bone
10	Squamous suture

8   In Figures 4.16 and 4.17, note the differences between the male and female skulls. The male's frontal bone is low and **sloping**, whereas the female's frontal bone is higher and more rounded. The male eye orbits tend to be square, whereas the female's eye orbits are more circular. The male's lower jaw is square, with an angle of about 90 degrees. The female's lower jaw is sloped, with an angle greater than 90 degrees. Males also have squarer chins; females' chins are rounder or more V-shaped. The occipital protuberance, a bony knob on the male skull, serves as an attachment site for the

sloping Use Figure 4.17 and your prior knowledge to determine what *sloping* means.

● As you read, note the difference between the male and female chin.

Figure 4.16 A side view of male and female skulls, noting the differences.

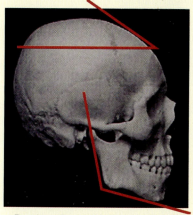 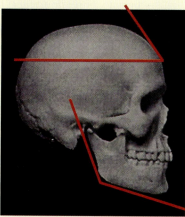

—Bertino, *Forensic Science: Fundamentals and Investigations,* 2009

Male: note the low sloping frontal bone and a jawbone set at 90 degrees.
Female: note the rounded frontal bone and jawbone greater than 90 degrees.

many muscles and tendons of the neck. Because the muscles in a man's neck are larger than the muscles in a woman's neck, the area of attachment needs to be thicker, creating the protuberance on the male skull.

Figure 4.17 Summary of male and female skull differences.

Male Front View	Male characteristics	Trait	Female characteristics	Female Front View
	More square	Shape of eye	More rounded	
	More square	Mandible shape from underside	More V-shaped	
	Thick and larger	Upper brow ridge	Thin and smaller	
Male Side View	**Male characteristics**	**Trait**	**Female characteristics**	**Female Side View**
	Present	Occipital protuberance	Absent	
	Low and sloping	Frontal bone	Higher and more rounded	
	Rough and bumpy	Surface of skull	Smooth	
	Straight	Ramus of mandible	Slanting	
	Rough and bumpy	Nuchal crest	Smooth	

—Bertino, *Forensic Science: Fundamentals and Investigations*, 2009

● Comprehension Questions

Write the letter of the answer on the line. Then explain your thinking.

Main Idea

_____ 1. Which of the following statements best describes the main idea of this passage?

   a. Joints contain three types of connective tissue.

   b. Bones are complicated, intricate parts of the body that make it difficult to understand human anatomy.

   c. There are many ways in which bones can help uncover the identity of a skeleton.

   d. How can one differentiate sex from bone fragments?

WHY? What information in the selection leads you to give that answer? _____

_____

_____

_____

____ 2. Which of the following sentences from paragraph 3 is the topic sentence?

    a. Throughout our lifetime, bones are being produced and being broken down.

    b. Children build more bones at a faster rate than the rate of bones being broken down.

    c. After 30 years, the process begins to reverse; bones deteriorate faster than they are built.

    d. This deterioration can be slowed with exercise.

WHY? What information in the selection leads you to give that answer? _____

_____

_____

_____

Supporting Details

____ 3. Which of the following is not mentioned in the reading selection as a trait that bones can help identify?

    a. Age

    b. Race

    c. Weight

    d. Sex

WHY? What information in the selection leads you to give that answer? _____

_____

_____

____ 4. Which of the following characteristics is a difference between the male and female skull?

    a. The male eye orbits are squarer.

    b. The male skull is more massive than the female skull.

      c. The female skull is more gracile.

      d. All of the above

WHY? What information in the selection leads you to give that answer? _____

_____

_____

_____

Author's Purpose

_____ 5. After reading the article, what would you say the main purpose is?

      a. To persuade the reader to become a forensic anthropologist.

      b. To inform the reader about how male skulls are bigger than female skulls.

      c. To entertain the reader with figures of the human skeleton.

      d. To inform the reader how bones tell us about people.

WHY? What information in the selection leads you to give that answer? _____

_____

_____

_____

_____ 6. What is the purpose of Figure 4.17?

      a. To explain why the male and female skull are similar.

      b. To contrast in table form the male and female skull.

      c. To list the traits of the human skull.

      d. To help the reader understand what his or her skull looks like.

WHY? What information in the selection leads you to give that answer? _____

_____

_____

_____

Relationships

_____ 7. What is the pattern of organization for the following sentence? *Because the muscles in a man's neck are larger than the muscles in a woman's neck, the area of attachment needs to be thicker, creating the protuberance on the male skull.*

a. Comparison

b. Cause and effect

c. Definition

d. Narration

WHY? What information in the selection leads you to give that answer? _____

_____

_____

_____

8. In paragraph 2, what is the pattern of organization?

a. Compare and contrast

b. Cause and effect

c. Classification

d. Time order

WHY? What information in the selection leads you to give that answer? _____

_____

_____

_____

Fact, Opinion, and Inference

9. Which best describes the following sentence? *The bones of a right-handed person's arm would be slightly larger than the bones of the left arm.*

a. Opinion

b. Fact

c. A mix of fact and opinion

d. None of the above

WHY? What leads you to give that answer? _____

_____

_____

_____

____ 10. Which of the following statements would the author agree with?

    a. Male skeletons are more different than female skeletons.

    b. Bones do not age.

    c. Although there are exceptions, usually female skulls are larger than male skulls.

    d. Some crimes would not be solved without the help of forensic anthropologists.

WHY? What information in the selection leads you to give that answer? _____

_____

_____

_____

● Vocabulary in New Contexts

Review the vocabulary words in the margins of the reading selection and then complete the following activities.

EASY Note Cards

Make a note card for each vocabulary word from the reading. On one side, write the word. On the other side, divide the card into four areas and label them E, A, S, and Y. Add a word or phrase in each area so that you wind up with an example sentence, an antonym, a synonym, and finally, a definition that shows you understand the meaning of the word with your logic. Remember that a synonym or an antonym may have appeared in the reading.

Relationships Between Words

Circle yes or no to answer the question. Then explain your answer.

  1. Could a diet **deficient** in vitamins cause your health to **deteriorate**?

    Yes   No

    Why or why not? _____

  2. Could an accident while on a ski **slope** cause **massive** head injuries?

    Yes   No

    Why or why not? _____

3. Could the habit of poor posture cause **deterioration** in a person's spine to the point he or she becomes **hunched** as a senior citizen?

Yes   No

Why or why not? _____

_____

Language in Your Life

Write short answers to each question. Look at vocabulary words closely before you answer.

1. Name a quality that you feel **differentiates** a good friend from a bad friend. _____

_____

2. Name a person in your family whose health has **deteriorated**._____

_____

3. Name an activity in which you could describe your posture as **hunched**._____

_____

4. Describe something you like to eat that is **deficient** in vitamins._____

_____

5. Name the biggest **slope** you have ever been on._____

_____

Language in Use

Select the best word to complete the meaning of each sentence.

deficient	deteriorate	differentiate	hunched	massive	sloping

1. Political relationships between countries can _____ just as relationships between individuals can.

2. A person might get tired of a partner's "issues," and break up with him or her; a government might view another power as being _____ in some way and decide to break off ties or even to threaten the other nation militarily.

3. It is a slippery _____ from military threats to actual war.

4. It seems that once threats have been made, the _____ egos of the leaders sometimes prevent compromise.

5. Two dictators at odds bring to mind a cartoon of a crazy world leader _____ over his nuclear missiles, with his finger poised over the red "launch" button.

6. Sometimes it is hard to _____ between reality and fiction when it comes to the world's political scene.

Spotlight on Word Parts: -Ate

As you have learned, *deteriorate* means "to become progressively worse." The word *deteriorate* is composed of two parts:

deterior- means "to get worse" + ate means "to cause or make"

The two parts together add up to the meaning of the whole word. Keep in mind that one possible job of a suffix is to change the grammatical part of speech of a word. The suffix -*ate* makes words into verbs.

The suffix -ate is used in many other words.

advocate = to speak for or defend

deviate = to cause to stray

exaggerate = to make more than it really is

emancipate = to make free from control

fascinate = to charm

Circle the correct word in each of these sentences.

1. When you are (advocated / fascinated / emancipated) with someone, you want to explore who they are.

2. Fishermen have been known to (exaggerate / deviate / fascinate) the size of their catch.

3. To gain equality, we must (deviate / exaggerate / emancipate) the world from poverty.

4. Harry is passionate about nature, especially animals; he (emancipates / advocates / exaggerates) for several endangered species.

5. There are people in every culture who (deviate / fascinate / advocate) from the accepted cultural norms. As a result, they are often seen as weird, undesirable, or even crazy.

PART 5

"You are not in Kansas anymore. . . ."

When Colonel Miles Quaritch, played by Stephen Lang, said this in *Avatar*, he was referring back to a famous line in the classic film *The Wizard of Oz*.

Critical Reading

What would you do if you woke up one day and found yourself transported to a strange land? Would you lock the door and stay inside? Or would you go out and explore, by listening to your senses, using your prior knowledge, and asking questions?

The next two lessons focus on improving your thinking and understanding. In Lesson 15, you learn to ask a series of questions about what you are reading. These questions help you gain a better understanding of the ideas you are reading about, give you the language to explain the ideas to others, allow you to evaluate why other people think the way they do, and maybe even allow your creative juices to flow and come up with some new ideas of your own.

The benefits of asking questions aren't limited to the classroom. Most people are going to end up in strange new places in life. College won't be the only new place you encounter. Are you going to lock the door, sit still, and not take any risks, or are you willing to ask questions, take the initiative, and be bold in your life?

. . . .

Share Your Prior Knowledge

Have you ever gotten lost? Or perhaps you have been a stranger in a new school, neighborhood, or country. Share this experience with a classmate and explain how you got back to familiar territory or how you acclimated yourself to a new environment.

Survey the Lessons

Take a moment to turn to the table of contents and survey Lessons 15 and 16 in Part 5 so you know what to expect. For each lesson, name one thing you think you already know about that topic:

Lesson 15: _____

Lesson 16: _____

Name one thing you want to read more about to understand better:

_____

Read and Talk

ONLINE ARTICLE

In college, reading is just the beginning of how you will share new ideas with others in your class. So the first reading in each part of this book is meant to give you the chance to talk about reading. Read the article, and then use the four discussion questions to talk about your ideas with your classmates and your instructor. Make this an opportunity to create new friendships and knowledge through the art of listening to the ideas of others, the enjoyment of discussing your thoughts, and the fun of reading something new.

Access the Reading CourseMate via **www.cengagebrain.com/shop/ISBN/1413033156** to hear a reading of this selection and view a video about this topic.

Failure Is a Good Thing

Jon Carroll

Walter B. McKenzie/Photodisc/ Getty Images

1   Last week, my granddaughter started kindergarten, and, as is **conventional**, I wished her success. I was lying. What I actually wish for her is failure. I believe in the power of failure.

2   Success is boring. Success is proving that you can do something that you already know you can do, or doing something correctly the first time, which can often be a problematical victory. First-time success is usually a **fluke**. First-time failure, by contrast, is expected; it is the natural order of things.

conventional Using your prior knowledge, what might you say to someone when he or she starts something new, like a job or school? Does *conventional* mean "common and expected" or "uncommon and unexpected"?

fluke Since *fluke* is contrasted with *expected* here, what does *fluke* mean?

credibility The term "street cred" is related to this word. Based on this entire paragraph, your prior knowledge, and your logic, what do you think *credibility* means?

3   Failure is how we learn. I have been told of an African phrase describing a good cook as "she who has broken many pots." If you've spent enough time in the kitchen to have broken a lot of pots, probably you know a fair amount about cooking. I once had a late dinner with a group of chefs, and they spent time comparing knife wounds and burn scars. They knew how much **credibility** their failures gave them.

inferior This sentence sets up a contrast with the previous sentence. What does *inferior* mean?

4   I earn my living by writing a daily newspaper column. Each week I am aware that one column is going to be the worst column of the week. I don't set out to write it; I try my best every day. Still, every week, one column is **inferior** to the others, sometimes spectacularly so.

5   I have learned to cherish that column. A successful column usually means that I am treading on familiar ground, going with the tricks that work, preaching to the choir or dressing up popular sentiments in fancy words. Often in my inferior columns, I am trying to pull off something I've never done before, something I'm not even sure can be done.

6   My younger daughter is a trapeze artist. She spent three years putting together an act. She did it successfully for years with the Cirque du Soleil. There was no reason for her to change the act—but she did anyway. She said she was no longer learning anything new and she was bored; and if she was bored, there was no point in **subjecting** her body to all that stress. So she changed the act. She risked failure and profound public embarrassment in order to feed her soul. And if she can do that 15 feet in the air, we all should be able to do it.

subjecting What action is taking place? The example is that "if she was bored, there was no point in *subjecting* her body to all that stress." What would be a good synonym for *subjecting*?

7   My granddaughter is a perfectionist, probably too much of one. She will feel her failures, and I will want to comfort her. But I will also, I hope, remind her of what she learned, and how she can do whatever it is better next time. I probably won't tell her that failure is a good thing, because that's not a lesson you can learn when you're five. I hope I can tell her, though, that it's not the end of the world. Indeed, with luck, it is the beginning.

Talking About Reading

Respond in writing to the questions here and then discuss your answers
with your classmates.

1. What do you usually say to people when they fail to achieve what they have
   attempted? What do you say to yourself when you fail? _____

   _____

   _____

2. Think about our culture's view of failure. How does it differ from the view that the
   author presents in this reading? _____

   _____

   _____

3. What example can you give of how a small failure led you to a bigger success?

   _____

   _____

4. Do you agree with the author that failure is a good thing? Why or why not? _____

   _____

   _____

Thinking Critically About What You Read

It's a habit for many people to read an article quickly, make a snap judgment about it, and then act on that judgment as though it is truth. In college, however, one of the most important things you can learn is to slow down and not come to such quick conclusions. If you take the time to examine an author's ideas closely and then form a conclusion based on the evidence you find, you will be thinking critically.

You could say that the whole purpose of college is to teach people to think critically. In all fields of study, instructors want to help you learn to go beyond impulsive reactions in order to reach a more thoughtful response. In Lessons 15 and 16, you will learn how you have been building critical thinking skills throughout the course. You will continue adding to that foundation by learning about the different levels of critical thinking and by learning how to sort out fact from opinion. Finally, you will spend some concentrated time on forming inferences from details, which you have also been engaged in throughout the course. Learning to make inferences is so central to so many reading skills that it seems worthwhile to look at it as its own separate topic.

Lesson 15

Reading is not an activity you can do on "auto-pilot." You need to:

- Actively question the author's words.

- Think about the ideas behind the words.

- Add your own thoughts into the mix.

- Make decisions or solve problems based on your understanding.

The best way to be involved in your reading is to ask questions. You were introduced to this idea in Part 1, Active Reading. You have also practiced turning titles and headings into questions and then marking the answer while you read in Lesson 8. As you work through Lesson 15, you will be refining the questioning process using critical thinking.

Critical Thinking Is a Learning Process.

To help you form the habit of using a critical thinking process, we are going to explore a series of six critical thinking levels. The levels are arranged according to a format of increasing complexity that Benjamin Bloom, a professor at the University of Chicago, devised. His critical thinking levels are often referred to as Bloom's Taxonomy. (Lorin W. Anderson and David R. Krathwohl revised the system. We use their labels for each level.) Figure 5.1 describes the six levels.

When you read or listen to lectures, you will learn more if you make it a habit to apply these six thinking activities to the subject.

Critical Thinking Level 1: Remember.

When you remember, you can recall and repeat basic information. You have actually practiced this level of critical thinking throughout this book, beginning in Lesson 1 when you learned the 5W's and H: who, what, when, where, why, and how. Level 1 is about remembering the basic information about the subject—important dates and places, bold terms, and other key details that stand out when you read.

Figure 5.1 Bloom's taxonomy with questions.

LEVEL 6 CREATE — You use the information to create something new or you draw conclusions. "What other explanations or solutions are there?"

LEVEL 5 EVALUATE — You decide what value the information has or make choices based on it. "What factors should I consider to decide whether these ideas are worthwhile?"

LEVEL 4 ANALYZE — You understand the parts and how they relate to one another. "How do the parts or sections fit together to make up the whole?"

LEVEL 3 APPLY — You can use the information in a new situation or solve problems with it. "How can I apply this knowledge or procedure to produce a certain result?"

LEVEL 2 UNDERSTAND — You understand the information and can explain it to someone else. "How can I retell this using my own words?"

LEVEL 1 REMEMBER — You can recall and repeat basic information. "Who? What? When? Where? How? Why?"

Read this figure starting at the bottom. Each thinking action depends on mastering the steps below it. In order to draw conclusions from your reading, for example, you need to recall it, understand it, use it, grasp how its parts work together, and evaluate its worth.

—Dole/Taggart, *Connect: College Reading*

Example of Remembering: Watch

You can **recognize** what a watch is; you can tell a watch from say, a bracelet, and you **remember** the purpose of a watch and what it is used for—to tell time.

INTERACTION 5–1   Practicing Critical Thinking Level 1: Remember

Read the passage and then answer the questions that follow.

1   If you asked citizens their opinions on matters of public policy, it would be reasonable to expect they knew something of public policy. If you asked for their choice of a candidate for public office, you'd think they had some knowledge of the candidates and their positions. An answer about the operation and institutions of government presumes they have sufficient knowledge and information to form opinions. In addition, it is reasonable to expect those opinions are based on real preferences. But Americans often do not know much about the details of their government or who represents them.

2   Many Americans are unable to identify important political personalities. Fourteen percent were unable to identify Vice President Dick Cheney, prior to his and George W. Bush's re-election in 2004. Only a small percentage of Americans can identify a single piece of legislation passed by Congress. In fact, more people can identify TV personalities than political ones. In spite of an increase in educational levels, knowledge of politics has not increased since the 1940s.

3   Americans revere the Constitution. They believe it is the blueprint for democracy. However, many do not even know what's in it. One-third think it establishes English as the country's official language. One-sixth think it establishes America as a Christian nation. One-fourth can't name a First Amendment right. (By the way, those rights are: freedom to assemble and petition government, freedom to practice any religion, freedom of speech, and freedom of the press.) Only 6 percent can name all four.

4   Misperceptions regarding government policies are also common. Polls show strong favor of reducing the size of the federal government. However, most polled do not even know whether the government is growing or shrinking. In one poll almost half had an opinion on a bill that didn't even exist. They gave an opinion though, just as they would for real policies they had never heard of.

—Adapted from Welch, Gruhl, Comer, & Rigdon, *Understanding American Government: The Essentials*

For each of the following statements, circle T for true or F for false.

1. Americans are knowledgeable about their government.   T (F)

2. Thirty-three percent of all Americans think that the Constitution establishes English as the official language.   (T) F

3. Knowledge of politics has improved since 2004.   T (F)

4. Most Americans are against big government.   (T) F

5. Twenty-five percent of Americans can't name a first Amendment right.   (T) F

6. Four percent of Americans can name all six of the First Amendment rights.   (T) F

7. Eighty-six percent of Americans were able to identify Vice President Dick Cheney prior to his and George W. Bush's re-election in 2004.   (T) F

8. In one poll, about 50 percent of Americans had an opinion about a bill that did not even exist.   (T) F

9. More Americans can identify political personalities than TV ones.   T (F)

10. One-sixth of all Americans think that the Constitution established the United States as a Christian nation.   (T) F

Critical Thinking Level 2: Understand.

When you understand, you can explain the ideas in a reading selection to someone else using your own words. You have been practicing this level when you answer the "Why?" questions in the Test: Reading Comprehension readings at the end of each part of this book. Level 2 is about demonstrating that you comprehend ideas. Your ability to create a MAPP, summarize, outline, or explain the information to someone else verbally is proof that you understand.

Con you outline

Example of Understanding: Watch

You can **explain** what a watch is and what it is used for, and you can **explain** to another person the concept of telling time.

INTERACTION 5–2	Practicing Critical Thinking Level 2: Understand

Read the passage and then fill in the APP that follows.

> A number of factors contribute to the current high rate of divorce in the United States. Demographic changes (shifts in the make-up of the population) are part of the explanation. The rise in life expectancy, for example, has an effect on the length of marriages. Some marriages that in an earlier time may have ended in death now end in divorce. Changes in women's roles are also related to the rate of divorce. Women today are more financially independent. As a result, the economic interdependence that bound men and women in a marriage is not as strong.
>
> —Adapted from Andersen & Taylor, *Sociology: The Essentials*, 4th edition

About: _____High rate of divorce_____

Point: _____Factor_____

Proof: 1. _____Demographic change_____

2. _____The rise in life expectancy_____

3. _____Change in woman's role_____

Critical Thinking Level 3: Apply.

When you apply information, you can use it in a new situation or solve problems with it. Think of Lessons 10, 12, and 13, in which you practiced finding the main idea and identifying patterns of organization. You practiced these skills in class, and then you were expected to find the main idea or organizational pattern in a new paragraph on your own. Applying what you have learned helps you solve problems you haven't seen before.

Can you diagram

Example of Applying: Watch

You can **demonstrate** how to tell time on any watch or clock. You can tell time on both digital and traditional clock faces.

INTERACTION 5–3 | Practicing Critical Thinking Level 3: Apply

Read the passage and then answer the questions that follow.

1   SeaWorld Orlando has always known that Tilikum, a 12,000-pound orca that killed trainer Dawn Brancheau on Wednesday, could be a particularly dangerous killer whale.

2   SeaWorld trainers were forbidden from swimming with Tilikum, as they often did with the resort's seven other orcas.

3   That was in part because of his size: At an average weight of nearly 6 tons, Tilikum—nicknamed Tilly—was the largest orca at any of SeaWorld's parks.

4   But it was also because of his ominous history.

5   In 1991, Tilikum and two female killer whales dragged trainer Keltie Byrne underwater, drowning her in front of spectators at Sealand of the Pacific, a defunct aquarium in Victoria, British Columbia.

6   Acquired by SeaWorld the next year to breed with female orcas, he was involved in a second incident in July 1999 when the naked body of a man who had apparently sneaked into SeaWorld after hours to swim with the whales was found draped dead across his back.

7   Authorities later concluded that the man, Daniel Dukes, likely suffered hypothermia in the 55-degree water and drowned, but they said it also appeared Tilikum bit the man's body and tore off his swimming trunks after he had died.

8   Still, Chuck Tompkins, the corporate curator in charge of animal behavior for SeaWorld Parks & Entertainment, said Tilikum was not an unusually violent orca.

9   "What you need to remember is, we've done thousands of interactions with this animal with no incidents whatsoever," Tompkins told the Orlando Sentinel. He also noted that Tilikum had fathered many calves at SeaWorld, calling him "a valuable asset not only from a breeding standpoint but from a behavior standpoint, too."

—Excerpted from Garcia, *Orlando Sentinel,* February 24, 2010

Mathieu Belanger/Reuters/Landov

b 1. Which of the following would make the best thesis statement for the passage?

    a. Tilikum—nicknamed Tilly—was the largest orca at any of SeaWorld's parks.

    b. Tilikum was considered dangerous because of his size and ominous history.

    c. Tilikum was not an unusually violent orca.

    d. In 1991, Tilikum and two female killer whales dragged trainer Keltie Byrne underwater, drowning her in front of spectators at Sealand of the Pacific, a defunct aquarium in Victoria, British Columbia.

b 2. What are the two patterns of organization in the following sentence? *Thousands of interactions have been done with Tilikum over the years with no incidents whatsoever.*

    a. Cause and effect, description

    b. Time order, cause and effect

    c. Description, process

    d. Comparison and contrast, cause and effect

c 3. What are the two main patterns of organization in this passage?

    a. Comparison and contrast, cause and effect

    b. Description, classification

    c. Time order, cause and effect

    d. Time order, description

c 4. How many major supporting details are in this passage?

    a. 1

    b. 2

    c. 3

    d. 4

c 5. What category does the following sentence fall into? *Authorities later concluded that the man, Daniel Dukes, likely suffered hypothermia in the 55-degree water and drowned, but they said it also appeared Tilikum bit the man's body and tore off his swimming trunks after he had died.*

    a. Topic

    b. Main idea

    c. Major detail

    d. Minor detail

Critical Thinking Level 4: Analyze.

When you analyze a reading selection (or anything else), you learn about its parts and how they relate to one another. For example, Lesson 4 asked you to analyze the parts of a word and then decide what they mean when they are combined. In Lesson 7, you learned how to identify the author's tone by analyzing five different factors. Critical thinking level 4 is about breaking a whole into pieces and analyzing the pieces to understand how they work together, and then putting them back together to see what you have learned about the whole.

Throughout the book you have learned to analyze various aspects of reading selections. Here are just some of the things you can examine if you are analyzing a paragraph or longer selection:

- The topic, main idea, and supporting details.
- What the author did to connect one sentence to the next or one paragraph to the next. *(look for singal words)*
- Signal words that indicate relationships between ideas.
- The author's word choices—synonyms, antonyms, and similar patterns.

Put all these pieces together

When you have examined these specifics, ask yourself what the overall effect is. Generalize from the details.

Example of Analyzing: Watch

You can examine a watch; you can explain what each piece is, how it works, and how the pieces fit together. You can take the watch apart, **analyze** how it works, and put it back together.

| INTERACTION 5–4 | Practicing Critical Thinking Level 4: Analyze |

The sentences of a paragraph have been rearranged. Analyze how each sentence fits together with the other sentences. Put the sentences in a logical order to make a paragraph. Indicate the order by numbering the sentences 1–8. Then answer the questions that follow.

PRNewsFoto/Heritage Auctions/Newscom

_____ The buyer and the seller both wish to remain anonymous.

_____ A comic book in which Batman made his debut sold at auction for more than $1 million.

_____ This price set a record for the highest amount ever paid for a comic.

_____ A comic that introduced Superman sold for $1 million just a few days earlier!

_____ What was the exact price for Batman's debut comic, you ask?

_____ The buyer and seller of the Superman comic also wished to remain anonymous.

_____ $1,075,500.

_____ However, this is not the only high-dollar comic sale in 2010.

9. What connection between sentences 1 and 2 led you to put them in that order? _____

_____

10. What connection between sentences 3 and 4 led you to put them in that order? _____

_____

11. Think about how sentences 1 and 2 and sentences 3 and 4 are connected. When you put these specific details together, what generalization can you

make about how some sentences are connected within paragraphs? _____

_____

_____

12–14. Look for three different kinds of connections between sentences 6 and 7 that offered clues to the order. Write down what you find.

- _____

_____

- _____

_____

- _____

_____

15. Find a logical place to divide this paragraph into two parts. Where would you divide it? Summarize the topic of the first part and then summarize the topic of the second part. _____

_____

_____

Critical Thinking Level 5: Evaluate.

When you evaluate a reading selection, you decide what value the information has, or you make choices based on it. Evaluating a selection involves answering questions such as "Does this make sense?" and "Does this author support the main ideas well?" and "What bias does this author have?" **Bias** refers to whether an author is for or against a certain idea, belief, or action. Depending on your evaluation, you may choose to agree with the author or not.

Example of Evaluating: Watch

You are able to **assess** the **value** of a watch—whether it is cheap or expensive. You can analyze what is causing a problem with the watch and decide whether it is **worth** fixing.

| INTERACTION 5–5 | Practicing Critical Thinking Level 5: Evaluate |

A. Read the following excerpt from Gracia Burnham's autobiographical account *In The Presence of My Enemies*. In it she tells of her and her husband Martin's kidnapping by an extremist group in the Philippines. While you read, circle any words that have connotations in their context, and then answer the questions that follow.

1   Just as Martin reached the door, it burst open. Three guys holding M16s charged into the room. All were short, and one was very young—probably in his teens. Another was perhaps twenty-three or twenty-four with long black hair. I could tell the third man was somewhat older.

2   Immediately they swept Martin out the door, while the older man began yelling at me, "Go, go, go!"

3   "No, no, no!" I replied, clutching the sheet around me. "I'm not dressed." I don't know how much English he knew, but I was not about to obey him in my present state regardless. Shaking, I began pulling on my shorts.

4   "Okay, okay," he answered. I continued dressing.

5   "Move, move, move!" came the order again. As I was hurried out the door, I grabbed our thongs, *tsinelas,* the common flip-flops that everyone wears in the Philippines. There wasn't time for me to grab my purse or anything else.

6   The young guy who followed me out wanted me to walk faster, even run. I knew from previous training that in the first few moments of a kidnapping, you're supposed to comply with orders in every way you can, until everybody's adrenaline calms down. But I was just so mad at this kid—I was *not* going to run!

7   "Faster, faster!" he said, jabbing me in the back with the barrel of his weapon.

8   With a calm voice, I replied through clenched teeth, "I'm walking fast enough." I kept my pace. He jabbed me again, and it did hurt, but I was determined to exercise my will.

1. Did you find this reading exciting?   Yes   No

Why or why not? _____

_____

2. Circle the tone word that best describes Burnham's emotions in this sentence: *With a calm voice, I replied through clenched teeth, "I'm walking fast enough."*

        relaxed   arrogant   angry   wry   reticent

3. What word or phrase gives you the clue? _____

4. Do you think Gracia Burnham's decision to exercise her will against the kidnapper was wise? Why or why not? _____

_____

5. How do you think you would respond in a kidnapping situation? _____

_____

B. Read the passage and then answer the questions that follow. While you read, circle any words that indicate the author's attitude or bias toward the topic or issue.

>   Female calves or heifers grow up to be dairy cows, but there is no use for most of the bulls. As a result, the veal industry grew out of the dairy industry as a way to use male calves. In addition to being unfair, the process of creating veal is also mean. Bulls are confined in small crates their whole lives. This is done in order to keep their meat tender. The less movement, the less muscle is developed. Bulls are also fed a diet low in iron. This low quality diet serves no other purpose than to give the veal its pink color that consumers have come to expect. How ridiculous!

6. What is the issue? _____

7. What is the author's bias? _____

8. Circle the word that best describes the author's tone.

             bored   cynical   outraged

9. List the information the author uses to support his thoughts. _____

_____

10. Do you agree with the author's position? Evaluate the supporting details and decide what your opinion is. Then support your opinion, adding details as necessary. _____

_____

Critical Thinking Level 6: Create.

When you create, you use information to draw a conclusion or come up with your own ideas. You might make a prediction or think of a question that the reading did not answer. You may also read several sources about the same topic and combine the ideas, or synthesize them, into a new form or new idea. Level 6 is about the type of work you do when you are writing a paper. Another application of level 6 would be reading information and then using that information to create a plan for improving yourself or some part of your life.

Example of Creating: Watch

You can **design** your own watch based on what you have learned through understanding, applying, analyzing, and evaluating information about watches.

INTERACTION 5–6 **Practicing Critical Thinking Level 6: Create**

Read the passage and then answer the questions that follow.

1   Being a good listener is an important part of good communication. It is vital for having successful relationships. However, it is hard to listen. There are many distractions that interfere with listening. It becomes even harder to listen to someone who is blaming us for something they think we have done wrong. We tend to become defensive and push back rather than listen. (It is hard to admit when you are wrong, and even harder to do so when you think you are right.)

2   It is also hard to listen if someone is stating something we disagree with. We want to interrupt, argue, and jump to conclusions, so we can correct their wrong thoughts with our right ones! For example, if you are pro-abortion and someone is pro-life (or vice versa), you will tend to not even listen to what the other person has to say, but rather become argumentative. If listening is such an important skill, how can you improve your listening skills, even when you disagree with the person you are listening to?

Think about this issue in relation to you and someone you have trouble listening to (parent, boyfriend, girlfriend, sibling, spouse, child, etc.). Ask yourself, "How can I become a better listener with _____?" List some strategies to try.

_____

_____

_____

INTERACTION 5–7   **Using the Six Levels of Critical Thinking**

Read the article and answer the critical thinking questions that follow.

1   Shocked Westerners call it a human zoo, but the residents of China's "Empire of the Little People" have a different name for the place where people pay to watch performing dwarves. They call it home.

2   When entrepreneur Chen Mingjing put out a call last year for China's little people to come live in the park he was building, he quickly got more than 100 applicants, none taller than the cut-off height of 4 feet, 3 inches. "People accuse me of exploiting them," Mingjing told NBC News' Ian Williams in a report that aired Friday on TODAY. "But we've given them a home."

3   The home is literally a theme park that recently opened in Kunming, in the mountains of southern China. Visitors pay $12 a head to watch the residents dress up as fairy-tale characters and perform musical numbers and slapstick comedy. To a Westerner, the spectacle is reminiscent of circus and carnival "freak shows" that were popular a century ago in America. "Yet," Williams reported, "the strongest support for the park comes from the dwarves themselves." "Our life became better," one diminutive resident told Williams. "It's better here?" Williams asked. "Yes. It's a place for us."

4   Williams reported that in China, people who are handicapped have not been mainstreamed into the general population as they have been in the West. "Disabled people, or those who are just different, are often shunned in China," he reported. "People would laugh at us, they looked down at us," a park resident, Bin Bin, told Williams.

5   Dwarf performers in the theme park say their lives there are better than in the outside world, where they are often shunned. But that was in the

outside world. Once Bin Bin and his fellow little people came to the park, they found a new sense of respect. They also found mushroom-shaped houses with furnishings all scaled to their proportions. "Everything in this place is designed for us," resident Xiao bu Dian said. The park has even provided a haven for romance. Two residents, Ling Ou and Xiong Ci Lun, met at the park, fell in love, and have scheduled an April wedding.

Chen Peijin/Chinafotopress/Newscom

6   The residents and featured attractions at the park earn the equivalent of $130 a month along with their room and board. On their day off, they go into Kunming and go shopping, enduring the stares of the curious that they've become inured to. They say that they know the park is using them to make money—but they are also using it to earn money and to improve their lives. Many take English lessons after their workdays are done. None complained of being exploited. Indeed, in a nation of a billion people, there are many like them who would like to join them. "Make of this what you will, it is a spectacle," Williams said. "And right now the park is snowed under with applications from across China from little people who all want to join this empire."

—Mike Celizic, "Dwarves Say Their Theme Park Isn't 'Human Zoo,'" www.msnbc.com, March 19, 2010. Copyright 2010 by MSNBC INTERACTIVE NEWS, LLC. Reproduced with permission of MSNBC INTERACTIVE NEWS, LLC in the format Textbook via Copyright Clearance Center.

CRITICAL THINKING LEVEL 1: REMEMBER

1. What is the topic of this passage? _____

2. Where does this story take place? _____

CRITICAL THINKING LEVEL 2: UNDERSTAND

3. Summarize the two sides presented in this reading regarding the "Empire of the Little People." _____

_____

CRITICAL THINKING LEVEL 3: APPLY

____ 4. Which of the following sentences is the best topic sentence for paragraph 5?

   a. Dwarf performers in the theme park say their lives there are better than in the outside world, where they are often shunned.

   b. But that was in the outside world; things were different in the park.

   c. Once Bin Bin and his fellow little people came to the park, they found a new sense of respect.

   d. Two residents, Ling Ou and Xiong Ci Lun, met at the park, fell in love, and have scheduled an April wedding.

____ 5. What is the pattern of organization of the following sentence? *They say that they know the park is using them to make money—but they are also using it to earn money and to improve their lives.*

   a. Contrast

   b. Cause and effect

   c. Classification

   d. Definition

CRITICAL THINKING LEVEL 4: ANALYZE

6. What evidence does the author present in favor of the "Empire of the Little People"? Write the paragraph number and then the evidence from that paragraph.

   • Paragraph __ : _____

   _____

   • Paragraph __ : _____

   _____

   • Paragraph __ : _____

   _____

   • Paragraph __ : _____

   _____

CRITICAL THINKING LEVEL 5: EVALUATE

____ 7. What is the purpose of this article?
  a. To persuade
  b. To inform
  c. To entertain

____ 8. What is the author's tone toward this topic?
  a. Objectively presents two views of the topic.
  b. Biased toward closing the park down.
  c. Biased against closing the park down.
  d. Sarcastic and not to be taken too seriously.

9. Do you think that the "Empire of the Little People" takes unfair advantage of

the dwarves?   Yes   No

Why or why not? _____

_____

CRITICAL THINKING LEVEL 6: CREATE

10. Write a letter to the editor about this article. Express your position for or
against the "Empire of the Little People." Make sure you support your
thoughts with specific reasons. Find a classmate who disagrees with you.
Debate (respectfully) with your classmate.

Review: Critical Thinking Is a Learning Process.

The six levels of critical thinking each play an important role in your learning process.

- Remember—you can recall and repeat basic information.
- Understand—you can explain information to someone else.
- Apply—you can use the information in a new situation.
- Analyze—you understand how all the pieces work together.
- Evaluate—you can judge or assess the value of information.
- Create—you can produce something new.

Understanding and applying Bloom's Taxonomy will help you take control of your learning
in and out of school.

Recognize Critical Thinking Verbs on Tests.

Understanding the six levels of critical thinking will help you improve your test-taking ability. When an instructor creates questions for a test, he or she may use verbs that refer specifically to different critical thinking levels. You can recognize which critical thinking level is being called for by paying attention to the verbs in the question. This will allow you to be more precise about how you answer the question.

The key verbs listed for each level indicate that the instructor is asking for that level of thinking. Sample test questions then show you how questions at that level might be stated.

Critical Thinking Level 1: Remember

Key Verbs

identify, list, reproduce, define, locate

Sample Test Questions

Who or *what* is the reading about?
Identify the topic of this passage.
What is the main subject of the reading?
Define the four italicized key terms.
List the order of events in this story.

Critical Thinking Level 2: Understand

Key Verbs

summarize, map, discuss, paraphrase, restate

Sample Test Questions

Which of the following best *restates* the main idea of the passage?
Which of the following statements best *summarizes* this reading?
Map the town based on the author's description.
Discuss the four key details that contributed to World War I.
Which of the following best *paraphrases* the issue of this reading?

Critical Thinking Level 3: Apply

Key Verbs
diagram, demonstrate, solve, illustrate, organize

Sample Test Questions

Solve the following problem.

The author's example in paragraph 1 *demonstrates* which of the following?

Organize the following ideas from most general to least general.

Diagram the author's experiment as described in paragraph 7.

Which of the following best *illustrates* the author's claim?

Critical Thinking Level 4: Analyze

Key Verbs
compare (which can also mean contrast on tests), examine, explain, investigate, imply

Sample Test Questions

Compare the protagonist and antagonist.

Which of the following does the author *imply*?

Explain how the following detail supports the author's main point.

Examine the following statements and decide which one is the fact.

Investigate and *explain* figure 2.3 in paragraph 5.

Critical Thinking Level 5: Evaluate

Key Verbs
assess, rank, critique, justify, judge

Sample Test Questions

Does the author do a *good job* of supporting her argument? Explain your thoughts.

Assess the author bias found in paragraph 1.

Rank the author's support of the claim from strongest to weakest.

If you were to *judge* the situation found in this reading, who would you find guilty?

Critique the author's plan. Do you think it will work? Why or why not?

Critical Thinking Level 6: Create

> ### Key Verbs
> *develop, design, adapt, imagine, plan*

Sample Test Questions

The author criticizes the current model. Can you *create* a new *design*?

Based on the information from this Web site, *plan* the perfect getaway.

Develop an alternate theory for why fashion changes.

Imagine that you were in the situation described in this story. What would you do?

Adapt the following short story so that it has a happy ending.

INTERACTION 5–8   **Determining Critical Thinking Levels**

Read the passage and then answer the questions that follow.

1   Test anxiety, an unpleasant emotional response to being evaluated in a classroom, is a common experience. It is often accompanied by physical manifestations characteristic of fear, such as rapid, shallow breathing. Is it any surprise that severe test anxiety can undermine your performance on tests? A certain amount of anxiety can help performance, but too much usually impairs it.

2   Recently, Guida and Ludlow (1989) conducted a cross-cultural study of test anxiety in U.S. and Chilean seventh- and eighth-grade students.

> When they compared test-anxiety scores along culture, gender, and socio-economic lines, they found significant differences on all dimensions. U.S. students had lower test anxiety than Chileans; boys had lower than girls; and higher-socioeconomic students had lower than lower-socioeconomic students.
>
> —Price & Crapo, *Cross-Cultural Perspectives in Introductory Psychology*, 4th edition

From the list below, choose the critical thinking level that each question calls for. Underline the words in the sentences that give you the clue.

a. Level 1: Remember
b. Level 2: Understand
c. Level 3: Apply
d. Level 4: Analyze
e. Level 5: Evaluate
f. Level 6: Create

____ 1. Which of the following does the author imply about test anxiety?

____ 2. Imagine you are from a very poor family. What factors do you think would cause you to have increased anxiety?

____ 3. What is the topic of the passage?

____ 4. Which of the following best illustrates the author's claim that boys have less test anxiety than girls?

____ 5. Which of the following answers do you think best explains why there are test-anxiety differences between the U.S. and Chilean students?

____ 6. Summarize the main idea of this passage.

____ 7. Define test anxiety.

____ 8. Which of the following does the author imply with this statement? *Is it any surprise that severe test anxiety can undermine your performance on tests?*

____ 9. Which of the following patterns of organization is illustrated in this reading?

____ 10. Which of the following best restates the author's findings?

> **Review:** Recognizing Critical Thinking Verbs on Tests
>
> Being skilled in recognizing key critical thinking verbs can help you:
>
> - Recognize the level of thinking for which the instructor is asking.
> - Answer the question with that level of thinking.

ACTIVATE YOUR SKILLS 1
Thinking Critically About Reading

A. Read the passage and answer the critical thinking questions that follow.

Ten Steps to Buying a New Car

1. Here is an overview of the new-car buying process.

2. **How Much of a Car Payment Can You Afford?** Begin by deciding how much you have to spend on a new vehicle. Your monthly car payment should be no more than 20 percent of your monthly net income. Many car or dealer websites have calculators that can help you figure this amount out.

3. **Will You Get a Car Loan?** Decide whether to pay cash, finance, or lease your new vehicle. Each method offers different advantages for different budgets and lifestyles. Again you can go online and play with down payment, trade-in, or interest amounts to find the right method for your budget.

4. **What Is the Right Car for You?** What are your needs in regard to size, performance, safety, and styling? Research cars that meet your needs—and are in your price range—by using multiple sources, including the Internet, which is a great resource for comparing or contrasting car models. Choose at least three "target cars" to consider buying.

5. **Setting Your Price.** Find the market value price for your target cars. Add the cost of options and subtract rebates and incentives. The resulting price should be a win-win for you and for the dealer.

6. **How to Test-Drive a Car.** Make an appointment (which can be done by phone or online) to test-drive the cars you are interested in. This is a chance to evaluate the salesperson too. Drive—then leave!

7. **Should You Trade in Your Used Car?** A dealer will rarely pay what your trade-in is worth. Still, some shoppers like the ease of a single transaction. Here's how to do it. Check the value

of your car at kbb.com or Edmunds.com and get offers from at least three dealers. If you get one you like, the others might be more willing to match it.

8   **Beginning Negotiations.** Be prepared to visit more than one dealer. Make your opening offer several hundred dollars below the market value.

9   **Closing the Deal.** Don't let yourself be trapped by verbal games some salesmen play. Raise your offer to market value but not above. If negotiations stall, go to another dealer. Play the dealers against each other until you get your price.

10   **In the Finance and Insurance Room.** You will move to the Finance and Insurance (F&I) room to sign contracts. Review the contract carefully and avoid high priced extras like rust-proofing and road safety kits. Check your new vehicle for scratches and dents before taking delivery of it.

11   **Alternative Buying Strategies.** Consider using Internet buying services or faxing your offer to local dealerships for competitive bids. This can save you money and avoid the hassle of going from dealer to dealer.

—Adapted from "10 Steps to Buying a New Car," SpendOnLife.com

CRITICAL THINKING LEVEL 1: REMEMBER

1. What is this reading about? _____

2. How many dealers should you consider? _____

3. Which Web site(s) should you check to find the value of your trade-in? _____

    _____

4. What should you do after you test-drive? _____

CRITICAL THINKING LEVEL 2: UNDERSTAND

5. Create a thesis statement for this reading: _____

    _____

6. How has the Internet changed the car-buying process? _____

    _____

    _____

CRITICAL THINKING LEVEL 3: APPLY

7. What does *stall* mean under "Closing the Deal"? _____

____ 8. Which of the following is the best main idea of this reading?

    a. Buying a car is tricky.

    b. If you do not follow the steps mentioned here, you will probably get ripped off.

    c. Buying a new car is a multi-step process.

    d. Always do your homework to get the best deal on the car you want to buy.

9. How many major details are there in this reading? _____

10. What is the main pattern of organization for this reading? _____

CRITICAL THINKING LEVEL 4: ANALYZE

____ 11. What is the purpose of this reading?

    a. To inform

    b. To persuade

    c. To entertain

12. In the following sentence, are *rust-proofing* and *road safety kits* used connotatively or denotatively? *Review the contract carefully and avoid high priced extras like rust-proofing and road safety kits.* _____

____ 13. Which of the following would the author agree with?

    a. It is a better idea to buy than to lease.

    b. Buying a new car can be a scary process.

    c. Knowing your budget can help you find the right car for you.

    d. New cars often have dents.

CRITICAL THINKING LEVEL 5: EVALUATE

14. Rate the importance of each of the following in determining the kind of car you would purchase. Use 1 for most important and 6 for least important.

_____ Affordability

_____ Operating costs

_____ Hybrid, gas, diesel

_____ New or used

_____ Design

_____ Reliability

CRITICAL THINKING LEVEL 6: CREATE

15. Pretend you are in the market for a new car. Answer the following questions and come up with three cars that would fit your budget, needs, and style. Be sure to take into consideration how you rated the items in question 14.

How much of a car payment can you afford? _____

_____

Will you finance your car or pay cash? _____

_____

Which of the three cars that you originally chose is right for you? _____

_____

B. From the list below, choose the critical thinking level that each question calls for. Underline the words in the sentences that give you the clue.

a. Level 1: Remember

b. Level 2: Understand

c. Level 3: Apply

d. Level 4: Analyze

e. Level 5: Evaluate

f. Level 6: Create

_____ 16. Who or what is this passage about?

_____ 17. How does Figure 3.1 relate to the main idea of this passage?

_____ 18. Come up with an alternative theory for the change in fashion trends.

_____ 19. Which of the following details is not listed in the passage as a reason for World War I?

_____ 20. Which of the following would the author agree with?

ACTIVATE YOUR SKILLS 2
Critical Thinking Applied to Real Life

Read the scenario and answer the questions that follow.

1   Here is your scenario: You need to buy a new laptop computer for your college classes. The one you really want to buy will cost $1,500 after tax, software, and a student discount. You do not have the cash to buy it now, but you do have an extra $150 a month in your budget if you tighten your belt a bit. However, you just received a credit card application in the mail. Should you wait to buy the computer once you have the cash, or should you use the card? Here are a few of the credit card offer details you will need to answer the critical thinking questions that follow.

2   The Annual Percentage Rate (APR) for your purchase will be 0.0% for the first year; then the standard APR will be a rate of 19.99% variable. Finance charges are deferred for the first 365 days (the promotional period) for the purchase of a single qualifying product $900 and above (inclusive of tax and shipping) that posts to your new account in the first 30 days of account opening, provided you make timely payment of at least the minimum due each month and the initial qualifying purchase balance(s) is/are paid in full on or before the 365th day.* If the balance(s) is/are not paid in full at the end of the promotional period, you will be charged interest from the date of the purchase(s) at the disclosed standard APR for purchases.

3   The standard purchase APR may vary monthly and equals the Prime Rate plus an amount between 8.74% and 16.74%. The default APR may vary monthly and equals the Prime Rate + up to 27.99%, but such rate will never exceed 29.99%; effective January 1, 2010, the default APR for purchases may vary monthly and equals the Prime Rate + an amount between up to 13.74% and up to 21.74%.†

—Based on Discover Card online application and Barclaycard
Financing Visa Terms and Conditions.

* If you are late making a payment, any introductory/promotional rates will end and we may increase all your APRs to a Default Rate of 29.99%.

† The Prime Rate used is the highest prime rate listed in *The Wall Street Journal* on the last business day of the month.

CRITICAL THINKING LEVEL 1: REMEMBER

1. How long does the 0% interest period last? _____
_____

2. What rate will your APR go to after the 0 percent interest has ended? _____

_____

3. What is the default APR? _____

4. To qualify for this offer, how much do you need to spend within the first month?

_____

CRITICAL THINKING LEVEL 2: UNDERSTAND

5. Explain what will happen if you do not pay off the balance within the one-year
   time period. _____

   _____

6. Explain how the Prime Rate is calculated. _____

   _____

CRITICAL THINKING LEVEL 3: APPLY

7. If you do not pay off the entire amount in one year, approximately how much
   interest will you accrue? _____

CRITICAL THINKING LEVEL 4: ANALYZE

8. Compare and contrast saving and paying cash or buying and charging the computer now.

Save	Buy now

9. Based on your analysis, weigh which direction you would go: save or buy now. Support your answer with your reasoning. _____

_____

10. Based on your decision to save or buy now, do one of the following:
    a. Create a reasonable payment plan that will avoid paying any interest.
    b. Create an amount you would need to save per month if you plan to pay cash. How many months would you need to save? (Make sure the monthly amount is reasonable based on your budget.)

_____

_____

_____

MASTER YOUR SKILLS 1
Applying Critical Thinking to Reading and Test Questions

A. Read the passage and answer the questions that follow.

The Olympics

1   The Olympic Games formally began in 776 B.C.E. (the earliest date that can be verified in ancient Greek history) at the temple to Zeus in Olympia, in the western Peloponnesus. In 720 B.C.E., one competitor started the race wearing some kind of garment but shed it by the end of the race; after his victory, no competitor ever wore clothes again.

2   At first competitors participated in only a 656-foot-long (200-m) footrace, but the number of events increased quickly. By the year 600 B.C.E., they included the 1,323-foot-long (400-m) footrace, the pentathlon of five different events in one, wrestling, boxing, and chariot races. At their height the games ran for five full days and included the first day, set aside for prayers and oath-taking, and a final day of competition and of feasting and crowning of the winners. Tens of thousands of people who did not participate traveled from all over the Mediterranean to see the races and to enjoy the feasting and drinking.

Hulton Archive/Getty Images

3   Only the victor of each event received a prize, always a single wreath of leaves. Although the award of a wreath makes the Olympics seem an amateur event, most winners also received tangible rewards from their home city-states. Athletes sometimes competed for city-states where they had not been born simply to attain the higher rewards they offered. Winners from Athens were particularly fortunate: the city-state awarded them the equivalent of two years' income, a permanent tax break, and free meals for life.

4   Cheating did occur, even though it was considered an insult to the gods and was punished severely by fines or beatings. Athletes lied about their age so they could compete in the boys' events, which were less competitive. Wrestlers rubbed oil on their bodies so that their opponents could not get a grip on them.

5   The Olympic Games occurred every four years until 393 C.E., when the Roman emperor forbade the worship of pagan gods. Inspired by the success of hundreds of festivals bearing the name *Olympics,* in 1896 a French aristocrat revived the games in Athens with the explicit intention of giving amateur athletes from all over the world a chance to compete. This inclusiveness, though, is new: the ancient games were for Greeks only.

—Hansen & Curtis, *Voyages in World History*

CRITICAL THINKING LEVEL 1: REMEMBER

1. When did the ancient Olympic Games begin? _____

2. When did the ancient Olympic Games end? _____

3. Why did the Olympic Games end? _____

_____

4. Who was allowed to compete in the original Olympic Games? _____

5. What events were part of the Olympic Games? _____

_____

6. Who revived the games to create the modern Olympics? _____

7. Where did the first modern Olympic Games take place? _____

CRITICAL THINKING LEVEL 2: UNDERSTAND

8. Explain why competitors in the original Olympic Games probably wore no clothes when competing. _____

_____

CRITICAL THINKING LEVEL 3: APPLY

____ 9. What does *inclusiveness* mean (paragraph 5)?

    a. Games

    b. Amateur athlete

    c. Including all

    d. Greek

____ 10. What is the primary pattern of organization used in this passage?

    a. Compare and contrast

    b. Time order

    c. Cause and effect

    d. Classification

CRITICAL THINKING LEVEL 4: ANALYZE

____ 11. What is the overall purpose of this passage?

    a. To persuade

    b. To inform

    c. To entertain

____ 12. What is the tone of this sentence from paragraph 2? *At their height the games ran for five full days and included the first day, set aside for prayers and oath-taking, and a final day of competition and of feasting and crowning of the winners.*

    a. Factual

    b. Sarcastic

    c. Irreverent

    d. Nostalgic

CRITICAL THINKING LEVEL 5: EVALUATE

13. If an ancient Greek were transported to a modern Olympic Games, what do you think his or her reaction might be? Support your thoughts with some details from the reading. _____

_____

_____

_____

14. List the values that you think the Olympics promote in the world. _____

_____

_____

_____

CRITICAL THINKING LEVEL 6: CREATE

15. The passage explained that ancient winners only received a wreath of leaves, although certain city-states, like Athens, gave greater rewards. Today, athletes get a gold, silver, or bronze medal, as well as high-dollar sponsorships. Imagine you are part of the Olympic Committee. The Olympic Committee is restructuring the awards for the next Olympics games. You and a few other committee members are given the task to come up with a new way to reward the winners. Create your plan and state the awards you would give out. _____

_____

_____

_____

B. From the list below, choose the critical thinking level that each question calls for. Underline the words in the sentences that give you the clue.

    a.   Level 1: Remember

    b.   Level 2: Understand

    c.   Level 3: Apply

    d.   Level 4: Analyze

    e.   Level 5: Evaluate

    f.   Level 6: Create

_____ 16. Which of the following is least relevant to the main idea?

_____ 17. According to the passage, which of the following events happened first?

_____ 18. Which of the following answers best summarizes this passage?

_____ 19. Based on the information given in the passage, which of the following ideas would the author agree with?

_____ 20. The writer's main purpose in writing this selection is to _____.

MASTER YOUR SKILLS 2
A Critical Thinking Project

Read the passage and answer the questions that follow. This project is best done by writing your answers on a separate sheet.

Develop Your Career Potential

1   What do you want to be when you grow up? Still not sure? Ask around. You're not alone. Chances are, some of your friends and relatives aren't certain either. Sure, they may have jobs and careers, but you're likely to find that, professionally, many of them don't want to be where they are today. Sometimes, people's interests change, or they may experience burnout or boredom. And some people are unhappy with their current jobs or careers because they were never in the right one to begin with.

2   Getting the career you want is not easy. It takes time, effort, and persistence. And even though you will probably follow multiple career paths in your life, your career-planning process will be easier (and more effective) if you take the time to develop a personal career plan.

CRITICAL THINKING LEVEL 1: REMEMBER

1. What job do you currently have?

2. How do you feel about your current job?

3. Write down a list of jobs or career fields you are (or might be) interested in.

CRITICAL THINKING LEVEL 2: UNDERSTAND

4. Ask at least three different people (your parents, relatives, friends, and/or employer) what they think about your strengths and weaknesses. Encourage them to be honest. Have them explain what they feel you would be good at and what you need to improve to get there.

5. Compile a summary of what you found out from the three people you chose.

CRITICAL THINKING LEVEL 3: APPLY

6. Based on the information you have gathered (the good and the not so good), find some ads for a job you might want to have when you graduate. Use employment ads from a Sunday paper or a job Web site like Monster.com as inspiration. Look at the specifics—the company, title, responsibilities, required education and experience, salary, and benefits.

CRITICAL THINKING LEVEL 4: ANALYZE

Take a moment to think about where you are now.

7. Describe your strengths. (What do you do well?)

8. Describe your weaknesses. (What can you improve upon?)

9. What do you need to do in the short term to be qualified for this job?

10. What major would you need to have for this job?

11. What classes do you need to take?

12. Do your strengths lie in this area?

13. What experience would you need to get to better prepare you for this job?

CRITICAL THINKING LEVEL 5: EVALUATE

14. Do you feel it would be worth pursuing the job you have looked at? Why or why not? Explain your reasoning.

15. Rank your top three reasons.

CRITICAL THINKING LEVEL 6: CREATE

16. Create a detailed plan for the next year. What can you accomplish in the next year in order to get closer to your goal?

17. What will you do first?

18. List two people who can serve as mentors or accountability partners for you in this process.

19. Decide how and when you will monitor the progress you are making. Career experts suggest evaluating your progress every six months. Set the date now, and come up with at least three specific and challenging goals you will accomplish in the first six months.

20. Create a reward system for yourself to help motivate you to accomplish your goals.

—Adapted from Williams, *Management*, 4th edition

Analyze Facts, Opinions, and Inferences.

Being able to identify and understand the difference between fact and opinion is an important part of comprehension. If you can clarify what is factual, what is an opinion, and the details that support or refute them, you will be better able to analyze the author's tone and purpose. In addition, you can keep your reactions to a reading separate from the author's tone or from the facts of the reading itself. The basics of fact and opinion as well as the issues that complicate them will be discussed in the first part of this lesson. The second part of the lesson is about inference, which is a process of adding up all the facts and drawing conclusions from them.

Facts Can Be Verified.

Verified means that something can be proven to be accurate, true, and correct. The ability to be verified is at the core of all facts. You can confirm facts by reading different sources on that topic, such as newspapers and magazines that check facts carefully, encyclopedias, nonfiction books, and textbooks. Facts can be verified by science, statistics, or specifics.

The tone word that goes with facts is *objective*. As you learned in Lesson 7, **objective** means "just the facts," not influenced by personal feelings or opinion. You are likely reading facts when the author provides a lot of details such as people's names, place names, events, specific dates and times, numbers, and other items that are observable and provable. Here is an example:

Escada's couture line includes a pair of jeans covered in designs made with Swarovski crystals, which the design house sold for $10,000.

The previous sentence is a fact. It can be verified by checking reliable sources, such as *Forbes* magazine, from which this information was taken, or maybe Escada's Web site. The sources used to verify a particular fact will vary. For instance, if you wanted to verify that the African country of Somalia is east of Ethiopia, you would use a globe, map, or encyclopedia.

INTERACTION 5–9	Finding Factual Sentences

Mark the sentences that are facts with an F. If you think a sentence is a fact, ask yourself, "How can the information be verified?"

_____ 1. More than 1,800 people died in Hurricane Katrina.

_____ 2. Agriculture arose on plateaus in the Americas and Mexico, unlike in Mesopotamia, Egypt, or China, where it arose in river valleys.

_____ 3. The ancient inscription was rather unremarkable.

_____ 4. Channing Tatum is one of Hollywood's hottest young stars.

_____ 5. People with nightmare disorder typically experience terrible dreams on a nightly basis and are often jarred awake.

_____ 6. There are five things that research has shown improves happiness: being grateful, being optimistic, counting your blessings, using your strengths, and being kind to others.

_____ 7. Kona coffee is one of the most balanced coffees of the world, with a smooth, medium body and crisp finish.

_____ 8. More than 1 million users include "John" in their profile name, making it the most popular name on Facebook.

_____ 9. Jim Carrey became a grandfather in 2010 at age 48.

_____ 10. Wearing lashes by UR Elegant Eyes brings out your inner Diva.

INTERACTION 5–10	Finding Facts in a Paragraph

Read the paragraph and answer the questions that follow.

> [1]United's Flight 634 was well into its final descent toward Newark Liberty International Airport on Sunday morning January 10, 2010, when it began a sudden climb. [2]There was a problem. [3]Only two of the three landing wheels had opened successfully. [4]After repeated attempts to fix the problem had failed, those aboard were instructed to prepare for a crash landing.
>
> —Adapted from Sulzberger & Schweber, "Jet Makes Emergency Landing at Newark Airport," www.nytimes.com, January 10, 2010

1. Is sentence 1 a fact?   Yes   No

2. Is sentence 2 a fact?   Yes   No

3. Is sentence 3 a fact?   Yes   No

4. Is sentence 4 a fact?   Yes   No

5. Can you prove this story is a fact?   Yes   No

6. If so, how? If not, why not? _____

_____

_____

Review: Identifying Facts

To decide if a sentence is factual, always ask, "Can this information be verified?"

- Facts are verifiable. They can be proven to be true and accurate.
- Facts are objective. They are independent of personal beliefs or feelings.
- Facts are observable. They can be seen or noted.

Opinions Cannot Be Verified.

Unlike facts, opinions cannot be verified. An opinion is a personal view or judgment about something. Opinions change from person to person and from one point in time to another. For example, you may hate onions, but your friend Cedric loves them. However, when Cedric was a kid he did not like onions. As he grew up, his taste buds changed, and as an adult he loves them. Taste is one kind of opinion. Opinions are **subjective.** They are based on personal feelings, tastes, imaginings, predictions, and judgments, and they may change over time.

Remember the crystal-studded Escada jeans that cost $10,000? The price tag was a fact. However, your reaction to paying $10,000 for a pair of jeans would be an opinion. Take a class poll:

- How many of you think that $10,000 is a ridiculous amount to pay for a pair of jeans?

- How many of you think it would be fine to pay $10,000 if you could afford it?

Each answer is an opinion, even if several of you have the same opinion.

| INTERACTION 5–11 | Finding Opinions in Sentences |

Mark the sentences that are opinions with an O. Circle the words you think make the sentence an opinion. If you think a sentence is a fact, ask yourself, "How can the information be verified?"

clue given

O 1. Lil Wayne's song lyrics are degrading to women.

Opinion 2. The Winter Olympics offered some fierce competition, especially in women's figure skating.

O 3. The BlackBerry is better than the iPhone for business.

F 4. In a speech, *volume* means the loudness of a speaker's voice.

O 5. Never trust a person who does not have at least one bad habit.

F 6. Daylight saving time allows people to use less energy by taking advantage of the longer daylight hours during spring and summer.

F 7. Las Vegas casinos do not have clocks in them.

F 8. Tablecloths were originally used as napkins where diners could wipe their face and hands.

F 9. According to the *Guinness Book of World Records*, the oldest goldfish in captivity was at least 43 years old.

 10. The HBO show *True Blood* is a <u>more believable</u> view of vampires than what you see in the *Twilight* movies.

INTERACTION 5–12 | **Finding Opinions in a Paragraph**

Read the paragraph and answer the questions that follow. Circle any opinions you find as you read.

> [1]My grandfather was an amazing man. [2]He was honorable, and always did what was right. [3]He taught me many things about life. [4]I try to remember each lesson when I visit his gravesite. [5]I really miss him.

1. Is sentence 1 an opinion?   Yes   No

2. Is sentence 2 an opinion?   Yes   No

3. Is sentence 3 an opinion?   Yes   No

4. Is sentence 4 an opinion?   Yes   No

5. Is sentence 5 an opinion?   Yes   No

Review: Identifying Opinions

- Opinions are personal. An opinion can be a viewpoint, judgment, or belief.
- Opinions are subjective. They depend on personal beliefs or feelings.
- Opinions can change. They can change over time, from person to person, and from culture to culture.

Facts and Opinions Often Appear Together.

Fact seems simple enough to understand; it is something you can prove is true. An opinion is based on someone's feelings or beliefs. What's so complicated about that? One issue that complicates fact and opinion is that they are often mixed together. Here's an example:

Clint Eastwood, who won best director at the Oscars for the films *Million Dollar Baby* and *Unforgiven,* is also a fantastic actor.

While it is true that Clint Eastwood has directed two Oscar-winning films, to say that he is a fantastic actor is an opinion.

In addition, facts can be misleading. For example:

In 2006 ExxonMobil had fewer oil spills than in 2005.

This information is factual. What Exxon neglected to say was that even though it had <u>fewer</u> spills, the <u>amount</u> of oil spilled in 2006 was more than three times greater than the amount spilled in 2005 (40,000 barrels vs. 12,200 barrels). This information can be found in the ExxonMobil *2006 Corporate Citizenship Report,* p. 7.

Moreover, opinions can be hidden in unexpected places sometimes. For example, here is a headline from the *New York Times:*

Sweeping Health Care Plan Passes House

It is a fact that a health care plan passed a House vote, but what does "sweeping" mean? Is this fact or opinion? The word "sweeping" suggests that the plan will cover and fix many issues. This might seem like a fact, but "sweeping" is an opinion. If the health care plan leaves out an issue you find very important, then you would not agree that it is "sweeping."

INTERACTION 5–13   Is It Fact or Opinion?

A. In each item, underline the sentence that is fact. Circle the opinion word(s) in the sentence you do not underline.

1. John Fitzgerald Kennedy was assassinated on November 22, 1963. To this day, JFK remains an extremely popular figure in history.

2. The *Mona Lisa* hangs in the Louvre in Paris, France. It is possibly the most beautiful painting in the world.

3. The beauty of sunsets and sunrises is amazing. Although, you know, the sun does not actually "rise" or "set;" rather, the earth rotates.

4. Reading is a required skill in many jobs. In fact, it is the most important skill for success.

5. Salespersons should avoid the use of slang in their speech. Guidelines for proper speech use can be found in the new employee handbook.

B. In each item, underline the part of the sentence that includes a fact. Circle the opinion word(s) that make the other part an opinion.

6. On average, a drunk driver in the United States kills a person every 40 minutes, making this one of the most serious social issues we face.

7. *Avatar* became the second-highest-grossing film worldwide in just four weeks, which is hard to believe.

8. A few cultures do not practice kissing, so kissing must be a learned behavior.

9. Monopoly, which first became available during the Great Depression, was probably popular because people could pretend they were wealthy.

10. Although dating experts hotly debate the precise timeframe, a standard time period in which to return a call after first meeting a person is two to four days.

A Fact Is a Fact, But an Opinion Needs to Be Supported by Proof.

Once proven, a fact remains a fact, except in cases in which scientific advances uncover new information. An opinion, though, needs to be supported by proof to be credible—that is, to be believable by others. The stronger the proof, the more likely others will agree with the opinion.

How do you get support for an opinion? Just because you believe aliens have visited Earth doesn't mean anyone else does. "Where is your proof?" your friends will ask. "Do you have an 'un-Photoshopped' picture of an alien at the mall? Is it possible there is another explanation for what you saw?" While the alien example might be a bit of a stretch, there are ways to lend credibility to opinions.

Credibility comes from strong proof. Strong proof does not make an opinion a fact, but it does make it easier to consider. The strength of proof is usually determined by the source. There are two types of sources that can lend credibility to an opinion:

- An expert
- Direct experience

Expert Opinions

An **expert** is a person who has extensive knowledge, education, or experience about a topic. He or she probably works or has worked in the field, and may have written a book about the topic. For example, a doctor is an expert on medical care. Your doctor has an opinion about what is wrong with you, but his or her experience and education provides support for that opinion and makes it credible. That does not mean doctors do not make mistakes. They do. That is why you get second opinions on more serious health issues.

In addition, a doctor is an expert in the field of medicine, but that doesn't automatically make him or her an expert in other fields. If you want your car repaired, you don't go to a doctor. An expert is an expert in his or her field only, not in all things.

Direct Experience

Direct experience refers to a person's firsthand exposure to something. For example, if a friend has been to Maui for vacation, he has direct experience of the island. His vacation does not make him an expert on Maui unless he has written a travel book, been there twenty times, or produced a TV show for the Travel Channel. However, his personal experience, stories, and tips about vacationing there do have a certain degree of credibility, especially if he is trustworthy.

A word of caution: At times, people try to pass off **secondhand information** such as gossip as credible evidence. An example is when someone starts by saying, "Well, I heard . . ." or "My friend said. . . ." In order for an opinion to be strongly supported, the proof or evidence needs to be reliable, direct, and credible (believable).

| INTERACTION 5–14 | Expert Opinion or Direct Experience |

For the following situations, decide if the source is expert opinion or direct experience. Write Expert or Direct. If it is secondhand information, then write NO!

_____ 1. A doctor sharing his opinion about the current state of the U.S. economy.

_____ 2. Your neighbor, who is a mechanic, giving you car advice.

_____ 3. A grandmother giving advice to a new mother.

_____ 4. A movie director critiquing a film.

_____ 5. A soldier talking about his war experience.

_____ 6. An accountant giving tax advice.

_____ 7. Information about Beijing from an Olympic athlete who participated in the 2008 Summer Olympics.

_____ 8. A senior in college giving academic advice to a freshman.

_____ 9. President Obama on the prospects of his favorite football team, the Chicago Bears.

_____ 10. A person you meet on the bus giving you a stock tip.

Review: Supporting Opinions

For an opinion to have credibility, it should be supported in one of the following ways:

- An expert's opinion, gained through education and/or skill.
- Direct experience, gained through personal exposure.

Certain Kinds of Words Indicate Opinions.

One way to identify a fact is to ask yourself, "Is this information verifiable?" Visualizing how you would verify it can help you answer that question. Can you see it, duplicate the results, or check a reliable source? If the information is not verifiable, then it is probably an opinion. Often when you decide something is an opinion, it is because it contains one of the following:

- A value word

- An all-or-nothing word

The first category is "value words." These words mainly consist of adjectives that place a value on something. Here are some examples:

best beautiful awful ugly cool great fantastic good bad awesome attractive hard easy interesting boring immature

- The book was **great.**

- That movie is **awesome.**

- His sister is **beautiful.**

- This game is **boring.**

- This test was **easy.**

As you can see in each of these sentences, not everyone would agree. The value word makes these statements individual opinions rather than verifiable facts.

The second category is "all-or-nothing words." These words do not automatically express opinions, but you should always be suspicious when you see them and visualize whether they are verifiable facts or just opinions. Here are some examples:

always all any every none never must have to will

- You are **always** late.

- I **never** win.

- **Everybody** is going!

- You **must** listen to me.

- I **will** be there.

As you can see, each of these sentences allows no room for chance. These words are absolute, meaning there is no middle ground. Words like *should, sometimes, usually, often, might,* and *frequently* are more reasonable. However, absolute words do not *always* mean that the sentence will be an opinion. For example, take these sentences:

- Molly is **always** on time.

- The sun **always** rises in the east.

Both sentences use *always,* but in the first one, there is a probability that Molly will be late once, even if she is usually on time. The second sentence is a scientific certainty: the sun does *always* rise in the east and set in the west. So again, determining whether something is a fact or an opinion usually comes down to this one thing: Can the information be verified?

INTERACTION 5–15	Finding Opinion Words

Circle any word that indicates an opinion. If the whole sentence is factual, circle F. If it is an opinion, circle O. Discuss your answers with a classmate and then with your instructor when you are done.

1. Macs are cooler than PCs.   F   (O)

2. David Beckham is married to Victoria Adams, a former Spice Girl.   (F)   O

3. Classical music is soothing.   F   (O)

4. Laughter is the best medicine.   F   (O)

5. The number of people in prisons has outgrown current facilities in recent years, causing overcrowding and increased public spending to build new prisons.

                                                                                      (F)   O

6. The Black Eyed Peas' song "Boom Boom Pow" was the most frequently downloaded song on iTunes in 2009.   (F)   O

7. Everyone needs at least eight hours of sleep per night for the body to function.

                                                                                      F   (O)

8. During his lifetime, Pablo Picasso had financial troubles and in the winter would burn his paintings to stay warm. **(F)** O

9. Americans must support the troops during times of war. F **(O)**

10. The "27 club" is a pop culture name for a group of famous musicians who all died at the age of 27. This club includes Jim Morrison of the Doors, Jimi Hendrix, and Kurt Cobain. **(F)** O

11. The government's involvement with attempting to socialize medicine angers all Americans. F **(O)**

12. Texting is <u>frustrating</u> when you don't know what <u>all</u> the abbreviations mean, like ALOTBSOL = Always Look On The Bright Side Of Life. F **(O)**

13. A film with the name *Hot Tub Time Machine* cannot be worth seeing. F **(O)**

14. A great time-saving tip for grocery shopping is to make a list before you go. F **(O)**

15. Kettle corn is tastier than regular popcorn. F **(O)**

16. South America has made many contributions to the pharmacopoeia (the storehouse of medicines) that help fight human disease. **(F)** O

17. Political stability has helped Botswana make the most of its economic resources, like diamonds. **F** O

18. The drug company Pfizer considers AIDS to be a serious health issue today. **F** **(O)**

19. Africa is a large continent. **(F)** O

20. *Condemned: Criminal Origins* is one of the most violent video games available. F **(O)**

INTERACTION 5–16 | All-or-Nothing Words: Fact or Opinion?

A. Circle the all-or-nothing word in each sentence.

B. Determine if the sentence is fact or opinion.

C. If the sentence is a fact, write F in the blank, and if it is an opinion, write O.

_____ 1. The applicants all want to get the job.

_____ 2. You should never mix chocolate and peanut butter together.

_____ 3. Bruce Willis's movies are always entertaining.

_____ 4. Camouflage is the must-have pattern of the season.

_____ 5. At the end of the movie everybody dies.

_____ 6. All people progress through the grieving process at the same rate.

_____ 7. You should never use an electrical appliance while in a bathtub.

_____ 8. When you are driving, your seat belt should always be on.

_____ 9. In order to take advantage of this special offer, you must call within the next twenty-four hours.

_____ 10. Everyone loves a baby.

INTERACTION 5–17   **Using Opinion Words to Indicate Opinion**

In each sentence, look for words that indicate an opinion. Circle any you find. Then indicate whether the sentence is a fact (F) or an opinion (O).

1. The supreme affluence of the United States means that all U.S. consumers have equal access to goods produced around the world.   F   O

2. A child's toy can represent this global system.   F   O

3. For young girls in the United States, Barbie™ is the ideal of fashion and romance.   F   O

4. Most young American girls have several beautiful Barbie dolls.   F   O

5. Each of the dolls comes with a specific role and costume.   F   O

6. Sold in the United States but produced overseas, Barbie is manufactured by those not much older than the young girls who play with her.   F   O

7. It is shameful that these same girls need all of their monthly pay to buy just one of the dolls that many U.S. girls collect by the dozen.   F   O

8. In China, more toys are produced than in any other country of the world.

      F   O

9. However, workers molding Barbie dolls in China only earn 25 cents per hour.

                                                                    F   O

10. Such violations of basic human rights are flagrant and inexcusable.   F   O

—Adapted from Andersen & Taylor, *Sociology: The Essentials,* 4th edition

---

Review: Words That Indicate Opinions

Certain words suggest opinions. They fall into two categories:

- Words that indicate a value or belief.
- Words that indicate "all or nothing."*

*Remember that "all or nothing" words do not guarantee that the sentence they are in is an opinion, but look closely because they often do indicate an opinion.

Inferences Are Made from the Author's Words and Your Logic.

Facts, as you have learned, are verifiable and observable. Facts are evidence. Sometimes, the author does not "connect all the dots" of the evidence—so you, the reader, have to. When you add up all the available evidence and draw a logical conclusion from it, you are making an inference.

Fact: Last night the temperature dropped below freezing.

Fact: I left my plants outside on the patio.

Fact: The leaves all shriveled and dried up.

Inference: My plants were damaged by the freezing temperatures and may have died.

The writer of the preceding statements inferred (made an inference) that because of the freezing temperature, his or her plants might have died.

When you are inferring from facts, it's important to be logical. You can't ignore any of the evidence, and you can't add any evidence if the author hasn't given it. Think about the inferences that doctors make when you visit them, for example. Doctors write a prescription or give a diagnosis based on the evidence they find when they examine you. A doctor would probably get sued pretty quickly if he or she simply ignored important symptoms you shared or recommended an operation without adequate evidence that you needed it.

The auto mechanic profession is another one that uses inference. The mechanic's job is to check the symptoms to diagnose what is wrong with your car. Mechanics probably wouldn't stay in business long if they ignored what needed to be fixed or started recommending expensive, unnecessary repairs without evidence of a real need.

You make multiple inferences every day. If clouds fill the sky, you infer that it's going to rain and you take along an umbrella. If traffic is backed up, you infer there is an accident and you take an alternative route. If you see a person eating only a salad for lunch every day, you might infer that he or she is on a diet or is a vegetarian. Each of these inferences is logical and based on evidence.

When you read, you make inferences based on what the author says. You may have heard this process referred to as "reading between the lines." You have used inference in every lesson of *Activate: College Reading.* For example, you have been using inference with the following skills:

- Lesson 1: Identifying an author's purpose

- Lesson 2: Predicting what the author will say

- Lesson 3: Thinking, talking, and writing about a reading selection

- Lessons 4 and 5: Defining vocabulary by using word parts and context

- Lesson 6: Using a dictionary effectively for understanding new words and connecting them to prior knowledge

- Lesson 7: Recognizing the connotation of words and how that connects to author's tone

- Lessons 8–11: Understanding the role of topics, stated main ideas and implied main ideas, and supporting details

- Lessons 12 and 13: Analyzing and using patterns of organization

- Lesson 14: Applying the MAPP annotating and reading strategy to textbooks

- Lesson 15: Developing your ability to think critically
- Lesson 16: Understanding the difference between a fact and opinion

Each of these skills involves inference. You are not given the answer directly, but through your logic and using the clues from the text, you are able to *infer* the answer.

INTERACTION 5–18	Using Details to Make Inferences from Situations

Read each situation. Use inference to answer the questions that follow.

Situation A

- Maurice plays soccer.
- Maurice had a soccer game last night.
- Maurice is limping this morning at school.

1. What is the best inference about Maurice?

_____ a. He stubbed his toe on his way to school.

_b__ b. He injured himself playing soccer.

_____ c. He is looking for attention.

Situation B

- You go to visit your grandmother.
- You walk in the door and it smells like fresh-baked cookies.

2. What is the best inference about your grandmother?

_____ a. She is burning a candle that smells like fresh-baked cookies.

_____ b. She is wearing a new perfume that smells of cookies.

_c__ c. She has baked cookies for you.

Situation C

- You pull up next to a Ferrari at a traffic light.
- The driver is dressed in the latest style.

3. Which of the following is the best inference concerning the driver?

___ a. She stole the car.

___ b. She is driving her dad's car.

_C_ c. She is successful.

Situation D

- Your roommate is a partier.
- She came home sometime in the middle of the night.
- You wake up to the sound of her throwing up.

4. What is the best inference about your roommate?

_a_ a. She drank too much last night.

___ b. She has the flu.

___ c. She is bulimic.

Situation E

- Shannon's mom is dying of cancer.
- Her health is declining quickly.
- Shannon gets a call in the middle of the night.

5. What is the best inference about the phone call?

___ a. It is a prank call.

_b_ b. Something has happened to her mom.

___ c. It is a wrong number.

INTERACTION 5–19 Inferring Main Ideas from Details

Read each group of details. Use inference to determine a main idea for each group.

Group 1

- Warren Buffett is worth more than $40 billion, but he still lives in a house he bought for $31,500 more than fifty years ago.

- Ingvar Kamprad, the founder of Ikea, is worth more than $30 billion, but drives a 15-year-old Volvo.

- Chuck Feeney, who co-founded the Duty Free shops found in airports around the world, is a billionaire who wears a $15 watch and doesn't own a home or car.

- Azim Premji, an Indian businessman worth $17 billion, drives a Toyota Corolla, flies coach, and stays in budget hotels.

What main idea can you infer from these details? *Bellionar are*

Cheap

Group 2

- Flavored milk commonly sold in schools can be just as high in sugar as soda.

- Flavored milk adds a significant amount of saturated fat in our children's diets.

- Many children's bodies are unable to process lactose, a naturally occurring sugar found in milk.

- Drinking flavored milk can increase cholesterol levels.

What main idea can you infer from these details? *Flavored milk are*

not health

Group 3

- Many violent video games reward players for committing acts of violence or cruelty.

- Violent video games desensitize the players to real-life violence.

- The FBI has linked playing violent video games to school shootings.

- Playing violent video games increases aggressive behavior.

What main idea can you infer from these details? *Violent video game*

increase aggressive behavior

Group 4

- Social networking sites allow people to create new relationships and strengthen old ones.

- Social networking sites bring people with similar interests together.

- Social networking sites provide many free services, such as blogging, photo sharing, games, and e-mail.

- Social networking sites can be a cause of social change, through grassroots movements and protests.

What main idea can you infer from these details? _Social networking_ _have benifiet_

Group 5

- Performance-enhancing drugs have long-term negative effects on the health of the user.

- Performance-enhancing drugs give the users an unfair competitive advantage.

- When professional athletes use performance-enhancing drugs, they are a negative influence on their fan base, who will see their behavior as being acceptable and maybe even use the drugs themselves.

- The use of performance-enhancing drugs damages the integrity of whatever game is being played.

What main idea can you infer from these details? _Performance enhancing_ _drugs are bad_

| INTERACTION 5–20 | Using Inference to Solve a Riddle |

Read the following riddle and use your critical thinking and inference skills to create a solution.

> A farmer is going to the market to sell a fox, a goose, and a bag of corn. But he has to cross a river in a boat that is only big enough for him and one of the other three at the same time. If he leaves the fox and the goose alone, the fox will eat the goose. If he leaves the goose and the corn alone, the goose will eat the corn. What should the farmer do?

_____

_____

_____

_____

INTERACTION 5–21 | Making Inferences from Paragraphs

Read the passages. Use inference to answer the questions that follow.

An Icon Creator

Steve Jobs is the co-founder and current CEO of Apple, Inc., the most respected company in the world, according to *Fortune* magazine. He has had a hand not only in creating world-renowned products, such as the iPod and iPhone, but also in changing the way the world accesses e-mail, the Internet, and music. In light of all his accomplishments and success, one interesting story about Jobs is that in the 1970s, he applied for a job at Hewlett Packard but wasn't hired because he had dropped out of college.

1. Can you infer why the author refers to the Hewlett Packard incident as "interesting"? _____

_____

2. Explain Hewlett Packard's view of education, as presented in this paragraph. ___

_____

_____

A Tiny Toy Gun or a Weapon?

Thinkstock/Comstock/Jupiter Images

Image copyright Picsfive. Used under license from Shutterstock.com

If you have a child who attends an American elementary, middle, or high school, beware of "zero tolerance" policies. Several kids have been suspended for bringing tiny toy guns to school. One brought a two-inch plastic LEGO gun. Another brought a policeman action figure that included a gun. A third had a small water gun in his backpack. Carrying any one of these violates a school's "zero tolerance" policy on "weapon possession."

—From www.thisistrue.com

3. What can you infer about the author's view of the zero tolerance policy on weapon possession? _____

_____

4. What pieces of information in the reading support your inference? _____

_____

_____

Composing Effective E-Mails

- Keep e-mails brief, concise, and to the point.
- Address one topic per e-mail.
- Avoid being antagonistic or critical.
- Ensure that all e-mails you send have value for the recipient.
- Be aware that there is no such thing as a private e-mail.
- Check spelling and punctuation for accuracy.
- Include a meaningful subject line.
- Respond to e-mails within 24 hours.

—Solomon, Tyler, & Taylor, *100% Career Success*

_____ 5. Using inference, determine the purpose of this reading.
   a. To persuade
   b. To inform
   c. To entertain

_____ 6. Using inference, determine the tone of this reading.
   a. Objective
   b. Subjective
   c. Ironic
   d. Emotional

A Bureaucratic Problem

1   Once bureaucratic organizations are created, they tend to resist change. This resistance not only makes bureaucracies virtually impossible to eliminate but also contributes to bureaucratic enlargement. Because of the assumed relationship between size and importance, officials tend to press for larger budgets and more staff and office space. To justify growth, administrators and managers must come up with more tasks for workers to perform.

2   Resistance to change may also lead to incompetence. Based on organizational policy, bureaucracies tend to promote people from within the organization. As a consequence, a person who performs satisfactorily in one position is promoted to a higher level in the organization. Eventually, people reach a level that is beyond their knowledge, experience, and capabilities.

—Kendall, *Sociology in Our Times*, 7th edition

_____ 7. Using inference, determine the best topic for the passage.

    a. Resistance to change

    b. Bureaucratic organizations

    c. Incompetence

    d. Larger budgets and staff

_____ 8. Using inference, determine the pattern of organization for the second paragraph.

    a. Process

    b. Classification

    c. Cause and effect

    d. Compare and contrast

INTERACTION 5–22   **Applying Inference to a Paragraph**

Read the paragraph. While you read, circle any opinion words or phrases. Then answer the questions that follow.

Childhood is a magical time. All young children have an extraordinary ability to captivate any adult's attention, especially ours. We apologize repeatedly to friends and strangers alike as we share every cute thing our kids do. Most wondrous of all are the rapid and momentous developmental changes of the childhood years. Helpless infants become curious toddlers in what seems like a very short time. Before a parent can blink, these toddlers are schoolchildren engaged in spirited play with young friends. Then suddenly, they are insecure adolescents, worrying about dates, part-time jobs, cars, and college. The whirlwind transitions of childhood are miraculous, so parents should enjoy every moment while they can.

—Adapted from Weiten, *Psychology: Themes & Variations,* 7th edition

1. Using inference, determine whose point of view this paragraph written from.

   _____

2. Using inference, determine the tone. _____

   _____

3. Based on the general context or your prior knowledge, infer what the word *captivate* means. _____

4. Using inference, determine the pattern of organization for this paragraph.

   _____

5. List the signal words that led you to the pattern you chose. _____

   _____

6. Which of the following is the best implied main idea of this passage?
   a. There is a certain magic associated with childhood.
   b. Parents with kids are annoying to listen to when they ramble about their kids.

    c. Parents should enjoy their children at every stage because they grow up so fast.

    d. When kids grow up they do not want anything to do with their parents.

____ 7. Using inference, determine the purpose of this passage.

    a. To inform

    b. To persuade

    c. To entertain

8. List the proof that led you to the purpose you chose. _____

_____

____ 9. Which of the following is a valid inference you could draw from the reading?

    a. The author believes that parents are prouder of their infants than they are of their teenagers.

    b. The author thinks that some parents do not take enough pictures of their kids.

    c. The author feels that children grow up too fast.

10. List the proof that led you to your answer for question 9. _____

_____

| INTERACTION 5–23 | Making Inferences from a Visual |

Look at the cartoon and discuss the clues with a classmate in order to figure out the answers to the following questions.

Patrick Corrigan, Reprinted with permission-Torstar Syndication Services

1. What does the artist mean by "Resolutions"? _____

   _____

2. Create a topic sentence that includes the implied main idea of this cartoon. _____

   _____

   _____

3. Using inference, determine the author's tone. _____

   _____

4. Does this cartoon indicate a fact or an opinion? Support your answer. _____

   _____

   _____

5. Using inference, determine the organizational pattern indicated in this picture.

   _____

ACTIVATE YOUR SKILLS 1
Identifying Fact, Opinion, and Inference

A. Read the following sentences and decide if they are fact (F) or opinion (O). Circle any opinion words you find.

   1. Walt Disney World is a magical place.   (F)   O

   2. Banks will be handing out bonuses to their upper management soon, which will bring the most vicious media attack the industry has ever seen.   F   (O)

   3. The International Student Club is scheduled to have a hot dog and snow cone sale on Wednesday, July 1st, at 11:00 a.m.   F   O

   4. Don't worry about cooking lunch; just stop by the bookstore area and buy a delicious hot dog.   F   O

   5. The price of hot dogs and snow cones is only one dollar.   F   O

   6. Please come and support the International Student Club in this amazing activity.   F   O

   7. I have provided a link to the program guide that will give you the information you requested.   F   O

8. Increased memory for your computer will make processing faster.   F   O

9. Our short five-question survey should take no more than a few minutes.   F   O

10. I've heard complimentary things about you and look forward to meeting you.

                           F   O

11. All of us at the Benevolent Insurance Group greatly appreciate your business.

                           F   O

12. Credit unions usually offer better interest rates on checking and savings accounts than banks.   F   O

13. The 8.8 magnitude earthquake that hit Chile on February 27, 2010, was the seventh strongest earthquake in recorded history.   F   O

14. American children eat more snacks per day than they should, which is contributing to their obesity.   F   O

15. A British man was fined and prohibited from driving for six months after he "walked" his dog from the driver's seat of his car.   F   O

Look at the following visual and then answer questions 16–20.

16. Using inference, determine the purpose of this cartoon. _____

_____

17. Using inference, determine the author's view of texting while driving. _____

_____

18. Using inference, determine the tone of this cartoon. _____

_____

19. List the key details of this cartoon: _____

_____

20. Create a topic sentence that expresses the implied main idea of this cartoon. ____

_____

_____

B. Read each situation. Use inference to answer the questions that follow.

Situation 1

- Valentina is three months behind on her car payments.
- She is at the mall shopping.
- When she comes out, her car is not where she left it.

21. What is the best inference about the missing car?

        ____ a. The car was stolen.
        ____ b. She forgot where she parked the car.
        ____ c. The car was repossessed.

Situation 2

- You come home from a hard day at work with a sandwich.
- You set the sandwich down on the counter out of reach of your dog.
- You run to the bathroom.
- When you come back the sandwich (wrapping and all) is gone.

22. What is the best inference about the sandwich?

        ____ a. You actually left the sandwich in the car.
        ____ b. The dog could reach further than you thought.
        ____ c. You have a mouse infestation.

Situation 3

- It is a hot summer day.
- Three teens are in a small shop.

- One is wearing shorts and a tank top; the second is wearing jeans and a T-shirt; the third is wearing shorts, a T-shirt, and an overcoat.

- The youth steal some merchandise.

23. Which teen should the owner chase to recover the stolen merchandise, and why?

_____

Situation 4

- John is waiting in the dentist's office.

- He is jiggling both of his legs up and down.

- He keeps sighing.

24. Which of the following is the best inference?

____ a. John is a nervous person.

____ b. John doesn't like visiting the dentist.

____ c. John has a date after this appointment and is anxious to go.

Situation 5

- A girl is waiting at a train station for a train.

- She looks at her watch to see the time.

- Many trains go by, and she is still sitting there.

- Suddenly she jumps up and cries, "Oh, no!"

25. Which of the following is the best inference about the girl's exclamation?

____ a. She forgot to eat lunch.

____ b. She left her passport at the hotel.

____ c. She realized she missed her train.

ACTIVATE YOUR SKILLS 2
Practicing Fact, Opinion, and Inference

A. As you read each of the articles in part A, circle any opinion words. Then answer the questions that follow.

Maserati's 2010 GranTurismo Convertible

Dimitrios Kambouris/
WireImage/Getty Images

1   Let's face it. It's dreary outside in most of the nation and we could all use a little fun. We have just the thing: Maserati's 2010 GranTurismo convertible. But fun doesn't come cheap. It was just priced at $135,800. For that kind of cash, here's what you get:

2   The GranTurismo convertible is a stunning four-seat droptop with a 433-horsepower, 4.7-liter V-8 engine, six-speed adaptive automatic transmission with 593 standard paddle shifters.

3   Inside, Maserati says the convertible has the most legroom of any convertible in the rear seat of any car in its class, enough for "two real adults." The triple-insulated soft top retracts fully in 24 seconds, leaving the rear seat and trunk space unchanged.

4   There's lots of ways to customize the convertible to suit your tastes—from the nine paint colors to 10 shades of upholstery to three different wood trims. There's even matching luggage by Ferragamo.

—Woodyard, "Maserati Prices GranTurismo Convertible at $135,800,"
USA TODAY. January 19, 2010. Reprinted with Permission

1. How many opinion words did you circle? _____

2. Using inference, determine the tone of this passage. _____

_____

3. Using inference, determine the most important purpose of this passage. _____

_____

4. Using inference, determine the author's bias or view of the GranTurismo convertible. _____

5. Share your opinions on the following:

   a. What do you think of this car? Why? _____

   _____

   b. What are your thoughts on paying $135,800 for a car? Support your opinion.

   _____

   _____

Troubled Economy a Boost for Repo Business

1　In a bad economy, fun is often the first casualty.

2　For James Hedrick, that means it's a busy time in his line of work. He's one of those dreaded repo men.

3　He spends his days scanning yachts, sailboats and fishing skiffs as he steers his dinghy through a marina west of the city's skyscrapers, looking for a piece of the American dream.

4　This particular piece is a gleaming white, 65-foot Hatteras with two master bedrooms, two full bathrooms and a full galley kitchen with glossy teak cabinets. The owner is $35,000 past due on his $1.5 million boat loan.

5　Hedrick is an agent with National Liquidators, considered by industry experts to be the world's largest marine repo company. The Fort Lauderdale-based company has tripled its business in the past three years, and now takes possession of about 200 boats a month in Florida, Ohio and California. The company's competitors also say they've seen similar increases in business.

6　"They're going to hang on to the car, they're going to hang on to the house. But they're going to give up on the boat," said Hedrick, whose employer has doubled its staff in two years to 85 repo agents so they can meet demand from the banks and lenders.

7　"A lot of this is self-inflicted. It's somebody who three years ago made $50–$60,000 and didn't save a penny," said Ray Jones, the owner of Long Beach Yacht Sales in California. "They thought the income would never end. But the income stopped and the toys went away."

—Reprinted with permission from THE ASSOCIATED PRESS,
"Troubled Economy a Boost for Repo Business," July 15, 2008

---

6. How many opinion words did you circle? _____

7. Using inference, determine the tone of this passage. _____

8. Using inference, determine the purpose of this passage. _____

9. How would you describe the bias of this article: positive, negative, or neutral?

   _____

____ 10. Which of the following sentences is an opinion?

    a. National Liquidators has tripled its business in the past three years.

    b. National Liquidators is the largest marine repossession company.

    c. National Liquidators hires quality employees who have to do a hard task.

    d. National Liquidators is located in Fort Lauderdale, Florida.

B. Decide whether each sentence is fact (F), opinion (O), or mixed fact and opinion (F/O). Circle any opinion words you find.

11. Bonsai (pronounced bone-sigh) is an ancient oriental horticultural art form.

                                                                       F   O   F/O

12. In both Chinese and Japanese, the word *Bonsai* literally means "tree-in-a-pot."

                                                                       F   O   F/O

13. Originally developed in Asia almost 2,000 years ago, today the sublime art of bonsai is practiced throughout the world.   F   O   F/O

—Questions 11–13 adapted from "What Is Bonsai,"
www.bonsai-bci.com/whatis.html

14. A PADI diver carries the most respected and sought after scuba credentials in the world.   F   O   F/O

15. Your PADI certification card will be recognized and accepted anywhere you choose to dive.   F   O   F/O

—Questions 14 and 15 adapted from "PADI Courses,"
www.padi.com/scuba/padi-courses/default.aspx

16. Mixed Martial Arts (MMA) is a competitive fighting sport that combines a variety of martial art techniques.   F   O   F/O

17. MMA has increased in popularity since it began in the early 90s and has become one of the most exciting modern sports.   F   O   F/O

18. Eastern Diamondback rattlesnakes have been rattling a long time, but they have been the main attraction at Opp, Alabama's Rattlesnake Rodeo for the past 48 years.   F   O   F/O

19. Mr. J. P. Jones was the mastermind behind this small-town community event.

                                                                     F   O   F/O

20. Mr. J. P. Jones and the Opp Jaycees first organized this event in 1962; they wanted a fun-filled, family friendly weekend with snake shows, arts and crafts, and good food.   F   O   F/O

—Questions 18–20 adapted from "The Opp Rattlesnake Rodeo,"
www.rattlesnakerodeo.com/history.htm

MASTER YOUR SKILLS 1
Finding Opinion Words and Understanding Inference

A. Read the following paragraph. Circle any opinion words as you read.

"General" Larry Platt became the subject of a must-see "viral video" after he gave an amazing performance of his original song "Pants on the Ground" during the *American Idol* season 9 tryouts in Atlanta, Georgia. His song brought a smile to my face. Not only did the tune make people feel good, but it also gave an accurate commentary on a silly street fashion, which no one should wear. Even though "General" Larry Platt may have gotten 15 minutes of fame from this catchy song, he has led a life he is proud of. He is a charismatic civil rights activist who marched with Martin Luther King Jr. himself! Civil rights leader Rev. Hosea Williams gave him the title "general" for his leading role in organizing sit-ins during the 1960s Civil Rights Movement. The state of Georgia even gave him his own day (September 4, 2001) in recognition of his "priceless and immeasurable contributions."

You should have circled ten opinion words or phrases. List them below and identify whether each one is a value word or an all or nothing word.

1. _must see_____all or nothing words_____
2. _amazing_____value_____
3. _accurate_____value_____
4. _silly good_____value_____
5. _no one_____All or noth_____

6. _Should_   _Value_
7. _Catchy_   _Value_
8. _Charismatic_   _Value_
9. _Priceless_   _Value_
10. _Immeasurable_   _Value_

B. Look at the cartoon and then answer questions 11–15.

© 2010 Cam Cardow, Ottawa Citizen, and PoliticalCartoons.com

11. What is the implied main idea of this cartoon? _the car got stuck in_ _the snow_

12. Using inference, determine the tone of this cartoon. _Entertaining_

13. Using inference, determine the cartoonist's view of global warming. _not a big deal_

14. Explain "global warming" in your own words. _global warming_ _different climate changes_

15. Using inference, determine what kind of job the man pushing the car could have. Support your answer. _teacher_

C. Circle the words that indicate an opinion in the paragraph, and answer the questions that follow.

Diamond prices were sinking at an alarming rate in 1938, so the De Beers mining company enlisted ad agency N. W. Ayer & Son to help reverse the trend. A year later, it launched the "diamond is forever" campaign, which brazenly promoted the idea that every marriage required a sizable gift of bling. It also invented the "two months' salary" spending rule. This marketing campaign remains one of the most brilliant in the history of marketing.

—Adapted from "10 of the Most Brilliant Marketing Ideas," Feb. 26, 2010. www.msnbc.com.

16. What can be inferred about diamond engagement rings before 1939? _____

they were not expensive

17. Using inference, determine which of the following best describes the author's view of the ad agency N. W. Ayer & Son.
   a. They were marketing frauds.
   b. They were marketing geniuses.
   c. They were presumptuous in their marketing claim.
   d. They were not the right ad agency for the job.

18. Which of the following is an opinion?
   a. N. W. Ayer & Son invented the "two months' salary" spending rule.
   b. The decrease of diamond sales caused De Beers to hire N. W. Ayer & Son.
   c. N. W. Ayer & Son is an ad agency.
   d. N. W. Ayer & Son created a triumphant ad campaign for De Beers.

19. Using inference, determine which of the following is the best definition for _brazenly_.
   a. Timidly
   b. Boldly
   c. Unknowingly
   d. Slowly

20. What kind of word is _brazenly_?
   a. A value word
   b. A fact
   c. An all-or-nothing word

MASTER YOUR SKILLS 2
Applying Your Knowledge of Fact, Opinion, and Inference

A. Decide whether each sentence is fact (F), opinion (O), or mixed fact and opinion (F/O). Circle any opinion words you find.

1. The Bodega del Fin del Mundo winery in Patagonia, Argentina, along with prominent wine consultant Michel Rolland, has won several international medals for its complex wines.   F   O   F/O

2. Studies show that males tend to be more physically aggressive than females.

    F   O   F/O

3. Exercise is hard for people to do.   F   O   F/O

4. All Europeans viewed Native Americans as simple people who lived virtuous lives.   F   O   F/O

5. Alfred Nobel was a Swedish industrialist who founded the Nobel Prizes in hopes that he could encourage peace and cultural development.   F   O   F/O

6. Herbs4U offers the best blend of premium herbs for your mental health.

    F   O   F/O

7. A number of years ago, social psychologist Jack Brehm demonstrated that telling people they cannot have something only makes them want it even more.

    F   O   F/O

8. The most important piece of finding quality resources online will always be your good judgment and critical thinking.   F   O   F/O

9. Studies of twins show that the IQ of identical twins is more similar than that of fraternal twins, suggesting that intelligence is at least partly inherited.

    F   O   F/O

10. People who have children are happier than those who do not have children.

    F   O   F/O

B. Read the passage and answer the questions that follow.

Antarctica

1   This may be the last year that Antarctica is open to mass tourism—not because the ice is melting too fast (though it is), but because of restrictions that would severely curtail travel around the fragile continent.

2   Until recently, most vessels passing through Antarctica were limited to scientific expeditions, but an exploding number of tourists now flock to what is arguably the world's last great wilderness. The tourism boom, scientists argue, poses a major environmental threat. Indeed, several passenger ships have run aground in recent years.

3   Countries that manage Antarctica are calling for limits on the number of tourist ships, for fortified hulls that can withstand sea ice and for a ban on the use of so-called heavy oils. A ban on heavy oil, which is expected to be adopted by the International Maritime Organization later this year, would effectively block big cruise ships.

4   With the new rules taking effect within two years, tour operators are promoting 2010 as the last year to visit Antarctica, while, at the same time, procuring lighter vessels that would be permitted. Abercrombie & Kent, for example, is introducing a new ship, *Le Boreal* (www .abercrombiekent.com), which its public relations firm argues "meets all the environmental regulations, so access to Antarctica via A&K will not be affected."

5   Launching this year, the compact luxury ship holds 199 passengers and features an outdoor heated pool, steam rooms and private balconies that offer intimate views of some of the world's remaining glaciers.

—From "The 31 Places to Go in 2010," www.nytimes.com, January 10, 2010

For questions 11–15, indicate which of the sentences from the "Antarctica" passage contain opinions. Mark them with an X and circle the opinion word.

_____ 11. This may be the last year that Antarctica is open to mass tourism.

_____ 12. Countries that manage Antarctica are calling for limits on the number of tourist ships.

_____ 13. The tourism boom, scientists argue, poses a major environmental threat.

_____ 14. With the new rules taking effect within two years, tour operators are promoting 2010 as the last year to visit Antarctica.

_____ 15. Private balconies offer fantastic views of some of the world's remaining glaciers.

16. Based on context clues or your prior knowledge, what does *curtail* mean? ___

_____

17. Based on context clues or your prior knowledge, what does *poses* mean? ___

_____

18. Based on context clues or your prior knowledge, what does *procuring* mean?

_____

19. What is the purpose of this passage? _____

20. Which of the following statements would the author probably agree with?
   a. Antarctica should not be visited by tourists.
   b. *Le Boreal* is the nicest cruise ship offering trips to Antarctica.
   c. The glaciers in Antarctica are more beautiful than the ones in Alaska.
   d. If you can go to Antarctica in 2010, you should because you might lose your chance after that.

Support your answer to question 20 with evidence from the passage: _____

_____

C. Read each group of details. Use inference to determine a main idea for each group.

Group 1

- Snuggies are blankets with sleeves.
- Snuggies are comfortable and convenient.
- Snuggies come in three great color choices.
- For a limited time, if you buy one Snuggie, you get one for free.

21. What main idea can you infer from these details? _____

_____

Group 2

- Cheerleading accounts for 65 percent of all female sports injuries in high school.
- About 30,000 cheerleaders are treated each year in emergency rooms for injuries.
- The average age for those treated is $14\frac{1}{2}$; most are just sent home to heal.

- Cheerleading injuries have increased 400 percent since the 1980s.

22. What main idea can you infer from these details? _____

_____

Group 3

- You should always attend class.
- You should do your homework before you go to class.
- You should study for a while every day rather than cram at the last minute.
- You should get to know your professors and visit them during office hours.

23. What main idea can you infer from these details? _____

_____

Group 4

- Eat three small meals and two to three healthy snacks per day.
- Move more.
- Eat smaller portions by using smaller dishes.
- Eat nutrient-rich foods like fresh vegetables, salmon, dark berries, and whole grains.
- Get at least eight hours of sleep per night.

24. What main idea can you infer from these details? _____

_____

Group 5

- Pay attention when puppies begin to sniff around or squat, and then scoop them up and rush them outside.
- Set a schedule to take your puppies outside every thirty minutes or one hour and encourage them to "go potty."
- Take your puppies outside about ten minutes after they eat or drink.
- Be consistent and praise your puppies when they go to the potty in the area you want them to go.

25. What main idea can you infer from these details? _____

_____

Summary Activity: Critical Reading

Part 5 has discussed how to think critically about what you are reading, including the six critical thinking levels, fact, opinion, and inference. Fill in the Reading Guide by completing each idea on the left with information from Part 5 on the right. You can return to this guide throughout the course as you complete other reading assignments.

Reading Guide to Critical Reading

Complete this idea	with information from Part 5.
The six levels of critical thinking from least complex to most complex are	1. remember 2. understand 3. apply 4. analyze 5. evalote 6. create
The **5W's and H**—who, what, when, where, why, and how—are examples of this critical thinking activity:	7. remember
When you use the skills you have already practiced in a new situation, you are using this critical thinking activity:	8. apply
Identifying an author's bias or making your own judgments is this critical thinking activity:	9. eveulote
Understanding tone, connotation or denotation, or fact and opinion is this kind of critical thinking activity:	10. analyze
When you write a paper, come up with an original idea, or create a conclusion from a reading, you are using this critical thinking activity:	11. Creating
If you are creating an outline or MAPP of a passage, you are using this critical thinking activity:	12. Understand
Which critical thinking activity do the following verbs indicate? *develop, design, adapt, imagine, plan*	13. Create

Complete this idea	with information from Part 5.
Which critical thinking activity do the following verbs indicate? *diagram, demonstrate, solve, illustrate, organize*	14. *apply*
Which critical thinking activity do the following verbs indicate? *assess, rank, critique, justify, judge*	15. *Evalote*
Which critical thinking activity do the following verbs indicate? *identify, list, reproduce, define, locate*	16. *remember*
Which critical thinking level do the following verbs indicate? *summarize, map, discuss, paraphrase, restate*	17. *Understand*
Which critical thinking activity do the following verbs indicate? *compare, examine, explain, investigate, imply*	18. *Analyze*
Facts can be	19. *Proven or objective*
Opinions need to be supported by	20. *proof*
The two types of evidence that can help support an opinion are	21. *exprert. rebired op* 22. *derect op*
The following adjectives—*awful, ugly, cool, great, fantastic*—are examples of	23. *Value ohing*
The following words—*every, none, never, must, have to*—are examples of	24. *all or nothing*
An inference is a	25.
Five skills you have used inferences for are	26. 27. 28. 29. 30.

Complete this idea	with information from Part 5.

Think about what your thinking and reading habits were before you read Part 5. How did they differ from the reading suggestions here? Write your thoughts.

Application: Critical Reading

● Pre-Reading the Selection

The following selection, "Lessons from the Oscars: Turning Obstacles into Opportunities" by Jill Koenig, is taken from an Internet magazine, ezinearticles.com.

Surveying the Reading

Survey the title and the first sentence of each paragraph, reading quickly. What is the general topic of the reading selection? _____

_____

Guessing the Purpose

Based on its title, what do you suppose is the article's main purpose: to persuade, inform, or entertain? _____

_____

Predicting the Content

Predict three things this selection will discuss.

- _____
- _____
- _____

Activating Your Knowledge

What experiences have you had in which you faced a setback but refused to give up?

- _____
- _____
- _____

Common Knowledge

Read these terms and their definitions to help you understand the reading selection.

5-octave range *(paragraph 2)* An octave is a musical range of eight notes. To have a 5-octave range is the ability to sing high, low, and all the notes in between (think Mariah Carey, Christina Aguilera, or opera singers). Most people only have a 1- or 2-octave range.

Calliope *(paragraph 3)* The name of a character (a Greek Muse—a goddess who inspires the arts) in the production of *Hercules: A Muse-ical Comedy.*

Simon Cowell *(paragraph 4)* A former judge on *American Idol*. He was known for his criticisms and negative remarks of contestants on the show.

Barry Manilow *(paragraph 4)* A popular singer-songwriter with a career spanning from the 1970s to today. He currently has a show in Las Vegas and is most famous for the songs "Mandy," "Copacabana," and "I Write the Songs."

Elton John *(paragraph 4)* One of the most successful musicians of all time. He has had a four-decade career with fifty-six top forty hits (including nine number-one hits). Some of his most popular songs are "Crocodile Rock," "Rocket Man," and "Candle in the Wind."

Clive Davis *(paragraph 7)* An American record producer responsible for signing, launching, or producing records from artists such as Santana, Pink Floyd, Billy Joel, Aerosmith, Whitney Houston, Sean "Diddy" Combs, and Alan Jackson. He was president of Columbia Records and founder of Arista Records.

● Reading with Pen in Hand

Now read the selection. Pay attention to and mark any ideas that seem important, and respond to the questions and vocabulary items in the margin.

Access the Reading CourseMate via **www.cengagebrain.com/shop/ISBN/1413033156** to hear vocabulary words from this selection and view a video about this topic.

Lessons from the Oscars: Turning Obstacles into Opportunities

Jill Koenig

1   For as long as I can remember, I have loved watching the Oscars. I enjoy seeing the best of the best being recognized by their peers and I love watching people live their dreams. I was **rooting** for my hometown girl and fellow southsider, Jennifer Hudson, who was awarded the Best Supporting Actress Oscar for her performance in *Dreamgirls*. Jennifer is an amazing example of persisting, following your passion, and turning obstacles into opportunities.

2   At the age of 7, Jennifer began singing in her church choir, following in the example of her late grandmother, Julia Kate Hudson, who sang in the choir. With a 5-octave range, Jennifer **attributes**

Reading Journal

● Imagine what it must be like to win an Oscar.

rooting *Rooting* is a verb. What is a synonym for *rooting*?

● Jennifer had her grandmother to encourage her; whom do you have?

attributes Based on the context, infer what *attributes* means.

Michael Germana/Everett Collection

everything including her vocal ability to her grandmother, who encouraged her to pursue her dreams.

● Paragraphs 3–6 organize Jennifer's experience in time order. Use them to visualize her steps to success.

3   Before *American Idol,* in 2003, Jennifer was signed to a 7-month contract to perform on a Disney cruise playing the role of Calliope. When that ended, she decided not to renew her contract and instead flew to Atlanta to try out for *American Idol.* She left a sure thing in order to take a chance at a bigger dream. The prize for the winner of *Idol* is a record contract.

stern Look at Simon Cowell's words and infer the meaning of *stern.* Or, if you have watched *American Idol,* use your prior knowledge.

4   Jennifer reached 7th out of 70,000 *Idol* hopefuls. In typical Simon Cowell fashion, he sent her away with the **stern** words, "You're out of your depth. I don't think you're capable of doing any better." Ouch. However, others, such as Barry Manilow and Elton John, recognized her amazing abilities. When season 3 of *Idol* ended, she went on tour with the top 10 finalists, and was grateful for having the opportunity.

obstacle Not winning *American Idol* is the obstacle being referred to. Infer the meaning.

5   For many people, that would be it, not winning *American Idol* would be enough of an **obstacle,** their one shot, and the end of their dream. But not for Jennifer Hudson. For her it would be the beginning. She did not lose sight of her goals. She said, "God has something in store for me. I don't know where or when but something big is coming." She went on and continued to pursue her dream of singing and sharing her voice with the world.

6   She was next chosen from 782 highly talented actor/singers for the role of Effie White in *Dreamgirls,* for which she received the

Best Supporting Actress Oscar. Jennifer said that losing on *American Idol* was a blessing because if she had won, she would have gone down a different path, which would not have allowed for parts such as the one in *Dreamgirls*. When Oprah Winfrey watched Jennifer's performance in *Dreamgirls,* she stood up and said, "Girl, go get your Oscar." Greatness recognizes greatness.

7   Three years ago she was singing on a cruise ship. She now has a record deal with Clive Davis. Big voice. Big goals. Big dreams. The lesson: When you don't get what you want, it means something bigger and better is right around the corner if you are willing to **persist** and turn that obstacle into an opportunity. Keep on keeping on.

8   Twenty five years old. First movie role. First nomination. First Oscar. "Look at what God can do." (Jennifer Hudson) Imagine what you can do if you apply the same faith and persistence to your goals. Live your dreams!

persist This word (and forms of it) is used several times to describe how Jennifer Hudson reached her goals despite the obstacles. What does it mean?

● Think about how persistence can help you reach your educational goal.

● Critical Thinking Questions

Critical Thinking Level 1: Remember

1. Who is this reading about? _____

2. What is the lesson this reading presents? _____

   _____

____   3. Which of the following is a setback Jennifer Hudson experienced?

   a. Being chosen to play Effie White after the first choice turned the part down.

   b. Losing her job with Disney.

   c. Being kicked off *American Idol.*

   d. Having to sing on a cruise ship.

WHY? What information in the selection leads you to give that answer? _____

_____

_____

_____

____   4. Which of the following people did not recognize Jennifer Hudson's potential?

a. Elton John

b. Oprah

c. Barry Manilow

d. Simon Cowell

WHY? What information in the selection leads you to give that answer? _____

_____

_____

_____

Critical Thinking Level 2: Understand

Fill in a time line of Jennifer Hudson's life as presented in this reading.

5. _____

6. _____

7. _____

8. _____

9. _____

10. _____

11. _____

Critical Thinking Level 3: Apply

_____ 12. Which of the following statements best describes the main idea of this passage?

a. Jennifer Hudson is unique in Hollywood because of her perseverance.

b. Jennifer Hudson is a good example to follow if you want to achieve success.

c. *American Idol* is a show that often does not end up with the best singers winning.

d. Failure always leads to success, so do not give up.

WHY? What information in the selection leads you to give that answer? _____

_____

_____

_____

____ 13. Which of the following details is *least* relevant to the main idea of this passage?

    a. For as long as I can remember, I have loved watching the Oscars.

    b. Jennifer said that losing on *American Idol* was a blessing because if she had won, she would have gone down a different path, which would not have allowed for parts such as the one in *Dreamgirls*.

    c. In typical Simon Cowell fashion, he sent her away with the stern words, "You're out of your depth. I don't think you're capable of doing any better."

    d. With a 5-octave range, Jennifer attributes everything including her vocal ability to her grandmother, who encouraged her to pursue her dreams.

WHY? What information in the selection leads you to give that answer? _____

_____

_____

_____

____ 14. What is the main pattern of organization in paragraph 3?

    a. Comparison

    b. Cause and effect

    c. Definition

    d. Time order

WHY? What information in the selection leads you to give that answer? _____

_____

_____

_____

____ 15. What two relationships are found in the first two sentences of paragraph 7?

    a. Time order and contrast

    b. Contrast and classification

    c. Classification and definition

    d. Definition and time order

WHY? What information in the selection leads you to give that answer? _____

_____

_____

_____

Critical Thinking Level 4: Analyze

_____ 16. Why does the author include details of Simon Cowell's comments to Jennifer Hudson in this passage?

    a. To explain Simon Cowell's personality.

    b. To help the reader see how rude Simon Cowell is.

    c. To demonstrate that Jennifer Hudson is a good example of persistence.

    d. To demonstrate how mean words can keep you from success.

WHY? What information in the selection leads you to give that answer? _____

_____

_____

_____

_____ 17. What is the overall purpose of this passage?

    a. To persuade you to become a singer.

    b. To inform you of Jennifer Hudson's difficult life.

    c. To inform you of Jennifer Hudson's struggles to reach her goal and persuade you to not give up on yours.

    d. To indicate that life is not always fair.

WHY? What information in the selection leads you to give that answer? _____

_____

_____

_____

_____ 18. What is the overall tone of this passage?

    a. Apathetic

    b. Harsh

    c. Encouraging

    d. Objective

WHY? What information in the selection leads you to give that answer? _____

_____

_____

_____

Critical Thinking Level 5: Evaluate

The author of this reading uses Jennifer Hudson to illustrate the following claim: *"The lesson: When you don't get what you want, it means something bigger and better is right around the corner if you are willing to persist and turn that obstacle into an opportunity."*

19. Does the author do a good job of supporting her claim?

    a. If you think so, support your reasons with evidence from the passage.

    b. If you do not think so, how could she have done a better job?

_____

_____

_____

_____

Critical Thinking Level 6: Create

20. Do you have an acquaintance, friend, or family member who is discouraged? Using the information from this reading combined with your own thoughts, write a letter of encouragement to this person. _____

_____

_____

_____

_____

Analyzing Fact, Opinion, and Inference

21. Which statement best describes the following sentence? *Jennifer is an amazing example of persisting, following your passion, and turning obstacles into opportunities.*

    a. Opinion

    b. Fact

    c. A mix of fact and opinion

    d. None of the above

WHY? What leads you to give that answer? _____

_____

_____

_____ 22. Which of the following sentences includes a fact and an opinion?

    a. Jennifer reached seventh out of 70,000 *Idol* hopefuls.

    b. At the age of 7, Jennifer began singing in her church choir, following in the example of her late grandmother, Julia Kate Hudson.

    c. When season 3 of *American Idol* ended, Jennifer went on tour with the top 10 finalists, and she was the best performer.

    d. Jennifer Hudson did not lose sight of her goals.

WHY? What information in the selection leads you to give that answer? _____

_____

_____

_____

Label the following sentences as Fact (F) or Opinion (O). If you choose Opinion, circle the word that makes the sentence an opinion.

_____ 23. For as long as I can remember, I have loved watching the Oscars.

_____ 24. Everyone enjoys seeing the best of the best being recognized by their peers.

_____ 25. I was rooting for my hometown girl, Jennifer Hudson.

_____ 26. At the age of 7, Jennifer began singing in her church choir.

_____ 27. With a 5-octave range, Jennifer attributes everything including her vocal ability to her grandmother, who encouraged her to pursue her dreams.

_____ 28. Jennifer reached seventh out of 70,000 *Idol* hopefuls.

_____ 29. Simon Cowell sent Jennifer away with stern words.

_____ 30. However, others, such as Barry Manilow and Elton John, recognized her amazing abilities.

_____ 31. Jennifer said she was grateful for having the opportunity to tour with the *American Idol* finalists.

_____ 32. Losing on *American Idol* turned out to be better for Jennifer than winning.

_____ 33. Jennifer Hudson is a lucky girl.

Test 5: Reading Comprehension   NONFICTION BOOK

Your instructor may ask you to take practice tests throughout the semester to help you decide which topics you need to study the most. All the tests in this book include questions about all the major reading comprehension skills after the reading selection.

● Pre-Reading the Selection

The following selection, "Joe Kapp: Life Lessons from a Football Superstar," is taken from a book in which a hundred famous Latinos and Latinas share true stories from their lives.

Surveying the Reading

Survey the title and the first sentence of each paragraph, reading quickly. What is the general topic of the reading selection? _____

Guessing the Purpose

Based on the title of the selection and the type of book in which it is published, what do you suppose is the selection's main purpose: to persuade, inform, or entertain? _____

_____

Predicting the Content

Predict three things this selection will discuss.

- _____
- _____
- _____

Activating Your Knowledge

What experiences of playing sports do you have? Explain any sacrifices you made to play. If you did not play a sport, what sacrifices did you make in order to participate in a different type of activity, such as playing in band, being in an organization, or pursuing a hobby?

- _____
- _____
- _____

Common Knowledge

Read these terms and their definitions to help you understand the reading selection.

San Fernando, Salinas, Newhall *(paragraph 2)* Towns located in central California near Los Angeles.

frijoles *(paragraph 3)* The Spanish word for "beans."

Cub Scouts *(paragraph 7)* A club for boys aged 8–10 that has the aims of "citizenship training, character development, and personal fitness" (according to the Cub Scout Web site).

● Reading with Pen in Hand

Now read the selection. As you read, pay attention to and mark any ideas that seem important, and respond to the questions and vocabulary items in the margin.

Access the Reading CourseMate via www.cengagebrain.com/shop/ISBN/1413033156 to hear vocabulary words from this selection and view a video about this topic.

Reading Journal

profound Joe says that his mom's saying was <u>not</u> *profound*. Is his mom's saying deep and insightful, or shallow and obvious? What does *profound* mean?

● Joe Kapp's mom had a saying he remembered that helped him. Do you have a saying from a family member that has helped you?

Joe Kapp: Life Lessons from a Football Superstar

1   My mother, Florence Garcia, would always say, "*Si vas a hacer algo, hazlo correcto*" (If you're going to something, do it right). It's not a **profound** message, but I have always remembered it. That message carried me through hours of football practice and school. She also taught me that there is a price for everything; that is to say, you must concentrate on your goal. I learned there is a price you pay for focusing on being an athlete—you give up art or you give up a musical instrument. You develop certain other skills. You have to maintain academic skills in order to play, so you have to work very hard on both the mental and physical front. And always, spoken and unspoken, is the message that if you want to be good at something, then you gotta keep doing it and doing it. The honest effort of spending the time to perfect certain aspects of the game is necessary. Since I was doing something I loved, it didn't seem like work at all.

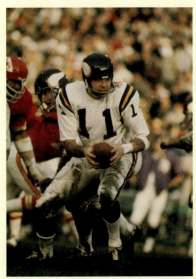

Focus on Sport/Getty Images

2   We moved a lot, like a lot of families in **rural** farming communities. I went through kindergarten to the third grade in San Fernando, from third grade to tenth grade in Salinas, and finished the eleventh and twelfth grade in Newhall. I learned to live with change. The only constant was football.

3   From my mother, I learned to eat all the **frijoles** on the plate. Translated to football, that means you never leave the plate empty. If you have a talent, use it. Fulfill your promise. My mother made **tremendous** sacrifices to even allow me to go on to college with three younger sisters and a brother still at home. She worked hard to allow me the luxury of getting that college education and participating in the crazy game of football.

4   A lot of people say, "Joe Kapp made it." In other words, I wasn't such a gifted **natural**, but I chose to work at football. I chose to work at it, and I chose to say, "Okay, you want to go to college? Okay." And I would tell myself, "If I play sports, I can go to college, and that's where I've gotta go."

5   You choose to pay the price of what it takes to be the best in your chosen position. You compete. I haven't paid the price for learning how to play the guitar, so the result is that all my friends get to hear me play badly. However, in my chosen field, I've paid the price of time and effort and focus and discipline. It's the same with

rural Joe lived in farming communities. Where would they be located? What does *rural* mean?

● Life is often changing. What is a constant you have had in your life?

● Are you using all of your talent?

tremendous Joe notes that his mother worked hard so he could go to college. What does *tremendous* probably mean?

● Is there a goal you have worked hard to achieve?

natural This word is often used to refer to nature, but it has a different context here. Joe says he was not a *natural*, but worked hard to make it in football. Based on the contrast, what does *natural* mean?

● How are you working hard to improve yourself?

● What are you afraid of?

conquer Later in the paragraph is a synonym for *conquer*. What does *conquer* mean?
● Can you think of a plan to help you overcome something you fear?

6   everything else. That's how you work through certain fears and weaknesses. You just work at it.

    We also have to work to improve ourselves in other ways. When I was growing up I wouldn't speak to the public, although I was captain of every team I ever played on, and the captain usually does the talking. Behind the scenes, I always made arrangements not to talk in public. Finally, in Canada, I saw that speaking was an opportunity, but I realized I was afraid to speak.

7   So I said to myself, "I can't do this anymore. I'm gonna look this fear in the eye and I'm gonna change. I'm gonna **conquer** this fear." I started speaking to kids, not twelve-year-olds, but third graders, Cub Scouts. I learned to speak to them, I graduated to the seventh graders, and so on. And, in the end, by working at it, I got over the fear of speaking in public. I spoke to a thousand people here recently. Imagine, the young man who was afraid to speak in public delivering motivational speeches. But I had to work at it.

—Adapted from Yolanda Nava, ed., *It's All in the Frijoles*
Fireside-Simon & Schuster, 2000

● Comprehension Questions

Write the letter of the answer on the line. Then explain your thinking.

Main Idea

    1. Which of the following statements best describes the main idea of this passage?

a. Joe Kapp is a football superstar.

b. If you are going to do something, do it right.

c. If you pay attention, you will learn some of life's biggest lessons from your mothers.

d. Football was Joe Kapp's ticket out of small-town poverty and into fame and fortune.

WHY? What information in the selection leads you to give that answer? _____

_____

_____

_____

_____ 2. Paragraphs 6 and 7 could be combined. What is the point of these two paragraphs?

   a. Public speaking.

   b. Public speaking is hard and takes practice to master.

   c. How it is important to be the captain of sports teams.

   d. It is important to improve yourself.

WHY? What information in the selection leads you to give that answer? _____

_____

_____

_____

Supporting Details

_____ 3. Which of the following is <u>not</u> a lesson Joe Kapp learned from his mother?

   a. If you are going to do something, do it right.

   b. Use all your talents.

   c. If you make a promise, keep it.

   d. Public speaking is nothing to fear.

WHY? What information in the selection leads you to give that answer? _____

_____

_____

_____

_____ 4. How did Joe Kapp overcome his fear of public speaking?

   a. He started speaking to young children and moved his way up to older and older audiences.

   b. He took some classes on overcoming his speaking fear.

   c. His mother gave him the advice and skills he used to overcome his fear.

   d. He learned how in Canada.

WHY? What information in the selection leads you to give that answer? _____

_____

_____

_____

Author's Purpose

____ 5. In your pre-reading of this selection, you were asked to predict its purpose. After reading the article, what would you say the main purpose is?

a. The purpose is to persuade readers to work hard at everything they do.

b. The purpose is to inform the reader about Joe Kapp's early life, as well as his successes and failures.

c. The purpose is to entertain the reader with stories from the life of a football superstar.

d. Even though the author's purpose is to persuade, the stories shared and lessons learned are entertaining.

WHY? What information in the selection leads you to give that answer? _____

_____

_____

_____

____ 6. Why does the author include the last sentence of paragraph 7?

a. It is an afterthought to show he did not really work at it.

b. The author is stating that it wasn't easy for him to overcome his fear of public speaking.

c. The author is being sarcastic because he really enjoyed public speaking.

d. To help readers understand that they, too, can overcome fear of public speaking.

WHY? What information in the selection leads you to give that answer? _____

_____

_____

_____

Relationships

_____ 7. Which pattern of organization is used in the following sentence? *I haven't paid the price for learning how to play the guitar, so the result is that all my friends get to hear me play badly.*

    a. Comparison

    b. Cause and effect

    c. Definition

    d. Narration

WHY? What information in the selection leads you to give that answer? _____

_____

_____

_____

_____ 8. Two main patterns of organization are used in paragraph 7. What are they?

    a. Comparison and contrast, definition

    b. Cause and effect, time order

    c. Classification, contrast

    d. Time order, comparison

WHY? What information in the selection leads you to give that answer? _____

_____

_____

_____

Fact, Opinion, and Inference

_____ 9. Which statement best describes the following sentence? *My mother made* <u>*tremendous*</u> *sacrifices to even allow me to go on to college with three younger sisters and a brother still at home.*

    a. Opinion

    b. Fact

c. A mix of fact and opinion

d. None of the above

WHY? What leads you to give that answer? _____

_____

_____

_____

____ 10. Which of the following can be inferred about the author?

a. Achieving goals was easy for Joe Kapp.

b. Joe Kapp is the best at everything he does.

c. Joe Kapp hates playing the guitar.

d. Joe Kapp admires his mom.

WHY? What information in the selection leads you to give that answer? _____

_____

_____

_____

● Vocabulary in New Contexts

Review the vocabulary words in the margins of the reading selection and then complete the following activities.

EASY Note Cards

Make a note card for each vocabulary word from the reading. On one side, write the word. On the other side, divide the card into four areas and label them E, A, S, and Y. Add a word or phrase in each area so that you wind up with an example sentence, an antonym, a synonym, and, finally, a definition that shows you understand the meaning of the word with your logic. Remember that a synonym or an antonym may have appeared in the reading.

Relationships Between Words

Circle the answer to each question. Then explain your answer.

1. Is a **profound** idea more likely to be **tremendously** important or a waste of time?

   Tremendously important   A waste of time

   Why? _____

   _____

2. If you have chosen to live in a **rural** setting, is it **natural** for someone to assume you do not like city life?

   Yes   No

   Why or why not? _____

   _____

3. Is it true that **conquering** a fear takes a **tremendous** amount of work?

   Yes   No

   Why or why not? _____

   _____

Language in Your Life

Write short answers to each question. Look at vocabulary words closely before you answer.

1. Name one thing you want that costs a **tremendous** amount of money. _____

   _____

2. Name one thing at which you are a **natural**. _____

   _____

3. Do you prefer **rural** or urban life? Why? _____

   _____

4. Name an idea that you think is **profound**. _____

   _____

5. Name one fear you have **conquered** or want to **conquer**. _____

   _____

Language in Use

Select the best word to complete the meaning of each sentence.

conquering   natural   profound   rural   tremendous

1. Constantine the Great had a _____ impact on the history of the Roman Empire.

2. He was emperor from A.D. 306–337 and became the single ruler of a unified Roman Empire after _____ his enemies, Maxentius and Licinius.

3. Constantine also had a _____ influence on Christianity becoming the dominant religion of the Roman Empire. The story goes that he had a vision of the "Christ symbol" the night before his battle with Maxentius. He saw this as a divine sign and painted this symbol on his soldiers' shields.

4. When he won the battle against the stronger army the next day, he saw it as his _____ right to be the emperor of the Christian people.

5. As the single ruler of a vast empire, Constantine changed many things, from laws that favored Christianity to limits on _____ farmers' freedoms, as well as reorganizing the government.

Spotlight on Word Parts: *Pro-*

As you have learned, *profound* means "deep and insightful." The word *profound* is composed of two parts:

pro- means "from, forward, forth, or before" + **found** means "bottom or deep"

When you put the two parts together, you get "from the deep."

The word part **pro-** is used in many other words.

proceed = move forward

progress = walk forward

profit = gain from

produce = bring forth

profuse = give forth in abundance

Circle the correct word in each of these sentences.

1. California vineyards have a reputation for (proceeding / producing / progressing) excellent wines.

2. Do people really (progress / profit / produce) if they gain wealth but lose their family?

3. (Profit / Proceed / Produce) at your own risk! Guard dog on duty.

4. Danielle is making great (profuse / progress / profit) on her goal to lose 30 pounds this year.

5. In past elections, celebrities have been known to offer (produce / profuse / proceed) praise for their favorite presidential candidate.

PART 6

"So many of my friends, that's all they do: text and watch videos on their phones."

Leeann Hellijas said this as she filmed a cell phone video with Dr. Rachel Jones of Rutgers College of Nursing

Jim Cummins/The New York Times/Redux Pictures

 Find chapter-specific interactive learning tools for *Activate,* including quizzes, videos, and more, through CengageBrain.com.

 Videos Related to Readings

 Vocab Words on Audio

 Read and Talk on Demand

Readings

Cell phone videos may mostly consist of entertaining content such as music videos and popular films, but in one of the readings in Part 6, "A Soap Opera's Sex Is All for a Good Cause," you will find out how cell phone videos are being used to help people form healthier habits. You'll also read about how doctors empathize with patients, how a lieutenant colonel averted disaster in Iraq, and how your Facebook relationship status can get complicated.

Part 6 is organized into two topics that concern every one of us: our connections with other people and our need to make healthy choices. The purpose of Part 6 is to give you more opportunities to discuss the ideas in readings, to practice your reading comprehension skills, and to exercise your critical thinking.

Survey the Readings

A "Read and Talk" activity is at the beginning of each theme. The reading is followed by four discussion questions. You can use these as springboards for discussion in your group or class.

Two "Reading Reflections" sections per theme can be used as opportunities for reading comprehension practice, class work, extra credit, tests, or individual study. However they are used, these readings, along with a full suite of vocabulary and reading comprehension questions and selected critical thinking questions, will help you solidify your skills.

Each theme ends with "Reading Connections" questions to help you connect ideas from the readings and to guide you if you want to conduct further research into the theme.

Review Reading Comprehension Skills.

Here is a brief review of the major reading comprehension skills. If you have studied all the comprehension skills, you can consult this list for a quick definition of each skill. Or, if you haven't yet gotten to a certain skill in your course, refer to the description of the skill to help you figure out the task.

Main Idea

Think of the main idea as the "point" of the paragraph or passage. To find the main idea, notice which sentence explains the author's most important point about the subject. The other sentences in the paragraph should offer explanations, examples, and details about the main idea. The details are more specific than the main idea.

Supporting Details

Think of the supporting details as the "proof" for the main idea. To locate the supporting details, find the main idea and then look for the information the author uses to explain it in more detail. Sometimes, if a main idea covers more than one paragraph, you will find the supporting details in several paragraphs.

Author's Purpose

The author's general purpose may be to persuade (change the reader's mind or behavior), inform (share information with the reader), or entertain (make the reader feel a certain way, often through stories), or it may be a combination of these purposes. At specific points in a text, an author may use a variety of methods to achieve the general purpose. You should always assume that the author has a particular reason for what he or she wrote.

Relationships

The ideas in a reading selection are related to one another in different ways. For instance, one sentence might discuss the causes of an event mentioned in a different sentence. Some relationships have to do with time, space, comparisons and contrasts, causes and effects, and so on.

You may see the relationships between the ideas in different parts of one sentence, in different sentences, or even in different paragraphs. Many times, these relationships are indicated with signal words or transitions such as *but, and, however, for example,* and so on.

Fact, Opinion, and Inference

A fact is a true statement that can be verified by using another source of information: "It is 85 degrees outside." An opinion is a person's personal reaction: "It's too hot to play baseball." An inference is an idea the reader gets from the other ideas that the author has stated: "That person must be from up north." To be valid, an inference must be a logical extension of what the author has written.

The better you become at working through the processes involved in each of these skills, the better reader, thinker, and test taker you will become.

Read and Talk

NONFICTION BOOK

The following reading is from the prologue (introduction) of Daniel Goleman's book *Social Intelligence: The New Science of Human Relationships*. The story illustrates that our brains are wired with social circuitry, which helps us navigate day-to-day social situations. As you read, imagine how your social circuits would respond to the following situation.

Access the Reading CourseMate via **www.cengagebrain.com/shop/ISBN/1413033156** to hear a reading of this selection and view a video about this topic.

A Tense Moment in Iraq

Daniel Goleman

Dean Conger/CORBIS

Reading Journal

1   During the early days of the second American invasion of Iraq, a group of soldiers set out for a local mosque to contact the town's chief **cleric**. Their goal was to ask his help in organizing the distribution of relief supplies. But a mob gathered, fearing the soldiers were coming to arrest their spiritual leader or destroy the mosque, a holy **shrine**.

2   Hundreds of **devout** Muslims surrounded the soldiers, waving their hands in the air and shouting, as they pressed in toward the

cleric Look for a synonym for *cleric* two sentences later.

shrine Use the words *mosque* and *holy* to help you figure out what a *shrine* is.

devout Look at the emotion expressed by the mob in the previous sentence to determine the meaning of *devout* in this context.

platoon Use the context to understand the general meaning of *platoon*.

heavily armed **platoon**. The commanding officer, Lieutenant Colonel Christopher Hughes, thought fast.

3   Picking up a loudspeaker, he told his soldiers to "take a knee," meaning to kneel on one knee.

4   Next he ordered them to point their rifles toward the ground.

5   Then his order was: "Smile."

morphed Look at the contrast in the next sentence. What happened to the crowd's mood as described by the word *morphed*?

6   At that, the crowd's mood **morphed**. A few people were still yelling, but most were now smiling in return. A few patted the soldiers on the back, as Hughes ordered them to walk slowly away, backward—still smiling.

7   That incident spotlights the brain's social brilliance even in a chaotic, tense encounter.

sinister Look at the context of *sinister* and think about what kids are taught concerning "strangers."

8   What carried Hughes through that tight spot were the same neural circuits that we rely on when we encounter a potentially **sinister** stranger and decide instantly whether to run or engage. This interpersonal radar has saved countless people over human history—and it remains crucial to our survival even today.

—From Goleman, *Social Intelligence*, Bantam, 2006

Talking About Reading

Respond in writing to the questions here and then discuss your answers with your classmates.

1. Was Lieutenant Colonel Christopher Hughes's response what you predicted it would be when you read "The commanding officer, Lieutenant Colonel Christopher Hughes, thought fast"? What response were you expecting? _____

    _____

    _____

    _____

2. What do you think would have happened if Hughes had responded differently?

    _____

    _____

    _____

3. Can you think of a time where you have thought quickly and thus avoided a bad or dangerous situation? Share your story with a classmate. _____

_____

_____

_____

4. In addition to the example given in this reading, discuss the power of the smile.

_____

_____

_____

Reading 6–1

● Pre-Reading the Selection

It used to be that when you committed yourself to a serious relationship, it eventually became known because you told all your friends and then they told all their friends. This selection from a *Time* magazine article called "Your Facebook Relationship Status" suggests a way of broadcasting your status that you may not have considered before.

Surveying the Reading

What parts of the reading selection should you survey? _____

_____

Go ahead and survey the reading that begins on page 635.

Guessing the Purpose

Based on the title of the article, what purpose do you suppose the author has: to persuade, inform, or entertain? _____

Predicting the Content

Based on your survey, what are three things you expect the reading selection to discuss?

- _____

- _____

- _____

Activating Your Knowledge

Search your memory for knowledge that you have on any of the following topics: Facebook, MySpace, and relationship statuses. Write down at least three of these pieces of prior knowledge.

- _____

- _____

- _____

Common Knowledge

Read these terms and their definitions to help you understand the reading selection.

Facebook *(paragraph 1)* A free social networking Web site, like MySpace, that people can join to exchange personal information, such as photos or profiles, with friends and family.

Jane Austen *(paragraph 3)* An English author who lived from 1775–1817; she is most famous for her novels *Sense and Sensibility, Pride and Prejudice,* and *Emma.* Several of her works have been made into movies. A recent movie about her is entitled *Becoming Jane* (2007), starring Anne Hathaway.

Miss Manners *(paragraph 3)* Miss Manners's real name is Judith Martin. She is a newspaper advice columnist who answers questions about etiquette.

● Reading with Pen in Hand

Now read the selection. As you read, pay attention to and mark any ideas that seem important, and respond to the questions and vocabulary items in the margin.

Access the Reading CourseMate via **www.cengagebrain.com/shop/ ISBN/1413033156** to hear vocabulary words from this selection and view a video about this topic.

Your Facebook Relationship Status: It's Complicated

Claire Suddath

Reading Journal

1   For many people, the manner in which they present themselves on Facebook has come to mirror how they see themselves in real life. Photos broadcast the fun they're having, status updates say what's on their mind and a change in relationship status announces their availability, commitment or something in between.

● How do online social networks like Facebook mirror real life?

2   Of these mini-declarations, relationship status is the only one that directly involves another person. That puts two people in the social-networking mirror, and that, to borrow a Facebook phrase, can make things complicated.

● You should have formed a question from the title of this article. What are two answers to your question, based on paragraph 3?

3   There are six relationship categories Facebook users can choose from: single, in a relationship, engaged, married, it's complicated,

Jonathan Ernst/Reuters/CORBIS

and in an open relationship. (Users can decline to list a status, but Facebook estimates that roughly 60% of its users do, with "single" and "married" the most common statuses.) The first four categories are pretty self-explanatory, but when should you use them? A Jane Austen of Facebook has yet to emerge, let alone a Miss Manners, and no one seems to have a grip on what the social norms ought to be.

● Do you agree or disagree with Liz Vennum? Why?

4   "You change your Facebook status when it's official," says Liz Vennum, a 25-year-old secretary living in Chattanooga, Tennessee. "When you're okay with calling the person your girlfriend or boyfriend. Proper breakup **etiquette** is not to change the status until after you've had the 'we need to talk' talk. Then you race each other home (or back to the iPhone) to be the first to change your status to single."

etiquette What does *etiquette* mean? The clue in this sentence is "proper."

● Compare and contrast the views of Annie Geitner and Trevor Babcock.

5   Not everyone agrees, of course. Some couples are together for years but neglect to announce their coupledom to their social network. "Some moron tried to convince me that [my relationship is] not **legitimate** because I don't have it on Facebook," says Annie Geitner, a college sophomore who has had the same boyfriend for more than a year. "So that made me even more determined to not put it up there." Others, like Trevor Babcock, consider the Facebook status a relationship deal-breaker. "I'm not willing to date anyone exclusively unless she feels comfortable going Facebook-public," he says.

legitimate Study the two sentences before this one, then reread this one. What does *legitimate* mean?

6   One common theme among romantically inclined Facebook users is that there are almost infinite ways for the Facebook relationship status to go **awry**. There's the significant other who doesn't want to list his or her involvement (causing a rift in the real-world relationship); the accidental change that alerts friends to a nonex-

awry Look at the three examples that follow the word *awry* to determine its meaning.

istent breakup (causing endless annoyance); but worse than both is when the truth spreads uncontrollably.

7   Lesley Spoor and Chris Lassiter got engaged the night before Thanksgiving. The couple thought about calling their families immediately, but instead decided to wait a day and surprise everyone at Thanksgiving dinner.

8   The problem, of course, was Facebook. The morning after the big night, Spoor changed her relationship status. "I got all **giddy** since I'm old and engaged for the first time," says Spoor of her switch from "in a relationship" to "engaged." "I thought it had to be confirmed by [my fiancé] before it would update, though. Apparently not."

9   The wife of a guy who went to high school with Spoor's fiancé—a woman Spoor barely knew—was the first to post a congratulatory message on Spoor's Facebook wall. Spoor realized her mistake and deleted the message, but by then it was too late; her future in-laws had seen the message, and the status update, and called to ask what was going on. How do you explain to your family that you told the Internet you just got engaged before you told them? "It caused a huge fight," she says.

10   But relationship status doesn't have to be a source of confusion and **despair**. Emily and Michael Weise-King were in complete agreement about their status: they decided to change themselves from "engaged" to "married" in the middle of their February 2009 wedding reception.

11   "It was after cocktails but before the first course at dinner," says Mrs. Weise-King. Still dressed in their bridal **attire**, the couple whipped out their iPhones—they'd done a test run ahead of time and determined that they had to use the web browser and not the simple iPhone app—and switched status in front of **bemused** wedding guests. (They also uploaded a photo.) Throughout the rest of the night, Weise-King would occasionally glance down at her Facebook profile, "the way I'd glance at my ring when I first got engaged." Their status has not changed since.

—Friday, May 08, 2009 Time Magazine. Copyright © 2009. Reprinted by permission. TIME is a registered trademark of Time Inc. All rights reserved.

● Has your relationship ever suffered because of problems with Facebook or some other social network site?

giddy What is an emotional response to getting engaged?

● How do you think your parents would feel if it were you in this story?

despair This word refers to an emotional response to the situation in the previous paragraph and then contrasted in this one.

● Imagine your thoughts versus your parents' or grandparents' if you were at a wedding where the bride and groom updated their Facebook relationship status as part of the ceremony.

attire What kind of clothes do the bride and groom wear at their wedding? *Attire* means:

bemused Because the guests had probably never seen this done, what do you think *bemused* means?

● Comprehension Questions

Write the letter of the answer on the line. Then explain your thinking.

Main Idea

_____ 1. What is the best statement of the main idea of this passage?

    a. One should avoid using Facebook because of its complications.

    b. The relationship status in Facebook can be complicated.

    c. Spoor got into a fight with her in-laws because she posted a notice of her engagement on Facebook before telling them.

    d. Facebook needs a Miss Manners.

WHY? What information in the selection leads you to give that answer? _____

_____

_____

_____

_____

_____ 2. Which of these sentences from paragraph 3 is the best main idea of the paragraph?

    a. There are six relationship categories Facebook users can choose from: single, in a relationship, engaged, married, it's complicated, and in an open relationship.

    b. Users can decline to list a status, but Facebook estimates that roughly 60 percent of its users do, with "single" and "married" the most common statuses.

    c. The first four categories are pretty self-explanatory, but when should you use them?

    d. A Jane Austen of Facebook has yet to emerge, let alone a Miss Manners, and no one seems to have a grip on what the social norms ought to be.

WHY? What information in the selection leads you to give that answer? _____

_____

_____

_____

Supporting Details

_____ 3. Which sentence provides supporting details for the idea that Facebook is essential to a relationship?

   a. "Some moron tried to convince me that [my relationship is] not legitimate because I don't have it on Facebook."

   b. "I'm not willing to date anyone exclusively unless she feels comfortable going Facebook-public."

   c. Lesley Spoor and Chris Lassiter got engaged the night before Thanksgiving.

   d. "Facebook is fun but what really matters is between the two in the relationship."

WHY? What information in the selection leads you to give that answer? _____

_____

_____

_____

_____ 4. Which of the following people is least likely to update his or her relationship status on Facebook?

   a. Lesley

   b. Annie

   c. Michael

   d. Trevor

WHY? What information in the selection leads you to give that answer? _____

_____

_____

_____

Author's Purpose

_____ 5. What is the author's overall purpose in this selection?

   a. To persuade you to use the relationship status in Facebook.

   b. To entertain the reader with funny relationship stories.

   c. To inform the reader on the best way to use the Facebook relationship status to avoid relationship issues.

       d. To inform the reader of some of the complications to relationship status that Facebook causes.

WHY? What information in the selection leads you to give that answer? _____

_____

_____

_____

_____ 6. What was the purpose of the story about Emily and Michael Weise-King?

       a. To underscore the issues that couples have with Facebook.

       b. To entertain the reader with a comical mishap this couple had.

       c. To illustrate that not all couples have conflicts based on Facebook's relationship status.

       d. To persuade couples to include Facebook updates in their wedding ceremonies.

WHY? What information in the selection leads you to give that answer? _____

_____

_____

_____

Relationships

_____ 7. What is the relationship between paragraphs 9 and 10?

       a. Contrast

       b. Cause

       c. Definition

       d. Listing

WHY? What information in the selection leads you to give that answer? _____

_____

_____

_____

_____ 8. This sentence is in paragraph 4: *"Proper breakup etiquette is not to change the status until after you've had the 'we need to talk' talk. Then you race each other home (or back to the iPhone) to be the first to change your status to single."*

What relationship does the word *then* indicate between the two sentences?

    a. The two sentences occur in time order.

    b. The sentences show a similarity or comparison.

    c. The second sentence is the cause of the first sentence.

    d. Space order links the two sentences.

WHY? What information in the selection leads you to give that answer? _____

_____

_____

_____

Fact, Opinion, and Inference

_____ 9. Choose the fact from the following statements.

    a. Worse than both is when the truth spreads uncontrollably.

    b. Some moron tried to convince me that [my relationship is] not legitimate because I don't have it on Facebook.

    c. Spoor realized her mistake and deleted the message, but by then it was too late.

    d. No one seems to have a grip on what the social norms ought to be.

What information in the selection leads you to give that answer? _____

_____

_____

_____

_____ 10. Which statement would the author most likely agree with, according to this article?

    a. Facebook is not worth the hassle.

    b. You and your significant other should agree how to display your relationship status to avoid issues.

    c. Lesley Spoor should not have updated her Facebook status because it caused her marriage to get off to a rocky start.

    d. Updated Facebook profiles will soon become part of traditional wedding ceremonies.

WHY? What information in the selection leads you to give that answer? _____

_____

_____

_____

● Vocabulary in New Contexts

Review the vocabulary words in the margins of the reading selection and then complete the following activities.

EASY Note Cards

Make a note card for each vocabulary word from the reading. On one side, write the word. On the other side, divide the card into four areas and label them E, A, S, and Y. Add a word or phrase in each area so that you wind up with an example sentence, an antonym, a synonym, and, finally, a definition that shows you understand the meaning of the word with your logic. Remember that a synonym or an antonym may have appeared in the reading.

Relationships Between Words

Circle yes or no to answer each question. Then explain your answer.

1. Would a person who feels **giddy** feel **despair** at the same time?

   Yes   No

   Explain. _____

2. Is a tuxedo considered **legitimate attire** for the groom at a wedding?

   Yes   No

   Why or why not? _____

3. If you showed up wearing Halloween costume **attire** to a dinner party requiring formal attire, do you think the other attendants would feel **bemused**?

   Yes   No

   Why or why not? _____

   _____

4. Would proper **etiquette** be to say "I'm sorry" if a water balloon you threw went **awry** and hit the wrong person?

   Yes   No

   Why or why not? _____

Language in Your Life

Write short answers to each question. Look at vocabulary words closely before you answer.

1. Name the **attire** you feel most comfortable in. _____

_____

2. Would you know the proper **etiquette** for a dinner at the White House?_____

_____

3. Name at least one thing that makes you feel **giddy**._____

_____

4. Think of an event that might cause you to feel **despair**._____

_____

5. What are some things that **bemuse** you? _____

_____

Language in Use

Select the best word to complete the meaning of each sentence.

> attire   awry   bemused   despair
>
> etiquette   giddy   legitimate

1. Sara was _____ after her boyfriend, Anup, proposed to her.

2. She now felt that their relationship was _____ and that her family would accept her decision.

3. However, things went _____. Her father was upset because Anup had not honored him by asking for his daughter's hand in marriage first.

4. Fortunately, Anup did not _____. He asked the father's forgiveness and then asked if he would give his consent.

5. Sara's father, impressed by Anup's newfound attention to _____ and knowing his daughter was in love, decided not to make this slip-up a bigger issue and granted his approval.

6. Once this major hurdle was overcome, the young couple was free to make grand wedding plans, including arguments about china choices and the proper _____ for the wedding party.

7. Anup was _____ when his future bride changed her mind several times before deciding on the bridesmaids' shoes.

Spotlight on Word Parts: *Be-*

As you have learned, *bemused* means "puzzled." The word *bemused* is composed of three parts:

> **be-** means "to intensify" + **muse** means "thought" + **-ed** means "past tense"

When you put the three parts together, you get "lost in thought."

> The word part **be-** is used in many other words.
>> **be**rate = to scold harshly
>> **be**stow = to grant
>> **be**trothed = to be engaged
>> **be**hoove = to carry out a responsibility
>> **be**reave = to experience the loss of a loved one

Circle the correct word in each of these sentences.

1. Despite the old-fashioned connotation, I do believe that I belong to my (berated / bestowed / betrothed), and he belongs to me.

2. John is (behooved / bereaved / berated). He lost his father due to a medical error a doctor made during a routine surgery.

3. The honor of knighthood was (bestowed / behooved / betrothed) upon Patrick Stewart and Peter Jackson in 2010 by Queen Elizabeth.

4. Something seemed wrong with this picture: the child (bereaved / berated / bestowed) the mother for not buying the doll she wanted.

5. It would (betrothed / bestow / behoove) you to pay attention in class.

● Reading Reflections

CRITICAL THINKING LEVEL 2: UNDERSTAND

Explain how online social networks like Facebook mirror real life for you, your friends, and your family members. _____

_____

_____

_____

CRITICAL THINKING LEVEL 4: ANALYZE

Think about how Facebook and other social sites have changed your relationships. In what ways has Facebook changed your relationships in the following categories?

Friends: _____

_____

_____

Family members: _____

_____

_____

Significant other: _____

_____

_____

CRITICAL THINKING LEVEL 5: EVALUATE

Share what you think the appropriate protocol for dealing with a relationship status on Facebook should be. _____

_____

_____

_____

Reading 6–2   NEWSPAPER ARTICLE

● Pre-Reading the Selection

This selection from the *New York Times* suggests that you do not have to experience the same thing as someone else to be able to empathize with him or her. Read the article to see what you think.

Surveying the Reading

What parts of the reading selection should you survey? _____

_____

Go ahead and survey the reading that begins on page 647.

Guessing the Purpose

Based on the title of the article, what purpose do you suppose the author has: to persuade, inform, or entertain? _____

Predicting the Content

Based on your survey, what are three things you expect the reading selection to discuss?

- _____
- _____

  _____

- _____

Activating Your Knowledge

Search your memory for knowledge that you have on any of the following topics: what empathy is, when you have been empathic or been shown empathy yourself, and how psychologists help patients. Write down at least three of these pieces of prior knowledge.

- _____
- _____
- _____

Common Knowledge

Read these terms and their definitions to help you understand the reading selection.

cardiologist *(paragraph 3)* A heart doctor.

oncologist *(paragraph 3)* A doctor who treats cancer patients.

Rotterdam *(paragraph 7)* The second largest city in the Netherlands. (Amsterdam is the largest.)

Stuka dive-bombers *(paragraph 7)* The Stuka was a two-seater German fighter plane used in World War II. Dive bombers got their name for diving straight down out of the sky toward their targets. This helped increase their accuracy.

● Reading with Pen in Hand

Now read the selection. As you read, pay attention to and mark any ideas that seem important, and respond to the questions and vocabulary items in the margin.

   Access the Reading CourseMate via **www.cengagebrain.com/shop/ ISBN/1413033156** to hear vocabulary words from this selection and view a video about this topic.

Understanding Empathy: Can You Feel My Pain?

Richard A. Friedman, M.D.

1   "Can I ask you a question?" the young woman **ventured**. "Have you ever been depressed? Do you have any idea how bad it feels?" The patient, a married woman in her late 20s, had been tearfully describing her symptoms of depression during a consultation when she suddenly popped this question. How could I possibly understand or help her, she seemed to be asking, if I had not personally experienced her pain?

2   Her question caught me by surprise and made me pause. O.K., I'll admit it. I'm a cheerful guy who's never really tasted clinical depression. But along the way I think I've successfully treated many **severely** depressed patients.

Reading Journal

ventured The woman is not just asking a question, but one that could be taken in a negative way. What does *ventured* mean?

● Predict how someone could help a person without having the same feeling or experience as they do.

severely *Severely* is made up of two word parts: *severe* + *ly*. What does this word mean?

Andy Cox/Stone/Getty Images

● Is shared experience necessary for a physician to understand or treat a patient?

competent The word *effective* is used as a synonym for *competent*. What does *competent* mean? That he or she is _____

● Do you feel better about a doctor you can identify with? Does it matter?

alleviate What is a doctor's job when it comes to pain?

● Does a common background or experience guarantee empathy? Why or why not?

adamant Look at the reason the patient gives in the next sentence to figure out what *adamant* means.

● What is empathy "all about"? Can you explain this in your own words?

empathy Look for a definition of *empathy* in the next two sentences.

3   Is shared experience really necessary for a physician to understand or treat a patient? I wonder. After all, who would argue that a cardiologist would be more **competent** if he had had his own heart attack, or an oncologist more effective if he had had a brush with cancer?

4   Of course, a patient might feel more comfortable with a physician who has had personal experience with his medical illness, but that alone wouldn't guarantee understanding, much less good treatment. Still, many patients want their doctor to be someone with whom they can identify, not just a technically competent professional who can **alleviate** their pain.

5   As a psychiatrist, I've met many patients who have made requests for a specific type of therapist: African-Americans who want a black psychiatrist, Orthodox Jews who insist on a Jewish psychotherapist, women who ask for a feminist therapist and so on. Not long ago, a gay man in his 30s called me to ask for a referral to a gay therapist. He was **adamant** about seeing only a gay clinician. "I can't take the chance of getting a homophobic shrink," he said. His assumption was that if a therapist shared his sexual orientation or ethnic group, there would be a kind of guaranteed basis for understanding or acceptance.

6   I did, in fact, refer him to an excellent colleague who happens to be gay, but the brief conversation left me troubled. All these patients who were searching for understanding had a misconception, I think, of what **empathy** is all about. What is critical to understanding someone is not necessarily having had his or her experience; it is being able to imagine what it would be like to have it. Thus, I do not have to be black to empathize with the toxic effects of racial prejudice, or be a woman to know how I would feel about being denied promotion on the basis of sex.

7   Contrary to what many people believe, being empathic is not the same thing as being nice. In fact, empathy can sometimes be put to a very dark purpose. When the Nazis were bombing Rotterdam in World War II, for example, they put sirens on the Stuka dive-bombers knowing full well that the sound would terrify and disorganize the Dutch. The Nazis imagined perfectly how the Dutch would feel and react. Fiendish, but the very essence of empathy.

> ● Can you think of any other examples of how empathy can be used for a bad purpose?

> **fiendish** This word is an adjective that describes the Nazis' behavior toward the Dutch. What is a synonym for *fiendish*?

8   In the right hands, empathy has tremendous positive therapeutic force and can narrow what looks like an unbridgeable gap between patients and therapists. A few years back, I saw an elderly woman who had just lost her husband to cancer. "Oh, I hadn't realized you were so young!" she exclaimed. "No offense, but maybe I need to see someone who's a bit older." I asked her, "Are you worried that I can't know what it feels like to lose someone you love and face life without him?" True, I had never lost a partner, but it wasn't hard to imagine her grief and anxiety about her future. That must have done the trick, because she stayed in treatment and never again mentioned my age.

> ● Have you ever shown empathy to someone and helped him or her?

9   Sometimes, though, patients should get exactly what they ask for in a therapist. One of my residents once saw a young woman from Africa who had survived hideous torture and rape and said that she didn't think she could see a male therapist. That struck me as entirely appropriate. Given her trauma, she simply could not have put her trust in a male therapist, no matter how empathic he might actually be.

> ● Summarize the author's conclusion about the young African woman. Do you agree with him?

> **hideous** Since this word is an adjective describing torture, what do you think it means?

10   What about patients whose demand for a particular therapist springs from nothing more than everyday prejudice? I remember a patient who once stormed into my office and demanded a white therapist to replace his therapist, who was black. That's a request I turned down, even knowing that this patient's biased beliefs were an appropriate target for treatment. To do otherwise would have vindicated his prejudice and fundamentally compromised the therapy from the start.

> ● Pretend you are a therapist. How would you deal with someone who is obviously prejudiced?

> **vindicated** This word is a verb. What would the action of changing this person's therapist have done to his prejudice?

11   In the end, empathy is what makes it possible for us to read each other. And it is the reason your doctor can understand your problem without actually having to live it.

—Reprinted with permission from *Understanding Empathy: Can You Feel My Pain?* By RICHARD A. FRIEDMAN, M.D.

The New York Times, April 24, 2007

• Comprehension Questions

Write the letter of the answer on the line. Then explain your thinking.

Main Idea

_____ 1. What is the best statement of the main idea of this reading?

a. Empathy is the reason your doctor can understand your problem without actually having to experience it.

b. As a psychiatrist, I've met many patients who have made requests for a specific type of therapist.

c. Patients should get exactly what they ask for in a therapist.

d. Is shared experience really necessary for a physician to understand or treat a patient?

WHY? What information in the selection leads you to give that answer? _____

_____

_____

_____

_____ 2. Which of the following sentences is the main idea of paragraph 9?

a. Sometimes, though, patients should get exactly what they ask for in a therapist.

b. One of my residents once saw a young woman from Africa who had survived hideous torture and rape and said that she didn't think she could see a male therapist.

c. That struck me as entirely appropriate.

d. Given her trauma, she simply could not have put her trust in a male therapist, no matter how empathic he might actually be.

WHY? What information in the selection leads you to give that answer? _____

_____

_____

_____

Supporting Details

_____ 3. Which of the following details is *least* relevant to the idea that "empathy is what makes it possible for us to read each other"?

    a. In the right hands, empathy has tremendous positive therapeutic force and can narrow what looks like an unbridgeable gap between patients and therapists.

    b. Her question caught me by surprise and made me pause.

    c. Thus, I do not have to be black to empathize with the toxic effects of racial prejudice, or be a woman to know how I would feel about being denied promotion on the basis of sex.

    d. Is shared experience really necessary for a physician to understand or treat a patient?

WHY? What information in the selection leads you to give that answer? _____

_____

_____

_____

    4. Which of the following is *not* mentioned as a patient requesting a specific type of therapist?

    a. An elderly woman who had lost her spouse.

    b. A gay man worried about discrimination.

    c. A prejudiced white man.

    d. A victim of torture and rape.

WHY? What information in the selection leads you to give that answer? _____

_____

_____

_____

Author's Purpose

    5. What is the author's overall purpose in this selection?

    a. To persuade the reader of the importance of having a therapist who has had similar experiences to your own.

    b. To inform the reader about the steps for choosing a good therapist.

    c. To entertain the reader with therapy anecdotes from an experienced therapist.

    d. To persuade the reader that empathy is what makes it possible for us to understand each other without having the same experiences.

WHY? What information in the selection leads you to give that answer? _____

_____

_____

_____

_____ 6. What is the purpose of this question at the end of paragraph 1? *How could I possibly understand or help her, she seemed to be asking, if I had not personally experienced her pain?*

    a. The author is trying to stress the importance of personal experience.

    b. This question illustrates the idea that most therapists are underqualified to conduct therapy.

    c. It sets up the discussion in the article and is the question the author ultimately answers.

    d. This question allows the author to prove that he did have similar experiences as his patients.

WHY? What information in the selection leads you to give that answer? _____

_____

_____

_____

Relationships

_____ 7. What relationship is found in the following sentence? *Not long ago, a gay man in his 30s called me to ask for a referral to a gay therapist.*

    a. Spatial order

    b. Comparison and contrast

    c. Cause and effect

    d. Time order

WHY? What information in the selection leads you to give that answer? _____

_____

_____

_____

_____ 8. What relationship does the following sentence show? *Empathy is the reason your doctor can understand your problem without actually having to live it.*

a. Comparison and contrast

b. Cause and effect

c. Definition

d. Description

WHY? What information in the selection leads you to give that answer? _____

_____

_____

_____

Fact, Opinion, and Inference

____ 9. Choose the opinion from the following statements.

a. In the right hands, empathy can have tremendous positive therapeutic force.

b. Many patients want their doctor to be someone with whom they can identify, not just a technically competent professional who can alleviate their pain.

c. All these patients who were searching for understanding had a misconception, I think, of what empathy is all about.

d. I remember a patient who once stormed into my office and demanded a white therapist to replace his therapist, who was black.

WHY? What information in the selection leads you to give that answer? _____

_____

_____

_____

____ 10. Which statement would the author most likely agree with, according to everything he has said in this article?

a. Empathy automatically makes a therapist good at his or her job.

b. Patients need empathy in order to find a good therapist.

c. Empathy is an unnecessary emotion.

d. Empathy can be used for purposes of good or evil.

WHY? What information in the selection leads you to give that answer? _____

_____

_____

_____

• Vocabulary in New Contexts

Review the vocabulary words in the margins of the reading selection and then complete the following activities.

EASY Note Cards

Make a note card for each vocabulary word from the reading. On one side, write the word. On the other side, divide the card into four areas and label them E, A, S, and Y. Add a word or phrase in each area so that you wind up with an example sentence, an antonym, a synonym, and, finally, a definition that shows you understand the meaning of the word with your logic. Remember that a synonym or an antonym may have appeared in the reading.

Relationships Between Words

Circle yes or no to answer the question. Then explain your answer.

1. If a person were described as "**fiendish**," could his or her behavior be considered **hideous**?

   Yes   No

   Explain. _____

2. Would hearing that she had been **vindicated** after being falsely accused **alleviate** a person's pain and anxiety?

   Yes   No

   Why or why not? _____

3. Would a person who is **adamant** about taking care of the environment be afraid to **venture** his or her opinion?

   Yes   No

   Why or why not? _____

   _____

4. Should the skill set of a **competent** physician include **empathy**?

   Yes   No

   Why or why not? _____

   _____

Language in Your Life

Write short answers to each question. Look at vocabulary words closely before you answer.

1. Name a couple of things you are **competent** at. _____

   _____

2. Name a monster or character from a movie that you think is truly **hideous**. _____

   _____

3. Name one ideal or belief you are **adamant** about. _____

   _____

4. Tell something that you think would **severely** limit a person's success in life. _____

   _____

5. What is your medicine of choice to **alleviate** a headache? _____

   _____

Language in Use

Select the best word to complete the meaning of each sentence.

adamant   alleviate   competent   empathy

fiendish   hideous   severely   ventured   vindicated

1. The Stuka was a little dive-bomber with a _____ wailing siren used by the Germans in World War II to intimidate and destroy their enemies.

2. For a short time, the Stuka _____ limited the ability of Europe to defend itself from the Nazis' advances or Blitzkrieg.

3. In Rotterdam, for example, the Stuka was responsible for a _____ attack that leveled about 1 square mile of the city.

4. The _____ flying and serious damage caused by the Stuka and its pilots led the Dutch army to surrender to the Nazis in order to avoid any further destruction of Dutch cities.

5. However, the Allied forces did not give up completely and struggled for a way to _____ the danger of the Stuka.

6. As it turned out, the terror caused by the Stuka was short lived because the plane was slow and didn't maneuver well, which added to the Allies feeling _____ that their side was the right side.

7. Despite the issues with the Stuka, the Germans were _____ about their continued use, since they had no other aircraft options.

Spotlight on Word Parts: *Em-*

As you have learned, *empathy* means "the ability to share someone else's feelings." The word *empathy* is composed of two parts:

em- means "in or into" + pathy means "feeling or emotion"

When you put the two parts together, you get "in feeling."

The word part em- is used in many other words.

embark = to begin a journey in a train or ship

embrace = to take into one's arms

empirical = knowledge based in experience

embroil = to be caught up in

emphasize = to put importance in

Circle the correct word in each of these sentences.

1. Dad had an intimidating way of jabbing his finger on your chest to (emphasize / embroil / empirical) his point.

2. Juries are often best convinced by (embroil / empirical / embrace) evidence.

3. It brought a smile to everyone's face to see the huge (embark / embrace / emphasize) the returning soldier received from her whole family.

4. The two sisters have been (empirical / embraced / embroiled) in a family feud for so long they no longer remember the issue.

5. Moms, wives, or girlfriends always want one more hug before their soldier (embraces / embarks / emphasizes) on a mission away from home.

● Reading Reflections

CRITICAL THINKING LEVEL 2: UNDERSTAND

Share a time you have shown empathy or empathy has been shown to you. Realize that empathy is different from sympathy. Sympathy involves a feeling; empathy involves understanding. Empathy means being able to understand someone else's emotions (to be in his or her shoes). _____

_____

_____

_____

CRITICAL THINKING LEVEL 3: APPLY

In paragraph 7, the author explains how the Nazis used empathy to spread terror during World War II. Think of other situations where empathy has been used for "dark purposes." _____

_____

_____

_____

CRITICAL THINKING LEVEL 4: ANALYZE

You should understand the difference between empathy and sympathy. Analyze each of the following situations to determine if empathy or sympathy is being shown.

1. Seven years ago, John's dad died suddenly. It hit him really hard. While his friend Sam felt bad for John, all he could do was sit helplessly by and watch his friend's sorrow.

Empathy   Sympathy

Support your answer choice. _____

_____

2. Zohab's friends call her "Z." She has successfully beaten cancer; it has been in remission for a couple of years now. A coworker just recently found out she has cancer. Z has a long conversation with her.

Empathy   Sympathy

Support your answer choice. _____

_____

3. Little 7-year-old Sophie just dropped her popsicle on the ground. While she stands there sniffling and feeling sorry for herself, her friend Emma comes up and gives her a hug and offers her a bite of her ice cream cone.

Empathy   Sympathy

Support your answer choice. _____

_____

● Reading Connections: Relating to Others

1. Imagine you are a family therapist. The Spoor and Lassiter families have come to you for help. Based on what you read in "Your Facebook Relationship Status: It's

Complicated" and learned about empathy in "Understanding Empathy: Can You Feel My Pain?", how would you deal with the family drama caused when Lesley Spoor updated her Facebook status about her engagement with Chris Lassiter before telling their parents?

As you explain how you would deal with this situation, remember that you need to show empathy to both sides. The parents are upset because they feel that they were not honored. Lesley is defensive about her actions and sees the whole situation as being made more important than it should be. _____

_____

_____

_____

2. Go online and do a search to find out who uses Facebook. What are the demographics of this group of people (their age, gender, geographical area, and similar information)? You can search for "Facebook Demographics" or "who uses Facebook." Be sure that your data is from the past year or two (the more recent the better). _____

_____

_____

_____

_____

Read and Talk

Social networking sites are so popular, you often hear them being discussed in everyday conversation: "Do you Facebook?" or "Twitter me" or "What's your MySpace?" You probably have an account with Facebook, Twitter, MySpace, or maybe all three! Think about your level of privacy on the social network site you use most as you read this article from The Associated Press.

Access the Reading CourseMate via **www.cengagebrain.com/shop/ISBN/1413033156** to hear a reading of this selection and view a video about this topic.

Bragging on MySpace

The Associated Press

Reading Journal

1   Dr. Megan Moreno went online to MySpace to see what kinds of information teenagers were posting on their profiles. She says that parents "should feel very comfortable looking up" their children's profiles on social networking sites like MySpace and Facebook. Doctors who care for teens should feel free to do that, too. It's not **creepy** or an invasion of privacy, she said, but more like reading posters on their walls or slogans on their T-shirts.

2   Moreno is a pediatrician and adolescent medicine specialist at the University of Wisconsin–Madison. She is the lead researcher of a study of lower-income kids that she says shows how parents and other adults can encourage safer Internet use. Young people don't consider the consequences of posting their drinking habits and sexual behavior online, Moreno said. She wondered if teens would change the information they had posted online if she sent them an e-mail warning.

creepy Does *creepy* more likely mean "causing a feeling of fear or uneasiness" or "causing a feeling of comfort"?

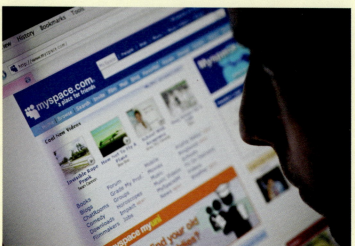

PSL Images/Alamy

3   The study shows that adult supervision of MySpace can raise teens' awareness of how accessible their pages are, she said. The researchers first located 190 MySpace public profiles in a single urban ZIP code. They **randomly** selected the ZIP code from the 10 U.S. Census areas with the lowest average income. Low-income areas were used because researchers wanted to target teens who might have less access to doctors than others do. All the teens said on their profiles they were 18 to 20 years old, and their pages included three or more references to sex, drinking, drug use or smoking. Half were sent an e-mail from "Dr. Meg." The other half weren't.

4   Moreno sent the e-mail to see what effect it would have on the teens' profiles. The message from "Dr. Meg" read in part: "You seemed to be quite open about sexual issues or other behaviors such as drinking or smoking. Are you sure that's a good idea? . . . You might consider revising your page to better protect your privacy." In response, some of the teens deleted mentions of sex and booze or they **boosted** their privacy settings. Several wrote back to "Dr. Meg" saying they had no idea their pages could be viewed by anyone. Such social networking sites have privacy settings, but they're not always used.

5   After three months, 42 percent of those getting a "Dr. Meg" e-mail had either set their profiles to "private," meaning only people they'd chosen as MySpace "friends" could view them, or they

removed **references** to sex or substance use. Only 29 percent of those in the group who had not been contacted by Dr. Meg made such changes over the three-month period. Moreno said the results suggest the e-mail intervention had a positive impact on "the hardest-to-reach teens, which gives us great hope that a similar intervention could be used to reach teens as a whole."

—Adapted with permission from THE ASSOCIATED PRESS, "Teens use MySpace to brag about sex, drugs & violence—but not if adults are watching: study," Tuesday, January 6th 2009

references *Reference* is made up of the word parts *refer* + *ence*. What does *references* mean?

Talking About Reading

Respond in writing to the questions here and then discuss your answers with your classmates.

1. Do you have a MySpace or Facebook page? Do you Twitter? If you do, which site do you prefer, and how much time do you spend on it? If you do not have an account, why not? _____

_____

2. Do you know what the privacy setting on your page is? Do you know how to check or change it? Is privacy important to you? Why or why not? _____

_____

_____

3. What are the advantages and disadvantages of having a social network page? _____

_____

_____

4. Would you be embarrassed if your parents saw your social network page? Why or why not?_____

_____

Reading 6–3

● Pre-Reading the Selection

The following article, "A Soap Opera's Sex Is All for a Good Cause," was published in the *New York Times*. As you start to read, ask yourself, "How can soap opera sex be for a good cause?"

Surveying the Reading

What parts of the reading should you survey? _____

_____

Go ahead and survey the reading that begins on page 663.

Guessing the Purpose

Based on the type of publication this article appears in, do you think its purpose is to

persuade, inform, or entertain? _____

Predicting the Content

Based on your survey, what are three things you expect the reading selection to discuss?

- ● _____
- ● _____
- ● _____

Activating Your Knowledge

Search your memory for knowledge you have about public health messages, films with a message of health, or examples of people making foolish decisions when it comes to sex. Write down at least three of these pieces of prior knowledge.

- ● _____
- ● _____
- ● _____

● Reading with Pen in Hand

Now read the selection. As you read, pay attention to and mark any ideas that seem important, and respond to the questions and vocabulary items in the margin.

Access the Reading CourseMate via **www.cengagebrain.com/shop/ ISBN/1413033156** to hear vocabulary words from this selection and view a video about this topic.

A Soap Opera's Sex Is All for a Good Cause

Jennifer V. Hughes

Reading Journal

Jim Cummins/The New York Times/Redux Pictures

1   The **scene** was set and the film crew was rolling. The actress playing Valerie was calling around, trying to find friends to go bar-hopping. She would end up in the arms of another woman's man, become pregnant and become infected with a sexually transmitted disease. But the soap-opera style film shot this month is not intended for entertainment—it's part of a research project designed to change attitudes about safe sex among young women. And the finished product will be distributed via cellphone videos.

2   Rachel Jones, an assistant professor at the Rutgers College of Nursing in Newark, created the project. During her years working as a nurse practitioner, Dr. Jones said, she saw that young women knew about the dangers of unprotected sex but still failed to use condoms. "Women say they know they should use condoms but they don't because they feel they need to hold on to the relationship," she said. "Women think 'If I ask him to use a condom, he'll think I've been messing around.'"

3   Dr. Jones said her research targets African-American and Hispanic women because statistics indicate they are most at risk for H.I.V. and AIDS. In New Jersey, about one-third of the 35,300 people living with H.I.V./AIDS are African-American or Hispanic women. The State Department of Health and Senior Services estimates that 8 out of 10 new infections will **afflict** women in those two groups.

scene Look at what happens in the next sentence. What is the *scene*?

● Do you know anyone who has had an experience similar to the character's?

● Evaluate the reason women give for not using condoms.

● Why do you think African American and Hispanic women are more at risk for HIV or AIDS?

afflict *Afflict* is a verb. Who is being *afflicted* with what? What does *afflict* mean?

insists Reread paragraph 2 and think about the purpose of the cell phone videos. Does *insist* probably more likely mean "request" or "demand"?

● Do you think Dr. Jones's idea for focus groups was a good one? Why or why not?

pioneer Look at the first sentence and the dates in the paragraph to figure out the meaning of *pioneer.*

● Have you ever seen any entertainment used to spread public health messages?

● Which method do you think will be more effective: the text messages or the soap opera episodes? Why?

● Evaluate the project: Is it worth the money?

medium Look at the context of the paragraph as well as how the message is communicated to determine what the word *medium* means.

● Do you agree that cell phones are a good medium to communicate a message like this? Why or why not?

4   In the film, after the character Toni learns about her boyfriend Mike's affair with Valerie, she **insists** they undergo tests for sexually transmitted diseases and use condoms. To create the film's dialogue and storyline, Dr. Jones held focus groups with young African-American and Hispanic women and pulled lines and plot twists from real-life experiences that they recounted. "The soap-opera format provides an opportunity to identify with the heroine and make more powerful choices after they see her make more powerful choices," Dr. Jones said.

5   Using entertainment to spread public health messages is not new. A **pioneer** in the field was Miguel Sabido, who created soap operas with messages about safe sex, family planning and education in Mexico in the 1970s. Since 1985 the nonprofit group PCI-Media Impact has created and broadcasted more than 240 radio and television dramas with social messages in 27 countries. "Public service announcements are very effective in getting people aware of an issue," said Michael Castlen, the group's executive director. "But they are not intended to actually change behavior."

6   In the New Jersey project, 250 women will be recruited from Jersey City and Newark and will be given cellphones. Half will receive weekly safe-sex text messages. The other half will receive weekly 20-minute episodes of the soap opera via cellphone video. Before, during and after the 12-week study, Dr. Jones said, the women will be surveyed about their H.I.V./AIDS risk behaviors. Dr. Jones said one of the benefits in using cellphones is that it will allow women to watch the soap operas repeatedly and in private.

7   The filming of the soap opera was paid for with a $154,400 grant from the Healthcare Foundation of New Jersey. The research is financed with a $2 million grant from the National Institutes of Health. Filming for the series began in September using professional actors, directors and crew. At a Jersey City apartment recently, the group shot scenes where Valerie learned she was pregnant and that she had gonorrhea.

8   Leeann Hellijas, who plays Valerie, said she thinks cellphones are an ideal **medium**. "So many of my friends, that's all they do: text and watch videos on their phones," she said. Martinique Moore, an assistant director for the film, said it is time for safe-sex messages to go beyond pamphlets and billboards. "A lot of young people get their cues from music videos," she said.

—Reprinted with permission from "A Soap Opera's Sex Is All for a Good Cause" By JENNIFER V. HUGHES. *The New York Times,* January 23, 2009

● Comprehension Questions

Write the letter of the answer on the line. Then explain your thinking.

Main Idea

_____ 1. Which of the following is the best statement of the main idea of paragraph 1?

    a. The scene was set and the film crew was rolling on a soap opera.

    b. Valerie is calling around, trying to find friends to go bar-hopping.

    c. Valerie ends up in the arms of another woman's man, becomes pregnant and infected with a sexually transmitted disease.

    d. The soap-opera style film is part of a research project designed to change attitudes about safe sex among young women.

WHY? What information in the selection leads you to give that answer? _____

_____

_____

_____

_____ 2. What is the best statement of the main idea of paragraph 6?

    a. In the New Jersey project, 250 women will be recruited from Jersey City and Newark and will be given cell phones.

    b. Half will receive weekly safe-sex text messages.

    c. The other half will receive weekly 20-minute episodes of the soap opera via cell phone video.

    d. Before, during, and after the 12-week study, Dr. Jones said, the women will be surveyed about their H.I.V./AIDS risk behaviors.

WHY? What information in the selection leads you to give that answer? _____

_____

_____

_____

Supporting Details

_____ 3. According to the passage, whose arms does Valerie end up in?

    a. Michael's

    b. Dr. Jones's

c. Toni's

d. Mike's

WHY? What information in the selection leads you to give that answer? _____

_____

_____

_____

____ 4. Which person is probably most responsible for the New Jersey project?

a. Leeann Hellijas

b. Michael Castlen

c. Dr. Jones

d. Miguel Sabido

WHY? What information in the selection leads you to give that answer? _____

_____

_____

_____

Author's Purpose

____ 5. What is the purpose of the soap-opera video project discussed in this selection?

a. To persuade people to use condoms.

b. To entertain its audience with soap-opera dramas.

c. To inform the targeted audience of the consequences of high-risk sexual behavior.

d. To change the behavior of its audience.

WHY? What information in the selection leads you to give that answer? _____

_____

_____

_____

____ 6. Why does the New Jersey project use cell phones as its medium?

a. The directors of the project feel it is the best way to communicate their message to their target audience.

b. Cell phones are the cheapest way to get the intended message across in this age of high-cost commercials.

c. Everybody has a cell phone.

d. Viewers can call a 1-800 help line if they have questions about the program.

WHY? What information in the selection leads you to give that answer? _____

_____

_____

_____

Relationships

_____ 7. What relationship is shown in the following sentence? *But the soap-opera style film shot this month is not intended for entertainment—it's part of a research project designed to change attitudes about safe sex among young women.*

a. Cause and effect

b. Comparison and contrast

c. Spatial

d. Time order

WHY? What information in the selection leads you to give that answer? _____

_____

_____

_____

_____ 8. What two relationships are found in the following sentence? *In the film, after the character Toni learns about her boyfriend Mike's affair with Valerie, she insists they undergo tests for sexually transmitted diseases and use condoms.*

a. Time and space order

b. Time order and cause and effect

c. Time order and comparison

d. Space order and definition

WHY? What information in the selection leads you to give that answer? _____

_____

_____

_____

Fact, Opinion, and Inference

_____ 9. Choose the opinion from the following statements.

a. Dr. Jones said one of the benefits in using cell phones is that it will allow women to watch the soap operas repeatedly and in private.

b. The filming of the soap opera was paid for with a $154,400 grant from the Healthcare Foundation of New Jersey.

c. "If I ask him to use a condom, he'll think I've been messing around."

d. A pioneer in the field was Miguel Sabido, who created soap operas with messages about safe sex, family planning and education in Mexico in the 1970s.

WHY? What information in the selection leads you to give that answer? _____

_____

_____

_____

_____ 10. Which statement would Michael Castlen most likely agree with, according to the information in paragraph 5?

a. Public service announcements are a waste of time because they do not really impact behavior.

b. Public health messages spread via cell phones would be more effective in changing behavior than those spread by TV.

c. In addition to social awareness, public service announcements intend to change people's behavior.

d. Michael Castlen is frustrated that all his work with public service announcements has been in vain.

WHY? What information in the selection leads you to give that answer? _____

_____

_____

_____

● Vocabulary in New Contexts

Review the vocabulary words in the margins of the reading selection and then complete the following activities.

EASY Note Cards

Make a note card for each vocabulary word from the reading. On one side, write the word. On the other side, divide the card into four areas and label them E, A, S, and Y. Add a word or phrase in each area so that you wind up with an example sentence, an antonym, a synonym, and, finally, a definition that shows you understand the meaning of the word with your logic. Remember that a synonym or an antonym may have appeared in the reading.

Relationships Between Words

Circle yes or no to answer the question. Then explain your answer.

1. Would a horror movie like *Nightmare on Elm Street, Halloween,* or *Saw* include **scenes** likely to involve **afflicting** pain?

   Yes   No

   Explain. _____

2. Would it make sense for a **pioneer** to **insist** on following the trails of others?

   Yes   No

   Why or why not? _____

3. Have **pioneer** directors like Ron Howard, Peter Jackson, Martin Scorsese, the Coen brothers, Clint Eastwood, and James Cameron expanded the quality as well as viewer expectations of the **medium** of film?

   Yes   No

   Why or why not? _____

Language in Your Life

Write short answers to each question. Look at vocabulary words closely before you answer.

1. Share your favorite movie **scene**. _____

   _____

2. Name a person you know who has an **affliction** that impacts his or her health. _____

   _____

3. Name several things you **insist** that you cannot live without. _____

   _____

4. Name a **pioneer** whom you respect. _____

   _____

5. What is your favorite **medium** of entertainment? _____

   _____

Language in Use

Select the best word to complete the meaning of each sentence.

afflictions   insist   medium   pioneers   scene

1. In my opinion, women are often not given enough credit for being among the first _____ _____ who came to America.

2. Imagine this _____: no running water, no toilet, no real shelter, no fuel, no doctors, no fineries, just hardship.

3. More often than not, women were responsible for gathering firewood or buffalo chips, cooking, cleaning, making and mending clothes, and tending the _____ of the family.

4. The _____ that many women used to express the hardships they experienced was a journal.

5. We should _____ that these women be given credit for their role as true heroines.

Spotlight on Word Parts: *In-*

As you have learned, *insist* means "to demand." The word *insist* is composed of two parts:

in- means "in" + sist means "to stand"

When you put the two parts together, you get "to stand in."

The word part in- is used in many other words.

influx = flowing in

interior = inside

incur = to bring in toward oneself

inflame = to cause violent emotion in someone

inception = the beginning

Circle the correct word in each of these sentences.

1. There has been a huge (interior / influx / inception) of Mexican immigrants to the United States since the 1970s.

2. Dan has a serious debt problem; even though he knows he will (incur / inflame / influx) large penalties, he feels forced to withdraw all his money from his 401(k) to maintain his lifestyle.

3. The (inception / interior / incur) of the cartoon character Mickey Mouse was 1928. Walt Disney had the name "Mortimer" in mind, but his wife, Lillian, suggested "Mickey." And the rest, as they say, is history.

4. The girl was so (inflamed / inception / influx) with envy over her classmate Lilli's new coat that she wrote on it with permanent marker.

5. The (influx / interior / inflame) of the county courthouse may have been shabby, but the old judge remained a strong believer in delivering timeless justice.

● Reading Reflections

CRITICAL THINKING LEVEL 3: APPLY

Based on what you have learned from reading this article, what could you do to get children aged 10 to 13 to not do drugs? Be sure to consider what kind of media this group uses a lot and what your message might be. _____

_____

_____

CRITICAL THINKING LEVEL 4: ANALYZE

Reread the last sentence of paragraph 4. What does Dr. Jones assume about how people learn? _____

_____

_____

CRITICAL THINKING LEVEL 5: EVALUATE

How effective do you think the cell phone videos will be in changing these women's behavior?

Very effective   Somewhat effective   Not effective

Why do you think that? _____

_____

_____

Reading 6–4

● Pre-Reading the Selection

The following reading, "Body Dysmorphic Disorder," is from a frequently visited Internet site on health: KidsHealth.org. It boasts around a half million hits each weekday. As you read, think what it would be like to live with this disorder.

Surveying the Reading

What parts of the reading should you survey? _____

_____

Go ahead and survey the reading that begins on page 673.

Guessing the Purpose

Based on the type of Web site that this article came from and the title of the reading, what purpose do you guess the article has: to persuade, inform, or entertain? _____

_____

Predicting the Content

Based on your survey, what are three things you expect the reading selection to discuss?

- _____
- _____
- _____

Activating Your Knowledge

Search your memory for knowledge you have about body image, self-image issues, or disorders such as body dysmorphic disorder. Write down three pieces of prior knowledge, even if what you know seems vague.

- _____
- _____
- _____

● Reading with Pen in Hand

Now read the selection. As you read, pay attention to and mark any ideas that seem important, and respond to the questions and vocabulary items in the margin.

Access the Reading CourseMate via **www.cengagebrain.com/shop/ISBN/1413033156** to hear vocabulary words from this selection and view a video about this topic.

Body Dysmorphic Disorder

Reading Journal

Erin Patrice O'Brien/Jupiter Images

Focusing on Appearance

1   Most of us spend time in front of the mirror checking our appearance. Some people spend more time than others, but taking care of our bodies and being interested in our appearance is natural. How we feel about our appearance is part of our body image and self-image. Lots of people have some kind of dissatisfaction with their bodies. This can be especially true during the teen years when our bodies and appearance go through lots of changes.

● Do you have any dissatisfaction with your body?

2   Although many people feel dissatisfied with some aspect of their appearance, these concerns usually don't constantly occupy their thoughts or cause them to feel tormented. But for some people, concerns about appearance become quite extreme and upsetting. Some people become so focused on imagined or minor imperfections in their looks that they can't seem to stop checking or obsessing about their appearance. Being constantly preoccupied and upset about body imperfections or appearance **flaws** is called body dysmorphic disorder.

● Do you know someone who obsesses about his or her appearance?

flaws What synonym is given before the word *flaws*?

What Is Body Dysmorphic Disorder?

- Can you explain body dysmorphic disorder in your own words?

intrude Think about other forms of this word you might know. Do you know what an *intruder* is? *intrude* is a verb, an action; what does *intrude* mean?

3   Body dysmorphic disorder (BDD) is a condition that involves obsessions, which are distressing thoughts that repeatedly **intrude** into a person's awareness. With BDD, the distressing thoughts are about perceived appearance flaws. People with BDD might focus on what they think is a facial flaw, but they can also worry about other body parts, such as short legs, breast size, or body shape. Just as people with eating disorders obsess about their weight, people with BDD become obsessed over an aspect of their appearance. People with BDD may worry their hair is thin, their face is scarred, their eyes aren't exactly the same size, their nose is too big, or their lips are too thin.

- Why has BDD been called "imagined ugliness"?

4   BDD has been called "imagined ugliness" because the appearance issues the person is obsessing about usually are so small that others don't even notice them. Or, if others do notice them, they consider them minor. But for a person with BDD, the concerns feel very real, because the obsessive thoughts **distort** and magnify any tiny imperfection.

distort If a person with BDD sees his nose as very large but others see it as normal sized, what is the person with BDD doing?

Behaviors That Are Part of BDD

compulsion Look at the definition and example that follow in the next two sentences to determine the meaning of *compulsion.*

5   Besides obsessions, BDD also involves compulsions and avoidance behaviors. A **compulsion** is something a person does to try to relieve the tension caused by the obsessive thoughts. For example, someone with obsessive thoughts that her nose is horribly ugly might check her appearance in the mirror, apply makeup, or ask someone many times a day whether her nose looks ugly. These types of checking, fixing, and asking are compulsions. Avoidance behaviors are also a part of BDD. A person might stay home or cover up to avoid being seen by others. Avoidance behaviors also include things like not participating in class or socializing, or avoiding mirrors.

- What do you think it feels like to have BDD?

6   With BDD, a pattern of obsessive thoughts, compulsive actions, and avoidance sets in. Even though the checking, fixing, asking, and avoiding seem to relieve terrible feelings, the relief is just **temporary**. In reality, the more a person performs compulsions or avoids things, the stronger the pattern of obsessions, compulsions, and avoidance becomes.

temporary Based on the context of paragraph 6, does *temporary* mean "permanent" or "short term"?

What Causes BDD?

7   Although the exact cause of BDD is still unclear, experts believe it is related to problems with serotonin, one of the brain's chemical neurotransmitters. Poor regulation of serotonin also plays a role in obsessive compulsive disorder (OCD) and other anxiety disorders, as well as depression. Some people may be more **prone** to problems with serotonin balance, including those with family members who have problems with anxiety or depression. This may help explain why some people develop BDD but others don't.

8   Cultural messages can also play a role in BDD by reinforcing a person's concerns about appearance. **Critical** messages or unkind teasing about appearance as someone is growing up may also contribute to a person's sensitivity to BDD. But while cultural messages, criticism, and teasing might harm somebody's body image, these things alone usually do not result in BDD. It's hard to know exactly how common BDD is because not many people with BDD are willing to talk about their concerns or seek help. But compared with people who feel somewhat dissatisfied with their appearance, very few people have true BDD. BDD usually begins in the teen years, and if it's not treated, can continue into adulthood.

Getting Help for BDD

9   Many people with BDD seek the help of a dermatologist or cosmetic surgeon to try to correct appearance flaws. But dermatology treatments or plastic surgery don't change the BDD. People with BDD who find cosmetic surgeons willing to perform surgery are often not satisfied with the results. They may find that even though their appearance has changed, the obsessive thinking is still present, and they begin to focus on some other imperfection.

10   If you or someone you know has BDD, the first step is recognizing what might be causing the distress. Many times, people with BDD are so focused on their appearance that they believe the answer lies in correcting how they look, not with their thoughts, but the real problem with BDD lies in the obsessions and compulsions, which are distorting a person's body image, making that person feel ugly. Because people with BDD believe what they are **perceiving** is true and accurate, sometimes the most challenging part of overcoming the disorder is being open to new ideas about what might help.

- What cause for BDD is given in paragraph 7?

prone This paragraph gives a couple of examples of why some people have BDD. Use this information to help you determine the meaning of *prone*.

critical There is a synonym for *critical* in the same sentence. What is the synonym?

- You may be saying to yourself, "I have BDD!" But what is the difference between BDD and normal body dissatisfaction?

- Why does plastic surgery not usually help someone with BDD?

- Imagine you have a friend with BDD; what would you do to try to help?

perceiving A major symptom of BDD is what a person with the disorder *perceives* concerning her physical flaws. What does *perceives* mean?

grip The first sentence of paragraph 11 gives some clues to the meaning of *grip*. In addition, you might be able to think of another context where the word *grip* is used (think sports). What does *grip* mean?

11   Body dysmorphic disorder, like other obsessions, can interfere with a person's life, robbing it of pleasure and draining energy. An experienced psychologist or psychiatrist who is knowledgeable about BDD can help break the **grip** of the disorder so that a person can fully enjoy life.

—Reprinted by permission from the Nemours Foundation/Kidshealth.
www.kidshealth.com

● Comprehension Questions

Write the letter of the answer on the line. Then explain your thinking.

Main Idea

____ 1. Which of these sentences from paragraph 5 is the best topic sentence for that paragraph?

   a. Besides obsessions, BDD also involves compulsions and avoidance behaviors.

   b. A compulsion is something a person does to try to relieve the tension caused by the obsessive thoughts.

   c. For example, someone with obsessive thoughts that her nose is horribly ugly might check her appearance in the mirror, apply makeup, or ask someone many times a day whether her nose looks ugly.

   d. Avoidance behaviors are also a part of BDD.

WHY? What information in the selection leads you to give that answer? _____

_____

_____

_____

____ 2. What is the best statement of the main idea of paragraph 2?

   a. Although many people feel dissatisfied with some aspect of their appearance, these concerns usually don't constantly occupy their thoughts or cause them to feel tormented.

   b. But for some people, concerns about appearance become quite extreme and upsetting.

c. Some people become so focused on imagined or minor imperfections in their looks that they can't seem to stop checking or obsessing about their appearance.

d. Being constantly preoccupied and upset about body imperfections or appearance flaws is called body dysmorphic disorder.

WHY? What information in the selection leads you to give that answer? _____

_____

_____

_____

Supporting Details

___ 3. Which of the following is not mentioned as a contributor to BDD?
   a. Cultural issues
   b. Genetics
   c. Vision issues
   d. Poor regulation of serotonin

WHY? What information in the selection leads you to give that answer? _____

_____

_____

_____

___ 4. Which of the following would not be considered a compulsion related to your body image?
   a. Repeatedly checking your hair in the mirror.
   b. Asking multiple people if your pants make you look fat.
   c. Reapplying makeup to your face every hour.
   d. Staying home to avoid people.

WHY? What information in the selection leads you to give that answer? _____

_____

_____

_____

Author's Purpose

_____ 5. What is the author's overall purpose in this selection?

    a. To persuade you to help friends or family with BDD.

    b. To convince you to feel empathy for people who have BDD.

    c. To inform the reader about the steps for getting successful BDD treatment.

    d. To explain what BDD is, as well as its causes and behaviors.

WHY? What information in the selection leads you to give that answer? _____

_____

_____

_____

_____ 6. What is the purpose of paragraph 9?

    a. To emphasize the importance of plastic surgery in the life of a person with BDD.

    b. To reinforce the idea that a person with BDD should seek professional help and not rely on the compliments of friends and family.

    c. To illustrate that cosmetic fixes do not solve the root problem for a person with BDD.

    d. To show that it is unethical for doctors to perform plastic surgery on people afflicted with BDD.

WHY? What information in the selection leads you to give that answer? _____

_____

_____

_____

Relationships

_____ 7. What is the relationship and the word that signals it in the following sentence? _BDD has been called "imagined ugliness" because the appearance issues the person is obsessing about usually are so small that others don't even notice them._

    a. Description; has been called

    b. Cause and effect; because

    c. Definition; BDD

    d. Spatial; small

WHY? What information in the selection leads you to give that answer? _____

_____

_____

_____

____ 8. What relationship is found in the following sentence? *Many times, people with BDD are so focused on their appearance that they believe the answer lies in correcting how they look, not with their thoughts, but the real problem with BDD lies in the obsessions and compulsions, which are distorting a person's body image, making that person feel ugly.*

    a. Contrast

    b. Time order

    c. Cause

    d. Space order

WHY? What information in the selection leads you to give that answer? _____

_____

_____

_____

Fact, Opinion, and Inference

____ 9. Choose the opinion from the following statements.

    a. Being constantly preoccupied and upset about body imperfections or appearance flaws is called body dysmorphic disorder.

    b. In reality, the more a person performs compulsions or avoids things, the stronger the pattern of obsessions, compulsions, and avoidance becomes.

    c. People with BDD who find cosmetic surgeons willing to perform surgery are often not satisfied with the results.

    d. Although the exact cause of BDD is still unclear, experts believe it is related to problems with serotonin, one of the brain's chemical neurotransmitters.

WHY? What information in the selection leads you to give that answer? _____

_____

_____

_____

_____ 10. Which of the following body parts might a person with BDD be least likely to obsess about?

    a. Lips

    b. Nose

    c. Skin

    d. Toes

WHY? What information in the selection leads you to give that answer? _____

_____

_____

_____

● Vocabulary in New Contexts

Review the vocabulary words in the margins of the reading selection and then complete the following activities.

EASY Note Cards

Make a note card for each vocabulary word from the reading. On one side, write the word. On the other side, divide the card into four areas and label them E, A, S, and Y. Add a word or phrase in each area so that you wind up with an example sentence, an antonym, a synonym, and, finally, a definition that shows you understand the meaning of the word with your logic. Remember that a synonym or an antonym may have appeared in the reading.

Relationships Between Words

Circle yes or no to answer the question. Then explain your answer.

1. Would a 5'5", 110-pound girl who **perceives** herself as fat have a **distorted** view?

    Yes   No

    Explain. _____

2. Would a person with BDD be **prone** to be more **critical** of the **flaws** of others than he

    is of the ones he sees in himself?

    Yes   No

    Why or why not? _____

3. Might parents have a **compulsion** to **intrude** into their child's e-mail account or cell phone records if they thought the child might be headed for trouble?

Yes   No

Why or why not? _____

4. Could duct tape be used as a **temporary grip** to keep a cracked car window together?

Yes   No

Why or why not? _____

_____

Language in Your Life

Write short answers to each question. Look at vocabulary words closely before you answer.

1. Name three **flaws** that would cause you to break up with a person you are dating.

_____

2. Have you ever **intruded** into a friend's life to help him avoid a problem he did not see?

_____

3. Do you think media images **distort** people's **perceptions** about what the human body should look like? _____

4. List one **compulsion** you have. _____

_____

5. If you could live **temporarily** anywhere in the world, where would you live? _____

_____

6. Name someone you know who is accident-**prone**. _____

_____

7. Name something you are **critical** about. _____

_____

8. On a scale of 1–10, how do you **perceive** your life right now? Explain. _____

_____

9. Name one or more reading concepts you feel you have a good **grip** on. _____

_____

Language in Use

Select the best word to complete the meaning of each sentence.

compulsion   critical   distort   flaws   grip

intrude   perceive   prone   temporary

1. It is fairly common to notice the _____ and blemishes of other people.

2. It seems to be human nature that we are _____ to criticize others first rather than praise them.

3. Of course, being negative is more of a _____ for some than others.

4. I am sure you could name someone who, given a choice, would rather be _____ than encouraging.

5. However, it is easy for all of us to fall into the _____ of negative thoughts toward others more often than we should.

6. The problem with being critical is that it _____ our views of how wonderful people can be.

7. If you are not careful, this type of outlook toward people in general can begin to change the way you _____ those you love.

8. These negative thoughts begin to _____ into your life, causing people to wonder what happened to the positive person you used to be.

9. So next time you find yourself drifting into negative thoughts about someone, make it a _____ visit, and then try to think two positive thoughts to wash the bad taste out of your mind!

Spotlight on Word Parts: *Dis-*

As you have learned, *distort* means "to twist out of shape." The word *distort* is composed of two parts:

dis- means "apart or away" + **tort** means "twist"

When you put the two parts together, you get "twist apart."

The word part dis- is used in many other words.

dispose = put away

disconcerted = did away with agreement

dissolve = release away

disregard = to do away with attention

dissect = to take apart or analyze

Circle the correct word in each of these sentences.

1. Despite what you may have heard, a tooth will not (dissolve / disconcerted / disregard) overnight in a glass of cola.

2. The criminal had neglected to carefully (dissect / dispose / dissolve) of all the evidence that linked him with the crime.

3. The sight of Jaime's ex-boyfriend walking arm-in-arm with her best friend greatly (disconcerted / dissolved / disposed) her.

4. The students were required to (dispose / dissect / disconcerted) the famous novel *The Pearl* in their literature class.

5. As drivers, we often (dissect / dissolve / disregard) traffic rules and then get angry at the police officer whose job it is to enforce them.

● Reading Reflections

CRITICAL THINKING LEVEL 3: APPLY

Give your own example of each term used in the reading selection.

obsession: _____

compulsion: _____

CRITICAL THINKING LEVEL 4: ANALYZE

Analyze which pattern of organization (for example, cause, effect, comparison, contrast, definition, example, classification, time order, space order) each sentence in paragraph 3 uses.

Sentence 1: Body dysmorphic disorder . . .   _____

Sentence 2: With BDD, . . .   _____

Sentence 3: People with BDD . . .   _____

Sentence 4: Just as people . . .   _____

Sentence 5: People with BDD . . .   _____

CRITICAL THINKING LEVEL 5: EVALUATE

Rate how effective this article was in teaching you about BDD:

Very effective   Somewhat effective   Not effective

Give three reasons to support your rating: _____

_____

_____

_____

_____

_____

● Reading Connections: Making Healthy Choices

1. Would a young woman with BDD be more or less likely to ask her boyfriend to use a condom? Would her BDD affect her relationship in some other way? Explain your answer. _____

_____

_____

_____

2. This theme has been about making healthy choices. Research other aspects of this topic in your library or online to find out answers to the following questions. Write down these ideas and the sources of information you used.

- What can you do to keep your heart healthy? _____

  _____

  _____

  Source: _____

  _____

- What can you do to keep your relationships healthy? _____

  _____

  _____

  Source: _____

  _____

PART 7

"Today a reader, tomorrow a leader."

—Margaret Fuller

More Tips for Reading and Taking Tests

Reading can be a gateway to success in school and your professional career; it can be a gateway to adventure via a great story; and it can be a gateway to staying informed about current topics and issues. Regardless of your ultimate destination, the journey of reading opens up new worlds of understanding and pleasure.

Activate has primarily focused on strategies for reading textbooks and other (mostly informative) sources. Part 7 expands the reading horizon by discussing other kinds of material students often like to read. The first kind, fiction, can be read with no assistance whatsoever, but we hope you have learned in this book that having strategies can help with any kind of reading. The second is online reading material. Reading and finding information online requires some specialized strategies that we cover briefly.

The last sections offer reading tips for two kinds of tests: general tests in any course area and specialized reading tests. These tips are intended to give you some ways to navigate through the tests in this reading class as well as tests in your other classes. We hope you will use these strategies to become confident test takers!

· ·

Find chapter-specific interactive learning tools for *Activate*, including quizzes, videos, and more, through CengageBrain.com.

Videos Related to Readings

Vocab Words on Audio

Read and Talk on Demand

Tips for Reading Fiction

Short stories and novels are fiction. A novel represents a story created through the development of character, plot, setting, theme, symbolism, as well as other methods. Reading fiction is different from reading nonfiction such as college textbooks.

Reading a novel sometimes requires more inference than reading nonfiction, especially nonfiction that is designed to inform readers. Novels have an entertainment purpose, so even if readers do feel they have learned something, the author's main purpose is to tell a story. Stories are often about how a character or characters change because of their experiences.

Your prior knowledge—the experiences you have had in life and the knowledge you have gained by living those experiences—is just as important to apply while reading a novel as it is nonfiction. Another kind of prior knowledge—knowledge of the different elements that literary authors use to develop a character and a story—is also helpful in reading fiction. In other words, knowledge of these elements will help you build a plan for reading novels.

A General Reading Plan

- **Beginning.** You need to understand what the situation is as the story begins: who the main characters are and when and where the action is happening. Every story has a conflict, and this should be identified clearly. The conflict might be a problem that someone faces, a decision that someone has to make, or a desire that someone wants to satisfy.

  Key question to examine: **What is it the character or characters want and what is keeping them from getting it?**

- **Development.** Once the story is set in motion and the main characters are introduced, new problems occur and additional characters may be introduced.

  Key questions to examine: **How do characters go about trying to get what they want? What new successes or complications occur?**

- **Resolution.** The characters may have gotten what they wished for (or not)—or sometimes they may have gotten what they deserved (or not). At this point you should be able to decide whether the characters have learned anything from their experiences and whether they have changed in any way.

Final key question to examine: **Did the characters get what they wanted, what they deserved, both, or neither?**

Literary Elements

- **Characters.** These are the fictional people in the story. The story is built around what the characters say, how they act, how they interact, how they look, and how they feel. At least one of the major characters usually changes over the course of the story, often in response to emotional or physical challenges, natural disaster, or personal tragedy.

- **Point of View.** The author usually shares the story through a narrator, who can tell the story from one of two different points of view: first person or third person. A first-person narrator is often a major character (but not always). First-person narrators tell the story from their own point of view. Third-person narrators tell the story from a different perspective. Some are omniscient: they know everything. Some are limited: they know what a single character knows. Some are objective: they know everything that happens between characters, but they can't see into characters' minds.

- **Plot.** The plot is how the main pattern of events in the story unfolds. The author reveals the plot by what characters say to each other and how they interact, by how the different events that occur are arranged, and by cause-and-effect relationships. The plot doesn't always happen in time order. Sometimes there are flashbacks (scenes from the past), flash-forwards (scenes from the future), or the same scene from several characters' perspectives.

- **Setting.** The setting is where and when the story takes place. Important elements of the setting may be the geographic area (desert), the historical time period (Middle Ages), and the city, country, or region (Paris, France) in which the plot takes place.

- **Symbolism.** A symbol can be a person, thing, or action that has two layers of meaning: a literal layer and a figurative layer. The person, thing, or action is exactly what it seems to be at the literal level. At the figurative level, it has a more complex meaning; it stands for something more abstract or more general. For example, the "fountain of youth" could be a literal fountain, and it can also figuratively represent a desire to live forever.

- **Author's Style and Tone.** The style and tone are based on some of the same aspects that you think about when reading nonfiction (see Lesson 7). How the author uses words and sentence structures creates a certain feeling. So do figures of speech such as metaphor (direct comparison), simile (indirect comparison), personification (giving human qualities to something nonhuman), and hyperbole (exaggeration). How the author uses symbols is part of the style, also. The author's tone toward the characters and the story might be optimistic, cynical, humorous, ironic, or any of the tones listed in Lesson 7 on page 186.

- **Theme.** Theme is the main point that the novel makes about life. Think about theme as an implied main idea (see Lesson 10). The author never states the theme, but it is there for readers who think about the novel and let it affect them deeply. The theme is different from the plot. The plot is the main action that drives the story; the theme is what must be true for the plot to happen. For example, in *New Moon,* the plot is the development of the story among three main characters—Isabella Swan, Edward Cullen, and Jacob Black—but the theme deals with the loss of true love.

Remember, whether you are reading fiction or nonfiction, reading is important because it exercises your mind!

Tips for Reading and Gathering Information Online

The Internet stores a tremendous amount of information. In fact, while many people do use the Internet as a source of entertainment, searching for information is the reason most of us access the Internet. This is why it is important to understand how to search, evaluate, and use information that you find from the Internet effectively in your college classes. The following suggestions will help get you started.

- Use search engines, such as Google or Yahoo!, and know how to use key word searches and Boolean logic (use of the words *and, or, not*) to limit or refine your search.

- Learn how to use databases, such as InfoTrac (check with the librarian for the database options at your school).

- Be aware of the purpose of the Web site you are on. The last part of the URL, or the URL extension, reveals what kind of Web site it is.

.com	Commercial or business	Persuade or offer products for you to buy
.edu	Educational	Provide information about a school
.org	Organizational (usually nonprofit)	Promote the organization
.gov	Governmental	Provide information about government services

- Three navigational aids can help you find your way around a Web site:

  1. Menus (the table of contents for the Web site, often found in drop-down menu style at the top or along the left side of the Web page);

  2. Links embedded in text (often blue or underlined, these hyperlinks take you to more information about the name or term that is linked); and

  3. Bread crumb trails (found at the top of the Web page, they let you know where you are within the Web site).

- To decide whether to trust the information you find on a Web site, consider three things:

  1. The author's credibility (What makes him or her believable?);

  2. The information's reliability (How do you know the information is accurate?); and

  3. The domain you are in (.com, .edu, .org, or .gov).

- Examine online text for three clues to decide whether the ideas seem worth considering:

  1. Does the site's organization or author show expertise in the area under discussion?

  2. Does the tone match the information?

  3. Does the site use correct grammar and spelling?

- The best way to know if a fact is trustworthy is to double-check it with another reliable source of information.

General Tips for Taking Tests

In college, the most common way to check your comprehension of an individual concept, a broad subject, or specific material is by testing. Because you will probably take tests in most of your classes, you should use strategies that help you approach tests in a clear, logical, and precise manner. The following list can help you lay a firm foundation for successful testing.

Before the Test

Survey the entire test before you begin.

- How many questions are there?

- How many points is each question worth?

- How much time do you have to complete each item?

- Read and pay attention to all directions.

During the Test

Start with what you already know. Work from what you know to what you don't know.

- Read each question carefully.

- Make sure you understand key words.

- Decide exactly what the question is asking for before you answer it.

- Read all the possible answers carefully before you choose one.

- Eliminate answers that you know are wrong first.

- Double-check the answer you think is correct.

- If you are unsure of an answer, mark the choice you think might be correct and then return to that question after you complete the test if there is time.

- Change your answer only if you have a good reason to believe that a different answer would be better.

After the Test

When you get the test back, you can evaluate your strategies based on the results.

- If you have done well, celebrate! Repeat those strategies for the next test.

- If you have done poorly, ask questions to find out why.

- Evaluate what you missed and ask yourself how you could have done better.

- Ask your instructor for suggestions about how you could do better on the next test.

- Ask students who did well on the test how they studied, and if they would be willing to help you prepare for the next test.

Tips for Taking Reading Tests

Questions on reading tests often cover specific skills. These can include understanding the main idea and supporting details; skills related to inference—vocabulary in context, literal versus figurative meaning, purpose, tone, or drawing conclusions; relationships between ideas; skills related to critical reasoning—point of view, assumptions, implied main idea, fact and opinion; or skills related to organization—understanding an outline or a summary or interpreting a table, chart, or graph.

Main Idea

- The main idea is the point that the author is trying to make.

- You need to understand the relationship between the topic, main idea, and supporting detail to effectively answer a main idea question.

- On multiple-choice reading tests, the possible answers to main idea questions generally fall into three categories:

  1. Too broad—the topic or an idea falls outside the scope of the passage.

  2. Too narrow—these are often the supporting details of the passage. A too-narrow answer will actually support the correct answer choice.

  3. Just right—this is an answer that both supports the topic and is supported by the details.

- Eliminate any answers that are too broad or too narrow.

- Double-check your chosen answer. Do this by turning the answer into a question. If it is the main idea, the details of the passage should answer the question.

Supporting Details

- Look carefully through the passage for the answer. Don't rush or lose patience.

- Pay attention to synonyms used. The answer is stated differently than the information in the passage, but the answer means the same thing.

- Be cautious of answers where two items from the text are put together but in an incorrect relationship.

- Be aware of "all or nothing" words (*all*, *never*, *always*, *none*). Make sure they have specific support in the passage.

- Make sure the detail in the answer isn't broader than what is supported by the text.

- When dealing with numbers or percentages, look carefully at the numbers stated.

  1. The text may say "75 percent will not," but the test answer might say "25 percent will."

  2. The text may say the words "twenty-five percent," but the answer might say "25%."

  3. The number stated in the answer does appear in the text, but it represents something other than what is stated in the answer.

Skills Related to Inference

- **Vocabulary in Context.** Always look for signal words and relationships between ideas.

  1. Examples—look for words like *for instance, such as,* and *for example,* but understand that even without a signal word, an author can still give an example.

  2. Antonyms—look for opposite relationships (*however, but, although, not*).

3. Synonyms—look for similar relationships (*also, similarly, and, that is*).

4. Your Prior Knowledge—focus on what you know and understand to help you figure out what you are not sure about.

- **Literal Versus Figurative Meaning.** Apply your understanding of denotative (the literal, dictionary definition) or connotative (the figurative, emotional meaning). Do the answers contain any of the following?

    1. Metaphor—a direct comparison (The sun is a big yellow ball.)

    2. Simile—an indirect comparison using "like" or "as" (The sun is *like* a big yellow ball.)

    3. Personification—the giving of human characteristics to non-human objects (The cool summer rain *kissed* my face.)

    4. Hyperbole—an exaggeration (My teacher gives a *ton* of homework.)

- **Purpose.** Remember PIE. The author's main purpose is often supported by the details, just as the main idea is.

    1. Persuade—the author wants you to change your mind or behavior and gives you reasons to support his or her opinion or claim.

    2. Inform—the author is giving you objective information about something that you can verify.

    3. Entertain—the author is trying to pull an emotion from you—laughter, fear, sympathy, dread, suspense, and so on. This is often done through stories.

- **Tone.** What emotion is the author using in his or her writing?

    1. Positive—the tone words are positive, showing the author likes or is in favor of something.

    2. Negative—the tone words are negative, showing the author does not like or is against something.

    3. Neutral—the tone words are objective, factual, and informative.

- **Drawing Conclusions.** The answer chosen must have proof in the passage.

  1. Pay attention to key words used.

  2. Turn your answer into a question.

  3. Verify the proof with details from the passage.

Relationships Between Ideas

Pay attention to relationships between ideas by asking questions and looking for signal words.

- **Time Order.** When did this happen? Look for information that takes place in a particular order of time.

- **Space Order.** Where are things located? Look for description and location.

- **Definitions.** What does this mean? Look for a key term, followed by a definition and examples explaining the term.

- **Examples.** What are the examples of this general idea? Look for multiple examples of the same general idea.

- **Cause and Effect.** Why? What made this happen? What does this lead to? Look for a direct relationship between a reason and result.

- **Comparison and Contrast.** How are these the same? How do they differ? Look for two or more items being talked about in terms of similarities or differences.

- **Classification.** What kinds are there? Look for groupings of items into categories or types.

Skills Related to Critical Reasoning

- **Point of View and Assumptions.** Both can be proven by details from the reading, paying special attention to tone.

  1. Decide what point of view the author is using, and whether that makes the selection seem more positive, negative, or neutral. Ask yourself, "How does the passage make me feel?" The author chooses a tone to make a certain impression on readers. So take that impression into account.

2. Look for subjective words (some reading tests call such words "biased") that indicate the author's attitude or opinion about the topic. In other words, look for words with positive or negative connotations. If there are several, think about what attitude they all add up to. If you don't find any, the author's point of view might be objective.

3. Look for any suggestions that the author is being figurative rather than literal. Do the words seem appropriate for the situation?

- **Implied Main Idea.** Use the topic and the details to determine the missing main idea.

    1. Look for the topic of the passage by noticing repeated words, phrases, and ideas.

    2. Find the details. Pay attention to how they are organized (the pattern of organization).

    3. Think about what all the details have in common.

    4. Create a sentence around this idea.

    5. See if one of the answers closely matches the answer you came up with.

    6. Turn the answer you chose into a question to see if the details of the passage support it.

- **Fact and Opinion.** Facts can be proven; opinions cannot be verified.

    1. Double-check for words that are suspicious, such as *all, none, beautiful, smartest, best,* and so on.

    2. Ask—can this be proven by observation, looked up, duplicated, or found?

    3. Just because it is stated in the passage does not make it a fact. ALWAYS ask, "Can this be proven? How?"

Skills Related to Organization

- **Understanding an Outline.** Each point of the correct answer must be directly supported by the text and follow the same order as it appeared in the text. Be patient with this type of question, and go point by point. Ask the following questions:

1. Are the points of the outline too broad, too narrow, or just right?

2. Do they have direct support in the reading?

3. Do the points of the outline match the order of the reading?

- **Proving Which is the Best Summary.** A summary usually needs the following:

1. The topic (a must);

2. The main idea (a must); and

3. The major supporting details (usually required but not absolutely necessary).

- **Interpreting a Table, Chart, or Graph.** Depending on what type of visual is presented, you will need to follow steps similar to these:

1. Read the title of the table, chart, or graph carefully (know the main idea).

2. Read the captions, categories or headings of rows and columns, or the labels on x- and y-axes carefully (understand how the information is organized).

3. Notice the meaning of each color used (understand what the colors represent).

4. Think critically about the implications of the headings, the numbers, and the way the information is presented.

5. Double-check that your chosen answer is supported by the details of the table, chart, or graph.

Credits

Part 1

4: Adapted from "Miami's Heat" by Francis Rodriguez, *The New York Daily News*, September 16th 2009. © New York Daily News, L.P. used with permission. **13:** "New Moon Delivers . . . Six Packs" from *Associated Content* online by Suzie Soule. November 21, 2009. Copyright © 2009 by Associated Content. Reproduced by permission of Associated Content in the format Textbook via Copyright Clearance Center. **25:** Linda Cook, "Love disaster and destruction? '2012' won't disappoint." From the *Quad City Times*, Davenport, IA Nov. 17, 2009. Reprinted by permission. **51:** From Bryant, "How to Survive a Plane Crash." From Howstuffworks.com. http://adventure.howstuffworks.com/how-to-survive-a-plane-crash.htm. Reprinted by permission. **62:** Sarah Kilff, "Crystal Renn's Disappearing Act: Why the 'V' Magazine Spread Sends Mixed Messages about Bigger Bodies." From *Newsweek* 12/23/09 issue. Copyright © 2009 Newsweek, Inc. All rights reserved. Used by permission and protected by the Copyright Laws of the United States. The printing, copying, redistribution, or retransmission of the Material without express written permission is prohibited. www.newsweek.com. **68:** Adapted from "Adam Lambert and Danny Gokey Dominate American Idol Final 13" from *Associated Content* online by Saul Relative. Copyright 2009 by Associated Content. Reproduced with permission of Associated Content in the formats textbook and Other book via Copyright Clearance Center. http://www.associatedcontent.com/article/1554550/adam_lambert_and_danny_gokey_dominate.html. **75:** "The Commercial," from *How to Watch TV News*, Revised Edition, by Neil Postman and Steve Powers, copyright © 1992 by Neil Postman and Steve Powers; © 2008 by Steve Powers. Used by permission of Viking Penguin, a division of Penguin Group (USA) Inc.

Part 2

89: From "Child Hero: Bethany Hamilton," by Tyler H. Reprinted with permission from The MY HERO Project. http://myhero.com. **150:** Copyright © 2007 by Houghton Mifflin Harcourt Publishing Company. Reproduced by permission from *Webster's New Pocket Dictionary*. **151:** Copyright © 2010 by Houghton Mifflin Harcourt Publishing Company. Adapted and reproduced by permission from *The American Heritage Dictionary of the English Language* Fourth Edition **151:** Copyright © 2008 by Houghton Mifflin Harcourt Publishing Company. Reproduced by permission from *Webster's New College Dictionary*, Third Edition. **152:** By permission. From *Merriam-Webster's Collegiate® Dictionary*, 11th Edition. ©2010 by Merriam-Webster, Inc. www.Merriam-Webster.com. **156:** Copyright © 2010 by Houghton Mifflin Harcourt Publishing Company. Adapted and reproduced by permission from *The American Heritage Dictionary of the English Language* Fourth Edition. **157:** Copyright © 2010 by Houghton Mifflin Harcourt Publishing Company. Adapted and reproduced by permission from *The American Heritage Dictionary of the English Language* Fourth Edition. **157:** Copyright © 2010 by Houghton Mifflin Harcourt Publishing Company. Adapted and reproduced by permission from *The American Heritage Dictionary of the English Language* Fourth Edition. **157:** Copyright © 2010 by Houghton Mifflin Harcourt Publishing Company. Adapted and reproduced by permission from *The American Heritage Dictionary of the English Language* Fourth Edition. **158:** Copyright © 2010 by Houghton Mifflin Harcourt Publishing Company. Adapted and reproduced by permission from *The American Heritage Dictionary of the English Language* Fourth Edition. **173:** Copyright © 2010 by Houghton Mifflin Harcourt Publishing Company. Adapted and reproduced by permission from *The American Heritage Dictionary of the English Language* Fourth Edition. **183:** From "I Can't Imagine Why Anyone Would Want to Stop Crying" The Onion, April 9, 2008, issue 44-15; http://www.theonion.com/content/opinion/i_cant_imagine_why_anybody. **207:** Kyle Busch, "Mistakes, I've made a few. (On The Fast Track)." *The Sporting News* 228.33 (August 16, 2004): 60(1). Reprinted by permission. **213:** Don Yaeger, "Winning every day: Pat Summitt's strategy centers on goal-Setting. (Lessons from Sports)." *Success* (Jan 2009): 74(3). Reprinted by permission.

Part 3

287: Adapted from http://www.akc.org/breeds/labrador_retriever/ by permission of the American Kennel Club. 288: Copyright © Oddity Central. www.odditycentral.com. Reprinted by permission. 292: Excerpt from Erin Thompson, "The dumbest generation." USA TODAY. June 3, 2009. Reprinted with permission. www.usatoday.com. 293: From Associated Press, "NBC sells out Super Bowl ads for record $206M." http://nbcsports.msnbc.com/id/28951579/ns/sports-super_bowl/. Reprinted by permission. 295: Copyright by Quintessential Careers. The original article can be found at: http://www.quintcareers.com/job_skills_values.html. Reprinted with permission. 323: Adapted from Tim Hanrahan and Jason Fry, FINGERS DO THE STUMBLING. THE WALL STREET JOURNAL ONLINE, February 14, 2005. Reprinted by permission of The Wall Street Journal Online, Copyright © 2005, Dow Jones & Company, Inc. All Rights Reserved Worldwide. License numbers 2432170770723/2432170902099. 330: Adapted from Dave Ramsey's article, "The 7 Baby Steps." http://www.daveramsey.com/new/baby-steps/. Reprinted by permission. 337: From Walter C. Willett and Anne Underwood, "Crimes of the Heart," *Newsweek,* Feb 5, 2010 http://www.newsweek.com/id/233006. 343: Adapted from Sue Shellenbarger, "Good News at Last in the Battle of the Sexes: Men are Helping More" with permission of *The Wall Street Journal,* Copyright © 1998 Dow Jones & Company, Inc. All Rights Reserved Worldwide. 2398380282200/2398380135966. 365: From Sting, "The Mystery of Music." Commencement Address, Berklee School of Music May 15, 1994, p. http://www.berklee.edu/commencement/past/sting.html. Reprinted by permission. 373: From the October 29, 2007 issue of Boston.com. Reprinted by permission of the author.

Part 4

413: Adapted with permission from Tara Parker-Pope, *New York Times Well Blog: Medical Bills Cause Most Bankruptcies,* June 4, 2009 422: From *Forces of Nature: ThinkQuest 2000* (Team #C003603) http://library.thinkquest.org/C003603/english/tornadoes/causesoftornadoes.shtml. Reprinted by permission from Oracle Education Foundation. 482: SOURCE: Reprinted by permission from Gallup Polls, reported in Public Opinion and updated at www.gallup.com.

Part 5

527: "Failure is a Good Thing" by Jon Carroll, copyright © 2006 by Jon Carroll. From the book THIS I BELIEVE II: MORE PERSONAL PHILOSOPHIES OF REMARKABLE MEN AND WOMEN, edited by Jay Allison and Dan Gediman with John Gregory and Viki Merrick. Copyright © 2008 by This I Believe, Inc. Reprinted by arrangement with Henry Holt and Company, LLC. 536: Adapted from Jason Garcia, *Orlando Sentinel,* February 24, 2010, http://www.orlandosentinel.com/business/tourism/os-sidebar-tilikum-the-whale-20100224,0,7926536.story. 544: Celizic, "Dwarves Say Their Theme Park Isn't 'Human Zoo,'" www.msnbc.com, March 19, 2010. Copyright 2010 by MSNBC INTERACTIVE NEWS, LLC. Reproduced with permission of MSNBC INTERACTIVE NEWS, LLC in the format Textbook via Copyright Clearance Center. 593: Woodyard, "Maserati Prices GranTurismo Convertible at $135,800," USA TODAY. January 19, 2010. Reprinted with Permission. 594: Reprinted with permission from Associated Press, "Troubled Economy a Boost for Repo Business," July 15, 2008. 600: Reprinted with permission from "The 31 Places to Go in 2010," The New York Times, January 10, 2010. www.nytimes.com.

Part 6

635: From Claire Suddath, "Your Facebook Relationship Status: It's Complicated" Friday, May 08, 2009 *Time Magazine.* Copyright © 2009. Reprinted by permission. TIME is a registered trademark of Time Inc. All rights reserved. http://www.time.com/time/business/article/0,8599,1895694,00.html. 647: Reprinted with permission from "Understanding Empathy: Can You Feel My Pain?" By Richard A. Friedman, M.D. *The New York Times,* April 24, 2007. 659: Adapted with permission from THE ASSOCIATED PRESS, "Teens use MySpace to brag about sex, drugs & violence - but not if adults are watching: study," Tuesday, January 6th 2009. 663: Reprinted with permission from "A Soap Opera's Sex Is All for a Good Cause" By Jennifer V. Hughes. *The New York Times,* January 23, 2009. 673: Reprinted by permission from the Nemours Foundation/Kidshealth. www.kidshealth.com.

Index